INTRODUCTION
TO DESIGNING AND
CONDUCTING RESEARCH

INTRODUCTION TO DESIGNING AND CONDUCTING RESEARCH

CLIFFORD J. DREW

Professor, Department of Special Education and
Department of Educational Psychology,
University of Utah, Salt Lake City, Utah

SECOND EDITION

with **67** *illustrations*

The C. V. Mosby Company

ST. LOUIS • TORONTO • LONDON   1980

SECOND EDITION

Copyright © 1980 by The C. V. Mosby Company

All rights reserved. No part of this book may be reproduced in any manner without written permission of the publisher.

Previous edition copyrighted 1976

Printed in the United States of America

The C. V. Mosby Company
11830 Westline Industrial Drive, St. Louis, Missouri 63141

Library of Congress Cataloging in Publication Data

Drew, Clifford J   1943-
  Introduction to designing and conducting
research.

  First ed. published in 1976 under title:
Introduction to designing research and evaluation.
  Includes references and index.
  1. Research—Methodology.   I. Title.
Q180.55.M4D73   001.4′2   79-25403
ISBN 0-8016-1460-0

C/CB/B 9 8 7 6 5 4 3 2   02/C/261

Preface

Many times during the preparation of this volume I have been asked the question, "Why are you putting so much effort into a second edition?" It seems that some would view a new edition primarily in terms of updating references and removing sexist language. Certainly I have attempted to accomplish these tasks, but the main purpose of preparing this second edition involved much more. Four new chapters have been written and others have been substantially expanded. These additions provide a view of research that is much broader than that presented in the first edition. Material has been added that addresses non-experimental research (e.g., questionnaires and interview studies) as well as the experimental research designs discussed in the first edition. Major attention has also been given to ethical issues related to conducting research such as consent, harm, privacy, and deception. These are topics of great concern to practicing researchers and clearly important to the beginning student.

Hopefully the additions and revisions in this volume will increase its usefulness. It should be noted, however, that the basic purpose remains similar to that of the first edition. This book provides an introduction to research that emphasizes the fundamentals of planning and design. The basic design of an investigation represents the foundation on which successful research endeavors are built. No single segment of the research process, such as sampling, sophisticated electronic measurement, or statistical computation, will result in meaningful results in the absence of sound research design and planning.

Many of the college courses that carry the title "Introduction to Research" should more appropriately be called "Introduction to Statistics." Furthermore, this statistics course is frequently all that is involved in a student's program of study, based on someone's arbitrary decision that "every student should have three hours of research." Such an arbitrary decision about course hours makes little sense, especially because statistics represent only one segment of the research process, a segment that must be preceded by several steps. Conducting research involves much more than the computation of statistical analyses. It involves a clinical process that includes decisions, often judgmental in nature, both as preparation for and as explanation of the results of statistical computation. The overall process, with each segment in its proper perspective, is something

v

for which schools often provide little if any preparation. When students are introduced to research at the statistical technique stage, they are beginning to study midway in a process in which much goes on before and subsequent to that phase. Students are often given answers (how to compute) before they even know what the questions are (what is being computed). The result is a population of frustrated students being taught by instructors who are equally frustrated because of their students' inability to grasp concepts whose meaningfulness is presumably self-evident. Such a situation is ironic, given what teachers are supposed to know about learning.

The purpose of this book is to provide that first step into the world of research. The book is not intended to be a statistical text, as shown by the absence of computational procedures. This material can serve as an initial conceptual framework for the student without a background in research. From this beginning the student may then proceed to more advanced work or terminate the study of research with a general working knowledge of what research involves.

Practice is one of the best teachers. This has certainly been my experience in teaching students how to conduct research. Yet in most courses there is neither sufficient time nor resources to permit application of the concepts and skills discussed. To at least partially meet this need, practice problems are provided to simulate as much as possible the situations faced by beginning researchers. These simulated problems provide the student with a paper-and-pencil substitute for application of the material presented.

In certain areas several simulations are presented on a given topic. This was done for two reasons. First, the simulations, in general, progress from the elementary to the more difficult. This sequence of difficulty has been determined over several years' use in introductory courses on research. Second, multiple simulations are included in certain areas simply to provide additional practice in applying the material. Frequently such practice is important to the beginning researcher.

The simulations may be used in a variety of fashions, depending on the instructor's preference. They may be effectively used in class sessions for both individual and small group participation. It seems to be more effective to complete the relevant simulations immediately after reading a given section than to wait until the entire chapter is read. These points in the text are "flagged" with instructions to the reader regarding which simulation is appropriate and where it may be found. Each simulation is accompanied by simulation feedback at the end of the book. Usually it is helpful for the student to read this feedback immediately after completing a given problem. The feedback provides a check on the student's performance for that problem and is useful before proceeding to the next simulation or further reading.

I am indebted to many whose wisdom and frustrations have contributed to the conceptualization of this volume. It is always risky to name specific individuals since some will undoubtedly be overlooked. Such practices are, however, customary and appropriate despite the risk. First and foremost are my students, who have helped me learn to teach about research and served as the primary impetus for the book. Sincere appreciation is also extended to my colleagues who have noted errors and areas that were unclear in the first edition and made suggestions for improvement. I am particularly grateful for the assistance and contributions of Don Logan, Dave Byrne, Mike Hardman, Karen Oberg, Mary Perry, Cathy Smith, and Dean Workman. Without their input and many hours of help, this volume would not have reached its present stage of refinement. Last but far from least, a special thanks to my wife, Robyn, whose patient prodding and able assistance in manuscript preparation were invaluable.

Clifford J. Drew

Contents

PART I

Overview

CHAPTER 1

Introduction and background

What is research? There are many different conceptions of what constitutes research. If you were to ask six different scientists what research is, you might well obtain six different answers. At least you would probably receive varying sets of words. Some may respond with very lofty and complex-sounding definitions. Others may be somewhat more casual in their responses, using terms that actually seem to be a part of the English language. Likewise, if you were to ask for a definition from six individuals who were not scientists, the result might be much the same.

For the beginning student an actual definition of research is often difficult to obtain. Many courses begin with a discussion of the content, and often that content focuses on a limited part of the research process (such as statistics). One might guess that the definition of research is supposed to become self-evident as the discussion progresses. Perhaps the assumption is made that you already know what research *is* and that your purpose in taking the course, or reading a research text, is to become thoroughly familiar with the intricacies of the process. In many cases, the purpose is probably that of meeting requirements for graduation. The course is probably required and the text is probably required (perhaps this text for that matter). Research design is not a topic that most students study as an elective.

Every author makes certain assumptions concerning the readers. That I am no different is obvious from the statement that was just made. Assumptions are necessary to function in daily life. They are based on a variety of factors such as knowledge about the world, past experience, and even faith. Assumptions become troublesome only when they are faulty for one reason or another. Perhaps the knowledge is incorrect or is only correct under certain conditions. Perhaps the past experience has been limited in some way and is not relevant to the current situation. Under such circumstances, these assumptions may not be very useful in helping people function.

My assumptions, faulty or not, are reasonably simple. They are based primarily on several years' experience in teaching research design (and my years as a student trying to learn about it). I believe that research has been taught for many years in a manner that is ineffective and, therefore, has had some unfortunate side effects. I also assume that many of you are *not* reading this book because of a life-long love affair with the topic. Additionally, I believe that research is something that is worth learning about (for reasons other than that it is a required topic of study). These assumptions, as well as others that may not be so prominent, have significantly shaped my approach to teaching research design and the nature of this book. Given this context, let us return to our initial question, What is research?

Research is a systematic way of asking questions, a systematic method of enquiry. The purpose of research is to obtain knowledge or information that pertains to some question. The question may be a very simple one (such as "Which of these teaching methods is most effective?") or it may be more complex. The emphasis of this definition is the term *systematic*. There are many ways of asking questions and obtaining information. Research is a method, however, that attempts to underake this task in a systematic fashion to obtain objective and unbiased information. The definition of research presented above is rather simple. Beyond this level of abstraction, there are many descriptive characteristics that are involved in research. At the outset, however, a general definition will serve quite well.

The term *research* has traditionally generated a variety of misconceptions on the part of the uninitiated. Whether purposefully or accidentally, a shroud of secrecy has been placed over the act of research. (In fact, many students would swear that professors teach as though the research process is something that *must* remain a secret—known only by those chosen few.) The net outcome of this situation is a generalized lack of information concerning what goes on in a research laboratory, the nature of the research process, and what research results mean. All of this has tended to generate both a mystique and a suspicion of the whole process by lay and student populations. The researcher has been caricatured as a strange sort of person, with rather solitary habits and preferences, somewhat of a mechanistic egghead. These are unfortunate misconceptions and stereotypes. The process of conducting research is anything but mystical, and it certainly is not mechanistic, as will become increasingly clear as you progress further into the content of this volume. While an individual researcher may indeed be somewhat different, strange, perhaps even weird, as a group, researchers are no more like that than the general population. In general, they exhibit no greater variation in terms of personality or preferences than do their neighbors next door.

Research has typically been an anxiety-producing topic for students. In fact, the most consistent description of what research is may be found among students. From a student perspective, particularly the beginning student, research is something that generates a certain amount of mental anguish, perhaps outright fear. Research is basically an academic hurdle that must be conquered but has little relevance to "the real world." For many students, research is synonymous with statistics, and that term in turn means mathematics (which *really* raises the anxiety level). These perceptions of research are, again, unfortunate misconceptions that must be corrected to fully understand the research process. For example, it is critical to understand from the outset that research is much more than statistics. Statistical analysis represents only one step in the overall research process. The statistics used in research should more accurately be viewed as tools, much as the automobile mechanic uses screwdrivers and wrenches. The mechanic's tools will be of little value if there is not a clear understanding of how an automobile operates. Likewise the researcher who does not know how to initiate the logical process of asking questions will have little meaningful use for statistical tools.

WHY READ AND LEARN ABOUT RESEARCH

This study of research began with some brief attention to what research is and is *not*. Hopefully this offsets, to some degree, certain commonly held misconceptions of research and researchers. The study also began with a general definition of research as a systematic method of enquiry. What has not been done thus far is to discuss some of the issues pertaining to why the study of research design is important. The purpose of this section is to address that question from two perspectives—the consumer and the professional.

It was noted earlier that research design is not a topic that students typically study by choice. It is usually required and there is no question that many students feel coerced and resent the whole process. I hate to think how many times I've heard comments such as: "I'm not going to be a researcher, so why should I take this class" and "Why can't I take something that is relevant to the real world." For many years I reacted to such statements very negatively, attributing such comments to what I thought was a generally poor attitude of a new breed of students. But eventually even crusty old professors have to listen. I realized that, in some ways, there had not been much serious thought given to why the study of research was important. There are some very important reasons for learning about research—beyond the fulfilling of requirements for graduation.

Research and the consumer

In discussing the issues related to why study research, it seems appropriate to initially focus on the consumer perspective. This view is seldom examined, and yet it may provide one of the most compelling rationales for becoming familiar with the research process. Like it or not, everyone is a consumer of research in nearly every facet of their daily lives. Oppenheimer (1959) maintained that science produces new knowledge and that new knowledge provides society with more choices. Providing more choices is most certainly a strong, consumer-oriented rationale for research *if* the consumer is equipped to take advantage of such an option.

From a general lay perspective, research often seems to be used more to control choices than to provide options. The student of research quickly becomes quite cynical concerning the manner in which research is used (mostly misused) to manipulate consumers. A few examples make this point painfully clear.

Some of the worst offenders in terms of misusing research are the people who develop and present advertising campaigns on television. It seems that the secret to selling a product on television is rather simple. Employ an actor (preferably someone who is not well known), put that individual in a white coat behind a desk (with rows of books on the wall), and the product to be sold suddenly appears scientifically credible. It always helps if the actor can also tell some sort of story to drive the point home. Often the line begins like this: "At a famous research center in the East, ..." An example of this type of selling is the commercial in which a well-known toothpaste is claimed to be "unsurpassed in the prevention of cavities when compared to the other leading brands of toothpaste." The wording of this line is quite carefully controlled. The obvious implication is that this brand (Brand X) is more effective in preventing cavities. However, that is not exactly what is said. The term *unsurpassed* specifically means that the other leading brands were not any better than Brand X. Most likely, there was no difference between them. Certainly if Brand X was really *more* effective it would seem that the advertisers would joyfully say so.

Another rich source of consumer-oriented "research" is the news media. A few years ago a headline appeared that captured the imagination of many who were rather sleepily gulping their morning coffee. (Headlines are worded just for that purpose.) It read *A Kiss Means Success.* The essence of the story was that a husband who kisses his wife good-bye in the morning lives longer and earns a great deal more money than a man who fails to perform that ritual. Although this is less serious, it exemplifies the same point as the television advertisement. One implication from this news story is that the kiss *causes* the husband to live longer and to make more money. Such an implication cannot be taken very seriously however, since it is obvious that this type of reasoning is more romantic than logical. In fact, it would be rather humorous if it weren't such an insult to one's intelligence.

The point of these examples is that lay consumers are inundated on a daily basis with what appears to be research information. Without some knowledge of the research process, they are at the mercy of those who present the information. Laws requiring truthful advertising will not help make intelligent decisions. After all, the toothpaste advertisement was not really untruthful.

Research and the professional

The research consumer perspective is also relevant to most professionals. Professional consumers are faced with situations similar to those confronting lay consumers. The content may be different, but professionals still have a strong need to be familiar with the research process. Once again, a few examples illustrate this point.

Most professional practitioners operate on a daily basis as service deliverers in one form or another. Counselors interact with clients, educators teach students, psychologists use tests to evaluate individuals, and so on. The question arises concerning the bases on which the practitioner selects the particular technique to be used. Which counseling method, teaching procedure, test should be used? These questions are not easily answered, particularly since the professional consumer receives a variety of sales pitches that often resemble the television advertisements noted earlier. Everyone wants you to use their test, their material, or their techniques. Although there are some consumer safeguards (e.g. the American Psychological Association's *Standards for Educational and Psychological Tests and Manuals*), the professional consumer still has the basic responsibility of evaluating the basis on which the procedure or technique was developed. Clearly some methods have been developed on a very sound basis with a solid research foundation, whereas others have not. It is equally clear that selection of materials and techniques by the professional consumer has not always been undertaken after careful consideration of the relevant research.

The selection of instructional material by teachers presents an interesting example of how some professional decisions are made. Many teachers decide which materials to use on the basis of second-hand information or suggestions by others. Their principal, or perhaps another teacher, may indicate rather casually that a particular material is "good." Quite often, the basis for the "good" rating remains unspecified. It may be that the individual making the recommendation mentions that ". . . the material was researched . . .," but this is not a typical basis for the suggestion. Further investigation concerning the research results and the technical soundness of such research (if it actually exists) is even less typical.

This all begins to sound very much like the sales proposition involving that infamous "research center in the East." In fact there are more similarities than many professionals would like to admit (and teachers certainly are not the only professional consumers involved). Professional practitioners (teachers, supervisors, psychologists) often find themselves inundated with salespeople and advertisements expounding the virtues of their products. The marketing process for professional products has the same goal as any other arena—selling. The same tactics are often used, and despite a reluctance to admit it, a large number of professional consumers are ill-equipped to question the "research" claims used to sell products.

The basic purpose of this section was to discuss some of the reasons why it is important to learn about the research process from a consumer perspective. There is no intent here to suggest that everyone has to become a researcher (a claim that many of my students have made). A contention *is* made, however, that some understanding of the research process is important to be an intelligent consumer. Certainly many decisions do not require an awareness of the scientific method. There are others, however, when it would be most helpful to be able to question some of the claims made by the people who are selling. The examples given in terms of professional consumerism are necessarily limited both in number and scope. It is difficult to imagine how one can intelligently keep abreast of the professional literature without an understanding of the research process. Most professionals have long since learned that they should not accept everything that is printed in an unquestioning fashion.

WHY CONDUCT RESEARCH

It was noted above that the intent of this book is not one of making everyone into researchers. There may, however, be some who do have such a goal or *might* be interested. Consequently there is some legitimacy to briefly discussing the reasons why research is conducted.

The reasons for conducting research are nearly as varied as the people who are involved. Some would suggest very grand and glorious motivations such as solving the ills of society. Others might be much more personal and indicate that research is just plain fun. Neither of these extremes should be ignored; they are both genuine and powerful reasons for conducting research.

Sidman (1960) has provided a most articulate discussion concerning the variety of purposes involved in undertaking research. Remaining cognizant of the value of research based on theory, Sidman cautions that the beginning student should not submit to a rigid insistence that all research "must derive from the testing of hypotheses [p. 4]." He discusses the value of several other reasons for performing experiments: (1) to try out a new method or technique, (2) to indulge the investigator's curiosity, (3) to establish the existence of a behavioral phenomenon, and (4) to explore the conditions under which a phenomenon occurs. Bailey (1978) examined social research in terms of studies that describe what is happening and those that explore why or how something happens.

It is clear from this discussion that research is conducted to solve problems and to expand knowledge. These are reasons that are commonly accepted by both lay and professional groups. However, Sidman's comment concerning curiosity raises a completely different area of justification that is not generally discussed. Some would vigorously argue that the curiosity of an investigator is not adequate rationale for conducting research. Such justification sounds too frivolous and all too much like the "ivory tower." This type of argument is very much a part of a way of thinking that demands that every piece of research must directly relate to the immediate solution of a practical problem. It ignores, however, the established fact that many problems cannot be immediately and effectively solved until a foundation of fundamental knowledge is present. Oftentimes the development of such a body of knowledge is only possible by the collective investigation of many researchers who may well be studying questions that seem rather removed from the "practical, real world." This type of argument also ignores the history of solutions to immediate problems that have resulted because some researcher was indulging a curiosity many years before. It is not uncommon to find answers that may be theoretically interesting but will not find their way into application until problems arise at a later time. Thus from my point of view, indulging an investigator's curiosity is a very good reason for conducting research. The benefits from a practical perspective may not be immediate, but such an immediacy is far less important than a more reasoned outcome at a later time that may ultimately lead to more effective decisions.

The foregoing discussion sounds much like a debate involving basic versus applied research. This is a popular argument in some circles and one in which I do not wish to engage. Basic research involves investigation of questions that are interesting but may have no application at the present time. This is occasionally termed *pure* research, but that term connotes a value judgment that is not particularly helpful (as compared with *impure* research?). Applied research, on the other hand, is used to designate investigations aimed at solving problems of immediate concern.

The debate concerning applied versus basic research has been a confusing one because the issues have been presented as both method issues and value judgments. This is unfortunate because a great deal of time and energy has been spent on the debate itself. Essentially the debate can be reduced to the value judgment issue that was discussed above (that is, whether or not research should be conducted that is not immediately applicable). If conducted carefully, the methodology is the same; only the content and the setting differ. The task here, however, is to explore technically sound research designs, not to debate value judgment issues. There is good reason to conduct research that is basic as well as that which may be characterized as applied. There is no reason for conducting research that is unsound in the way it is designed regardless of the topic being investigated.

It is clear from this discussion that I am a strong advocate of Sidman's approach regarding the purposes for research. All of his reasons are powerful justifications. Most active researchers seem to, at one time or another, be involved in all of his reasons for undertaking investigations. This places the question of "Why conduct research?" on a very personal level and that seems quite appropriate. I have already noted that research is fun (not discounting the fact that it is also work). It is most assuredly a pleasurable experience to obtain an answer to a question that one has, regardless of whether it is one of curiosity or theoretical importance or one that solves an immediate social problem. There is tremendous personal satisfaction in gathering your own data—much more than reading someone else's report. I will never forget the exhilaration that occurred when I received my first questionnaires back for my Sociology study as an undergraduate. (The Dean of Women, however, was less excited—my topic was dating and sexual behaviors. This was a very small college and more years ago than I like to recall.)

As the years have passed, I have begun to appreciate other personal benefits of conducting research. As a researcher, a natural part of the process is writing. Clearly, the expression of thoughts, ideas, and findings, *in writing,* is one of the most demanding tasks a person can undertake. It requires a completeness and clarity of communication that is simply not involved in routine conversation. Spoken communication, even if it is rather formal conversation, often includes a great deal of nonverbal gesturing to accentuate, provide emphasis, and complete thoughts that are only partially expressed by the actual words. Most persons do not even notice these behaviors since they are so accustomed to both using and experiencing them. Although these nonverbal aids may be acceptable in verbal communication, writing does not include such luxuries. Consequently it is very challenging for most people to write in an articulate fashion. Despite the struggle that is often involved, a great deal of satisfaction accompanies the completion of a particular piece of research.

The entire research process, from designing the study to writing the report, can be one of the most growth-producing experiences available. Each step requires the exercise of disciplined thought balanced with an appropriate dose of creativity. I have often thought that the conduct of research has many similarities to the writing of poetry. You can nearly feel the mental growth each time a successful study is completed. For me, this is a very compelling, personal reason for conducting research and one that is as powerful as any of the more lofty justifications that are typically offered.

THE RESEARCH PROCESS

Reference has previously been made to the research process although only certain portions of it have been described. As a whole, the research process can best be conceptualized in a circular or closed loop fashion in the manner illustrated in Fig. 1-1. Initially there is the research question or problem. The research question may arise from theoretical dilemmas presented by other research, a practical problem needing solution, or the curiosity of the individual undertaking the study. In most cases, the research idea must be distilled into a very specific question, which tends to take the form of a hypothesis or several hypotheses. Once this has been accomplished, the study must be designed in a manner that will avoid potential difficulties and permit the researcher to answer the question. The research design part of the overall process is critically important and essentially involves a rigorous and meticulous planning procedure. This planning should include the operational details of actually conducting the study. You are now ready to begin. Data are collected and then analyzed. Once this is done, the results must be interpreted in terms of the research question that

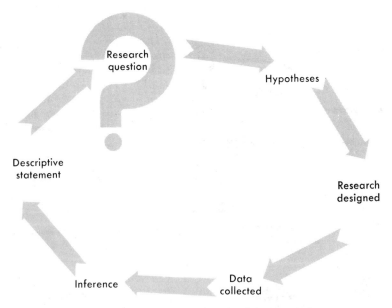

Fig. 1-1. Closed loop conceptualization of the research process.

completes the loop. If executed properly, the question should be answered, the problem solved, or at least a first step taken toward achieving this end.

Obviously the discussion above presents a simplified view of the overall research process. A variety of obstacles may intervene at each step and many details have been omitted. These will be discussed in greater depth throughout this volume. What has been examined, however, is the research process as a whole. We have often been guilty of focusing on one portion or emphasizing one step to the exclusion of others. Such a limited perspective has frequently given laypersons and beginning students an inaccurate view of what is really involved in research. Creating such perspectives (knowingly or unknowingly) has generated many misconceptions that have often created unfavorable opinions about research. As an introductory book, it is hoped that this volume will serve to inform as well as correct misconceptions in cases when that is appropriate.

FOUNDATION TOPICS RELATED TO RESEARCH

Several topics should be considered before discussing the central design aspects of conducting research. Although these topics are peripheral to the major concern of designing and executing research, they serve to round out the introductory information required for a full understanding of the process. As noted earlier, the purpose of research is to obtain knowledge or information. It is a systematic method of asking questions. As such it involves the scientific method, which warrants some discussion. The scientific method is, to some extent, different from the way in which people generally conduct their everyday lives. This section is aimed at placing research in perspective with other approaches to knowledge about the world.

Differences between science and common sense

According to Kerlinger (1973), science is essentially a "systematic controlled extension of common sense [p. 3]." Kerlinger, however, also outlined several differences between them. These are useful in placing the scientific method in the context of everyday functioning. There is a general theme that threads its way through the differences that will be discussed. For the most part, the scientific method is characterized by a more systematic approach to problems than common sense.

There tends to be a distinct difference between science and common sense in the use of theoretical structures and concepts. Science systematically constructs theories and conceptual schemes, uses them, and submits them to repeated tests. A layperson who operates primarily on a common sense basis generally does not use theory and concepts in the same fashion. Often theories and conceptual structures are applied loosely and not systematically at all. Explanations for the occurrence of events may not be endowed with the logic relating that explanation to a conceptual scheme.

A second difference, closely related to the first, speaks to the issue of theory testing. The method of science systematically tests theories, hypotheses, and ideas. The term *systematic* here again becomes the key. If a given theory is presumed to be operative under conditions X, Y, and Z, science demands the systematic examination of events under conditions X, Y, and Z. A common sense approach to testing, on the other hand, tends to be much less concerned with systematically testing an idea under all relevant conditions. Selection bias frequently enters into the choice of test situations and the viewing of test results. Often an idea such as "All Republicans are conservative" is tested unintentionally under conditions that ensure the support of a preconceived notion. Information that does not support the hypothesis may be discounted or ignored and not fed in as a part of the test. Proverbial "mother-in-law" stories exemplify this type of information bias.

A third difference between science and common sense involves the concept of control. This concept will become a central focus in later chapters. Here again, the systematic approach is relevant. Science is built on the concept of control, which essentially involves eliminating possible influential variables except *the one being tested*. Common sense, to the contrary, may operate in such a loose fashion that several factors are allowed to vary at once. This may mean that any one of two or three influences *might* have generated the results observed, in addition to the one being tested. Under such circumstances, scientists would probably throw up their hands and view the data as uninterpretable, certainly not attributing the results to any one influence. From the less systematic framework of common sense, the interpretation may suggest a result caused by one influence, which, since two or three are operating, may well be in error.

A fourth distinction between science and common sense involves the interest level concerning relationships between phenomena. The layperson is interested in relationships between phenomena in a somewhat loose and unsystematic fashion. Primarily, interest is generated only when there is great personal relevance involved. To the contrary, the scientist becomes almost obsessed with the relationships between phenomena, personally relevant or not. There seems to be a continual question-asking process in operation (for example, "I wonder if this material would be more effective if . . ." or "I wonder if that behavior is influenced by . . ."). Such an enquiry approach seems to frequently spill over into the nonprofessional life of the scientist. It is not clear whether this curiosity is a part of the animal (that is, whether individuals with such a bent gravitate to science) or whether the nature of the training generates such behaviors in those who choose science. Such curiosity is, however, apparent and reported frequently in the everyday lives of scientists. (This is certainly *not* meant to imply that all scientists are this way or that it is always the case even in some scientists.)

The fifth difference between science and common sense relates to explanations of phenomena. Explanations of events that emanate from the method of science tend to be stated in terms of the observable, the logical, and the empirically testable. A common sense explanation frequently involves reference to metaphysical influences. Metaphysical explanations cannot be tested. Such statements as "Working hard is good for one's moral character" and "Suffering builds character" are metaphysical statements. Although occasionally amusing, such explanations do not fit well into the observable empirically testable framework.

As noted previously, science is in one way a systematic extension of common sense. There is certainly a conceivable continuum between the two, and they are probably not best thought of in an all-or-none fashion. The primary factors that seem to be involved are concepts of systematic enquiry, logic, objectivity, and observable phenomena.

Four ways of knowing or fixing belief

Kerlinger (1973) cites the philosopher Charles Peirce as the source in distinguishing four different ways of knowing or fixing belief. Each approach (tenacity, authority, a priori, and science) involves a different set of characteristics and sources of information. Additionally, each of these methods is used to a greater or lesser degree by different sectors of the population. As with the previous discussion concerning science and common sense, the different ways of fixing belief are useful in placing research in perspective with regard to other approaches to enquiry.

The first method of fixing belief is known as the method of *tenacity*. Utilizing the method of tenacity, derived from the idea that an individual holds tenaciously to existing beliefs, something is thought to be true because "it has always been true." If something is known by the method of tenacity, essentially a closed system exists. It is closed in that it is not particularly amenable to the input of new information. In fact, the very nature of tenacity may prompt the individual to hold to a belief even in the face of nonsupportive evidence.

The second approach to knowing or fixing belief, *reference to authority*, involves the citing of some eminent person or entity as the source of knowledge. If someone who is well known (an authority) states that something is the case, then it is so (at least according to some people). Reference to authority relieves the believer from having to consider alternative information. As will be evident later, the method of authority is not clearly and definitively a "bad" method of knowing. Much depends on the authoritative source, and even more depends on the way in which the believer uses the method. If it is used totally in a non-thinking, closed-system fashion, there are obvious weaknesses. Used in this manner, there is no consideration given to nonsupportive or conflicting evidence. If this is the case, the progress of knowledge and ideas is painfully slow and depends totally on the progress of the authority.

A third way of knowing or fixing belief is called the *a priori method*. A priori, by definition, refers to "before the fact" and is primarily based on intuitive knowledge. In subscribing to the a priori method, one knows that something is the case before the gathering of information by experience or even in the absence of experiential data. Usually the a priori approach is logical or in harmony with reason. The weakness in the method, as Kerlinger notes, lies with the question of whose reason is used. Humans have certainly been known to commit errors of reason or logic. Unless the information system is open to data from experience (experimentation or observation), such an error of logic may initiate a line of thought that is characterized by progressive errors.

The fourth method of knowing is called the *method of science*. As reflected in earlier discussions, the method of science is characteristically different from the other three ways of fixing belief. It is based on experience external to the knower, in that observation that is presumed to be objective is the primary source of information. The method of science has a *built-in self-correction factor*, which distinguishes it rather dramatically from the other ways of knowing. This self-corrective factor is operative because the system is open and public. The work of the scientist is public not only in terms of end products but also in the means by which those ends were attained. As is evident from reading the literature, a researcher must describe in considerable detail the procedures, materials, and subjects and must even show the path of logic used to reach the question or conclusion involved. This degree of openness or public exposure attempts to ensure that subsequent investigators may know as much as possible about previous work to be able to replicate (duplicate) the investigation. It is the process of independent replication that operates the self-correction factor of the science method.

Research has its foundation in the method of science. Nevertheless, one has only to read a research article to observe the use of at least segments of two other methods of knowing. Certainly reference to authority is operative in research. The researcher is continually citing the work of others. This use of the method of authority, however, is considerably different from utilizing authorities solely in a closed system in which conflicting evidence is not acknowledged. Furthermore, research serves to openly challenge authority when evidence is not in agreement. Research also uses basic components of the a priori method of knowing, logic, and reason. Again, the way in which it is used in research is considerably different from the use of the a priori method as the sole source of knowledge. It was noted that the researcher is usually required to openly show the path of reason by which conclusions are reached. If the logic is faulty or in conflict with experiential evidence, it is challenged in the method of science. By virtue of its public nature, science can effectively make use of portions of the other methods of knowing and avoid pitfalls inherent in them.

Inductive and deductive reasoning

Reasoning and logic represent vital components of the research process, elements that, if absent, weaken and jeopardize the process so severely as to render it useless. Without the input of reasoning, knowledge would not progress at all, since the relationship of one idea to another, or of data to an idea, is based on this essential element.

Two rather distinctive types of reasoning are involved in the broad spectrum of research efforts—deductive and inductive reasoning. *Deductive reasoning* uses logic that moves from the general to the specific. Deductive reasoning is characterized by statements that were initiated from a general idea, model, or theory, and from these statements something is inferred about a specific case ("If this [general] theory is correct, then I should be able to observe the [specific] behavior in children"). *Inductive reasoning*, on the other hand, reflects the reverse type of logic. Inductive reasoning uses logic that is launched from a specific case or occurrence and moves to inferences concerning the general ("If this [specific] behavior occurs, then this [general] theory is supported").

Both types of reasoning are used in behavioral research. Examples of deductive reasoning may be found in introductory statements of research articles. When researchers are examining a theory, model, or body of knowledge (general) and hypothesizing a specific behavior that they expect to observe, deductive reasoning is the mode of logic being used. Inductive reasoning is the primary means by which data generalization is accomplished. When a researcher is writing the discussion section of a research report, the discussion is primarily based on the data obtained. From the data (specific behavioral occurrences), inferences are drawn back to the theory or model (general) that was mentioned in the introduction. Additionally, generalizations are usually being made about the population (general) from the subject performance observed (specific).

Rationalism versus empiricism

Throughout the history of human existence, various methods of enquiry have been used as the search for knowledge has proceeded. It is already evident that one may think of methods of enquiry in a number of different fashions. One manner in which enquiry may be categorized is in terms of the source of knowledge: internal or external. This conceptualization is relevant from a historic viewpoint and may be distinquished as rationalism versus empiricism.

Rationalism is a method of enquiry that primarily uses an internal source of knowledge. Characteristic of enquiry in ancient Greek times, rationalism views the intellectual examination of ideas as *the* means by which knowledge progresses. Little if any emphasis is placed on that which is external and observable except as the objects are to be manipulated. Instead the emphasis is on logic, reasoning, and intuitive intelligence. Rather than observing a phenomenon to see if a given event occurs, the user of rationalism may draw conclusions as to whether it occurs by using a logical progression of ideas.

To the contrary, the empirical approach emphasizes knowledge that comes through factual investigation, with the facts discovered through sources external to the investigator. The primary means by which information is obtained involves direct experience through the senses for a particular situation.

Different phases of history have been characterized by different modes of enquiry and knowledge seeking. In reaction to the introspective, intuitive approach of rationalism, enquiry has occasionally swung to the other extreme, empiricism, with the *only* acceptable source of knowledge being that which is directly observable. The rationalistic approach to enquiry, in isolation, is subject to considerable possibility of error because of the virtual absence of a monitor on the progress of ideas, using observation or experiential checkpoints. It is possible for progressive error to operate if a series of ideas are generated from the foundation of a false or weak assumption. Thus, although rationalism may permit rapid progress, the probability of error is high. Strict empiricism, on the other hand, progresses painfully slowly if it is used in isolation. The strict empiricist is reluctant to infer to any degree and is more inclined to merely view the data as a behavioral description. Progress will be infinitesimal if behavioral descriptions must result from observations under all possible conditions without permitting the use of logic or reason to draw inferences between pieces of data. The strength of empiricism is its constant contact with the reality of experience. This substantially reduces the error potential that is so high with pure rationalism. Current research approaches tend to represent a blend of rationalism and empiricism. Reason and logic are used to draw inferences from empirically derived data. Such a blend fortunately combines the strengths of the two approaches as each tends to offset the pitfalls of the other.

Nomothetic net

Related to the discussion of empiricism and rationalism is a topic that is concerned with the manner in which theories are constructed. A theory or model usually involves a descriptive explanation of why some phenomenon occurs. In such an explanation, certain aspects of the theory are frequently observable, or have been observed, whereas other aspects are either not directly observable or have yet to be observed. Theoretical structures are usually formed by drawing intuitive or logical connections between such aspects. The points and their connective links together become the theory and form what is known as a nomothetic net, a nomologic network or nomologic structure. Cronbach and Meehl (1955) describe the nomothetic net in the context of test validity as an "interlocking system of laws which constitute a theory [p. 290]." In the context of research, the points or behavioral events, which may relate within the network as (a) observable properties or quantities to each other; or (b) theoretical constructs to observables; or (c) different theoretical constructs to one another [p. 290]."

The nomothetic net conceptualization of a theory is analogous to a fishnet. The knots or points where the strings join may be thought of as the points (either observed data on performance or hypothesized behavior expected before observation). The linking strings between knots are analogous to intuitive or logical links that suggest relationships between known behavioral data points and hypothesized behavioral performances. Fig. 1-2 illustrates the nomothetic net that represents a behavior theory. Points A, B, C, K, L, and M represent results of investigations. The other points, D, E, F, G, H, I, and J, represent hypothesized

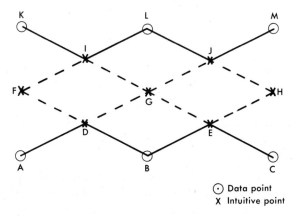

⊙ Data point
X Intuitive point

Fig. 1-2. Hypothetical representation of a behavior theory as a nomothetic net.

or expected behaviors. In accomplishing this, the theory builder may scrutinize known points A and B, essentially saying that "if A is the case and likewise B, then perhaps the child's memory operates like D." Similarly the theoretician may inspect B and C and hypothesize a composite picture of the child that looks like E. The question might then be raised concerning the existence of both D and E, supposedly composite pictures of the child from known data. The process is not unlike that of photographically describing an object. One might take three different photographs, each from a different angle and thus each providing a different piece of information. If one looks at any two of the photographs, a somewhat different mental image of the whole may be generated.

Further inspection of Fig. 1-2 indicates three intuitive points (F, G, and H) that are two steps or intuitive links removed from observed data points. These are examples of what Cronbach and Meehl (1955) described as relationships of "different theoretical constructs to one another [p. 290]." Such intuitive points may represent attempts to hypothesize more completely what the phenomenon will look like from two or more previously hypothesized constructs. The logic links that proceed to these second-order constructs are represented in Fig. 1-2 by broken lines. This is intended to suggest a weaker inference than those that are only one step away from observed data points. Because known information is further away from intuitive points F, G, and H, their soundness must be viewed as much more tenuous than those that are more closely linked to existing evidence. The further the theorist moves away from known data, the weaker the inferences must be considered. The intuitive points then may become studies to be conducted. As investigations are subsequently completed, there are more knowns and fewer intuitive points, placing the theory on an increasingly firmer evidence base. Certainly, it is also to be expected that the nature of some of the intuitive points will be altered as data are obtained that suggests theory modification.

The nomothetic net conceptualization of theory construction illustrates nicely the manner in which empirical and logical processes work together in research. It is in this fashion that empiricism and rationalism blend in current research and theory. Actually the fishnet analogy is descriptive of the way in which theory serves to generate research and the theory is, in turn, tested by empirical investigation. If one has made accurate inferences in generating the nomothetic net, it ought to function as a sound fishnet would in scooping fish. Assuming that point G is a solid knot, it ought to "catch" or predict the behavior of a child. This would be either substantiated or negated by the data from an investigation of point G. If, instead, point G was shown not to be an accurate inference, the knot is unsound and the child will slip through the hole in the theory net (i.e., the theory will "miss" or not predict performance). This situation would then suggest a change in the theory, assuming that the experiment was executed in a fashion that was appropriate to test the theory in the first place.

This chapter has discussed a variety of topics representing background information concerning research. These concepts form a substantial portion of the foundation necessary to learn about research.

REFERENCES

Bailey, K. D. *Methods of social research.* New York: The Free Press, 1978.

Cronbach, L. J., and Meehl, P. E. Construct validity on psychological tests. *Psychological Bulletin,* 1955, *52,* 281-302.

Kerlinger, F. N. *Foundations of behavioral research* (2nd ed.). New York: Holt, Rinehart & Winston, 1973.

Oppenheimer, J. R. The importance of new knowledge. In D. Wolfle (Ed.), *Symposium on basic research.* Washington, D.C.: American Association for the Advancement of Science, 1959, 1-15.

Sidman, M. *Tactics of scientific research: evaluating experimental data in psychology.* New York: Basic Books, Inc., Publishers, 1960.

CHAPTER 2

Different research approaches

Chapter 1 began with a relatively simple definition of research as a systematic method if enquiry. This is a rather broad definition that essentially identifies the purpose of research as one of obtaining information pertaining to some question or set of questions. Obviously there may be many different types of questions. As might be expected, there are a variety of approaches to obtaining answers. The approach that is selected depends on several factors including the nature of the question, the setting in which the research is to be conducted, and the background and disciplinary orientation of the researcher. Although each approach is different in some rather significant ways, all involve the basic components of the research process as outlined in Chapter 1. The research question or problem must be specifically identified and distilled into researchable form, the study must be designed in a technically sound manner, the data must be collected and analyzed, and the results must be interpreted. The purpose of this chapter is to discuss different approaches to conducting research.

DISTINCTIONS BETWEEN RESEARCH AND EVALUATION

Differences between evaluation and research have been subjects of discussion and debate for many years. Early considerations of this topic often seemed to be unproductive and characterized more by debate than by serious examination. However, significant progress has been made in recent years, and a brief discussion appears warranted to place both in perspective.

There are many situations in which the distinctions between evaluation and research are minimal, if they exist at all. In fact, Hemphill (1969) posed the question of whether or not evaluation should "be considered simply a subset of the more general set of activities denoted by the term 'research' [p. 189]." As this discussion continues it will become evident that this question remains relevant to some degree today.

One of the distinctions between research and evaluation involves the generic purposes for which such an effort is initiated. Hemphill (1969) notes that evaluation is presumably undertaken ". . . to provide a basis for making decisions . . . [p. 189]." Such decisions might pertain to selecting the most effective procedure, material, or organizational structure. Evaluation studies may also address such questions as "Does this technique (material, treatment) work?" These purposes obviously involve questions of immediate utility. Answers to these questions are sought to solve immediate problems, which seems to be a fundamental purpose of evaluation. Some research efforts also share this type of purpose. The earlier discussion of applied research clearly suggested similar, if not identical, goals. However, the broader concept of research included other purposes. Although applied research is aimed at solving more immediate problems, basic research is primarily focused on knowledge acquisition. The immediate application of such knowledge is a secondary consideration.

The preceding discussion may suggest that evaluation can be considered as synonymous with applied research. This thought was broached by both Hemphill (1969) and Stake and Denny (1969), although they were somewhat tentative in their assertion and suggested that more was actually involved. Stake and Denny viewed evaluation as a *form* of applied research. They identified the principal difference between research and evaluation as ". . . the degree to which the findings are generalizable beyond their application to a given product, program, or locale [p. 374]." Certainly this remains as a prominent distinction since research is nearly always concerned with generalizability to some degree, whereas evaluation primarily focuses on the immediate situation. However, recent advances in evaluation methodology have made it more distinct from research than it once was (e.g., Cooley and Lohnes, 1976; Anderson and Ball, 1978; Guttentag and Struening, 1975; Popham, 1974; Struening and Guttentag, 1975). It is clear that generalizability can no longer be viewed as the *principal* difference.

Provus (1969) presented a description of evaluation that began to emphasize its conceptual distinctions from research and served as a forerunner of further model development in the field. Provus' concept has since developed into what is known as the Discrepancy Evaluation Model (DEM). He outlined evaluation as the process of "(a) agreeing upon program standards, (b) determining whether a discrepancy exists between some aspect of the program and the standards governing that aspect of the program, and (c) using discrepancy information to identify the weaknesses of the program [p. 245]." This notion highlights one of the distinctions that often differentiates research and evaluation. Essentially the DEM compares performance with some agreed upon standard to identify potential discrepancies. By virtue of the fundamental purpose of research, predetermined performance standards are not involved when the goal is primarily knowledge acquisition.

Evaluation may still be considered a form of applied research at the most abstract level. However, the gap between the two appears to be widening. As the technology has developed and the conceptualizations matured, evaluation has become a credible field of study. The distinctions between evaluation and research have become more evident over the past few years and may be even more notable in the future.

DIFFERING RESEARCH PERSPECTIVES

Different approaches to conducting research were noted at the beginning of this chapter. These differing approaches are the result of a number of factors including the wide variety of questions, the settings in which the research is to be conducted, and the disciplinary background of the individual undertaking the investigation. Obviously this is only a partial list of the influences that contribute to divergent research perspectives. Even such matters as the investigator's personal preferences may strongly affect the particular method selected. Such specific differences are far too numerous to completely catalog and such an inventory serves little purpose in an introductory text. There are, however, some generic characteristics of various approaches that are important to consider to become fully acquainted with the research process.

Disciplinary perspectives

There has been a great deal of discussion about the nature of a discipline, the characteristics of a discipline, and the vast differences between disciplines. Occasionally the tenor of such discussions has been reduced to consideration of whether or not a particular field warrants the status of a discipline (e.g., education, the "soft" sciences in general). Although such debates may serve to inflate some professional egos and deflate others, they are not helpful in furthering the primary purpose here—to more fully understand the research process from various disciplinary perspectives.

It is patently obvious that there are vast differences between many disciplines (medicine, anthropology, psychology). What is seldom noted is that there are a number of similarities as well. For example, many of the problems faced by medical research are similar to those encountered in psychology, sociology, and education. In some cases the specific context or content may differ, but viewed broadly the problems are quite similar. All researchers are faced with complex ethical problems as they attempt to conduct research. There are ongoing and vigorous debates within several disciplines concerning the philosophical approach to research, preferred methodologies, and the perennial debate regarding applied versus basic research. Consequently an examination of disciplinary perspectives must go beyond issues concerning what is or is not a "true" discipline (discipline has been defined simply as a field of study). If people are to profit from the advances of science in general, it is important to explore various disciplinary differences and similarities regarding the general character of research in the disciplines, methodologies used, and the fundamental views of research in the larger disciplinary mission.

It is neither feasible nor productive to discuss every possible field of study in an introductory text. My purpose here is to be illustrative rather than exhaustive. There is much to be learned regarding the general scientific process by reviewing the techniques, problems, and perspectives of various fields. All too often one's perception of a problem and the approach they use to examine that problem are unnecessarily narrowed by a single disciplinary focus.

It will become evident that certain disciplinary distinctions are more ambiguous than they might appear on the surface. For example, if someone is investigating the practice of medicine and studying the physician in the process, is that person engaged in medical research? Perhaps, but depending on the perspective, it may be considered psychological research or sociological research. It may also be that it is not important to determine exactly what *type* of research is being conducted. In the last analysis the most important consideration is whether or not the investigation is designed and executed in a sound manner.

General disciplinary image. The general image of research in different disciplines varies nearly as much as the number of fields of study that one can imagine. In some disciplines research efforts are viewed very favorably and represent high status activities. In other fields research does not have such a favorable image. Although the general scientific image may not be a prominent concern to the individual researcher, it does impact rather substantially on the ability to conduct research in several ways. (1) it serves to promote or diminish funding available to support investigations, (2) it impacts dramatically the importance attached to findings that are reported, and (3) it influences, in a rather circular fashion, the current and future view of research held by professionals within the discipline (that is, attitudes and inclinations of both practitioners and potential scientists). It is difficult to separate these matters since they truly interact in a circular and progressive manner. Attitudes within a discipline affect significantly the amount and type of research undertaken, which, in turn, influences the importance attached to reported findings. Additionally, all of these impact on the support and funding available to facilitate research and vice versa. It is not at all clear whether they are really a *cause* or an *effect* with regard to disciplinary image. What is clear, however, is the general impact on science within a field.

The general attitude of a discipline toward any activity, in this case research, is largely formed and perpetuated by the training programs that prepare individuals to work in that field. This process has been characterized as professional socialization and basically follows the general notion of socialization, but places it in the context of the professional environment (Clark and Guba, 1976). The socialization of professionals regarding research varies dramatically between disciplines and the impact is equally dramatic. This discussion will focus on medicine, psychology, and education to illustrate the issues involved.

One very important indicator of socialization is found in the attitudes and publicly expressed views concerning research by the practitioners in a given field. It is clear that research in the medical field is generally considered a valued activity even by most physicians who are not actively involved. One very seldom hears a physician complain about those who are conducting medical research or berate their efforts as having little value. This is a very enviable situation and one that brings into bold relief some of the differences between disciplines. Such conditions do not exist in all fields and may best be illustrated by the status of research in education where practitioners seem continually at odds with those who are conducting research. One does not have to search very far to find educators who are complaining about "those ivory tower researchers," claiming that such efforts are worthless and a waste of money. In many cases those who are most vocal with such judgments have no solid basis to support their assertions. (Often one wonders how long it has been since they have read a professional journal.) It is clear that the field of education is not one that is favorably socialized toward research. This is not a recent phenomenon, although it is a continuing problem. In 1969 Ausubel highlighted this difficulty when he stated: ". . . there is both little general acceptance of the need for educational research and little appreciation of the relevance of such research for the improvement of education. A tradition of research does not exist in education as it does, for example, in medicine or in engineering, where both professionals and consumers commonly agree that research and progress are almost synonymous [p. 6]."

Not all behavioral science views research in the same manner as described above for education. Psychology, for example, is a behavioral science discipline in which research has a much more favored status. Drew and Buchanan (1979) attribute this phenomenon to disciplinary socialization and note that "the professional socialization of educators, with regard to research, seems to be much different than psychology . . . where research is a *routine* and *ongoing activity* [p. 50]." Because research is more of a way of life in psychology, students become accustomed to both reading and conducting investigations very early in their academic careers. The process and terminology of research is an integral part of their program and therefore becomes favorably incorporated in their attitudes and conceptual view of the discipline. This represents a very important source of support for research in the field and one that should serve as an important lesson to those fields in which scientific socialization is less effective.

It was also noted above that there are substantial differences between disciplines regarding the importance attached to research findings that are reported. These differences are particularly evident in the lay public. Once again the great diversity is probably best illustrated by medicine and education. Within the lay public, medical research seems to have a very high status and create a great deal of interest. In some ways this aura appears warranted, whereas in others it seems merely another manifestation of society's sacred view of the physician. Regardless of the causes, most people are simply much more interested in advances related to the physical status of humans than they are in areas pertaining to social, psychological, or educational progress. A new discovery in the field of medicine seems to be more of a newsworthy event than a discovery in these other fields. The lay public will generally continue to watch television as the newscaster describes a new surgical procedure even if they do not understand the technical terms being used. On the other hand, a discussion of some piece of educational research is more likely to serve as a signal to raid the refrigerator (despite the fact that the refrigerator bandit may have children in school and may never need surgery).

It was noted earlier that our society has historically viewed the physician and the medical field in a somewhat sacred manner. Most persons have complained at one time or another about this doctor or that hospital—even belittled the entire medical field from time to time. Despite these complaints, there is no denying that the physician and the medical field continue to be symbols of prestige. This type and degree of status is not something that is likely to be achieved by other social or behavioral science fields regardless of efforts toward that end. The impact of this lay perspective is extremely potent and has a substantial influence on the funding and support for research. Members of Congress are unlikely to vote for funds to support activities that are not valued by their constituents. If they did, the unemployment lines would be even longer.

The purpose of this section was to discuss some disciplinary differences with respect to the general image of research and scientific effort. Some of this examination drew comparisons that illustrated strengths and weaknesses in certain disciplines. For example, the field of education did not fare very well in terms of research image. This in no way should be interpreted as a suggestion that educational research is an undesirable career to pursue. To the contrary, it is a rich and fertile field that has a great need for additional scholarly emphasis. This discussion was meant to suggest how other disciplines have addressed research image problems. <u>Any discipline, if it is to remain and grow in vigor, must achieve a balance between scholarship and application</u>. The imbalance that has occurred in education is a result of many factors not the least of which has been the pressure to produce trained personnel on the practitioner level. Although that pressure remains to some degree, the vigor of education is currently in need of a serious scholarly thrust. Many professionals view the future as involving more research than ever before, particularly that which includes collaborative efforts between the disciplines.

Research methods and settings. There may be no area in which disciplinary differences are so well known as the methods used and the settings in which science is conducted. Stereotyped characterizations place the anthropologist in the field studying uncivilized cultures, the psychologist in a laboratory studying rats, and the biologist huddled over a microscope studying "Lord knows what." Although stereotyped views are always somewhat misleading, they are often based on fact to some degree. The purpose of this section is to briefly discuss differing research methods and settings. Where appropriate, notations will be made regarding characteristic use of one method or another by specific disciplines. However, the major agenda here is not one of furthering stereotypes. All methods have applicability in certain situations. Selection of an appropriate method will primarily depend on the question under study and the setting in which the research is being conducted. The fully equipped scientist must have a variety of tools on hand to effectively pursue the diverse questions that arise.

Research methods can be categorized in a number of different manners depending mostly on the perspective being used. Scientists with a sociological background often divide them into two major groups—survey and nonsurvey methods. Those with a background in psychology tend to view methodology in terms of experimental and nonexperimental techniques (as will be done here). Such perspectives are clearly more a function of disciplinary socialization than any priority of one over another.

Experimental approaches. Experimental approaches to conducting research have a long and rich history that has crossed many disciplinary boundaries including early work in agriculture and psychology. Sir Ronald Fisher is often cited as the father of experimental methodology for his work during the early part of the twentieth century (1925, 1926, 1935). There was, however, another author who actually predated Fisher in describing experimental methodology with still another field in mind—education. The work of W. A. McCall (1923), although not cited frequently, must be viewed as a classic in experimental methodology and has had a significant impact on current thinking regarding this approach to research. Although experimental approaches have been stereotypically associated with certain disciplines, McCall's methodology has been used by many researchers in medicine, biology, and many others. It is a powerful tool when the topic and setting are appropriate for its use; sufficiently powerful that some disciplines not often associated with experimentation are beginning to incorporate it into the research tool kit (e.g., anthropology).

Experimentation is most often described in terms of a tightly controlled investigation in which the researcher manipulates the particular factor under study (e.g., treatment) to determine if such manipulation generates a change in the subjects. This type of research is most commonly associated with laboratory investigations in which the experimenter tightly controls all the outside influences that might contaminate the results. If this is successfully accomplished (i.e., controlling all extraneous influences), any change observed in the subject(s) is presumed to be caused by the variable that was manipulated and is being studied. It will become evident in this volume that controlling all influences except the one under study is a major problem confronting researchers and is of central importance. It will also become evident that there are many variations of the experimental approach and that the stereotype of a precise laboratory investigation does not always hold true. However, the experimental approach remains a very powerful technique.

It was noted above that the experiment involves a study in which the re-searcher *manipulates* the factor under study. A brief discussion of this idea is needed to further examine experimentation, even in this introductory section. The factor under study—the variable that the experimenter manipulates—is known as the *experimental variable*. It is also called the *independent variable,* but in this book the term *experimental variable* will be used to avoid confusion with certain other research concepts. Obviously if the researcher is going to observe change in the subjects, there must be some means of measuring that change (e.g., improved reading performance, faster time in running the mile relay, reduced number of classroom disruptions). The measure of change is known as the *criterion measure*, that is, the process by which the researcher determines if change has occurred. It may be a test in which the number of correct responses are recorded, it may involve a stopwatch to measure time, or it may include any number of other techniques depending on the study. The criterion measure is often called the *dependent variable,* since the change (if it occurs) is presumably dependent on the researcher's manipulation of the experimental variable. For purposes in this book, the designation of the criterion measure will be used to avoid a term that often confuses the beginning researcher.

The experimental variable, in terms of the previous discussion, is thus the factor that the researcher manipulates. It may be a particular treatment in pharmacy research such as drug A compared with drug B. It may involve the comparison of teaching methods (e.g., programmed instruction compared with reading a book). In any case, the idea that has been expressed involves the fact that the researcher *manipulates* the treatment. In the literal sense, this is not always the case. Sometimes a researcher is interested in a variable that cannot be easily manipulated or has already been "manipulated" by nature. An example of such a situation might be found if the researcher were interested in studying brain damage. In this case an investigation might be designed whereby subjects who were brain damaged were compared with subjects who were not brain damaged. Obviously the researcher does not have the freedom to sample a large group of subjects and "inflict" brain damage on half of them. Instead it is more likely that the brain-damaged subjects will have to be sampled from a group of individuals who are already known to be so afflicted and the non–brain-damaged subjects from a group known not to be so afflicted. In this type of situation, the experimental variable is formulated on the basis of preexisting differences between the groups as distinguished from circumstances in which the researcher creates differences by actually manipulating the treatment. Such a format is known as a *quasi-experimental* design, whereas the term *true experiment* (or just experiment) is reserved for cases involving actual manipulation of the variable under study.

The discussion of experimental methodology has thus far focused on, and used examples of, studies in which groups of subjects are used. Variations on this theme will be explored in greater depth later in this volume. There is, however, another approach that must be mentioned under the general topic of experimentation—*time-series designs.* Time-series experiments have come into more frequent usage in the past few years and are often associated with operant conditioning or behavior modification research. In fact, time-series designs have often been labeled as single-subject designs because of their frequent use with individual subjects. Actually such a label is somewhat misleading since they can be and are used in situations in which more than one subject is studied. The particulars of this type of experimentation will be treated in greater depth later in this volume although some brief discussion is warranted here. Since time-series experiments often use a single subject (in terms of current application), this abbreviated discussion will be couched in those terms.

Time-series experiments involve investigations in which the experimental variable is basically studied across different phases of treatment. Essentially these phases compare a subject's performance without treatment (baseline) and with treatment. The fundamental purpose is to determine whether the initiation of treatment will generate a change in the subject's performance or behavior. The simple diagram in Fig. 2-1 illustrates the basic concept underlying time-series designs.

Fig. 2-1 illustrates a data display that might result from a time-series format that is known as an A-B design. In this type of experiment, the researcher records data on the subject for a time without treatment involved (phase A, known as baseline). After the researcher has enough data to reliably indicate the subject's untreated performance level, phase B (treatment) is initiated. The experi-

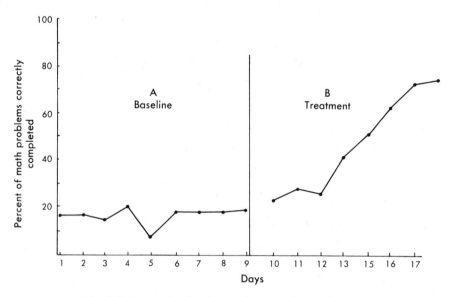

Fig. 2-1. Example of a time-series experiment format.

mental variable in this case is the treatment with two specific conditions in that variable—treatment absent and treatment present. Time-series experiments represent situations in which the researcher actually *manipulates* the experimental variable. A variety of specific time-series formats may be used in different situations. These will be explored in greater depth in later chapters.

Advantages and disadvantages of experimental approaches. There are advantages and disadvantages to all research approaches. In most cases the selection of one method over another is a matter of discretion depending on the question, the setting, and a variety of other considerations. No particular approach is uniformly inferior or superior for all research questions.

Experimental approaches to research have several advantages over nonexperimental procedures. First of all, the very nature of experimentation involves a greater degree of control exercised by the researcher. The basic aim of the investigator is one of controlling all extraneous influences and manipulating the experimental variable. Regardless of which specific design is used, the experimenter wants to arrange matters so that the factor under study varies and others do not. Thus one of the advantages of experimentation involves the amount of *control* that can be imposed.

Because of the control exercised in experimental research, this approach comes as close as any to establishing *causality.* In this case causality refers to the notion that manipulation of the experimental variable *caused* any change observed in the criterion measure. Such an idea is very appealing since it represents the firmest type of evidence that could be obtained in an investigation and therefore is a definite advantage of experimentation. However, as strong as this advantage is, it must be viewed in a relative sense and is subject to misinterpretation by those unfamiliar with the scientific process. Researchers are reluctant to assume causality with a great deal of certainty—particularly in the behavioral sciences. Notice that the word "prove" is seldom used by researchers at all (except those alleged scientists selling toothpaste on television). Despite all the care taken to control extraneous variables, there is always the possibility that somewhere there was an uncontrolled outside influence. Even the statistical analyses used in research are based on chance. (There is some probability that the results could be caused by chance.) The process of experimentation is one of coming as close as possible to establishing causality, although a single study in no way accomplishes this end. Later portions of this volume will examine this process in much greater detail.

The disadvantages of experimentation are closely related to the advantages noted above. Because of the control involved, experimental research is often conducted in somewhat of an *artificial environment.* Obviously the degree to which the environment is artificial varies greatly depending on the manner in which the study is planned and executed. A laboratory experiment may represent an extremely artificial setting, whereas an experiment conducted in the field may be less so. Results of an investigation may be substantially different in an artificial environment than they would be if the same topic was studied in a natural setting, and it is the researcher's task to determine the most appropriate situation. In certain instances steps can be taken to offset this disadvantage as will be seen later.

A second disadvantage to experimental research is closely related to the first and may even be thought of as a subtopic under the broader concern of artificiality. Experimentation, by its very nature, often involves activities, people, and materials or apparatus that are unfamiliar to the subjects. Consequently these factors may be considered artificial and alter the manner in which the subjects behave. As before, such an influence may make the results different than they would be if the subjects were performing activities and encountering people or materials with which they were familiar. This is why experimental research is often thought to be "reactive" in the sense that subjects may *react* to these influences and not perform normally. These matters can also be overcome to a considerable degree if the researcher is thorough in planning ahead.

Disciplinary utilization. Many different disciplines have used experimentation as a cornerstone of research in the field. Certainly "hard sciences" such as biology, chemistry, and physics have long found experimental research to be a basic approach to enquiry. In behavioral science the field that is most frequently associated with experimentation is psychology, although there are clearly vast differences between the subdiscipline areas of psychology. Researchers in the field of education have also used experimental research heavily, although, as with psychology, there is great variation between subareas of study in the general field of education.

Experimental research is beginning to emerge in certain social science areas that have traditionally been associated with nonexperimental investigation. Perhaps the most notable are sociology and anthropology in which considerable attention is now being given to experimentation (e.g., Bailey, 1978; Brim and Spain, 1974). Experimental research is essentially a new and (to some) foreign approach in these disciplines. Such changes do not occur easily, and there are some interesting perceptions and arguments being advanced both pro and con. Anthropology serves as an excellent example.

As noted earlier, the sterotype view of anthrolopolgical research often involves a caricature of an individual in a pith helmet and khaki shorts busily recording field notes in an uncivilized part of the world. Although this perception is obviously a popularized one, it has certain elements that are also shared by professionals in the field. Spindler and Spindler (1973) describe the work of the anthropologist as: ". . . primarily to apply a trained mind to the observation and analysis of behaviors in cultural settings other than his or her own—to epitomize, to characterize, to communicate the meaning of a way of life across cultural boundaries. Anthropology in this tradition is careful observation and careful analysis, but it is also humanistic and even poetic [in Brim and Spain, 1974, p. *vi*]."

The preceding statement captures much that has been involved in the concept of traditional anthropological research. Such research has been known as "participant observation" wherein the researcher participates in the environment being observed. Brim and Spain (1974) have proposed more experimental approaches to research as a logical progression of the field from ". . . pure description to explanation [p. 104]." Obviously a revolutionary move, this development has resulted in what is termed the "emic" versus "etic" debate (phonemic versus phonetic). Brim and Spain (1974) believe that the emic perspective in anthropology involves the contention that the "concepts used and found meaningful by the native actors themselves will be more useful in the analysis of human behavior than will concepts and distinctions not meaningful to them [p. 106]." The etic view, on the other hand, holds that scientific data should be analyzed in terms of the concepts developed by the researcher. There are appealing points to both sides. The purpose of this section, however, was not to debate but to indicate that experimental research is now being considered as a part of the investigative framework in fields in which it has previously been ignored. Such changes do not come easily since our disciplinary narrowness often eliminates many potentially useful techniques. The statements below are presented as an epilogue to this section. They have seriously been advanced as arguments against using experimental designs in anthropology. Some have been encountered and overcome by other fields (those more accustomed to experimentation), whereas others seem merely to echo the growing pains of any discipline as it begins to reach out for new ideas and methodology. Certainly such pains are not the sole property of anthropology.

1. The well-designed research necessarily brings with it a reluctance to deal with phenomena not amenable to powerful and efficient research design. Thus vital, relevant, but often less manageable phenomena will tend to be avoided since they are unsuited for the "elegant."
2. An emphasis on rigorous research design, with its implied commitment to "scientific neutrality," will result in a decrease in civic commitment or involvement. Some anthropologists see such neutrality, or any neutrality, as the ultimate dehumanization of the most human of the sciences.
3. An emphasis on well-designed research will contribute to the erosion of ethical standards, as there will be a strong tendency for the anthropologist committed to well-designed research to sacrifice ethical principles for the principles of research design.*

Nonexperimental approaches. There are a variety of nonexperimental approaches to conducting research. Like experimentation, nonexperimental methods have a long history of use by many disciplines and have been the basis for

---

*From *Research design in anthropology: paradigms and pragmatics in the testing of hypotheses* by J. A. Brim and D. H. Spain. New York: Holt, Rinehart and Winston, Inc., 1974, p. 106.

enquiry in many different settings. In some ways nonexperimental research may be thought of as the mirror image of experimentation. Nonexperimental researchers tend to observe, analyze, and describe what *exists* rather than manipulating the variable under study. Nonexperimental researchers do not use direct control (such as in a laboratory) in the same fashion that is characteristic of experimentation. Additionally, nonexperimental research is more often conducted in the natural environment than experimentation. These points represent rather substantial distinctions between experimental and nonexperimental research. However, it is important to emphasize that the overall research process described in Chapter 1 (see Fig. 1-1) remains intact; only the methodology changes. Two different nonexperimental methods will be discussed in this section — survey research and observation.

1. Survey research involves asking questions of a sample of subjects who are presumably representative of the group being studied. The questions are related either directly or indirectly to the topic under investigation, and the answers provided by the subjects represent the data. Surveys are conducted using questionnaires or interviews and may investigate a broad range of topics. Most people have been involved as subjects in surveys of one type or another. Some surveys are designed primarily to collect descriptive information such as age, annual income, and political affiliation. Others are aimed at determining attitudes or opinions concerning some particular topic (e.g., type of automobile preferred, perceptions of the President's effectiveness). In many cases both descriptive and attitudinal questions are included in the same survey if the purpose of the study requires both. Examples of this latter type of survey can be found in marketing research in which the goal is to determine what products appeal to certain segments of the population.

As suggested above, survey research may be undertaken for a variety of purposes. The researcher who conducts a descriptive survey may wish only to describe what exists in a given population at a particular time. In this type of study, the descriptive information obtained represents the answer to the research question. On the other hand, a comparative survey may be conducted to see if there is a difference between two groups of subjects or between two times. This type of study may be undertaken, for example, to test some sociological theory concerning the two groups. There are many variations of survey research and a number of considerations that must be involved in planning and executing such investigations. These will be explored in greater depth in later chapters.

2. Observation is the second nonexperimental method to be examined. Actually classifying observation as a separate method and purely nonexperimental is somewhat misleading. It is being described here simply because manipulation is not inherent in the process. Observation is basically a data collection technique that is used in many different types of research and is *not* the exclusive property of nonexperiemental research. Many investigations that clearly involve experimentation also use observation as a means of collecting data. Therefore, since observation cuts across different research methods it is necessary to examine various types of observation.

One way of classifying observation techniques involves viewing the observer as either a participant or nonparticipant. In participant observation, the individual conducting the investigation actually *participates* in the setting or activities being observed. As the term suggests, the nonparticipant observer plays an outsider role and does *not* actively participate in the environment. Participant observation has long been the traditional method of conducting field research in anthropology as studies have been undertaken on various cultures. (The term *ethnography* is also used in such investigations.) Research of this type is most often associated with the study of primitive cultures (perhaps the classic being Margaret Mead's *Coming of Age in Samoa*). It is also being used, however, to investigate subcultures within contemporary societies (e.g., Spradley's *You Owe Yourself a Drunk: An Ethnography of Urban Nomads*, 1970). In participant observation, it is typical for the observer to literally become a *member* of the culture of group under study. Data are often recorded in the form of "field notes," which represent the observer's perceptions. It is not uncommon for the participants in the study to be unaware that they are being investigated since the observer either becomes or appears to become (to the group being studied) a part of the environment. Nonparticipant observers, as noted above, do not actively become involved in the environment under investigation. In this role, the observer does *not* become a member of the culture or group. Data collection through nonparticipant observation may be either unknown or known to the group being studied. In some cases the observer is evident (since there is no pretense of group membership), whereas in others the observer may not be obvious (such as observations through a one-way mirror).

A second method of classifying observation involves the amount of structure imposed on the study. Structure can be viewed in terms of both the observer and the environment for the investigation. The observations may be arranged so that little or no structure is imposed on the manner in which the data are collected (e.g., field notes recorded without any guidelines). On the other hand, the observer may be given a great deal of structure, such as a protocol or checklist used for counting and classifying behavior frequency. The structure of the setting may be similarly viewed. The observer may record data in a completely unstructured environment—that setting in which the subjects habitually live. The opposite end of this continuum would be when subjects are observed in a totally artificial or foreign setting such as in a laboratory experiment.

Observation is a very useful and powerful data collection procedure that spans many disciplines and many settings. Although observation has been discussed briefly, many specific details must also be discussed before an investigation of the procedure can be started. These specific details will be examined in greater depth in Chapter 6.

Advantages and disadvantages of nonexperimental approaches. To some degree, the advantages and disadvantages of nonexperimental research have already been encountered. Almost by definition, nonexperimental investigations are described in terms of what experimentation is *not*. Consequently the advantages of experimentation partially represent the disadvantages of nonexperimental research and vice versa. However, it is important to note the word "partially"; it will become evident later in this volume that *characteristic* advantages and disadvantages are being discussed. The ingenious researcher will be able to circumvent problems to some degree by the manner in which procedures and instrumentation are planned.

One of the disadvantages noted previously under experimentation involved the artificial environment in which such studies often occur. As discussed earlier, such an artificial setting may influence the manner in which subjects behave and therefore alter results. What is a disadvantage of experimental research here becomes an advantage for certain nonexperimental investigations. Some nonexperimental research involves the primary purpose of studying subjects in their natural habitat (e.g., the anthropological field study). To the degree that this is accomplished, the subjects being investigated should behave in a natural manner and the study itself will not influence the data. Clearly not all nonexperimental research is conducted in a naturalistic setting, in fact, some may be as contrived and artificial as a laboratory experiment. In such circumstances, the advantages discussed here would obviously be lost.

Many advantages and disadvantages of nonexperimental research depend on the type of data collection technique being used. For example, a survey study may be quite economical if the data are collected with a mail-out questionnaire. The expense of reproducing questionnaires and postage may be rather minimal. On the other hand, a survey conducted using interviewers might be very expensive. Personnel costs for trained interviewers can be quite high not to mention transportation and living expenses (if the interviewer is away from home). However, there are notorious problems with mail-out questionnaires that must also be considered.

Similarly there may be difficulties in quantifying certain types of observation data (e.g., field notes recorded without specific guidelines), whereas in other observational studies the data may be easily quantified. This latter case may exist when the observer used a carefully designed protocol or behavior checklist to record data.

One area in which nonexperimental research is at somewhat of a disadvantage is in the general area of control. Although the use of control varies from technique to technique and from study to study, nonexperimental research does not ordinarily involve as much control or the same types of control as is the case with experimentation. The survey respondent may complete a questionnaire at a convenient time, but it is unlikely that the mood, time of day, or setting will be consistent between respondents. Unstructured observations in field settings may literally exert no control on the data collection. (Although control may be very evident in certain other observational studies.)

It is clear that there is great variation regarding advantages and disadvantages of nonexperimental research depending on the particular method used. In many cases the particular data collection procedure must be considered in isolation to fully explore the method and its specific benefits or problems. Such a complete and detailed discussion far exceeds the scope of this section but will be addressed in considerable depth in later chapters. This brief section has served to illustrate that *no* given approach or method is totally free of problems. Each has certain strong points that must be weighed against its weaknesses in determining how the research question is to be studied. This also emphasizes the need for the fully equipped researcher to have knowledge of a variety of investigative techniques. Otherwise the studies conducted (questions explored) will be severely limited and actually determined by the tools available. This is no more acceptable in research than it is in auto repair.

Disciplinary utilization. Many different disciplines have and continue to use nonexperimental research approaches. It is obvious from the discussion above that participant observation has been a traditional means of conducting enquiry for anthropology. It has also been used in sociology, psychology, and education. As these different disciplines are noted, it is important to recall the earlier point that it is not always clear exactly *what* type (in terms of discipline) of research is being conducted. If a researcher (sociologist by training) is studying the subculture of a junior high school, is that individual conducting educational research, sociological research, or psychological research?

Survey research has often been undertaken in sociology, but it is also conducted in education, psychology, business, and political science. Without proceeding further it becomes abundantly clear that, in general, each discipline has used every type of research at one time or another. Despite the disciplinary stereotypes that are held, it also becomes evident that disciplinary narrowness creates many problems for the scientist who wishes to examine a variety of research questions. The optimal situation would favor researchers who were conversant with many methodologies, perhaps sufficiently knowledgeable that investigations could actually be implemented in the various modes. If this cannot be accomplished, the minimal hope would be that researchers can at least understand approaches to enquiry other than that typically associated with the discipline in which preparation occurred.

REFERENCES

Anderson, S. C., and Ball, S. *The profession and practice of program evaluation.* San Francisco: Jossey-Bass, Inc., Publishers, 1978.

Ausubel, D. P. The nature of educational research. In W. J. Gephart and R. B. Ingle (Eds.), *Educational research: selected readings.* Columbus, Ohio: Charles E. Merrill Publishing Co., 1969, 5-13.

Bailey, K. D. *Methods of social research.* New York: The Free Press, 1978.

Brim, J. A., and Spain, D. H. *Research design in anthropology: paradigms and pragmatics in the testing of hypotheses.* New York: Holt, Rinehart and Winston, Inc., 1974.

Clark, D. L., and Guba, E. G. An inventory of contextual factors and conditions affecting individual and institutional behavior in school, colleges and departments of education. Bloomington, Ind.: RITE Occasional Papers Series, Indiana University, 1976.

Cooley, W. W., and Lohnes, P. R. *Evaluation research in education.* New York: Irvington Publishers, Inc., 1976.

Drew, C. J., and Buchanan, M. L. Research on teacher education: status and need. *Teacher Education and Special Education,* 1979, *2*(2), 50-55.

Fisher, R. A. The arrangement of field experiments. *Journal Min. Agriculture,* 1926, *33*, 503-513.

Fisher, R. A. *The design of experiments* (1st ed.). London: Oliver & Boyd, 1935.

Fisher, R. A. *Statistical methods for research workers* (1st ed.). London: Oliver & Boyd, 1925.

Guttentag, M., and Struening, E. L. (Eds.) *Handbook of evaluation research* (vol.2). Beverly Hills: Sage Publications, Inc., 1975.

Hemphill, J. K. The relationship between research and evaluation studies. In R. W. Tyler (Ed.), *Educational evaluation: new roles, new means.* Chicago: NSSE, 1969, 189-220.

McCall, W. A. *How to experiment in education.* New York: The Macmillan Co., 1923.

Mead, M. Coming of age in Samoa. In *From the south seas: studies of adolescence and sex in primitive societies.* New York: William Morrow & Co., Inc., 1939.

Popham, W. J. (Ed.) *Evaluation in education: current applications,* Berkeley: McCutchan Publishing Corp., 1974.

Provus, M. Evaluation of ongoing programs in the public school system. In R. W. Tyler (Ed.), *Educational evaluation: new roles, new means.* Chicago: NSSE, 1969, 242-283.

Spradley, J. P. *You owe yourself a drunk: an ethnography of urban nomads.* Boston: Little, Brown and Co., 1970.

Stake, R. E., and Denny, T. Needed concepts and techniques for utilizing more fully the potential of evaluation. In R. W. Tyler (Ed.) *Educational evaluation: new roles, new means.* Chicago: NSSE, 1969, 370-390.

Struening, E. L., and Guttentag, M. (Eds.) *Handbook of evaluation research* (vol. 1). Beverly Hills: Sage Publications, Inc., 1975.

Vickers, G. The promotion of psychiatric research. *British Journal of Psychiatry,* 1968, *114*, 925-934.

CHAPTER 3

Ethical issues in conducting research

OVERVIEW

Consideration of ethical issues related to research is not a new phenomenon, although it has clearly surfaced in a more prominent fashion in recent years. As with many issues, the ethics of science have received greater attention as a result of a variety of influences. One of these influences involves abuses committed by some researchers who have operated either in a state of ignorance or with a lack of regard for the rights of others. A second influence that has contributed to increased attention to research ethics is closely associated with general societal awareness. Our society has experienced a greatly heightened sensitivity to the rights of individuals during the past 20 years. In some cases this sensitivity has been broadly based and related to issues far removed from the conduct of science. As might be expected, however, research activities have not escaped this trend. The purpose of this chapter is to explore some of the ethical issues involved in conducting research. Throughtful consideration of these issues is extremely important for both the beginning and experienced researcher as well as the consumer of research.

The importance of ethics in research is most dramatically illustrated by highly public and repugnant abuses or social value violations. Perhaps the most serious and widely known examples of such abuses occurred in the experiments conducted with Nazi concentration camp prisoners during World War II. These experiments involved grossly inhumane activities that were essentially viewed as unthinkable in civilized society. Perhaps because of the context of these experiments, general sensitivity of the lay public was not substantially heightened on a long-term basis. More recent evidence, however, has clearly indicated that concern for ethics in research (and potentially harmful outcomes) cannot be limited to wartime mentality related to prisoners. For example, information has recently come to light concerning what seem to be serious health problems resulting from nuclear testing in Nevada during the 1950s. Was this a violation of what was ethical research practices? Such questions are not easily answered, but it is obvious that certain additional precautions should have been taken.

Most of the topics to be discussed in this chapter are not nearly as dramatic as the examples presented above. *Most* do not involve death to the subjects by immersion in ice water or death from cancer caused by nuclear fallout. (Note the emphasis on "most"; some abuses are only different by subtle degrees.) The discussion in this chapter will be focused primarily on issues, activities, and situations that are far from black and white in terms of ethics; some that more liberal researchers may think do not warrant discussion. In all cases, a balanced presentation remains the goal. There are no simple answers and solutions; no pat answers. Although some guidelines are suggested, the burden of consideration for each investigation remains with the scientist.

The problem of ethical issues in research has been alluded to only in general terms, with a few specific examples. If not now, certainly by the end of this chapter, you may begin to have somewhat of a defeatist view. With all these problems, why should one even try to conduct research? This is not an uncommon response and is frequently voiced by young researchers who are encountering difficulty obtaining subjects for their studies. This topic was articulately and delightfully addressed in a paper by Carl Haywood (1976), which was appropriately titled "The ethics of doing research . . . and of not doing it." This paper was contexted in the discipline of psychology but has great relevance to all research. Haywood begins by noting that "the chief function of research is to dispel ignorance, a commodity that is in plenteous supply. . ." He continues and discusses how some (psychologists) may be guilty of unethical conduct in their research. However, the essential point of Haywood's comment is that researchers (psychologists) ". . . may also be guilty of unethical conduct if they fail to conduct important research. The latter part of this statement may be especially true. . .(of researchers who work in areas). . .that are so characterized by ignorance that the systematic acquisition of new knowledge is especially critical [p. 311]." Haywood's statements capture why one should conduct research even when faced with a variety of problems that seem to block such efforts. Additionally, as will be seen in later portions of this chapter, the ethical considerations do not make research impossible. While investigations may require a little extra thought and effort, they can be successfully undertaken.

This chapter will not provide a "complete ethical checklist" that will cover all questions, settings, or concerns. Such a task would be impossible and would not be helpful in your ability to thoughtfully consider and decide about each research situation you might encounter. Although there are certain guidelines that are relatively firm, for the most part the best insurance against unethical research practices is the knowledgeable individual scientist who can intelligently consider the circumstances being faced. Ethical issues will be discussed in three major categories: (1) ethical issues related to subjects, (2) ethical issues related to particular research approaches, and (3) ethics and professionalism. It will become evident that certain issues (e.g., consent) are relevant concerns in more than one of these categories. In fact, the categories of discussion are interrelated in a variety of fashions with separation here for instructional convenience.

ETHICAL ISSUES RELATED TO SUBJECTS

One of the areas that has received the most attention in recent years involves ethical issues related to subjects. This is not surprising in view of the generally heightened concern for individual rights. Ethical issues related to subjects will be examined in four major ways—consent, harm, privacy, and deception.

Consent

Consent, in the context of research, involves the procedure by which the subjects choose whether or not they wish to participate in a study. Although this may appear to be a rather simple concept on the surface, its complexities will become abundantly evident. Consent has received a great deal of attention recently and is most often referred to as *informed consent,* which is actually a misnomer. From a legal standpoint consent involves three elements: *capacity, information,* and *voluntariness.* For the most part, all three elements must be present for consent to be effective. It is also important to understand that consent is seldom (if ever) permanent and may be withdrawn at any time. (The act of withdrawing consent must also include the elements of capacity, information, and voluntariness.) To fully examine consent, each of the component elements must be discussed.

Turnbull (1977) has provided a detailed examination of consent and discussed each of the elements from a legal perspective. The first element, capacity, is viewed as "the present ability to acquire or retain knowledge; the ability to do something, a faculty or aptitude; the legal qualification or authority to perform an act [p. 6]." These general terms basically refer to two factors—the legal qualification factor and the ability factor. Legal qualification is most often viewed in terms of age; individuals under the age of majority (generally 18 years) are usually considered to be legally unable to make certain decisions. The ability factor is most often thought of in terms of mental competence to give consent. (Does the individual understand the nature and consequences of giving consent?) Clearly the capacity element is not simple even from this brief discussion. It often becomes even more complex in the context of implementation, which will be discussed further in later sections.

The element of information must also be carefully examined. Turnbull (1977) discusses this in the following manner: ". . .the focus is on *'what' information is given* and *'how' it is given* since it must be effectively communicated (given and received) to be acted upon. The concern is with the *fullness* and *effectiveness* of the disclosure: is it designed to be fully understood, and is it fully understood?

The burden of satisfying these two tests rests on the professional [p. 8]." From the perspective of the researcher, the last sentence of this quotation has great importance. Literally interpreted, this statement suggests that it is the researcher's duty to see that the information given to the potential subject is designed to be fully understood and *is* fully understood. This perspective places a great responsibility on the investigator and makes assurance that effective consent has been obtained even more complicated.

As noted above, the third element of consent is voluntariness, which, again, may be more complex than it appears on the surface. Obviously the notion of voluntary consent implies that the subjects must consent to participate in the study of their own free will. There are, however, certain subtleties involved in implementation that warrant attention. Turnbull (1977) examines voluntariness and notes that the consenting individual must be "so situated as to be able to exercise free power of choice without the intervention of any element of force, fraud, deceit, duress, over-reaching or other ulterior form of constraint or coercion [p. 10]." Furthermore, it is clear that the intent of this interpretation is that any such "constraint or coercion" must not be either explicit or *implicit* on the part of the investigator.

The collective consideration of all three elements of consent has great impact on the manner in which a study is planned and executed. Each research situation presents a different set of circumstances, and consent procedures must be adapted accordingly. For investigators in certain areas (e.g., child development, mental retardation, mental health), the type of subjects frequently studied present particularly perplexing problems. Keith-Spiegel (1976) identified three types of subjects typically involved in behavioral research as ". . . nonhuman organisms, 'free-agent' adult humans, and a variety of other human beings who by virtue of some characteristic (such as age, institutionalization, physical illness, mental disability, or the like) need special consideration and protection (p. 53)." Each type raises different consent issues, but the third category represents a particularly difficult situation because of the need for *special consideration and protection*. Such subjects will receive repeated attention in the discussion and examination of the consent issues regarding *who* and *when*.

Consent: who. The question of who may give consent is not a difficult one for Keith-Spiegel's second category of subject "types." Obviously for "free-agent" adult humans, *they* (the subjects) can and must give consent to participate in research. It is also clear that they must do so on a voluntary basis and with complete information concerning the nature and consequences of participation. Research with the first category of subjects—nonhuman organisms—raises an entirely different set of questions and issues that will receive attention in a separate section later in this chapter. However, Keith-Spiegel's third category of subjects, humans in need of special consideration and protection, must be a major focus of the current discussion regarding consent.

Many individuals in our third category of subjects are generally thought to be unable to give consent on their own. They may be lacking in capacity because of mental handicap or because they are legally too young. They may appear very vulnerable to either explicit or implicit coercion (thus violating the truly voluntary element of consent). They may have a combination of these and other characteristics that render them relatively powerless in terms of exercising free will and making decisions. For individuals in such circumstances, the question becomes one of who can give consent on their behalf (and what considerations must receive attention in the process).

The first possible answer to this question is obviously the parent, guardian, or other agent who is legally responsible for and authorized to act in the person's behalf. Although this may seem simple it is not, and the prerogative of consent is not constant. It varies greatly from situation to situation and between subjects. For example, legal and ethical writing seems to suggest that parents may generally give consent that permits the withholding of treatment from (and ultimate death of) infants who are defective at birth. However, literature and the courts have also suggested that it is *not* the parents' sole prerogative to give consent for sterilization of their retarded offspring (Chinn, Drew and Logan, 1979). This seems rather paradoxical since in one situation the outcome may be death and in the other the individual is merely rendered incapable of procreation. The qualifying word "merely" is not meant to suggest that the latter situation is deemed insignificant. It does, however, seem somewhat less dramatic than a decision to let someone die.

Although the above examples are somewhat removed from our central concern, they serve to illustrate the complexities of consent rather openly and also to highlight the difficulty in determining *who* can consent on behalf of those who cannot themselves. It is interesting to examine the differences between the consent situations in these cases. It seems that the parent, guardian, or other agent (e.g., institutional administrator) can probably give consent until it comes to someone's attention that the *interest of the consentor are at odds with what may be the interests of the subject.* This is exactly the case with sterilization. Some have thought that (and become vocal about) the fact that "parents or guardians often have interests that conflict with those of the retarded child. The parents of a retarded child may have understandable fears that the grandchild will also be retarded. Moreover, the parents may perceive a danger of their retarded child proving to be an unfit parent, and might wish to avoid the risk of shouldering responsibilities of grandchildren . . . [Murdock, 1974, p. 917]." This notion has not gone unnoticed, and Baron (1976) cites a noticeable tendency in terms of court intervention in parental decisions regarding sterilization consent. This illustrates clearly an area in which the expected avenues of consent have become less clear because of (and sensitivity being heightened to) potential conflict between legal guardians and the individual involved. For situations in which subjects cannot provide their own consent, the researcher should not automatically assume that "parental" consent is sufficient. Although it is for the most part, one should constantly be vigilant in situations in which it may not be.

Considerations concerning who should give consent in the case of "high-risk" subjects are clearly not simple. The most obvious place to turn is the legal guardian, although the points made above suggest that there are situations when this is not sufficient. The researcher should also *not* automatically eliminate input from the subjects themselves, even if they are in this special consideration category. For example, despite the legal incapacity, subjects who are 16 or 17 years of age should be consulted regarding their willingness to participate in a study. In fact, subjects of a much younger age may have definite opinions concerning whether or not they want to be involved. These are illustrations of where any single source of consent (e.g., parents) may be necessary *but not sufficient*. For example, consent for participation of young children may not be truly voluntary if only the parents or guardians are consulted (similarly for institutionalized subjects where the administrator may be the authorizing official). Children may feel coerced by parental pressure, either implicit or explicit. Keith-Spiegel (1976) illustrates this point nicely when she notes what might well be one of those "old rules to live by": *"Obey thy Mother and Father—and anyone else bigger than you are* [p. 56]." Although the letter of the law may suggest that parental consent is all that is necessary, the researcher would be foolish, and likely unethical, if input from the subjects themselves is not included. Such considerations may even be appropriate and advisable for "risk" areas other than age (such as mild retardation, mild mental health problems, and so forth). Investigators must use their best professional judgment in determining who should be involved in the consent process.

Consent: when. The generally accepted view of when consent must be obtained dictates that it is *necessary* ". . . whenever subjects are exposed to substantial risks or are asked to forfeit personal rights [Diener and Crandall, 1978, p. 34]." The notions of risk and personal rights are interpreted with great variability. Some research circumstances clearly require consent, whereas others are more subject to debate. The concept of risk to the subject may include a number of different situations ranging from actual physical harm in the form of pain to potential psychological harm such as emotional stress. Similarly the forfeiture of personal rights may vary greatly from a serious invasion of privacy to a situation in which the subjects' rights are not threatened in any significant fashion.

The factors involved in when consent should be obtained are similar to those regarding who can provide effective consent. There is no specific checklist for guidance; researchers must exercise their best professional judgment. Some would strongly maintain that consent should be obtained in all research, while others take a more moderate view. Diener and Crandall (1978) tend to subscribe to the latter position and hold that mandatory consent in studies that are entirely harmless is probably an unrealistic and unnecessary requirement. It will become increasingly evident that the factors under consideration are fluid at best. If it is unclear whether or not consent is needed, it may be prudent to err on the side of caution (again, depending on the circumstances surrounding the investigation).

Consent: how. The method of obtaining consent will vary greatly depending on the situation involved and the degree of potential risk for the subjects. If the study creates little or no risk or potential invasion of privacy, consent may be obtained less formally (i.e., verbally). In such circumstances, subjects may be verbally informed of the nature of the investigation (assuming that the capacity element is present) and can probably give consent verbally. In other situations when subjects are placed in a more "risky" position (e.g., potential harm, stress, substantial invasion of privacy), consent should be obtained in writing. This is typically accomplished by providing both written and verbal explanations of the study, and the subject indicates consent by signing the written form. In certain cases the provision of both verbal and written explanations is not possible such as in a survey using mailed questionnaires. Usually the subject's willingness to complete the questionnaire is adequate indication of consent. It is important, however, that a written explanation of the survey is included with the questionnaire (often as a part of the instructions *on* the questionnaire) with a clear indication that responses to the questions are voluntary. In all cases, the researcher must remain cognizant of the three elements of consent and also remember (and so inform the subject) that consent can be withdrawn at any time.

Harm

Perhaps the most central concern in all research ethics is that individuals *not be harmed by serving as subjects in an investigation.* In the context of research ethics, harm must be viewed much more broadly than a surface perspective may connote. Certainly we are speaking of extreme physical harm as illustrated in the World War II Nazi experiments. Additionally, harm in this context includes such factors as psychological stress, personal embarrassment or humiliation, or any of a myriad of influences that may adversely affect the subjects in a significant way.

Vulnerable types of research. Certain types of studies appear to present particular difficulties in terms of potential harm to subjects. Obviously research that involves physically dangerous treatment may present very real possibilities of harm if the treatment is "inflicted" on the participants. Unfortunately there are examples of such investigations in which ethical principles were violated in an extreme fashion. Some of these include such acts as the injection of live cancer cells into humans (without the consent or even knowledge of the subjects) and experimental infection of subjects with syphilis (without treatment and, in fact, resulting in death among some of the participants). Hopefully these types of studies are not being conducted currently, but they must be noted as examples to keep us mindful of the extreme acts that may occur and must be guarded against.

There are other areas of research that must also be viewed as "high risk" in terms of potential harm to subjects. For example, some studies are specifically designed to investigate the effects of psychological or emotional stress. Such research represents extremely difficult circumstances, especially when the procedures involve actual "infliction" of such stress. From the outset there is always the possibility that some subject may have a heart attack as a result of the stress. Additionally there is also the distinct possibility that the stress itself may be harmful to subjects from a psychological standpoint. This might be a particular concern with subjects who have a high degree of vulnerability (e.g., either identified or unidentified mental health problems)—a topic that will receive further attention.

Clearly science in general cannot ignore or avoid programs of research that are vulnerable to potential subject harm (although some would declare such efforts inappropriate for investigation). Since one of the basic aims of science is to "improve" society, these are the very topics of study that *need* attention. However, the manner in which such investigations are planned and executed is extremely important and, at times, must be undertaken with great caution. Even embarrassment or humiliation may represent a serious harmful effect and may draw strong ethical criticism.

Vulnerable subjects. A study that has a high risk regarding potential harm may be thusly characterized because of the particular subjects being studied. This becomes a more obvious problem when dealing with Keith-Spiegel's (1978) third category of subjects often used in behavioral research. This type of participant involves those human beings ". . . who by virtue of some characteristic (such as age, institutionalization, physical illness, mental disability, or the like) . . ." are rendered relatively powerless with regard to exercising free will in choosing whether or not to serve as research subjects [p. 53]. Such subjects may be less capable of understanding potential harm, or they may feel openly or implicitly coerced in some fashion. In a very real sense, they are disadvantaged and relatively powerless in our society (Kelman, 1972). Institutionalized individuals, such as criminal prisoners, mentally retarded persons, or those persons with serious mental illness, may agree to participate in a study either because they "should to show evidence of good behavior" or to gain approval of their institutional supervisors. Unfortunately, some of our worst examples of ethical violations (noted earlier) occurred with such subjects.

Highly vulnerable subjects should not be taken advantage of, and researchers investigating topics involving such individuals must exercise particular care in executing their studies. Very young children, elderly citizens, retarded or mentally ill individuals can be easily convinced that most activities are important, are of little harm, and should be engaged in for the benefit of society. The scientist who is seriously concerned with research ethics must remain especially alert to ethical concerns regarding harm when studying such subjects. This often raises a problem encountered previously. These are the problems (and subjects) that desperately *need investigation* to improve the culture and their lot in life and to benefit society. Consequently, these difficulties *will* likely be encountered by all scientists sooner or later. As before, thoughtful and knowledgeable consideration provides the primary source of guidance for procedures.

How much is harmful? The discussions in this section, as well as others in this chapter, have used many qualifying adjectives that are open to great variation in interpretation. Questions continually arise regarding what is meant by a *high degree* of vulnerability and a *potential, substantial,* or *significant* risk. These are not easy questions to answer. Although the terms suggest quantification, they refer to topics that are very difficult to quantify precisely. Basically they represent qualifying terminology that is primarily related to perceptions, values, or judgment. There is little likelihood that there will be widespread agreement concerning exactly what is meant. However, the topic cannot be ignored; it must be examined at least in terms of some broad perspectives. The question is reduced to one of attempting to determine "how much (harm) is harmful?"

Some of you may have already decided, for yourself, how much threat, stress, or pain can be considered harmful. If you have, it would not be unusual for your determination to be near one end or the other of the continuum (that is, nothing should ever be done in research that would possibly pose the slightest imposition of threat of stress on a subject versus the interests of science and the betterment of society should be paramount; an individual subject's distress or harm should largely be discounted in favor of the potential benefit for the larger number). Although both of these viewpoints have been argued and thoughtfully considered, current writing seems to suggest that neither extreme can be accepted as a blanket rule (Diener and Crandall, 1978). The topic is simply too complex, and the continuum must be explored more completely (and ultimately judicious caution exercised).

Some researchers have fallen back on *consent* as a means of dealing with the harm issues. The notion here has been that potentially harmful studies can only be undertaken if the subjects have effectively consented (have the capacity to understand the potential risk, full information concerning any harm to them that may occur, and voluntarily agree to subject themselves to such harm). Since consent is an essential prerequisite to such investigations, this would seem to afford little in terms of fully attending to the problems of harm to subjects. The complexities of consent were reviewed earlier, and even under the most careful precautions, an investigator would not be free to assume no further responsibility regarding potential harm.

Another approach to addressing the issue of harm to subjects has been called the *cost/benefit ratio* concept. This notion involves a comparison of the potential benefits of a given study with the potential risks to the participants. Presumably if the benefit of the study outweighs the potential harm, the study is considered ethical and vice versa. For example, suppose an investigation were proposed that had potential for solving the inflation problem in the United States. However, to conduct the study, a sample of 1000 participants would be required to divulge personal details concerning amount of income, sources of income, and the manner in which every dollar is spent. Certainly this represents a substantial invasion of privacy—but clearly the inflation problem badly needs a solution. Do the benefits outweigh the harm? Obviously this becomes a matter of judgment, like so many other issues discussed here. It also points up some of the difficulties with the cost/benefit ratio concept.

The idea of assessing costs and benefits has considerable appeal, but how does one accomplish this task? It may be a rather simple matter in business, but in many cases we are confronted with factors that defy measurement. How does one evaluate and predict the harm that might be inflicted on a subject? An equally difficult question involves how one measures and predicts benefit, and further, how does the process of balancing subject harm with potential benefit proceed? These are problems without precise solutions and must be considered in a very thoughtful manner. The evaluation process must involve a careful review by professionals other than the investigator proposing the study (often an institutional or agency "human subjects committee"). If assessments were solely the prerogative of the researcher, an obvious conflict of interest may influence the decision. (After all, the researcher has a vested interest in the study.)

This discussion of some of the difficulties involved in the cost/benefit ratio approach to addressing the problem of subject risk is in no way meant to suggest that it is not a useful concept. It cannot, however, stand by itself as a sufficient safeguard. A combination of consent and cost/benefit assessment provides additional insurance, but even here there are further steps that can and should be taken. As much as possible, research should be planned and executed in a manner that reduces the probability of harm to subjects. A study is always more ethically justifiable when there is little likelihood or risk. If there is a possibility of harm to the participants, it should be as minor as possible. Additionally, if there is potential harm to subjects, the researcher must be concerned about how long the effects will last after the study is completed and if they are reversible. Obviously it is desirable to deal with an effect that can be easily reversed and one that has a short postinvestigation duration. It is also desirable, if there is a potential harmful effect, that it be detectable early so that the study can be terminated if necessary.

Potential harm to subjects must always be a concern when an investigation is being planned and executed. As we noted earlier, it is an important goal that no harm of any kind be imposed on subjects as a function of participating in research. There are circumstances, however, when subjects are placed at risk to some degree. How much risk should be considered harmful is a difficult question as this discussion has indicated. It is hoped that the risk not be any greater than the subjects experience in their daily routine.

Privacy

The value attached to individual privacy has varied throughout history and vast differences still are evident from one country to another. It has, however, become a "right" that is highly treasured in contemporary western society. As with other ethical considerations, privacy has become an increasingly valued right because of serious abuses as well as a generally heightened sensitivity to individual prerogatives in recent years.

Ruebhausen and Brim (1966) examined this issue and stated that "the essence of privacy is . . . the freedom of the individual to pick and choose . . . the time and circumstances under which, and most importantly, the extent to which, his attitudes, beliefs, behavior, and opinions are to be shared with or withheld from others [p. 426]." Obviously total privacy does not exist, and people are required on occasion to yield a certain amount of privacy for one reason or another. In some cases this is done voluntarily to obtain something in return (e.g., a person divulges certain personal information to obtain a loan or credit card). Even in these circumstances, there have been rather dramatic changes recently in terms of the types of information that can be requested. There are, however, other situations in which it is not so clear that the information is being obtained voluntarily. It is this latter type of action in which an individual's free choice to privacy is endangered.

Science is based on the collection and analysis of data or information. In particular, the behavioral and social sciences often collect and analyze data concerning humans, both as individuals and groups. This is the point at which the goals of research and the right of privacy may emerge in conflict. Frequently research of this nature is aimed at obtaining information concerning attitudes, beliefs, opinions, and behavior—those very items that Ruebhausen and Brim defined as the essence of privacy. Thus it becomes a complex issue to pursue the goals of science and, at the same time, guard against unnecessary invasion of subjects' privacy.

In discussing privacy, several factors must be addressed regarding any research project. Obviously one must consider how sensitive the data are to the individual or group being studied. For example, certain types of information may be considered sensitive under any circumstances. Data concerning sexual experiences or preferences probably represents information that many people would want to keep private in most cases. Other information might be less sensitive, such as one's name. Additionally there are many types of information that would be considered situationally sensitive; information that would be divulged under certain conditions but not others (e.g., age, weight, personal income). There is a greater probability of privacy invasion when the data being collected are sensitive or potentially sensitive. Under such conditions, the researcher must exercise extra precaution and always proceed with great care.

The setting in which the research is being conducted may also be an important factor in considering potential privacy invasion. Diener and Crandall (1978) have viewed the setting in terms of a somewhat fluid continuum much like sensitivity. On one end, there are those settings that are nearly always considered private, such as a person's home. The other end of the continuum might be represented by a setting in which privacy is not generally assumed, such as a public park. As before, some settings may be only situationally private—a person's home cannot be considered private when a realtor is showing it to a prospective buyer. Clearly the researcher must consider the setting in which the data are collected if undue invasion of privacy is to be avoided.

A final point to be addressed regarding privacy involves how public the information is going to be. As a subject, you may not believe that your privacy has been seriously threatened if only one or two people know (e.g., the researchers collecting the data). It is a totally different story, however, if the investigators publish your name and personal opinions in the local newspaper. In so doing, they have made the information (which may be very sensitive) available to the general public and made it possible for those reading the newspaper to identify *you* as the individual holding those opinions. Hopefully such a breach of confidence would not occur, but this example is not without some base in reality. The researcher must remain very alert concerning the degree to which private information becomes known to others, particularly when such information is of a sensitive nature.

Obviously certain types of research have a higher risk in terms of potential invasion of subjects' privacy than others. Those studies that are focusing on information that might be sensitive clearly fall into the higher risk category. Investigations that record information in a setting that may be considered private by the subjects are also more vulnerable. Basically the researcher cannot ignore privacy in any study. If there is a potential problem, consent should always be obtained. Additionally the subjects should be assured that the data will be held in strict confidence to protect anonymity. There are few studies in which there is any need to maintain (certainly not publish) data in a form in which subjects can be personally identified. In general, researchers should invade the privacy of subjects as minimally as possible. If there is potential of a privacy risk, the investigator should take all precautions possible. Any study that substantially invades privacy may obviously place the subjects in a risk position. Such procedures also place the conduct of science at risk by reducing the public trust level that is vital to the successful pursuit of knowledge.

Deception

Research deception involves a misrepresentation of facts related to the purpose, nature, or consequences of an investigation. In the context of this discussion, it refers to either an omission or a commission on the part of the researcher in terms of interactions with subjects. Regarding an omission, deception might mean that the investigator simply does not inform subjects, either completely or at all, concerning important aspects of the study, he or she withholds part or all of the information. A commission, on the other hand, involves a situation in which the researcher gives false information concerning the investigation, either partially or totally. In the first case, subjects may not even be aware that a study is in progress or they may be only informed about a portion of the investigation. In the second situation, subjects generally are aware that they are involved in some type of study or activity out of the ordinary but may be given misleading information regarding the true purpose or nature of the study or activity. In either case, the researcher is misrepresenting the study.

Regardless of the precise nature of deception, it has become a very prominent problem for investigators concerned with the ethics of conducting research. It seems that deception of one type or another has become rather widespread in behavioral and social research. Diener and Crandall (1978) cite figures ranging from 19 to 44 percent of recent psychological research that involves ". . . direct lying to subjects [p. 74]." Viewing the matter somewhat more broadly, Menges (1973) believed that there was complete information given in *only three percent* of the psychological studies that he examined. Although the accuracy of such estimates can always be questioned, it is clear that deception presents a major problem. Many subjects believe that they are being told false information regarding studies in which they participate, whether or not they are really being deceived. Thus where there is smoke there may well be fire, or even if there is not fire there is perceived smoke.

The latter statements above illustrate clearly some of the difficulties of deception (real or perceived). Research subjects have become "test-wise," if you will, and often believe the "real" purpose of a given study is hidden. This is true more for certain types of participants than other (notably college sophomores, the most "studied" group around), but by no means limited to them. (I remember all too well the large number of mentally retarded *children* who mentioned, in passing, that they "figured out" what I was really testing.) If subjects are *that* suspicious, they may be expected to answer, perform, or generally respond in an atypical manner. Such responses, if widespread, may seriously threaten the soundness of an investigation as will be seen in later chapters. Subjects may attempt to respond in a manner that they think the researcher desires, or they may try to outguess the researcher and "foul up" the study. It must be remembered that some types of subjects are studied frequently and others are even professional research participants. (Many college students earn part of their monthly sustenance by serving as subjects in response to advertisements.) There is even some evidence that subject *un*naiveté is on the increase.

The methodological problems with deception have been alluded to and will be examined further in terms of potential weakness to sound research throughout this volume. Subjects simply are affected by the process of being in an investigation and may therefore react differently (*Hawthorne effect* in terms of internal validity and *artificial research arrangements* in external validity—discussed in Chapter 7). Although some of these topics have not yet been discussed in this book, the discussions thus far suggest that deception is a serious problem—both ethically and from a methodological point of view. One must then ask the question of why it occurs.

Deception is often undertaken for one of the same reasons that it represents a problem—a methodological one. Some studies involve purposes, activities, and actions that, if known to the participants, might be seriously compromised. For example, suppose a study were being conducted on group control of individual actions. In this type of investigation, the question might be one involving the amount of influence that a group had on individuals regarding differences of opinion concerning the use of drugs. This might be the type of study that would involve deception to a considerable degree. If the subject being observed (the rest of the "group" might be confederates in the study) were suspicious concerning the purpose of the investigation, he or she might be more or less resistant to group pressure than normally. Thus it would not be unexpected that the researcher would attempt to adapt for such an influence by deceiving the subject. The individual may be directly told that the purpose of the study was something else, or information may simply be withheld. Clearly if the subject were openly informed about the nature of the study, the outcome might be jeopardized. In this case, the reason for using deception might also become its greatest enemy. Obviously the researcher cannot reveal the exact nature of the investigation, but the participant may be generally suspicious and thereby alter behavior because of those suspicions (in a manner unknown to the investigator). Deception is used to control certain matters important to the study, but suspicion of deception creates problems for control.

The control exerted in the preceding discussion may relate to the technical soundness of the study or it may relate to the generalizability of the findings (matters that will be examined in detail in later chapters). If one group of subjects receives particularly different treatment (deception) than another, the comparison may not *really* involve what the researcher intended. Likewise, if deception is either real or perceived on the part of the subjects, results might not be generalizable to the outside world. Methodological reasons for using deception represent a double-edged sword; they have both advantages and disadvantages. Like the other issues discussed in this chapter, the judgment of the investigator is likely to be tested.

Other reasons are involved in the use of deception beyond methodological soundness of the study. Often the reasons are purely pragmatic. Limitations regarding finances, time, and the convenient availability of data sources have often led researchers to use deception. For example, if it is too expensive, time consuming, or not feasible to observe a particular phenomenon in terms of a natural occurrence, it might be best studied by creating a simulated incident. Such a situation may arise when the researcher is studying something that only occurs rarely or that creates dangerous circumstances when it does occur (e.g., emergencies). This type of deception might involve a staged purse-snatching or mugging with observations being focused on the reactions of witnesses. Such an example would necessarily involve deception (and also no prestudy consent) if the witnesses are to behave naturally.

The previous discussions have indicated some of the reasons why researchers use deception and also some of the problems involved in its use. But is deception ethical? Although this may seem to be a simple question, the answer is anything but simple. One of the most fundamental arguments against deception is that it *is* unethical and degrading to the subjects involved. Lying is generally viewed unfavorably in our society and even deemed immoral. This type of posture places the conduct of science in a dilemma. Science is presumably undertaken for the benefit of society, so should it be associated with acts that are generally thought to be evil? This is a question that has no direct answer since it is couched in such polar terms.

Most people would agree that research cannot be clearly declared either ethical or unethical. Like most of the topics discussed so far, there are many shades of gray and many matters that must be considered. One of the most serious issues facing research using deception is the issue of consent. If participants are involved in activities that present potential risk to them, consent is necessary. In studies using deception, effective consent has considerable probability of being absent. If a study is using deception, subjects must at least be given enough information to know the possibility of risk and may then voluntarily decide whether or not to participate. Additionally, deception exists on a continuum from a relatively minor omission of information to direct lies of major proportion. Clearly studies that use major deception are more ethically questionable than those involving minor deception. A final matter that must be considered is the research setting. Diener and Crandall (1978) note that deception in a laboratory is generally viewed as being more ethical than in other situations. They believe that if deception is to be used, it should at least be used in restricted settings. There would, however, seem to be another facet of logic in this view. If subjects are participating in a laboratory investigation, it is at least more obvious that they are serving as subjects, which decreases the magnitude of deception to some degree. All of these issues, plus those discussed in earlier sections, still leave the primary ethical responsibility on the shoulders of the researcher. Obviously the greater imvolvement of deception creates more questions regarding ethics. Investigators must attempt to balance their scientific aims with the ethical constraints in all cases.

Nonhuman subjects

Nonhuman research subjects clearly represent a separate set of issues in terms of ethical issues. Although some very sensitive and idealistic individuals would disagree, the same concerns do not functionally apply. (It is rather difficult to obtain effective consent from most animals.) Researchers should not, however, consider themselves free to disregard ethical concerns with such subjects. Although nonhuman subjects will not be examined extensively in this volume, they do require brief discussion. Certain points *are* somewhat familiar in terms of earlier sections.

The National Institutes of Health (NIH) has published information that is helpful to the researcher using animals as subjects (1971; 1978). Although this information specifically pertains to investigations funded by NIH, these documents are frequently viewed as relevant guidelines for studies that are conducted without such funding. In some senses, these guidelines are more specific than many of the published ethic codes applying to human subjects. For example, a distinction is made between the practices to be used with warm-blooded and cold-blooded animals. (Occasionally there are some of our human subjects for whom we might appreciate having such guidelines.)

The principles for using animal subjects in research attend to several factors including the personnel conducting the investigation, housing, the nature of the research, and even transportation. These guidelines are interesting, both in terms of topics addressed and the specific language used. Consequently portions of the specific text are presented below:

The personnel

1. Experiments involving live, vertebrate animals and the procurement of tissues from living animals for research must be performed by, or under the immediate supervision of, a qualified biological, behavioral, or medical scientist.
2. The housing, care, and feeding of all experimental animals must be supervised by a properly qualified veterinarian or other scientist competent in such matters.

The research

3. The research should be such as to yield fruitful results for the good of society and not random or unnecessary in nature.
4. The experiment should be based on knowledge of the disease or problem under study and so designed that the anticipated results will justify its performance.
5. Statistical analysis, mathematical models, or *in vitro* biological systems should be used when appropriate to complement animal experiments and to reduce numbers of animals used.

6. The experiment should be conducted so as to avoid all unnecessary suffering and injury to the animals.

7. The scientist in charge of the experiment must be prepared to terminate it whenever he/she believes that its continuation may result in unnecessary injury or suffering to the animals.

8. If the experiment or procedure is likely to cause greater discomfort than that attending anesthetization, the animals must first be rendered incapable of perceiving pain and be maintained in that condition until the experiment or procedure is ended. The only exception to this guideline should be in those cases where the anesthetization would defeat the purpose of the experiment and data cannot be obtained by any other humane procedure. Such procedures must be carefully supervised by the principal investigator or other qualified senior scientist.

9. Post-experimental care of animals must be such as to minimize discomfort and the consequences of any disability resulting from the experiment, in accordance with acceptable practices in veterinary medicine.

10. If it is necessary to kill an experimental animal, this must be accomplished in a humane manner, i.e., in such a way as to insure immediate death in accordance with procedures approved by an institutional committee. *No animal shall be discarded until death is certain.*

The facilities

11. Standards for the construction and use of housing, service, and surgical facilities should meet those described in the publication, *Guide for the Care and Use of Laboratory Animals,* DHEW No. [NIH] 74-23, or as otherwise required by the U.S. Department of Agriculture regulations established under the terms of the Laboratory Animal Welfare Act [P.L. 89-544] as amended 1970 and 1976 [P.L. 91-579 and P.L. 94-279].

Transportation

12. Transportation of animals must be in accord with applicable standards and regulations, especially those intended to reduce discomfort, stress to the animals, or spread of disease. All animals being received for use as experimental subjects and having arrived at the terminal of a common carrier, must be promptly picked up and delivered, uncrated, and placed in acceptable permanent facilities.*

Comments

Ethical issues related to subjects obviously present some very complex considerations for research. Subject-oriented concerns represent the most evident ethical problems for all scientists and clearly those that result in the most serious operational dilemmas regarding undertaking an investigation. Despite the visibility of these difficulties, they are not the only ethical problems facing the conduct of science and scientists themselves. Some of the topics remaining to be discussed are even more embarrassing (if not more serious). Some relate to topics already examined but must be highlighted in terms of particular research approaches. Others become very personal. All must be discussed.

---

*From NIH Guide for grants and contracts, Appendix I. 7, (17), 5-6, November 10, 1978.

ETHICS RELATED TO PARTICULAR RESEARCH APPROACHES

Research ethical problems have been examined in some detail in this chapter, specifically issues related to participants. This provides considerable background regarding the planning and execution of an investigation and represents a significant foundation for this section. Many details related to recurring topics will be abbreviated because of this. The central purpose of this section is to examine those ethical considerations that are of particular concern in the context of various approaches to research. Such a focus is presented to especially alert those investigators who are anticipating utilization of a particular approach. Although the text will be brief, an attempt will be made to sensitize and refer you to other sources that may address a given method in depth.

Chapter 2 discussed two major approaches to conducting research—experimental and nonexperimental. As the earlier discussion indicated, these approaches have rather substantial differences in both general designs and operational procedures. Each presents some unique ethical questions.

Experimental research

The experimental research involves studies in which the investigator manipulates the factor under study (the experimental variable). Frequently the manipulated variable represents some sort of intervention or treatment (e.g., medical, psychological, educational) that is being studied with regard to effectiveness. It is this very manipulation of "treatment" that raises certain ethical questions and dilemmas.

Part of the difficulty regarding an experimental treatment pertains to those subjects that *receive* the intervention. For example, the intervention may represent training in group communication that includes a great deal of self- disclosure. Self-disclosure is a procedure used by some counselors that promotes individuals talking about their feelings, attitudes, and experiences (some of which may be quite personal). Let us suppose that you are a subject and you tend to be a rather private person. The question then is raised concerning what right the researcher has to impose the treatment on you. After all, the manner in which you deal with such matters is really your own business and represents part of your personal value structure. This example illustrates the problem nicely but does not necessarily answer the question. Certainly the researcher should have fully informed you regarding the nature of the activities in the process of obtaining consent. It was also the investigator's responsibility to clearly indicate that your consent could be withdrawn and you could elect to discontinue the activities at any time. Assuming that the investigator handles consent in an appropriate manner, both in planning and execution of the experiment, the problem with those receiving the treatment should be lessened to a certain degree, although this does not completely eliminate ethical concerns.

An additional problem related to subjects receiving the experimental intervention involves the issues of potential harm, the probable duration of that harm, and its reversibility. These matters have been encountered before but must be reexamined briefly here. As noted earlier, research of any type should be designed and executed in a manner that reduces the risk of harm as much as possible. Furthermore, if there is a potential harm risk, it should (1) be as minor as possible, (2) be reversible, and (3) have a postexperimental duration that is as short as possible. All of these qualifications are particularly relevant to ethical questions regarding subjects who receive an experimental treatment. If harm *is* incurred by such an intervention, the researcher should take precautionary steps to reverse the problem and see to it that the reversal is effective as quickly as possible. Unfortunately there have been examples when such precautions were not taken.

The discussion thus far has focused on problems related to subjects who *receive* the experimental treatment. There are equally difficult ethical problems involving subjects who do *not* receive the treatment (e.g., placebo comparison or control groups). This begins to sound like "you're damned if you do and damned if you don't." There are, however, some distinct and interesting questions related to this part of the problem. Let's suppose, for the moment, that you have discovered a very effective treatment that may significantly reduce depression. Everything so far has suggested that it is a very promising procedure. You need to conduct further investigation and want to form two groups—one that receives the treatment and one that receives a placebo activity. The ethical question raised concerns what right you have to *not treat* the placebo group (deny them treatment). The conflict becomes evident—you need a group that does not receive treatment for comparison, but do you have the right to *not* give them what appears to be a promising treatment for depression?

The ethical perspective noted above would hold that it is the researcher's responsibility to provide treatment to all subjects. This argument is particularly emphasized if the "treatment" appears very effective as in our depression example above. As you can well imagine, there are those on the other side of this issue who have a very different view. This opposing perspective is often called the "natural state argument" and basically contends that the untreated subjects are not being denied a benefit they already have, they are merely being left in their natural state.

Clearly neither extreme position can be generally accepted for all research. In the depression example, you probably do have some responsibility to provide treatment to the placebo group, particularly if it is as effective as you think. However, there is still the need to conduct a scientifically sound test. One approach to this dilemma represents a compromise that attempts to meet the goals of research and also the ethical need for providing benefit to all subjects. It may be possible to first conduct the study as initially planned—with a treatment group and a placebo comparison group. Then, after the investigation is complete and the data collected, you could provide the treatment to those depressed individuals who were subjects in the comparison group. In this way you are not withholding the treatment from anyone in the study and yet the data are not contaminated. Although this is a reasonable compromise, there are some minor problems. Some would contend that the delay in treatment is still harmful to the placebo group. This may be true if the duration of the study is *very* extended, but if not, such an argument loses much of its potency. Another problem may be expense; if the treatment is quite expensive the researcher may have difficulty funding treatment for the second group. Although this may be a problem, it is not a very compelling argument. To remain clearly ethical the researcher should simply plan the budget to allow for treatment of the comparison subjects. None of this has great significance for interventions or treatments that are of questionable effectiveness but becomes more relevant as evidence of promise accumulates for any given treatment.

As before, there are no simple or clear guidelines that account for every ethical concern regarding experimentation. Some of the more prominent difficulties have been illustrated, but most specific planning must remain accomplished by the researcher's good judgment.

Nonexperimental research

Many of the ethical concerns associated with nonexperimental research—consent, deception, privacy—have already been discussed. They do, however, take on some unique meanings in the context of any particular research approach. Chapter 2 discussed observation as one important nonexperimental approach to research. Observation has been used widely in the social sciences as a means of collecting nonexperimental data in natural settings. In particular, both anthropology and sociology have used what is known as *participant observation* in which the researcher actually becomes a member of the culture or group being studied. Participant observation presents some perplexing ethical difficulties regarding consent, privacy, and deception and thus serves very well to exemplify some of the unique ethical problems encountered in nonexperimental research.

In most cases effective consent is necessary for an ethical study using participant observation. This view is expressed for several reasons. Potential harm, in terms of an actual risk of danger to subjects, although not unheard of, is not frequently a problem in participant observation research. For the most part, a treatment per se is not inflicted on the subjects. There may, however, be a substantial invasion of privacy. It is not uncommon for the observer to live, eat, and sleep on a daily basis with those being observed. The purpose of such a study is often to record a broad range of details regarding the subjects' cultural mores, interaction patterns, social structures, and daily behaviors. This type of research may therefore be probing into many facets of the lifestyle of the subjects—public, private, and often sensitive. With such a pervasive scope of observation, it is very difficult to imagine that privacy invasion does not occur. It is this probable invasion of privacy that makes consent so obviously necessary.

The very nature of the investigation also raises some serious difficulties concerning consent. From whom should consent be obtained? Is it adequate to obtain consent from the group leader (e.g., the tribal chief, the fraternity president)? This technique is occasionally used, but it also raises serious questions regarding the effectiveness of consent from other group members. Another problem in participant observation involves the effect of obtaining consent *on the behavior of those being studied.* One of the major advantages of this type of investigation is that it attempts to study the routine behaviors of the subjects in their natural environment. Does obtaining consent serve to alter the natural behavior? There is no doubt that it may. The researcher must exercise great care in attempting to distinguish natural from altered behavior, and some would maintain that it is impossible to do so. There is another potential difficulty with participant observation even if consent is obtained very carefully. By virtue of the observer's participant role, the subjects may forget that they are still being studied. Does this mean that they are no longer consenting just because they are not continually aware of the study? These are not easily answered questions, but they certainly represent areas of concern about which the researcher must be cautious.

The issue of privacy has been mentioned before in the context of consent. Privacy invasion represents a substantial risk in participant observation research. The areas of data collection often involve very sensitive information. After all, a serious description and analysis of a primitive culture or contemporary group cannot avoid such topics of enquiry. One of the factors in privacy issues concerns how public the information will become. This also speaks to one of the traditional methods of circumventing privacy problems—anonymity. Participant observation studies have often used fictitious names to disguise the actual identity of individuals, groups, agencies, and locations being investigated. Although this may be adequate in some circumstances, there have been several examples of when it was not. One of the best known involved Vidich and Bensman's book entitled *Small Town in Mass Society* (1960). Anonymity was not protected despite the fact that fictitious identities were used in the publication. Some of the information published involved behavior that could be considered embarrassing and potentially damaging to the individuals being studied. Clearly privacy represents a difficult ethical problem for participant observation studies and, for that matter, for many types of nonexperimental research.

Deception has not yet been mentioned in this section, but the aura of deception is very present in what has already been discussed. In one sense, the participant observer is an automatic deceiver to some degree. Even if consent is openly and carefully obtained, the role of the observer as a participant might be viewed as a deception by some. This is a serious problem that cannot be ignored by researchers using such an approach. It also raises the complex questions regarding the potential of harm if deception is involved. (There have been examples when the potential of harm even involved political spying.) Basically researchers using such procedures have to ask themselves (and the appropriate review committees) "What harm may be incurred by the deception involved in my study?"

This section has focused primarily on ethical concerns encountered in participant observation. Earlier chapters clearly indicated that there are other types of nonexperimental research. The discussion here has been illustrative rather than exhaustive. A complete examination of ethical issues, with any type of research, is far beyond the scope of an introductory text. Many of the references cited in this chapter may provide additional information for the student interested in pursuing a particular topic.

ETHICS AND PROFESSIONALISM

Some of the ethical issues associated with research participants and some that are uniquely problematic for particular research approaches have already been discussed. This section focuses basically on the researcher in the context of the profession. Many of these topics are not often openly addressed in print, although they are frequently the topic of debate in the hall or staff lounge. These are also topics that seem to be of great interest to students as they observe the "professionals" whom they intend to join as colleagues. This area could easily consume an entire volume, but that is not possible with this text. Three areas of discussion will receive special focus: (1) integrity during the execution of the study, (2) integrity related to publishing, and (3) sanctions for breaches of integrity. Hopefully these topics will provide a background and sensitivity that will prompt further thought and enquiry by the beginning researcher when a question arises.

Integrity during execution of study

Diener and Crandall (1978) call it "honesty and accuracy," Rosenthal (1966) discussed it in terms of "experimenter effects in behavioral research." In all cases *it* refers to a breach of integrity resulting in errors or inaccuracies in the data or results of a study. Such acts range all the way from minor unintentional errors to outright falsification of the data or results.

One of the most basic purposes of science is the acquisition of objective and accurate information regarding the world. Perhaps one could be so bold as to say that the ultimate goal of science is the seeking of truth. Everyone knows that "truth" is fluid, situational, and certainly variable depending on one's perspective. But somewhere underlying the conduct of science there is a philosophical assumption that some "truths" can be determined. This places a very important responsibility on science and scientists to undertake their efforts in a totally honest fashion. This is not a statement that reflects a value judgment or moralizing. It is simply a statement that reemphasizes a fundamental principle on which scientific investigation is based.

This chapter has emphasized the importance of integrity in research—focused thus far on execution. The question that is naturally raised in this context relates to why breaches of integrity occur. Although there are a variety of influences that result in these problems, none make such acts justifiable. However, their discussion helps to more fully understand them and take preventive precautions.

One of the factors influencing breaches of integrity involves some rather powerful social pressures, particularly among beginning researchers. There is great value placed by many on the "elegant" investigation; the study that is designed in a clever manner to investigate a particularly difficult question. I am *not* discounting the value of such research, it is to be admired and a sought-after goal. It does, however, seem to be overemphasized at times to the exclusion of other matters. Additionally, ethical problems arise when there is such strong pressure (often implicit) that it leads to inaccurate data collection. For example, such pressure may occur when a research assistant believes that significant results *must* be obtained and either consciously or unconsciously alters the data. Other circumstances may have the same net outcome. Often the data collection process is laborious, boring, and even extremely difficult. This has led to incidents in which research assistants actually record fictitious data rather than conscientiously observe subjects (sometimes known as *dry labbing*).

The examples and discussions thus far have involved research assistants. It needs to be made *very* clear that research assistants and beginning researchers are not the only scientists vulnerable to committing breaches of integrity. In fact, there have been some very prominent individuals, with widely known reputations, who have been discovered in or accused of unethical research execution. A recent example concerns the work of Sir Cyril Burt, a noted British psychologist. This is a particularly difficult case since the allegations of scientific misconduct against Burt were made after his death, making it difficult for him to respond. The controversy is further complicated by two factors: (1) there is no question that Burt was a very well-known scientist, he was knighted in 1946 in recognition of the importance of his work, and (2) the topic of his investigations was, and remains, very controversial—the heritability of intelligence. The allegations include: (1) estimating certain levels of intelligence (parents of certain twins) but later reporting such estimates as solid data, (2) listing individuals as co-authors on research papers who may have never existed, and (3) producing data that represented answers supporting his theoretical beliefs that are unusually "precise" fits to predictions (some say impossible). These points have been countered by supporters of his work on the basis that while the inconsistencies may represent a degree of carelessness, basically the errors are trivial, do not seriously undermine the strength of the heritability of intelligence position, and certainly do not warrant the accusations of fraud. Obviously the arguments have been intense on both sides (e.g., Gillie, 1977; Jensen, 1977), often representing varying perspectives on the intelligence issue as much as the problems involved in the ethics of science. Clearly, however, one cannot ignore the difficulties and suspicions generated in relation to the conduct of research. In some senses the scientific endeavor is as much on trial as the work of Burt, which illustrates very well the fundamental problems involved with breaches of integrity (confirmed or alleged). It should be noted that this is not the only example—other fields of science also have their unfortunate incidents or allegations.

All researchers must take precautions against integrity breaches related to the execution of research. However, it is impossible to have *every* data collection effort fully supervised or observed by more than one researcher. Ethical integrity in science, as in many other fields, is mainly an individual undertaking. Hopefully one precaution that may have an important influence is a more open discussion of the resulting problems and the potential outcomes. The interested reader should consult the references to this chapter for a more complete discussion.

Integrity related to publishing

Publishing is an integral part of the overall research process. Fig. 1-1 characterized the research process in a closed loop fashion. An investigation is undertaken to answer a question of presumed importance. The process is not completed until the results are interpreted in relation to the question that closes the loop. It was also noted in Chapter 1 that the work of a scientist is public and publishing is the means by which it is made public. For the most part, a published research report describes the closed loop. The research question is presented, followed by the rationale concerning why the question should be studied, the results, and an interpretation of those results related to the question. As noted earlier, considerable detail (e.g., subjects, procedures, analysis) is included in such a report, which basically makes the researcher's work open for public scrutiny by the scientific community. It is this public scrutiny that helps to make science objective and why publishing is such an important part of the research process.

Because publishing is an important part of research, it is also an important factor in the career of a scientist. It is one means of determining the capability and performance of a researcher. If a researcher has completed an investigation and been successful in having it published, there is at least some evidence that the work has withstood some review by the scientific community. Such evidence clearly enhances the researcher's employability, rank, and salary status. In fact certain agencies (e.g., some universities) will terminate professors if they have not published during the first few years of their employment (often the first 5 to

7 years). All of these matters place a certain amount of pressure on researchers to publish. Although the pressure is not undue (5 to 7 years is a substantial period), some tend to exaggerate the intensity of this pressure and ethical problems may result.

One of the ethical problems that may arise relates to some of our earlier discussion of integrity during execution. There may be a temptation to report the investigation in a somewhat different manner than the data collected would indicate. This may be a situation in which significant differences are reported but the data did not actually show statistically significant differences. Such incidents have ranged from circumstances in which "it was close" and the data were changed slightly, all the way to "dry labbed" results. Obviously this type of act represents a serious breach of professional integrity and hopefully it seldom occurs. Some reports, however, suggest that the frequency may be disturbingly high (Diener and Crandall, 1978).

Another ethical problem related to publishing involves multiple publication of the same article. This difficulty would present itself if, for example, you conducted a survey, wrote an article reporting the study, and then published the same article in two different professional journals. In fact, the rule of thumb that I was taught does not even permit submitting the same article to two different journals at the same time. This view would hold that you submit the article to one journal, and if it is rejected, you are free to resubmit it for review by another journal.

The multiple publication issue noted above is much different than an article (already published) that is *reprinted* in another journal or a book of readings. In this latter situation, the journal or publisher desiring to reprint your article must request permission from the first journal before the article can be reprinted. (A credit line must also be listed in the reprinted publication clearly indicating that it is reprinted from another publication and the name of that publication.) Additionally, such a reprinted piece is *not* claimed by the author as a separate and new publication; it is merely noted as having been reprinted.

Authorship also presents several serious ethical problems in publishing. This is an area in which graduate students and beginning researchers may be particularly vulnerable. One of the first questions relates to who should be listed as author or authors. Any individual making a major contribution to the project should be listed as an author. Obviously the phrase "major contribution" is open to different interpretations. In this context, it is being used to reflect a contribution involving the conceptualization, design, data collection and analysis, and writing of the manuscript. One can insert several combinations of "and/or" between these activities to determine whether or not authorship is warranted. Once again this is an area in which one's best ethical judgment must prevail. The problem is mentioned because it seems that integrity occasionally wears thin when it comes time to list authors. All too often graduate students have been taken advantage of by unscrupulous professors who only give them·a footnoted credit line, if that. (A credit line may be appropriate for minor contributions; it is *not* appropriate for substantial efforts involving conceptual and writing efforts.)

It is obvious from this discussion that a publication may have multiple authors. This raises the question regarding the order of authorship. Who is to be senior author (listed first) and who will be junior author(s) (those listed second, third, and so on). The order of authorship should be determined in relation to the amount of contribution. The person making the greatest contribution should be senior author and the others listed in order of their relative efforts. If the contribution is relatively equal, order should be determined by mutual agreement, a flip of the coin, or some other method that is acceptable to those involved. Do not be deceived by someone's claim that order is accomplished alphabetically; typically the one making such a claim has a last name that is early in the alphabet. Also disregard the argument that order is a trivial matter—after all with three authors the citation is usually "Senior et al., 1979." Do you really want to be *et* or *al* if you did most of the work? Unfortunately not everyone adheres to fair and ethical principles when determining the order of authors. The main precaution that one can take is to be aware that such breaches of integrity occur and to be firm for your own rights (and do not take advantage of someone else).

Sanctions for breaches of integrity

Some of the sanctions for unethical conduct are self-evident in the earlier discussion. Certainly a breach of ethics that is made public is personally embarrassing and causes professional disgrace. It may cause one to loose a job and be unable to obtain other employment in the research community (word travels rapidly even if the publicity is not a major exposé). Most scientists belong to professional organizations such as the American Psychological Association, the American Sociological Association, or some other disciplinary organization. Many of these organizations have formal codes of ethics to guide members' activities. Such organizations may expel a member for unethical conduct, which is essentially an expulsion from the profession. Sanctions can be very harsh for the person who is unethical, but such harshness is clearly warranted. Each time a breach of ethics occurs, the entire field of research is disgraced to some degree. At times it may seem that ethical conduct is at odds with the aims of research. Although inconvenience may result, it is important to remember that ethical principles are not only in harmony with science but also represent the basic fiber from which the process is made.

REFERENCES

Baron, C. H. Voluntary sterilization of the mentally retarded. In A. Milunsky, and G. J. Annas (Eds.), *Genetics and the law.* New York: Plenum Publishing Corp., 1976, 267-284.

Chinn, P. C., Drew, C. J., and Logan, D. R. *Mental retardation: a life cycle approach* (2nd ed.). St. Louis: The C. V. Mosby Co., 1979.

Diener, E., and Crandall, R. *Ethics in social and behavioral research.* Chicago: The University of Chicago Press, 1978.

Gillie, O. Did Sir Cyril Burt fake his research on heritability of intelligence? Part I. *Phi Delta Kappan,* 1977, *58,* (6), 469-471.

Haywood, H. C. The ethics of doing research . . . and not of doing it. *American Journal of Mental Deficiency,* 1976, *81,* 311-317.

Jensen, A. R. Did Sir Cyril Burt fake his research on heritability of intelligence? Part II. *Phi Delta Kappan,* 1977, *58,* (6), 471, 492.

Keith-Spiegel, P. Children's rights as participants in research. In G. P. Koocher (Ed.), *Children's rights and the mental health profession.* New York: John Wiley & Sons, Inc., 1976, 53-81.

Kelman, H. C. The rights of the subject in social research: an analysis in terms of relative power and legitimacy. *American Psychologist,* 1972, *27,* 989-1016.

Menges, R. J. Openness and honesty versus coercion and deception in psychological research. *American Psychologist,* 1973, *28,* 1030-1034.

Murdock, C. W. Sterilization of the retarded: a problem or a solution? *California Law Review,* 1974, *62,* 917.

NIH Guide for Grants and Contracts, 1971, *1,* (7), 3-5.

NIH Guide for Grants and Contracts, 1978, *7,* (17).

Rosenthal, R. *Experimenter effects in behavioral research.* New York: Appleton-Century-Crofts, 1966.

Ruebhausen, O. M., and Brim, O. G., Jr. Privacy and behavioral research. *American Psychologist,* 1966, *21,* 423-437.

Turnbull, H. R., III (Ed.) *Consent handbook.* Washington, D.C.: American Association on Mental Deficiency, 1977.

Vidich, A. J., and Bensman, J. *Small town in mass society.* New York: Doubleday & Co., Inc., 1960.

PART II

Basic design considerations

CHAPTER 4

The research process

Thus far the research process, various research approaches, and ethical issues involved in the conduct of research have been discussed. These topics serve as the backdrop for the remainder of this book. In some areas, more attention must now be focused on what has previously been discussed in a cursory fashion. In other areas, such as ethical issues, only a quick reference or brief elaboration will be made concerning what has already been stated. A review of the basic conceptualization of the overall research process seems appropriate at the start of this part of the book.

The research process has been conceptualized in a closed loop or circular fashion (Fig. 4-1). It is clear from the earlier discussions that there may be vast differences in methodology from study to study and between various disciplines. These differences do *not* change the overall research process. Every investigation begins with an idea that becomes the research question. The research question may then lead to some hypotheses or "guesses" about the topic under study, which in turn leads to the design or plan for the investigation. Data are then collected and analyzed to answer the question (which hopefully closes the loop).

This is a very simple conceptualization of the research process—one that often does not fit the stereotyped notions concerning science. Many of the perceptions and misconceptions that are frequently held by beginning students and laypersons regarding research were discussed previously. These popular views of science do not help at all, and in many cases they serve to interfere with the teaching-learning process. It is important to go beyond the introductory explanations presented thus far to more fully understand research and, in turn, discard these misconceptions. One of the best places to begin is with the research idea.

THE IDEA FOR RESEARCH

Not all the problems confronting the teaching of research are generated by misconceptions from outside the research community. Considerable interference results from misconstrued philosophies coming from within the profession.

Students are often required to conduct research as a part of their academic preparation program. Such research is generally expected to result in a docu-

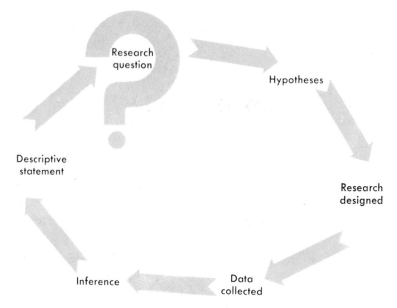

Fig. 4-1. Closed loop conceptualization of the research process.

ment or report that represents a senior project, master's thesis, or doctoral dissertation. In most cases, well-articulated guidelines for the students are not available, which makes the task extremely difficult, contributes to the "mystique" perception, and renders the experience most distasteful. Perhaps the students are presented with a mimeographed document that outlines format, reference forms, and other such critical items concerning how large the type is to be and what rag content is necessary in the paper to be used (heaven forbid that the wrong rag content might be used). With these wonderful guidelines, the students begin what is perhaps their first piece of research. Completely lost at this point, they may seek assistance by turning to the college catalog to find a written description of what the thesis should be.

Although a college catalog *is* a logical place to turn, unfortunately it may serve to hinder rather than help. The descriptive statement generally says something to the effect that the thesis "must be an original contribution to the field in which the student is seeking academic preparation." This is indeed a formidable task, particularly when viewed through the eyes of a student with little research experience who may interpret it literally. The anxiety that may be generated by such a statement may be debilitating and probably inhibits the student's progress. In the first place, the statement that the research must be "original" (which may imply that it must arise out of an *original* idea) is frightening enough. Placed in the context that this research must represent a "contribution to the field," the task becomes even more formidable. This situation may contribute substantially to the often-asked question, "Is this (idea) enough to be a thesis?" Although the student's interpretation may be too literal, it is very real and not infrequent. (After all, no one told you that you shouldn't believe *all* of what is in the college catalog.) The issues of educational pragmatism, realistic educational objectives, and relevance concerning how research is conducted by practicing researchers loom very prominently in this situation and should be carefully considered by professors directing student research.

Initially it seems necessary to consider what educational objectives are involved in the production of a thesis. It makes considerable difference whether such student research is viewed as a learning experience or as an examination of competency. Unfortunately, the latter framework is implied by such statements as the catalog example and by the manner in which many faculty members approach such a subject. If it is kept in mind that this is an early, if not the first, research experience for the student, the competence examination philosophy becomes ludicrous. Early student research projects should be viewed primarily as learning experiences; it often takes the practicing researcher many years to actually make a "contribution" that is even partially original. From this philosophical stance, one must not be overly concerned about the source or ultimate impact of the research idea.

It also seems reasonable that the world of practicing researchers should be explored briefly. The source or originality of the majority of research ideas investigated by professionals in behavioral science is certainly not as it is perceived to be by most students beginning their thesis work. In many cases the experienced researcher obtains ideas for investigation by reading articles written by other people and noting that a gap exists in the information presented. Such an information gap might involve a variety of topics. For example, it may be that the study being reported did not focus on children of a particular age group (say 10 to 12 years of age). If the researcher reading this report thinks that the study would be improved if such children were included, this represents a perceived information gap. Often such gaps are explicitly mentioned in the discussion section. Implications for future research are an integral part of many published articles and are nearly standard in theses and dissertations. In most cases these implications are easily identified, since the author typically uses such phrases as "future research should . . . ," "additional study is needed . . . ," and "further investigation might. . . ." If these gaps and projections are of interest to the individual, they will most probably become *the idea* on which to work. What about the source? Are such ideas "original?" According to the apprehensive, literal interpretation frequently used by the student, they may not appear to be *original;* but, in fact, the practicing researcher working within the context of a subject area would consider them to be a *contribution.* Thus inexperienced beginning researchers may give themselves an apparently more rigorous task than practicing researchers generally require for their own investigations.

The ideas for research come from everywhere. The student who really becomes involved in a subject will find not a shortage of ideas but rather an abundance of them. Problems are generated in other people's publications, but they also appear in nearly every corner of the daily environment. Someone who is working on an idea or problem tends to assume ownership of that idea or problem. If an idea has been specifically mentioned by someone else as having implications for future research, the publication in which it was mentioned should be cited. Building on someone else's work does not reduce the value of the current work and does make good sense from a programmatic research standpoint.

Turn to p. 88 and complete Simulations 4-1, 4-2, and 4-3.

FOUNDATIONS OF RESEARCH: THE SCIENTIFIC METHOD

Research has previously been defined in this book as a "systematic method of enquiry." Many descriptive characteristics of research that are not obvious in this definition must be discussed to obtain a comprehensive perspective of the process. This section will examine some of these characteristics, which serve to conceptually undergird the research approach to enquiry.

In examining the process of research, it is often useful to express the assumptions underlying the scientific methods. Underwood (1957) has discussed two basic concepts that he considers to be assumptions of science, *determinism* and *finite causation*. In his terminology, determinism involves the assumption that "there is lawfulness in the events of nature as opposed to capricious, chaotic, or spontaneous occurrences. Every natural event (phenomenon) is assumed to have a cause, and if that causal situation could be exactly reinstituted, the event would be duplicated [p. 4]." Finite causation, the second general assumption of science, involves the idea that "every natural event or phenomenon has a discoverable and limited number of conditions or factors which are responsible for it [p. 6]." Determinism presumes that a certain level of predictability may be achieved regarding the occurrence of natural events. Finite causation essentially presumes that everything in nature is *not* influenced by everything else. These assumptions are essential to the scientific enterprise.

To see these assumptions so blatantly stated, preserved in the form of ink and paper is often somewhat disconcerting for researchers, particularly those in behavioral science. (The issue of causality has already been noted as a difficult one in Chapter 2.) These assumptions do not enjoy public and universal acceptance among behavioral scientists. Many researchers who would endorse these assumptions in principle would have difficulty accepting formal use of the term "cause." In fact, a perusal of the research in behavioral science reveals a substantial reluctance to speak in terms that even approximate causation. The discussion of results often gives the impression that a researcher is a master of the elastic phrase (evidenced by such statements as "these results might suggest" and "these data would seem to indicate"). However, such an apparently indecisive approach to research reporting is warranted by the nature of the tools used. As noted earlier, designs are often imperfect and statistical analyses are developed on the basis of probability, and consequently discussions of results are usually stated in terms that are not ironclad in their certainty. Thus a given behavior can be thought of as occurring, with a given probability, as a function of the treatment (which also means that such a result may have occurred because of chance, with a certain probability). Working within these contingencies and considering the highly complex interaction of behavioral influences, it is not surprising that many researchers become somewhat nervous about total and complete acceptance of the assumptions of determinism and finite causation. These assumptions do, however, remain as useful foundation concepts even if in behavioral reality their precise operation is difficult to observe.

Perusal of discussions concerned with the scientific method seems to result in a situation similar to that encountered in defining research; emerging are a variety of descriptions of what is involved. Perhaps the most frequent citation in such discussions involves the work of Dewey (1933) who suggested that it is a systematic manner of thinking and enquiry. From this conceptualization, a variety of dimensions within the scientific method warrant examination.

The scientific method has often been characterized as a sequence of events or activities that are initiated at a given point and proceed through several steps in a given order. Although they are useful at times for teaching about research, such descriptions often give the impression that science is guided by a rigid checklist similar to that used by an airline pilot preparing for takeoff. To a certain degree, the checklist impression is useful. However, the idea of rigid adherence to a set sequence of fully articulated stages is somewhat out of phase with reality in the world of research; furthermore, deviation from some sequential checklist does not push one's work into a nonscientific category. For example, it is common for researchers to begin with a fairly specific problem or question and to subsequently think their way back through a chain of logic or a rationale to a larger theoretical model. On other occasions, the actual formulation of complete and refined hypotheses may not be executed. Consequently this book discusses the scientific method in terms of three broad areas of activity rather than a sequential examination of steps. These areas of activity include (1) the problem, (2) the data, and (3) the inference. At times, however, certain sequential dimensions of the method will become evident or may be specifically mentioned as a precautionary note to the beginning student.

The problem

The first broad area of consideration in discussing the scientific method is the problem. Two subactivities are involved within this area, problem identification and problem distillation. Problem identification, in this context, refers to the process of finding or determining what research idea is to be studied. Problem distillation refers to the process of refining the problem or idea and making it sufficiently specific so that it is amenable to investigation.

Problem identification. Considerable curiosity is evidenced by the beginning research student concerning the source of research problems and ideas. A recurring theme that is evident in conversation with many students suggests that, at least from their own perception, they feel as if they are in an idea desert. There are no ideas around at a time when they are so badly needed. Progress beyond this point is often inhibited by an understandable reluctance of some students to admit their dilemma. (You may recognize this feeling of reluctance. After all, why emphasize to all those smart people what your weaknesses are?) It is essential, however, that the beginning student move beyond the "idea-desert" stage as quickly as possible. Most researchers would agree that once this movement is made the difficulty arises in selecting rather than identifying problems and ideas.

Kerlinger (1973) discusses problem identification with respect to what he calls a notion of "problem-obstacle-idea." In this context he reflects an impression that is echoed repeatedly in examinations of the scientific method, that the problem is often generated by an obstacle to understanding. Prompted perhaps by some behavioral observation, a problem may be identified by researchers as they ask how or why a given behavior occurs. This question may then become the research problem that is to be studied. It has already been noted that problem identification frequently occurs as the researcher reads the work of others. Often authors of journal articles will facilitate the problem identification process by specifically suggesting implications for future research.

Classical research design has traditionally couched the conduct of research in the context of theory. From this vantage point, the statement of a problem is often viewed more comfortably if it is aimed at testing some part of a theory (such as some particular aspect of a learning theory or some part of a theory of forgetting).

Several changes in philosophical contingencies have legitimized research efforts that may not be couched in such a firm theoretical base, however. One example of this is represented by recent developments in program evaluation, which is seldom based on much beyond a desire to assess effectiveness. Certainly this does not constitute an attempt to test a full-blown theory.

In addition to the items mentioned above, the points made by Sidman (1960), which were discussed earlier, warrant repetition because of their relevance to problem identification in its broadest sense. He contended that research should be conducted to (1) try out new methods or techniques, (2) indulge the investigator's curiosity, (3) establish the existence of behavioral phenomena, and (4) explore the conditions under which phenomena occur. Certainly these points cover a great deal of territory. The point to be made for the beginning student is that problem identification comes from several fronts. The time has passed when the only source of problems for research lay within the boundaries of major theories.

Problem identification is usually the result of a gap in the information available in an area. Such a gap in information was involved in the earlier example in which the researcher was interested in children 10 to 12 years of age. An information gap may be the result of no previous investigation, or it may be the result of previous work that was poorly executed and thus did not provide any information. Most students have little difficulty identifying a broad problem, yet from that point on they find themselves in a quandary regarding transforming it into a researchable question. This process, essential to launching an investigation, usually involves a distillation or definition of the problem into a testable form.

Problem distillation. The point in research at which problem identification ceases and problem distillation begins is vague. Some would contend that the problem has not been truly identified until operational definitions and hypotheses have been stated. In reality, problem identification and distillation are probably a continuous process. They are distinguished here somewhat artifically for the convenience of instruction. For the experienced researcher, they are often indistinguishable.

As the problem becomes identified, it is often in the form of a fairly general question. For example, in reading an article you may encounter something that makes you ponder, "What are the types of influences that affect learning?" The investigation that you have been reading studied the effects of response time, but something seems troublesome with that. It is at this point that you may recall (from your own experience) that response time seems to have different effects depending on how meaningful the material is. This would seem to represent a stage of preliminary problem identification that tends to focus and guide additional reading and search of existing studies. At this point you are beginning to distill the problem into more specific form.

Problem specification. One of the first tasks in problem distillation is a precise specification of the topic under study. Although this may sound rather redundant, the key term here is "precise." As noted above, the research idea is frequently in very general terms—often even vague and nebulous. To successfully design and execute an investigation, the researcher must be very clear (and specific) about what is being studied and the nature of the research question.

A point needs to be made here about the nature of the research question. It is obvious from the discussion thus far that a variety of different questions may be investigated. To list examples of each *specific* type would be impossible. It is possible, however, to examine the *general* types of questions in terms of three basic categories: *descriptive, difference,* and *relationship.* Descriptive questions essentially ask *what is;* what does this culture look like or what does this group look like. Descriptive studies are basically static in that manipulation does not occur and are frequently undertaken in surveys (and anthropological field studies). *Difference questions* essentially make comparisons and ask the question "Is there a difference?" Comparisons may be made either between groups or between measurements within a group. In many cases these comparisons are made between the mean scores (average) of the groups. The question may be phrased "Is there a difference in the average scores between these groups (or treatments)?" Difference questions tend to be most frequently used in experimental research, although nonexperimental studies may also be comparing groups or cultures. *Relationship questions* explore the degree to which two or more phenomena relate or vary together. If the researcher were curious about the relationship between height and weight, the question would basically be "As height varies, what *tends* to happen to weight?" More specifically, if height increases, does weight *tend* to increase or decrease (or is there no systematic tendency)? Rather than comparing groups, the researcher records data (both height and weight measures) on a sample of subjects. With two measures on each subject, the investigator then computes a correlation coefficient, which provides an estimate of the degree to which the variables relate.

One very important part of problem specification is determining exactly what type of question is being asked. Although this is a seemingly simple task, it is one that repeatedly baffles the beginning research student. It is also crucial; if the researcher does not know what type of question is being asked, there is a very poor likelihood that the study can be planned.

Problem specification for an experimental study involves determination of the experimental variable. The earlier discussion stated that the experimental variable refers to the phenomenon under study, that factor which the researcher manipulates to see what the effect is. For example, if you were interested in which of two teaching methods was more effective, you might design a study in which two groups were taught, one using method 1 and one using method 2. After the two groups had been taught with their respective methods for a specified time, you would then test both of them to find out which group had learned more. If other influences between the groups are equal, you are likely to suggest that the method used to teach the group that performed better is more effective. In this example the experimental variable is the *method of teaching* (which is what you were investigating).

Anderson (1966) discusses an important point in the problem of defining the experimental variable for an investigation, which he calls the *principle of generality*. He notes that the *experimental variable* should be expressed in terms of "a descriptive statement . . . [that refers] . . . to abstract variables" rather than the specific treatments being studied. Referring back to the earlier example, the experimental variable was stated in terms of the abstract variable of *method of teaching*. This is the appropriate way to state the experimental variable as op-

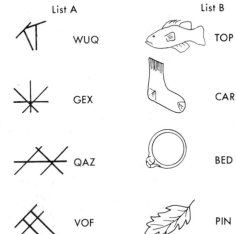

Fig. 4-2. Example of a paired associate task.

posed to stating it in terms of the particular treatment conditions (which in this case would have been something like "method 1 versus method 2"). As a further example, Logan (1969) used two lists of paired associates in a learning study. A portion of those lists is presented in Fig. 4-2. Logan's results indicated that list B was learned more rapidly than list A. In harmony with the principle of generality, Logan did not speak in terms of lists A and B. Instead, he defined his research problem in terms of the abstract variable of the *meaningfulness* of the list material. From this framework, the lists are the particular stimuli that represent the experimental variable of meaningfulness. List A is characterized in terms of being less meaningful than list B. Results may then be discussed regarding meaningfulness, which provides more generalizable information and generates more predictive power regarding other materials. However, if Logan had discussed the experiment merely by referring to list A versus list B, no information would have been contributed beyond the fact that list B was learned more rapidly than list A. Nothing would have been available to permit prediction concerning the learning of other material.

Problem specification for nonexperimental research is equally as important as it is for experimentation. Once again the same principles apply as discussed before. The topic under study must be clearly in mind before the planning can begin. For example, if you were interested in learning about dating behaviors of college sophomores, a survey might be an appropriate method for conducting the research. In such a situation, *dating behaviors* would be the problem and you would then have to specify the specific behaviors to be studied (much like specifying the teaching methods 1 and 2 before). Without this type of consideration (before the study is begun), the survey is likely to be analogous to a fishing expedition; you may end up on the lake simply pulling in anything that bites.

The discussion in Chapter 2 clearly indicated that some nonexperimental researchers do not agree that the problem should be specified before the study begins. This is particularly evident in anthropology where some are arguing strongly against experimental methods and in favor of a more traditional view of the participant observation approach. Such a perspective is represented by the "emic" position discussed earlier. Those subscribing to the emic approach believe that the observer should attempt to view the problems to be investigated through the eyes of the subjects being observed. Although masses of descriptive data can be obtained using this approach, it is quite limited in terms of explaining phenomena or testing theory (Brim and Spain, 1974).

Operational definition. Another important task involved in problem distillation relates to operational definition. Concerning this part of distillation, Anderson (1966) states that "all terms in a descriptive statement must be carefully defined in terms of the steps (operations) that were carried out in the observation or measurement of their referents [p. 12]." This is an essential step in problem distillation and must precede implementation of the experiment. Suppose for the moment that the researcher is going to further study the effects of material meaningfulness on learning, which was investigated by Logan (1969). Full distillation of the problem will require operational definition of all terms, operations, and measures that will be involved in the study. The definitional process can be demonstrated with the term "learning." Since learning cannot be measured directly, it must be inferred that a certain amount of it has occurred based on some performance dimension. Will the focus be on the rate of acquisition? If so, how is this to be measured? A variety of measures might be used, some preferred over others for differing circumstances. The point to be made is that learning must be rigorously defined in terms of what is observable. Similar definitional efforts would be required for the survey on dating behaviors. In all cases the definitions will have to include operational terms that are translatable into procedure. Beyond this, each aspect of the idea must also be operationally defined in the same manner to fully distill the problem. In this sense a research problem is much like liquor: it is not usable until it is fully distilled. The distillation process, as discussed above, involves two essential activities: (1) specification of the experimental variable and (2) complete operational definition of all necessary terms. Once this is accomplished, the researcher is ready to plan the steps necessary for implementing the study.

 Turn to p. 92 and complete Simulations 4-4, 4-5, and 4-6.

The hypothesis. Descriptions of the scientific method are frequently written in a fashion that heavily emphasizes hypotheses. As a consequence, the beginning student often forms an idea of the scientific method primarily from a hypothesis formulation standpoint.

The hypothesis as development of theory. In one form, a hypothesis represents one dimension of theory development. Within this framework, the hypothesis is a theoretical conceptualization or, more informally, an idea or guess regarding how the researcher thinks the results will look. Used in this way, the hypothesis may take the form of a fairly general statement, occasionally written but often merely exchanged verbally with colleagues. The statement is usually linked to the theory being tested (for example, "if the interference theory of forgetting is accurate, then the subjects should . . ."). Used in this fashion, the hypothesis becomes a part of the logic underlying the execution of a study, thus linking data to theory.

The hypothesis as a testable prediction. Hypotheses made for a second purpose take a much different form than do those of the "theory-logic" type described above. This second type represents the ultimate in problem distillation. It demands that the statement be made in specific terms and that it take the form of a statistically testable prediction. Hypotheses of this second type might appear in the following form:

1. Subjects will not differ in mean trials to criterion as a function of high versus low meaningful material.
2. Subjects will not differ in mean trials to criterion as a function of 5-second versus 20-second response time.

These hypotheses were adapted from a study that compared subject learning rate on two types of material and under two response time conditions. Indicative of the level of specificity is the fact that a testable hypothesis is generated for each experimental variable (material meaningfulness and response time). With the research problem distilled to this level of detail, conceptualization of the study is facilitated since it is broken into its most fundamental components, two experimental comparisons.

One factor that often introduces confusion involves the use of null and directional hypotheses in experimental research. *The null hypothesis predicts no difference between comparison groups.* Examples of null hypotheses are found in those presented above concerning material meaningfulness and response time. *Directional hypotheses,* on the other hand, *do predict a difference and indicate the expected direction of that difference* (that is, which group will perform at the higher level).

From a pragmatic standpoint, hypotheses primarily are used in research for statistical testing and problem distillation. For the beginning researcher, the hypothesis is most valuable for clarifying the question and serves little other purpose. Under these conditions, the important concern is dealt with well using null hypotheses and nothing is to be gained by predicting the direction of differences. The prediction of a directional hypothesis becomes functional in the context of theory development (the first purpose for hypotheses). In this framework, the "guess" of prediction becomes relevant from the standpoint of how well the theory logic functions in the clinical or applied setting of real subjects.

However, for statistical testing and problem distillation purposes, the null hypothesis serves well and is probably used more frequently by practicing researchers than the directional hypothesis. For theory purposes, the directional prediction is more often used.

Unstated hypotheses. A student who turns to the journals for examples of the uses of hypotheses by practicing researchers may experience considerable difficulty identifying or even *finding* formally stated hypotheses. In most cases, the formal hypothesis or even reference to one's existence is not evident in the published research report. This does not mean that such problem distillation is not used by experimenters who publish their work. In most cases, the experienced researcher has a backlog of experience that makes problem distillation nearly an automatic process. In such situations, hypotheses more often take the form of mental notes or written records that are so much second nature to performing the overall research act that they seldom appear in the published report. Formal hypotheses do, however, appear frequently in theses and dissertations. This phenomenon relates to the third purpose of the hypothesis, which somewhat overlaps the first two.

The hypothesis as an aid in teaching. The third purpose for the hypothesis tends to overlap the others because it primarily involves a *use* rather than a substantive component or addition to the research process. Hypotheses are, within this context, of considerable value in the process of teaching beginning research students how to conduct research. Many beginning researchers meet with difficulty conceptualizing the research problem. In addition, there is frequently a strong tendency for the beginning investigator to identify a research target that is far too broad and vague to be a viable research question. In both of these general areas of difficulty, the use of hypotheses is helpful. As noted earlier, two practical purposes of hypothesis formulation include theory development and problem distillation. Both of these purposes tend to combat the beginning researcher's difficulties. Problem distillation (using a testable prediction), to the extent exemplified by the hypotheses presented previously, serves to strongly counter the student's implicit belief that a study must be complex (synonymous with big) to "qualify" as research. Initially, specific testable hypotheses tend to break a given investigation into its most simple and fundamental components. This facilitates conceptualization by simplifying the concept being studied. The "theory-logic" use of hypotheses helps problem conceptualization by forcing a step-by-step articulation of the logic base for predictions.

It is thus not surprising to find formal hypothesis statements in student theses and dissertations. For beginning researchers, the hypothesis becomes an instructive device to guide them through the processes that have become second nature to the experienced investigator. It is desirable that the student place hypothesis formulation in proper perspective, however. It is useful for instruction, yet it is often not mentioned on paper by the practicing researcher. Additionally, the important points made by Sidman (1960) should be kept in mind. Research aimed in testing hypotheses related to theory is simply *not* the only legitimate type of scientific investigation.

Comments. The first broad area within the scientific method has been identified generically as *the problem*. Referring to the research problem, the two subactivities of problem identification and problem distillation are seen as necessary elements in the eventual formulation of a researchable question. Although a variety of specific activities may be involved across the broad spectrum of possible research topics, these activities seem essentially to serve either the identification or distillation function. With the problem distilled to the point at which it becomes a focused, specific, researchable question, the next area to be considered is the data aspect of the scientific method.

The data phase involves a number of subparts including design and planning activities, data collection, and data analysis. It is important to remember that *issues involving the problem must be settled before entering the data phase of a scientific investigation.* Frequently a student has data in hand and "wants to do something with it" or "hates to see all this data wasted." Perhaps it is a stack of cumulative testing records from a school district or counseling center. Regardless of the individual's emotional attachment to the data (or the strength of his or her belief that this is a quick way to complete a thesis), to launch a study in this fashion is to launch a study destined for innumerable difficulties. Often such activity is a waste of time from the standpoint of both research information obtained and knowledge gained by the student about the research act. Further discussion of these types of studies and difficulties encountered is found in Chaper 7 under the heading of experimental mortality in follow-up studies. At this point, it is sufficient to state that the sequence of the scientific method essentially places problem issues before data issues.

The data

Once the problem is adequately distilled, the researcher is ready to enter the next phase of activities, which coincides with the second general area of the scientific method. The second area focuses on issues related to the data to be collected. The data dimension of the scientific method probably most nearly represents the lay person's total conception of research. By now, however, you are well aware that the data portion of the scientific method constitutes only one factor in a set of related activities.

Design and planning. Perhaps the most important decisions affecting the soundness of an experiment are made *before initiating data collection*. In fact the strength of any datum is directly influenced by the preexperimental planning that determined how it was to be gathered. The more clearly the problem is articulated (distilled or defined), the easier the data-related planning will be accomplished.

A basic concept that influences the data is that of *control*. As other aspects of the scientific method are discussed, the focus will be on interpretation of what the data or results mean. Of course it is desirable to be able to say that the data reflect the experimental variable (if we are conducting experimental research). The researcher will be able to do this *only if there is confidence that the data do, in fact, reflect the variable of interest* and *not some other influence that has not been eliminated.* Anderson (1971) has discussed this dimension of the scientific method as the principle of controlled observation. In his terminology, one can make the statement that *"a change in variable A causes a change . . . [in the data]" only if all variables other than A can be discounted as causes of the change [p. 27].* This principle is an essential aspect of research design and an important consideration in the data area of the scientific method. It is a central issue that underlies all research in one form or another.

A second consideration involved in data planning relates to the generalizability of results. In discussing this aspect of the scientific method, Anderson (1966) indicates that before a given finding "can be generalized . . . [to a chosen population] . . . it must be shown to hold for an adequate sample drawn from this population [p. 16]." This point has considerable relevance for concerns of external validity, which will be discussed in Chapter 7. To what degree are the results generalizable beyond the specific subjects and exact setting used in the research? Essentially the topic being addressed involves the reliability of data obtained. How reliably can one obtain the same or similar results?

A variety of influences are operative in the reliability of data. Perhaps the most evident influence involves the *subjects in the study.* If it is desirable that results be applicable to a given group of individuals, the subjects in the investigation must be representative of that group. (Such profoundness! Yet this is frequently a problem.) Usually this larger group is defined as the population to which generalization is desired. The researcher wants generalizability, that is, to be able to observe the same or similar performance in the general population that was evident in the sample of subjects. To obtain this data reliability between subjects and population, the experimenter must be able to assume that the subjects are representative of the larger population. This is primarily accomplished through the procedures used in drawing the sample of subjects. Sampling procedures will be discussed in detail in Chapter 8.

A second factor to be considered in data reliability involves the *stability of measures being used in the research.* Although this factor is related to generalizability, the discussion of generalizability focused primarily on sample considerations and did not involve measures. Measures are, however, a vital concern in the data aspect of design as related to the scientific method. In the context of data reliability, the primary concern is that the measure is sufficiently stable that a *subject in the same status* (such as physiological, motivational, or anxiety status) and *performing at the same level as an individual in the broader population, will obtain the same or a similar score on the measure* (or provide the same or similar answers on a survey questionnaire). Thus, for the results of an investigation to be generalizable, the measures recorded must be stable enough that a given score or answer is likely to recur under the same conditions. If the measure is highly unstable, the data may indicate two different scores for the same subject status. Although behavioral science is somewhat plagued by measurement problems, it is usually possible to select or contrive measures that are adequately stable. This, of course, does not mean that there is no variation in the behavior. Instead the concern is that the measure is sensitive to variations in performance and not capriciously variable when performance is not changing (that is, the variability in measure is coincidental to performance variation).

Many investigations involve situations in which the data are collected via observation. In these types of studies, measure stability is very closely tied to the nature of the observation. More specific tasks requiring less judgment from the observer usually result in greater measure stability. These often translate into specific, overtly evident responses that may be counted or easily placed into discrete categories. Binary decisions are the most easily counted. Either the subject does or does not respond. Either the response is correct or incorrect. Such measures, when easily observed and counted, can minimize potential error in judgment and result in stable data. Similarly, measures utilizing relatively precise instrumentation, such as time as assessed by a stopwatch, do not tend to be highly subject to error when the observer has easily observable cues for instrument operation. Less stability may result if it is less obvious when to initiate or terminate instrument operation.

Instrumentation may be used in another fashion that may contribute to measure stability. Devices are available that, if the experimental procedures permit, may be used to permanently record actual subject responses. Such approaches then allow the recorded responses to be removed to another site and analyzed later in a careful manner, without the pressure of ongoing procedures. The types of recording instruments vary, and new techniques are currently being technologically perfected. Audio tapes may serve well to record verbal responses, and video tape equipment may similarly be appropriate for video records of ongoing behavior sequences. Additionally a variety of physiological instruments, such as the electroencephalogram, polygraph, and others, may be used if that type of data is desired. The advantages of such devices have already been implied. The data may be permanently recorded, and analysis or categorization may be accomplished in a relaxed and cautious fashion. Such recording of responses also permits the review of performance if any uncertainty exists concerning the nature of the response. This allows multiple checks to be made on the categorization of responses, which, in turn, serves to improve potential data stability.

The use of permanent recording devices seems to be desirable insurance for research in situations in which such procedures are possible. I have used permanent mechanical recorders as well as human observers many times. As a consequence of such experiences, a note of caution seems in order. Permanent recording devices are not a panacea. Their utility is only as good as the mechanical soundness of the equipment. More than one experimenter has been dismayed when the recordings were prepared for viewing and there was no record because of mechanical failure that was undetected. This unfortunate situation, of course, means lost subjects, lost data, lost time, and occasionally a completely aborted experiment. It is always prudent to double-check equipment before it is used in a study. Perhaps nowhere in research is Murphy's Law more applicable than with equipment.*

Several examples have been given of measures or procedures that may be used to improve data stability. There is also a variety of measurement situations that may be viewed as conditions of higher risk in terms of instability. The probability of greater measure instability is raised substantially when more reliance is placed on observer judgment concerning the nature of a subject's response. This may occur under several conditions. Probably the greatest variation is generated when the observer is requested to categorize behaviors that are not well defined or easily observable. The fewer distinct cues that are available, the more difficult the task of recording data. Likewise when rating scales are used to assess constructs that are ill defined (for example, attitudes, self-concept, anxiety), the observer is presented with a more difficult task, and often greater data instability results. Such situations may be encountered in interviews or mail-out questionnaires. Four basic approaches can help minimize such difficulties. First, the behavior or performance to be measured must be as well defined as possible. Second, when more distinct cues are defined for the observer, there is greater chance that accurate response records will result. Third, multiple observers can be trained to a point at which reliability is high among the group of judges as a whole. In this latter technique, the several observers serve as checks on each other, which places less reliance on a single individual's judgment. Finally, when rating scales are used (such as the Likert or 1 to 5 scale), each point on the scale can be as tightly anchored as possible. A tightly anchored scale might involve very specific descriptors (e.g., $1 = 0$ days per week, $5 = 7$ days per week). Such arrangements can greatly increases data stability simply because the respondent's interpretation of vague descriptors (e.g., seldom, often) is less involved.

Planning or design aspects of the data component are extremely important functional dimensions of the scientific method. It is easy to see how investigations may be seriously jeopardized by errors in this area. Since the data become the central representation of subjects' behavior under the experimental conditions, its soundness must be ensured to every extent possible.

---

*Murphy's Law of Research simply says that "anything that can go wrong will."

Collection. The collection phase refers to the actual execution of the investigation and thus involves data collection. This may include the process of administering a questionnaire, conducting an interview, or presenting an experimental task to a subject and recording responses. *This is the point at which the study is implemented.* The activities involved in this area are those that are most frequently described in the "procedures" section of a research article.

Perhaps the most critical aspect of data collection is performed before the actual initiation of subject testing—detailed planning of each step. This has been stressed throughout the discussion thus far and is being raised once again to emphasize its importance. At least two types of factors warrant attention before data collection begins. First, there are many details that should be planned ahead of time and that are so much a part of research that they are almost givens. They are present in nearly all data collection procedures. The second type of factor is much less predictable. Planning in this area is precautionary, an attempt to head off occurrences that are sporadic but may jeopardize the soundness of data collection procedures. (In laboratory vernacular, this planning is aimed at keeping things from getting screwed up.)

In planning for both types of details, the best preparation is research experience. Frequently these items become second nature to the practicing researcher, almost to the point that it becomes difficult to recall and teach the research student about them. The most effective method of learning about such factors is to work with a researcher over a period of time on different investigations and to note carefully the types of details that receive attention. (This is the most effective manner in which to learn research.) In lieu of accomplishing this at present, some areas will be suggested that may warrant preliminary planning.

Regarding the more nearly standard concerns, probably the most effective planning device is to *mentally rehearse* the entire procedure in detail. A series of questions is usually helpful:

1. *Where are you going to administer the task to subjects?* This is a question that is more expansive than may be apparent at first. The actual attention to place is certainly important. If a study is being conducted in a school, will there be a room available in that school, or will you have to make other arrangements? Suppose you have a room; what is its proximity to the source of subjects? This has certain ramifications for later questions involving transporting subjects to the test area.

The question also has ramifications for the characteristics of the test site. What are the characteristics of the test site that are desirable for your purposes? Should it be a relatively distraction-free room? What about air circulation; might that be important? Final decisions on many of these details must await the site visitation. They should receive advance attention, however, for you to have in mind what will or will not suffice. Frequently the advance planning involves the assessment of general tolerance levels that are acceptable regarding the characteristics (for example, just how stimulus-free *must* it be?). Air circulation may not generally be a problem, but when the principal shows you the room (which turns out to be a walk-in food locker that is no longer used), it suddenly presents a difficulty.

2. *Where are the subjects, and how do you gain access to them?* Again, if the study is being conducted in a school, do you contact the teacher(s) with a prear-ranged list, or do they merely send children as they are free? This could present some sampling problems unless precautions are taken. (See Chapter 8.) The distance from the subject source to the test site is usually not a big problem. One must be concerned, however, about the set that the subject receives during the walk to the experimental room. If the experimenter is accompanying the child, the nature of conversation may be rather influential.

3. *What furniture is necessary in the research room, and how should it be arranged?* Do you want a table between yourself and the subject for materials?

4. *Are your record or data sheets in order for the subject's appearance?* Do the data sheets contain space for complete and convenient recording of descriptive infor-mation concerning the subject (for example, name or code, age, sex, and test data)? Are the data sheets designed for complete and convenient recording of data? Often this may have to be performed with one hand while the other hand manipulates the research materials. Can this be done if necessary?

5. *Are your materials in order for the subjects when they arrive?* How should this be accomplished to save time and not make the subjects nervous? Is instrumenta-tion, such as a stopwatch, in place and in good working order?

6. *What are your instructions going to be to the subject?* It is often a sound proce-dure to have these typed out and either memorized or read verbatim. Never send a questionnaire out without a carefully constructed cover letter. The word-ing is crucial to the response.

7. *What is the time interval that is to be used for the subject to respond?* Is it five seconds in an experiment or three weeks for a mailed questionnaire? (Do not forget to allow for the mail delivery.) What do you say and/or do if this interval is exceeded?

8. *What is your response to the subject if an error is committed?* Likewise, what is to be said if a correct response is made? (This is of obvious importance in research in which the subject is actually face-to-face with the researcher.)

9. *How do you dismiss the subject when the task is completed?* Again this is most crucial when the researcher is in direct contact with the subject(s). What is to be said?

These questions are merely examples. They are relevant in a high proportion of research procedures but may not include everything that should be consid-ered in a given investigation.

Beyond the mental rehearsal, there is one procedure that will provide fur-ther safeguards and, in fact, is so essential that it should be a standard rule (it is with my students). In preparation for data collection and where possible, *the researcher should actually try or practice the entire procedure from start to finish.* Pretest the questionnaire on a few individuals who are similar to the subjects to be used. Practice the experimental procedures or interview in a similar fashion. This rehearsal will serve two important purposes. First, it will usually highlight procedural questions that may not have received attention. Such decisions and preparations can then be accomplished before the time that the study is begun, which minimizes the risk of losing subjects because of procedural error. The second purpose served is that of giving the researcher practice and self-confidence and of polishing the performance of experimental procedures. This is essential, and it is surprising how much improvement is usually evident in the first few practice trials.

As noted previously, it is often not possible to anticipate every contingency even by following a checklist of standard procedures. Unexpected situations usually arise when the procedural rules are stretched by deviant subject performance or behavior. Tales of subject antics are exchanged in research laboratories much in the same way that the proverbial fish stories are circulated among sports enthusiasts. In many cases, the researcher's judgment is tested to a considerable extent to preserve order in the study setting. It is also not uncommon to lose subjects because of deviant behavior, responses, or performance. This possibility can also be circumvented, to some extent, by preinvestigation planning. Such planning usually takes the form of attempts to anticipate, on an a priori basis, the possible performance or behavioral extremes. In most cases this anticipatory planning takes the form of a series of "what if" questions. Some possible decision questions are suggested.

1. What if the subject indicates openly (or subtly) that participation in the study is no longer a desirable activity? This is sometimes referred to (in cynical laboratory vernacular) as "withdrawing consent." This is a real possibility and presents a definite decision point for the researcher.

2. What if the subject asks to have the instructions repeated? Is this permissible?

3. What if the subject makes an error and then *immediately* corrects it ("Oh no, the answer is . . .") in a fashion that gives the impression that the correct answer *may* have been known in the beginning?

4. How many consecutive incorrect responses are permissible before the subject is deleted, and is deletion the appropriate action? Subjects with certain learning problems may persevere far beyond what is imaginable before they are deleted.

5. What should be done if someone knocks on the door or even enters the room without knocking while the study is in session? (This is guaranteed to happen at least once.)

6. Should records be kept out of sight of the subject? How should this be

accomplished? In fact, should the timing (if this is a part of the procedures) and data recording be performed surreptitiously (and is this ethical)?

7. What is to be the response if the subject rises and walks around the table to see the materials?

Turn to p. 93 and complete Simulations 4-7 and 4-8.

It is impossible to anticipate all the contingencies that will occur during data collection. It is evident, however, how helpful it is to have considered even the few suggested here. Data collection may be exhilarating and nerve-wracking, somewhat like athletic competition. It may also be repetitious and boring in certain cases. There must be, however, something addictive about data collection, since researchers keep returning to it again and again.

Analysis. Once the data are collected, the next step is analysis. This step will be treated in considerable detail later in the text and will only be discussed briefly here in the context of the scientific method.

Data analysis probably carries with it more negative connotations than any other single part of the overall research process. Most beginning research students visualize data analysis somewhat like a baptism by complete immersion in Greek symbols that make up complex formulas. Actually, most analyses are merely combinations of elementary arithmetic operations. In most cases, if one is reasonably prepared with the skills of addition, subtraction, multiplication, and division, the essential elements are present. The actual performance of these operations may be guided by any one of a series of step-by-step analysis handbooks on the market. Such handbooks (known as "cookbooks" in the profession) are based on a philosophical position that it is of little value for the researcher to memorize formulas. I subscribe to this position with considerable vigor. Consequently the discussion of analysis procedures in later chapters will include several references to computational handbooks.

Data analysis computation, in most cases, is nearly foolproof. First of all, the task has been made considerably easier in recent years by computers and sophisticated calculators. Additionally, there are mathematical checkpoints that will usually tell the researcher if a computational error has been made. Selection of the appropriate analysis is often more troublesome than performing the computation. This question involves a variety of considerations, which are discussed in Chapters 10 through 13.

The inference

The data are not an end but merely a means by which behavioral descriptions may be made. Such a statement may appear somewhat pedantic, but it is not unusual for the impression to be given that once the data are analyzed, the study is completed. To the contrary, one of the most exciting processes has just begun, that of data interpretation and inference.

Inference is the third general area of discussion under the scientific method. In a specific sense, inference *is the intuitive process by which the experimenter derives a descriptive statement from the data;* it is the *explanation* of the results. Principally based on logical conclusions from the data (related back to the theory or question that prompted the study), the outcome of the inference may be found primarily in discussion sections of research articles.

In addressing the task of making an inference, it is not appropriate to use a "shotgun" search for explanations. In the inferential part of the research method, the data are fed back into the total process in a fashion that attempts to close the information loop. At the outset, there was a research question. Some hypotheses were generated, whereupon an investigation was designed and executed to gather data relevant to that question. The process of inference essentially translates numbers back into behavioral descriptions of what happened to propose an answer to the original research question. Fig. 4-1 illustrates the closed loop conceptualization of the research process and the role of inference in that model.

One important point needs to be considered regarding the inferences drawn from data. For the uninitiated, there is a common tendency to conceive of results as "proving" that a descriptive statement is the case. The problems of "proving" a theory or statement were discussed earlier. There is probably no single term that makes a researcher shudder as much as "prove." Behavioral science has its foundation based on chance or probability theory. A consequence of this is that results *tend* to confirm or support a descriptive statement, or, alternatively, the results *tend* to be in disagreement with or negate a statement.

Results of statistical analyses are no more than probability statements. The statistical statement of $P < .05$, frequently encountered in research reports, means that "the results obtained may be expected to occur due to chance alone only 5 times out of 100." The converse of the same statement speaks to the presumed effects of the treatment. The results obtained may be expected because of influences other than chance (inferring the treatment) 95 times out of 100. Thus inferences in discussion sections of research articles are usually written in such terms as "These results would seem to suggest . . . ," rather than saying that the results "prove" certain statements. Researchers write in such a fashion because they are working from probability bases, not because they are that unsure of their work.

In the process of designing an investigation and interpreting the results, researchers attempt to eliminate alternative explanations. If this is not accomplished and there are multiple logical explanations for a given result, the investigation has not been efficiently designed and a meaningful interpretation cannot be expected.

Such an essential relationship between study design and study outcome also points up something that will be reflected throughout this text. Although the total research process is composed of several component functions, a crucial relationship ties each component into an integrated operation. A serious weakness in any part of the research method threatens the worth of the total effort. Thus each segment must be addressed with equal seriousness and with consideration for its bearing on every other segment.

REFERENCES

Anderson, B. F. *The psychology experiment* (1st ed.). Belmont, Calif.: Brooks/Cole Publishing Co., 1966.

Anderson, B. F. *The psychology experiment* (2nd ed.). Belmont, Calif.: Brooks/Cole Publishing Co., 1971.

Brim, J. A., and Spain, D. H. *Research design in anthropology: paradigms and pragmatics in the testing of hypotheses.* New York: Holt, Rinehart and Winston, Inc., 1974.

Dewey, J. *How we think.* Boston: D. C. Heath & Co., 1933.

Kerlinger, F. N. *Foundations of behavioral research* (2nd ed.). New York: Holt, Rinehart and Winston, Inc., 1973.

Logan, D. R. Paired associate learning performance as a function of meaningfulness and response times. *American Journal of Mental Deficiency,* 1969, *74,* 249-253.

Sidman, M. *Tactics of scientific research: evaluating experimental data in psychology.* New York: Basic Books, Inc., Publishers, 1960.

Underwood, B. J. *Psychological research.* New York: Appleton-Century-Crofts, 1957.

SIMULATIONS

SIMULATIONS 4-1, 4-2, AND 4-3

Topic: Research ideas

Background statement: Many research ideas come from previously published articles, dissertations, and theses. Frequently the author will either allude to or specifically note research gaps and investigations that need to be conducted in the area of interest.

Tasks to be performed

1. Read the stimulus material and list any research idea or ideas that are suggested by the authors in the discussion. Write the idea statements in as complete a form as possible.

2. Copy verbatim or underline the sentence, phrase, or allusion in the passage that generated the idea.

Stimulus material for Simulation 4-1

Simulation 4-1 excerpted from Henderson, R. W., & Garcia, A. B. The effects of parent training program on the question-asking behavior of Mexican-American children. *American Educational Research Journal,* 1973, *10,* 193-201. Copyright, 1973, American Educational Research Association.

Discussion

The results indicated that instruction by an experimenter using modeling procedures had a significant effect on Mexican-American six-year-olds' production of casual questions, and that this behavior generalized to new stimuli without significant loss. Although not a direct replication of Rosenthal, Zimmerman, and Durning's (1970) work, these results support their findings that modeling procedures provide an effective means of teaching children to produce generalized categories of questions, and thus the present investigation has general implications for the design of strategies for direct instruction in information-seeking skills.

The most striking set of findings was that children whose mothers were trained and instructed to use social learning principles, directed toward the modification of their children's question-asking behavior, produced significantly more casual questions in each of the three trial phases (baseline, instruction, and generalization) than children whose parents were not trained and instructed to use these procedures. The implications of these findings for education may be made apparent through an analogy. Consider the baseline measurement as a reflection of a child's school entry behavior on a specific academic skill. Further consider instruction on question-asking provided by the classroom teacher. The teacher might well assume that the change in performance from baseline to instruction is attributable to her teaching. . . . We can note, however, that the experimental and control samples, drawn from the same population, appear to represent two different populations; high achievers and low achievers on the specific tasks investigated in this study. The differences here, however, are not attributable to differences in the abilities of the children. Rather, they are attributable to the fact that the experimental group of children received instruction and support at home and the control group did not. This situation may be parallel to the natural circumstance in which children's school performance is facilitated by the efforts of parents or siblings at home, the so-called hidden curriculum in the home.

Considering the data already available which indicates that differences in home environments are highly related to differences in children's intellectual growth (Dave, 1963; Henderson, 1966, 1972; Henderson and Merritt, 1968; Wolf, 1964), the results of this study indicate that parenting skills relating to the development of intellectual competence can be learned and used effectively by parents who have relatively little formal education. The effectiveness of such parental intervention is clearly evident in the results of this investigation. Anecdotally it should be noted that the mothers of the so-called "disadvantaged" children in the experimental group for this investigation were highly motivated to participate in the training program once the rationale and purposes became clear to them.

The relationship between question-asking behavior under controlled conditions such as those reported in this study and curiosity-motivated question-asking of the sort which is of principal concern to educators remains to be examined through controlled investigation. While we do not have hard data on transfer of skills studied in this investigation to more curiosity-motivated question-asking in natural environmental settings, some anecdotal information is available to suggest that generalization may occur. At the conclusion of the study, the mothers and children who participated in the experiment were taken to a facility housing wild life indigenous to Arizona and Sonora. The mothers remarked that their children were asking far more questions than usual, and many of the questions could be answered by neither the mothers nor the project staff. The mothers spontaneously began to record the children's questions. A meeting was scheduled with an employee of the Museum at the end of the tour, and the questions were answered. Furthermore, at the beginning of the study very few of the participants had library cards. By the conclusion of the program every mother in the experimental group had obtained a library card for the child involved in the study, and for other children in the family.

Susan Gray's (1971) report on the longitudinal results of the Early Training Project at the Demonstration Research Center for Early Education, suggests that improved educational programs are necessary but not sufficient conditions for dealing with the problem of progressive retardation in the school performance of disadvantaged children. Gray indicates that, "Unless the home circumstances of the child can be changed, the adverse environment which created the original problem will continue to take its toll [p. 13]." The results of the present study indicate that the efforts of parents to influence a specific set of behaviors in their children can be effective in producing in those children a significant increment of performance, over the results of instruction by outsiders.

Further research should be directed toward the problem of determining how parents may be encouraged to generalize the social learning principles, which they were trained to use for this study, to other child behaviors facilitative of intellectual development. Applied experimentation of a longitudinal nature should also be pursued to identify appropriate procedures to maintain the use of parenting skills for which training may be provided, and to determine the specific and general effects of home intervention over time.

For feedback see p. 321.

Stimulus material for Simulation 4-2

Simulation 4-2 excerpted from Tang, F. C., and Chagnon, M. Body build and intelligence in Down's syndrome. *American Journal of Mental Deficiency*, 1967, 72, 381-383.

Conclusion and summary

The findings partly confirm Goldstein's empirical observations: there is a tendency for shorter and fatter mongols to have higher IQs than those of taller and thinner bodies, with CA controlled. However, in predicting IQ from body build in two extreme groups, forty-two percent of the total group would be incorrectly identified.

Goldstein associated other variables with the two considered in this study. Heavier subjects would suffer from thyroid deficiency and be emotionally more stable while lighter and less intelligent subjects would have pituitary disturbances and be more restless. Further research would employ more refined criteria of body build and take into account a greater number of variables as described by Goldstein.

For feedback see p. 322.

Stimulus material for Simulation 4-3

Simulation 4-3 excerpted from Skiba, E. A., Pettigrew, L. E., and Alden, S. A behavioral approach to the control of thumb-sucking in the classroom. *Journal of Applied Behavior Analysis*, 1971, *4*, 121-125.

Discussion

The initial objective of the study was to attempt to control a socially undesirable response in a classroom. The results show that this attempt was somewhat successful.

An initial disadvantage that faces any experimenter attempting such a study is the physical size of the class. With class sizes ranging from 25 to 35 children, management of routine lessons can in itself be quite arduous. Attempting to control experimentally the behaviors of specific children becomes an even greater task. It is easy to see, therefore, that control of variables in such a classroom situation may be quite difficult to maintain. Some of these variables were identified during the course of the study and will presently be discussed.

The experimenter was able to observe the subject for only two 50-minute sessions per week. Effects of behavior of the subjects' parents and regular teacher towards the thumbsucking was not controllable in this study. It would be interesting to note how the thumbsucking would be affected if the regular teacher provided reinforcement contingency every day throughout the week. Even more interesting would be the effects of combined control by both the parents in the home setting and the teacher in the school setting. Further research is needed in this area.

Another important variable of interest in furthering the control of the child's behavior is that of random reinforcement by classmates. Wahler (1967) suggested that peer reinforcement may possibly take over when social reinforcement is not provided by the teacher. Although the measurement of such reinforcement would be quite difficult to obtain, the need for investigating its effects is important.

Equally important areas not covered in this study were the effects of the number of reinforcements given and also the method of presentation of such reinforcements. Research has shown the importance of schedules of reinforcement in conditioning behavior. No attempt was made to schedule the frequency of reinforcements in this study.

The use of reinforcement contingency in eliminating undesirable behavior presents a wide range of research possibilites. Control of behaviors ranging from simple idiosyncratic (calling out) to more overt (aggression) can be attempted by the teacher in the classroom. The results as shown in this study describe an attempt to control such a behavior (thumbsucking) within a classroom in a public school.

For feedback see p. 322.

SIMULATIONS 4-4, 4-5, AND 4-6

Topic: Problem distillation

Background statement: One of the most crucial operations in the early planning stages of research is problem distillation. This is the process of refinement that changes a general, frequently vague idea into a specific, researchable question.

Tasks to be performed

1. Read the following statements, which represent research ideas stated in somewhat general terms.
2. For each simulation, restate the idea in a distilled form that makes it more specific and a researchable question. Your restatement may be rather lengthy. In the statement specify what is necessary to indicate the experimental variable (keeping in mind the principle of generality). Make the statement as specific as possible in terms of operational definitions.

Stimulus material for Simulation 4-4

The idea to be distilled reads as follows: "Assess the effects of variation in teaching experience on material evaluation."

For feedback see p. 323.

Stimulus material for Simulation 4-5

The idea to be distilled reads as follows: "Compare the effectiveness of different methods of teaching reading."

For feedback see p. 324.

Stimulus material for Simulation 4-6

The idea to be distilled reads as follows: "Assess the effects of number of reinforcements given."

For feedback see p. 324.

SIMULATIONS 4-7 and 4-8

Topic: Data collection

Background statement: The text emphasized the importance of preexperimental planning for data collection. Such precautions frequently save an investigation from being aborted (remember, Murphy's Law is the enemy of thesis completion!).

Tasks to be performed

1. Read the following stimulus material, which concerns a study you are planning.

2. Make notes to yourself concerning the preexperimental planning or decisions that need attention. To the degree possible, write out those plans or answers to decision questions (realizing that the study is hypothetical). Accompany those plans or answers with a rationale as to why you elected the response given.

Stimulus material for Simulation 4-7

You are conducting a learning experiment on third- and fourth-grade children. The subjects are to learn a set of eight words with which they are not acquainted and which are on flash cards. You are going to administer the task to each subject individually. After one exposure of each word in the list, during which you will say the word for the subject, you will require the subject to read each word to you as presented.

For feedback see p. 325.

Stimulus material for Simulation 4-8

You are conducting an investigation on the dating practices of college students. You are primarily interested in their responses to questionnaire items. These items are statements to which they respond on a scale of 1 to 5 (highly agree to highly disagree). You want your sample to be equally distributed between men and women.

For feedback see p. 325.

CHAPTER 5

Designing experimental research

The previous chapter emphasized the idea that the research process involves a number of interrelated steps. It also noted that this research process is basically the same regardless of what type of investigation is being undertaken. A wide variety of influences exists as the researcher proceeds toward the implementation of a study. Some of these forces are at odds with the basic aim of research as suggested in earlier chapters. However, it is under just such contingencies that research must be conducted and completed in as rigorous a fashion as possible. The research design or plan has already been mentioned as being an extremely crucial aspect of the total research process. The purpose of this chapter is to present the basic foundation of research design for one major approach to investigation—experimentation.

The source of appropriate research designs is frequently a bewildering problem for beginning students. Existing designs or prepackaged plans often do not fit either the research question or the situation in which the study is being conducted. This is the case even in relatively sterile laboratory settings. Consequently, researchers frequently find that they must modify basic designs or even contrive a totally new plan using components from several basic arrangements.

This chapter presents certain foundation concepts of research design and a variety of design formats that are used in experimental investigations. In accomplishing this task it is necessary to present several basic design arrangements. Although some of these basic designs may serve well for a particular investigation, they are not presented as a comprehensive catalog of all possible arrangements. Instead they are presented as sources for useful components that may be combined in a variety of fashions to suit the need of a research question.

THE CONCEPT OF CONTROL

Perhaps the most nearly central idea in research, basic to all design efforts, is the concept of control. Although it was mentioned earlier, this concept is such an essential concern in design that it warrants repetition. When a study is completed, the researcher will want to attribute the results to the treatment. To accomplish this with any confidence, all other possible explanations must be eliminated, or their probability must be minimized. Thus the researcher wants to *control* or hold constant all influences except that which is under study. If, for example, the researcher is setting out to evaluate the effectiveness of a reading program, this will be accomplished only if the other possible influences are controlled, leaving the influence of the reading program free to generate an impact. Control is the essential element in sound research design, and it will be a primary part of the discussion in Chapter 7. The fashion in which the concept of control is implemented varies a great deal depending on the circumstances involved in the research setting.

Turn to p. 111 and complete Simulations 5-1 and 5-2.

TWO APPROACHES TO EXPERIMENTATION

Experimental research in recent years has been characterized by two divergent approaches to designing studies as noted in Chapter 2: time-series experiments and traditional experimental designs. Time-series experiments have come into more frequent usage in the past few years, often in operant conditioning or behavior modification research. Traditional experimental design, on the other hand, has long been used in a variety of settings ranging from psychology and education to medicine and pharmacology. Traditional experimental research was developed primarily in the context of early agricultural research, whereas time-series experimentation has come into popular usage essentially in the realm of behavioral science.

There are several differences with regard to both philosophy and approach between time-series designs and traditional experimental research. Some of these differences are plainly evident (for example, application of time-series experimentation frequently involves small numbers of subjects or even research on a single subject, whereas traditional experimental approaches are usually characterized by much larger groups of subjects). There are, however, some much more subtle distinctions that hold greater importance as well as some similarities that are often overlooked. With the broad range of research problems that face the practicing researcher (or even the consumer of research), it is no longer the case that one can afford to be equipped with a narrow range of tools. The purpose of this section is, therefore, to present an overview of the basic concepts of design, both time-series and traditional experimental approaches.

Initially, it is important to note the similarities and differences between time-series and traditional experimental designs. From the outset both methods have *the same goal,* that of producing information. Since this is the basic objective of all science, it is not at all surprising that this is a commonality. It should be mentioned, however, that because of the different manners in which questions are addressed, the type of data generated is different. Additionally, because of the various settings involved in their typical applications, the data tend to be put to different use.

A second similarity between the two methods involves use of the *concept of control*. As was mentioned previously, this is an essential component in sound research design. Consequently, both time-series and traditional experimental designs are vitally concerned with the concept of control. The researcher must be able to attribute any effect observed to the treatment being studied. However, the ways in which the concept of control is implemented differ greatly between the two approaches.

A variety of differences between time-series experiments and those using traditional experimental designs have been alluded to previously. Research using time-series designs tends to be concerned with the behavioral process as well as the product. The terms "process" and "product" should be clarified. Time-series researchers record several sets of observations over a specified period, under both baseline and postintervention conditions. As a consequence of these procedures, investigators not only have information regarding the influence or product of the treatment, but they also have considerable information concerning the behavioral characteristics of the subject as change was occurring (process). This concern for process as well as product is an important strength of the multiple data points gathered (often continuous measurement) in time-series designs. Traditional experimental designs, on the other hand, tend to focus more on the behavioral *result* or *product* of the treatment being studied. Fewer measurements are usually taken in investigations using traditional experimental approaches. The method, in general, involves formulation of the sample, administration of a treatment, and assessment of treatment effects. From this standpoint, a single performance measure is the source of information. (If more than one measure *is* obtained, such data are certainly much less frequent than in time-series designs and are not usually in sufficient number to observe the process.)

An additional distinction between time-series and traditional experimental designs relates to the *generalization of results*. Traditional experimental research involves standard procedures that focus on generalizing descriptive statements to broader groups of individuals than those used in the actual study. This will become more evident in Chapter 8 with the discussion of sampling procedures. Time-series experiments, because of restricted numbers of subjects as well as subject selection, are less focused on generalization of results. Although time-series researchers usually do not openly deny a concern for generalization, the nature of the method used tends to seriously detract from it. It must be admitted that when working with a single subject or with small numbers of subjects, the probability of such subjects being unrepresentative is considerably greater than with a larger group. Additionally, the manner in which a subject is selected must be considered. Time-series investigations tend to be pragmatically responsive to needs in naturalistic settings (such as controlling undesirable behavior in the classroom) rather than attempting to gather knowledge with samples that represent a characteristic population. This frequently results in problems and subjects being presented to the *experimenter* rather than the experimenter taking a given problem to a *population*. Consequently, generalization of results tends to be limited and is somewhat of an abstraction that might be stated as "relevant to all those like . . . (the subject)." This problem is not insurmountable even in the time-series method. It does, however, require numerous replications of single-subject experiments that are conducted with generalization as a focused purpose. It is also important to note that results of traditional experimental investigations are not automatically generalizable merely because of the approach. Generalization must be a concern of the researcher in designing the study if results are to be generalized, regardless of method. This topic is further explored in later discussions of external validity.

Both time-series and traditional experimental designs have important strengths and problematic pitfalls. Neither should be systematically viewed as being preferable over the other. There are myriad problems and situations involved in the settings in which research must be conducted. Under certain conditions, time-series approaches will serve more effectively than traditional experimental designs, and vice versa. It is imperative that researchers be aware of the various design characteristics so that they can be less restricted with regard to what can be investigated.

TIME-SERIES EXPERIMENTAL DESIGNS

Time-series or continuous measurement research is not totally without a history of usage. It has been used for a considerable period in economics (Davis, 1941) and was implemented occasionally in earlier behavioral science work (Thomas, Loomis, and Arrington, 1933; Arrington, 1943). Its popularity, however, as well as methodological sophistication, has grown dramatically in recent years with an increasing interest in behavior modification. It is beyond the scope of this book to explore in depth all the dimensions and details involved in designing continuous measurement investigations. It is possible, however, to provide an overview of basic design concepts. Readers interested in further study should consult sources devoted exclusively to time-series experimentation (Hersen and Barlow, 1976; Kratochwill, 1978).

Several initial factors must be considered, since they are essential elements in continuous measurement research. It is suggested by the term that this approach to research involves *continuous or at least nearly continuous measurement*. In actuality it involves a series of observations taken on the subject over a specified period. This is a distinctive feature in relation to other research approaches, in which a single (or at least far fewer) data point(s) represent the source of information. The number of measures taken varies considerably depending on the situation, which leads to a second basic consideration. Usually there are a number of phases in any experiment, each one representing a different experimental condition. The number of measurements or data points within any phase must be sufficient to determine a *stable* performance estimate. The purpose of changing from one phase to another is to demonstrate behavior change presumably caused by the new condition. This cannot be established with any degree of certainty unless the behavior rate or performance level is stable (neither accelerating nor decelerating) before the change. The different phases are important and correspond to various experimental conditions. Before demonstrating the effect of any special treatment, it is necessary to determine what the performance level is without the treatment influence. This is usually accomplished by recording the performance level of the subject in a natural or nontreated state. Such a condition and the data generated are called the *baseline*. When sufficient data have been recorded to establish the usual or stable baseline performance level, the experimenter then begins experimental treatment. For purposes of this discussion, the initiation of treatment will be called the *intervention*. (In actual experiments, it is usually labeled by the specific treatment term such as "extinction" or "reinforcement.")

The A-B design

The A-B design is essentially a two-phase experiment. Although it was frequently used in early work, the A-B design involves some very serious weaknesses. Expansions that were developed to circumvent these pitfalls have essentially replaced its use entirely. It is presented here only because of its conceptual simplicity, which facilitates basic understanding of time-series formats in general.

The two phases constituting the A-B design are baseline (A) and intervention (B). The baseline condition is implemented first and continued until a satisfactory estimate of pretreatment performance level is obtained. *After a stable rate of baseline behavior has been established, the intervention or treatment condition is begun.* Fig. 5-1 illustrates a data display that might result from an A-B design experiment.

The vertical center line in Fig. 5-1 represents the time of intervention or phase change. Basic to the A-B design is an assumption that performance change after intervention is a result of the treatment. The major difficulty with the A-B design lies in the absence of supporting evidence for this assumption. Suppose, for the moment, that baseline data are stable, and then a rather dramatic performance change is evident, which occurs at the same time as the intervention. In viewing such data, one might be compelled to attribute the performance change to the treatment. This may, in fact, be the case. There are, however, some alternative explanations. It could be that other influences occurred simultaneously with the initiation of treatment. In the example in Fig. 5-1, the intervention involves Johnny being fitted for glasses. The experimenter would therefore like to say that the dramatic improvement in math performance in phase B is because Johnny is now wearing corrective lenses. Suppose, how-

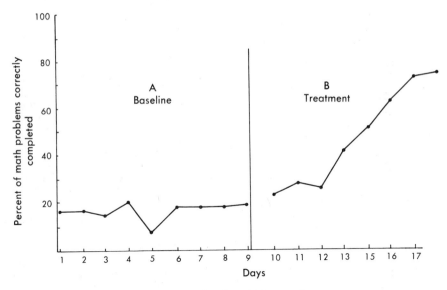

Fig. 5-1. Example of an A-B experiment.

ever, that about the time that Johnny was fitted for glasses, the teacher (bless her soul), distressed by his poor performance, also began to provide him with one-to-one tutorial assistance. Is the performance change caused by the glasses, the tutoring, or both? The experimenter really cannot say with certainty. Here is a situation in which the change in performance might be caused either in part or wholly by influences other than the experimental treatment. Without additional convincing evidence, the researcher will find it difficult to be assured that the treatment alone resulted in the behavior change. Such difficulties are discussed in greater detail in Chapter 7.

One additional note must be made. It has repeatedly been mentioned that the baseline data *must be stable before intervention.* This is an *essential* element in any time-series experiment. Otherwise, performance change evident in the data may merely represent an extension of an already existing trend and may not be the result of the intervention at all.

 Turn to p. 111 and complete Simulations 5-3 and 5-4.

The A-B-A-B design

In an effort to circumvent some of the pitfalls of the A-B design, researchers have extended that basic model into a four-phase format, the A-B-A-B design. Frequently called the "reversal design," the A-B-A-B essentially involves a sequential replication of baseline–intervention–second baseline–second treatment intervention. Fig. 5-2 illustrates a hypothetical data display for an A-B-A-B design.

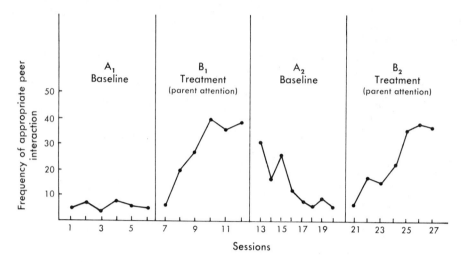

Fig. 5-2. Example of an A-B-A-B design.

The purposes of the first two phases in the design are the same as for the A-B design. The B_1 condition is terminated at the time that the performance level or behavior rate is stable. At that time, the condition is reversed such that the pretreatment baseline contingencies are reestablished (A_2). The assumption underlying this procedure is that if the treatment being studied is the influential or controlling variable, that which generated behavior change in B_1, then removal of said treatment condition ought to reestablish the behavior at the baseline level. The A_2 condition is then continued until the performance level returns to or nears the A_1 baseline level or stabilizes. If this occurs, it is presumed that the treatment is the factor influencing the behavior. At this point, the experimental treatment contingencies are reinstituted (B_2). If behavior returns to the first intervention level, this is taken as further confirmation that the treatment is controlling the behavior.

The A-B-A-B design is not without weakness. First of all, the assumptions concerning the controlling variable are supported only if the data reverse nicely to or near the initial baseline level when A_2 is instituted. Likewise, as noted previously, if condition B_2 reestablishes the performance at or near that evident in B_1, further strength is provided for the assertion that the experimental treatment is controlling the behavior. However, such support is not available if the data do not fall nicely into this pattern. Suppose the behavior does not reverse in A_2. There may be several reasons for this. The first involves the possibility that the experimental treatment is not controlling the behavior. Other influences occurring at about the same time as the intervention at point B_1 may have changed the performance level (as in the previous example). Alternatively, the treatment may be so powerful that the effects are not reversible even with treatment withdrawn. A third possible contaminant might be operative. Some unknown influence may have intervened to maintain the B_1 performance level at the same time that the experimental treatment was withdrawn. Another possibility is that the behavior itself is not reversible. Certainly the reinforcement history of the subject has changed, and it is doubtful that the subject in A_2 is the same organism that existed before treatment was ever instituted. This is most pointed in target behaviors in which obvious learning is involved as a function of B_1. Acquisition of skills is rather difficult to reverse.

The A-B-A-B design must be used with considerable caution. It is of doubtful utility if the target behavior involves obvious learning or skill acquisition (e.g., academic areas). It may be used effectively in behavior is being maintained by contingencies in the environment, perhaps an undesirable behavior, and those contingencies may altered to decelerate the emission rate. The primary strength of the design is visible when the data evidence reversal under A_2 and reestablish a changed level under B_2. Without this evidence, the researcher is left primarily to speculation concerning the treatment effectiveness.

Beyond the interpretation difficulties that may be presented by nonreversal, other considerations must receive attention in use of the A-B-A-B design. It has previously been mentioned that time-series experiments are frequently conducted for pragmatic purposes rather than primarily for knowledge progress. Under these conditions, it is not unusual to encounter situations in which reversal of changed behavior is undesirable. If, for example, a child is exhibiting self-destructive behaviors, it is not likely that the experimenter will be inclined to reestablish such behaviors to strengthen confidence in what controlled the behavior. (A parent is not likely to be impressed by the contribution to science when the child has bruised head or broken bone because of A_2.) The danger simply may be too great to permit reversal. Consequently, under such conditions the A-B-A-B design is not desirable.

Turn to p. 112 and complete Simulations 5-5, 5-6, and 5-7.

The multiple-baseline design

In situations in which the reversal design format is either undesirable or has a low probability of effective demonstration, alternative designs must be used. One such alternative, the multiple-baseline design, has received considerable attention recently by researchers conducting time-series experiments.

In the multiple-baseline design, data on more than one target behavior are recorded simultaneously. Termination of baseline on the different behaviors is staggered in a fashion illustrated by the hypothetical data display in Fig. 5-3. As is evident in Fig. 5-3, the baseline condition on behavior 2 is not terminated until the experimental condition data for behavior 1 has been established. Likewise the phase change for behavior 3 is conducted in a similar fashion regarding the

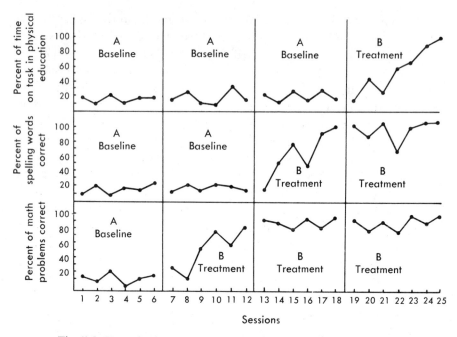

Fig. 5-3. Hypothetical data display for a multiple-baseline design.

data for behavior 2. The assumption undergirding multiple-baseline designs is that the second behavior serves as a control for behavior 1, and the third behavior serves similarly for behavior 2. Presumably the continued baseline level on behavior 2 (after B has been instituted on behavior 1) represents what would have occurred with the treated behavior had the experimenter not intervened. Thus, if the intervention on behavior 2 also results in a rate change (as exemplified in Fig. 5-3), this is viewed as confirmation that the treatment was the influence that generated change in behavior 1. Similarly, behavior 3 is viewed as a checkpoint for behavior 2. If the base rate remains stable and then intervention results in a rate change (again as in Fig. 5-3), this is viewed as further confirmation concerning the treatment being the controlling agent. The absence of rate changes in behaviors 2 and 3 under continued baseline conditions (the staggered portion) is of vital importance to this design. Continuation of stable base rates is presumed to indicate the absence of coincidental influences other than the treatment that might have generated changes in the respective treatment conditions.

As with most designs, both in time-series and traditional experimental research, the multiple-baseline design is not without vulnerability to certain pitfalls. Similar to reversal designs, the multiple-baseline approach shows strongest support for basic assumptions when the data fit nicely into the pattern exemplified in Fig. 5-3. The two foundation assumptions involved in the design are that (1) the continued or staggered base rates on behaviors 2 and 3 will remain stable while other respective behaviors are under treatment, and (2) the control behaviors will change rates when treatment is specifically applied to them. (The present discussion is worded in terms applicable for three or more behaviors; there are also applications in which two behaviors are used.) Several difficulties may be encountered with these assumptions. First, suppose continued base rates on the control behaviors do not remain stable (i.e., they also change when treatment is applied at intervention points in other behaviors). One explanation might involve influences other than the treatment that occur coincidentally with intervention. If this were the case, such other influences (e.g., unknown reinforcers in the environment) would probably not be applied only to the target behavior (e.g., behavior 1 in Fig. 5-3) but more generally and thus might generate rate change in control behaviors. Under these conditions, the experimenter would have no way of knowing whether the treatment was powerful enough to generate rate change at all. An alternative explanation would leave the researcher in an equally confusing situation. Perhaps the treatment was so powerful or the control behaviors so sensitive that the observed base rate change in control behaviors was caused by generalization of influence. Regardless of which alternative actually occurred, change in rate when baseline condition is in effect seriously jeopardizes the strength of multiple-baseline designs and frequently leaves the researcher with uninterpretable results.

Failure of those behaviors that were previously control behaviors to exhibit rate change on intervention also presents the researcher with problems. Suppose, for example, that the rate of behavior 2 did not increase when B (treatment) was applied to it. Again several possibilities might be operative. It may be that the treatment is effective only for certain behaviors (in this instance, behavior 1). This would simply mean that all the behaviors under study are not controllable with the same treatment. One essential assumption of the multiple-baseline design is that the target behaviors *are* all amenable to control by the experimental treatment. A second possibility might involve absence of control of the treatment at the beginning. If the change in behavior 1 was caused by some other coincidental influence and *not* the treatment, the treatment might also not change behavior 2. This possibility is somewhat remote, since it is doubtful that a coincidental influence would be so specific as to affect behavior 1 and not 2 or 3, which were under baseline.

Despite the difficulties noted above with a multiple-baseline design, it is one of the most powerful available for time-series experiments. When the researcher is using this design, it is important that the target behaviors not be closely related or dependent on one another. If behaviors are closely related, the chances of generalized rate change during staggered baseline are substantially increased. As with most basic designs, many variations may be generated that permit investigation in a broad spectrum of situations. Such variations involve expansions as well as combinations of other design components. The example and discussion presented above involved multiple behaviors in a single subject. However, the basic design may also be used to study the same behavior across multiple environmental conditions or may be applied using multiple subjects.

Turn to p. 114 and complete Simulations 5-8 and 5-9.

TRADITIONAL EXPERIMENTAL DESIGNS

Traditional experimental methodology has held a position of prominence in research efforts for a considerable period. As noted earlier, many of the basic design formats were developed primarily in agricultural research and were subsequently modified or applied directly to other areas of investigation. Used in a somewhat broader spectrum of research endeavors than time-series designs, traditional experimental research may still be understood in terms of a few basic design formats. Beyond this core of basic designs, a multitude of variations and expansions have been used in particular situations. This section presents an overview of traditional experimental designs.

Traditional experimental research is usually characterized by a single data point on a group of subjects in contrast to the continuous measurement found in time-series studies. When multiple measures are taken on the same subjects, they involve far fewer than is characteristic of time-series approaches. (More than two or three repeated measures are unusual.) As with time-series research, traditional experimental designs involve several distinctive formats.

Independent group comparisons

One of the most commonly used designs involves independent group comparisons. The term "independent," in this context, simply refers to different groups for each condition. Since, for example, group A is made up of different subjects than group B, there is little reason to expect the scores in one group to be influenced by scores in the other. Since they are different subjects and not related, that is, since the scores in one group are presumed to be independent of the scores in the other group, the term "independent" is applicable. This term is used primarily to distinguish the separate group designs from those in which more than one measure is recorded for the same group.

Beyond the dimension of group independence, the number of experimental variables is an essential determinant of design configuration. The experimental variable, of course, is that factor or question that is under study. In the study by Logan (1969) in which he was attempting to determine the effects of material meaningfulness on learning rate, the experimental variable was material meaningfulness. If the experimenter were interested in what the effects of teaching experience are on instructional effectiveness, the experimental variable would

Fig. 5-4. Hypothetical independent group comparison with one experimental variable.

be teaching experience. Simply, it is that which is being investigated.

Fig. 5-4 illustrates a hypothetical design for an independent group comparison with one experimental variable, frequently called a single-factor design. This example uses material meaningfulness as the experimental variable and illustrates a study in which two groups are compared; group A received highly meaningful material, and group B received material of low meaningfulness. The basic single-factor design may include more than two groups; it is not uncommon for it to involve three, four, or more groups. Each of the groups or conditions within the independent variable is called a *level* within the experimental variable (for example, two levels of meaningfulness, high and low, are involved in Fig. 5-4).

One basic assumption is essential to the independent group design regardless of how many levels or groups are being used. *The groups must be equivalent before the administration of the treatment.* The usual procedure is is to constitute the groups and then to administer the experimental treatment, there being a difference in the treatment given to groups A and B. Usually the performance score is generated either in the process of treatment administration or on some type of test given immediately after the treatment. If groups are not equivalent before treatment, any differences observed in the performance measure may be a result of group differences before the treatment rather than the treatment itself. Therefore, if the study is to actually investigate the effects of a treatment, the only difference between the groups *must be the treatment.* This is the essential concept of control mentioned previously. Various means of forming equivalent groups primarily involve the way in which subjects are assigned to the respective groups. This will be discussed in detail in Chapter 8.

Frequently the researcher is interested in investigating two experimental variables in the same study. This may be accomplished conveniently by using what is known as a two-factor design. (The number of "factors" indicates the number of experimental variables, for example, a single-factor design has one experimental variable, and a two-factor design involves two experimental variables.) Fig. 5-5 illustrates a hypothetical two-factor design. Note that this discussion is still focused on independent group comparisons, which means, for the design in Fig. 5-5, that the experimenter must constitute four different subject groups. The experimental variables in Fig. 5-5 are material meaningfulness and amount of practice. There are two levels of each variable (high and low meaningfulness on comparison A; ten and twenty trials on comparison B). Consequently, this design is frequently labeled a "2 by 2" or "2 × 2," which refers to the number of levels in each variable.

The two-factor design is flexible with regard to the number of levels in each factor. It is not necessary that the two experimental variables include the same number of levels; one may use three on A and two on B or any number of combinations (e.g., 3 × 2, 2 × 3, or 3 × 4). The assumption of pretreatment group equivalence is also necessary for the two-factor design, as it is for group comparisons in general.

Fig. 5-5. Hypothetical independent group comparison with two experimental variables.

More complex group designs may also be used if three or four experimental variables are studied simultaneously. These are merely logical extensions of what has already been discussed and also may involve a variety of levels within the experimental variables (e.g., three factor, $2 \times 4 \times 2$, or $3 \times 3 \times 5$). If three experimental variables are involved (A, B, and C), the pictorial representation is three dimensional, as in a representation of a cube. More complex designs, if used in a totally independent group comparison format, require a large number of subjects. More complex designs also present interpretation difficulties simply because of the complexity of results with several experimental variables. Although useful on occasion, the simpler experiment provides a more clear-cut demonstration of effect and is therefore preferable when possible.

Repeated-measures comparisons

There are situations in which the experimenter either does not desire or is not able to compare independent groups. Under such circumstances, the researcher may choose to record data on the same group under two or more different conditions. Because the same subjects serve as the data source more than once, this type of experiment is known as a repeated-measures design (sometimes called nonindependent, again because the scores are on the same subjects, and the performance at time 2 is certainly not independent of the performance at time 1).

Several different applications are used in the general repeated-measures design. Frequently the experimenter will administer two different tests with either a treatment or time lapse intervening between them. This may take the form of a pretest followed by the treatment and then a posttest. Known as a pre-post design, this arrangement is illustrated in Fig 5-6. As indicated in Fig. 5-6, the data (frequently mean scores) are compared between the pretest and posttest performance to determine if significant change has occurred in subject performance. If there is a difference in the mean scores between administrations, the researcher is then inclined to attribute this difference to the intervening treatment.

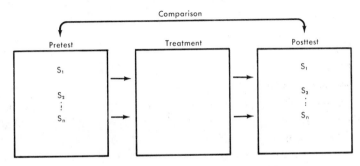

Fig. 5-6. General pre-post design format.

The basic assumption underlying the pre-post design is that the treatment is the *only* influence that intervened between measurements. If this is actually the case, the researcher may accurately infer that the treatment generated the performance change. This assumption, however, is somewhat difficult to substantiate. The only data usually available are the performance scores on pretests and posttests. The researcher often has little firm evidence that test scores would not have changed had no treatment been administered. In using the simple one-group pre-post design, there is always the unknown influence that may have occurred between tests to plague interpretation. There is also no evidence concerning how much improvement may have resulted from test practice. Problems that threaten the soundness of this design and suggestions for circumventing them are discussed in greater detail in Chapter 7.

The researcher is not limited to two data points in repeated-measures designs. It may be desirable to obtain multiple assessments over a period to trace performance change in a more specific fashion than is permitted by only two measures. The condition that occurs between measures may merely be time passage, or it may involve some active intervention such as the treatment suggested above. In either case, the repeated-measures design is still plagued by the same assumption weaknesses that were noted with the pre-post format. Depending on the actual circumstances surrounding the experiment, repeated measures with more frequent assessments may be more vulnerable to test practice than is the case when only two data points are used.

Despite the problems confronting repeated-measures designs, they are an essential part of the researcher's repertoire. Frequently the nature of the research question demands observation of performance change on the same subjects. Many expansions and variations are used to circumvent the problems discussed above. Usually such variations involve the addition of comparison groups, which permits measurements that will substantiate or assess the soundness of the basic assumptions.

Turn to p. 115 and complete Simulations 5-10 and 5-11.

Mixed-group designs

Mixed-group designs involve *two or more experimental variables with independent groups on one or some of the variables and repeated measures on the remaining variable or variables.* This type of design is called "mixed" because of the use of both independent groups and repeated measures. Fig. 5-7 illustrates a mixed two-factor design in which material meaningfulness is the independent variable and recall time is the repeated variable. As illustrated by Fig. 5-7, this merely means that two groups are formed with one being administered condition A_1 (material of high meaningfulness) and the other A_2 (material of low meaningfulness) and

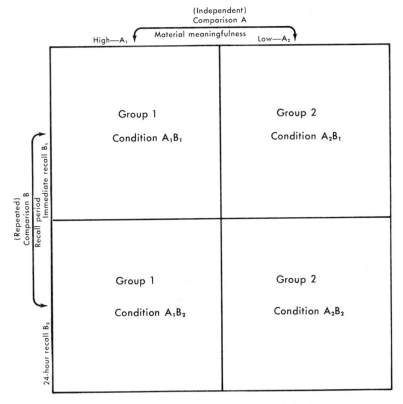

Fig. 5-7. Hypothetical two-factor mixed design.

that both groups are tested for recall immediately and after 24 hours (B_1 and B_2).

The mixed-group format is extremely flexible. If three experimental variables are being studied, the researcher may design the investigation with one variable independent and two repeated or with two independent and one repeated. Fig. 5-8 illustrates both of these options.

The same basic assumptions are operative with mixed designs as with other group comparison formats. More complex designs may be used on occasion, although interpretation of results becomes more difficult.

DESIGN ALTERNATIVES: COMMENTS

This chapter outlined a wide variety of options regarding experimental research designs. There is no single answer to the question that is frequently asked: which is the best? Each approach has its strengths and weaknesses as we will see in even greater detail in later chapters. They serve different purposes and operate under different situations. The researcher must assess the contingencies that are operative in a contemplated investigation. The task then becomes selection and, usually, modification of the basic design format to be used.

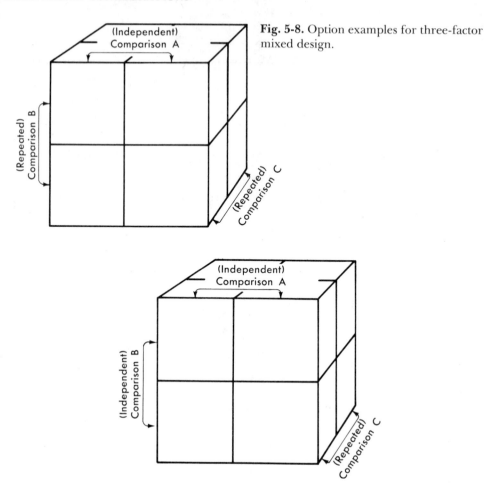

Fig. 5-8. Option examples for three-factor mixed design.

 Turn to p. 116 and complete Simulations 5-12, 5-13, and 5-14.

REFERENCES

Arrington, R. E. Time sampling in studies of social behavior: a critical review of techniques and results with research suggestions. *Psychological Bulletin,* 1943, *40,* 81-124.

Davis, H. T. *The analysis of economic time-series.* Bloomington, Ind.: Bloomington Press, 1941.

Logan, D. R. Paired associate learning performance as a function of meaningfulness and response times. *American Journal of Mental Deficiency,* 1969, *74,* 249-253.

Hersen, M., and Barlow, D. H. *Single case experimental designs: strategies for studying behavior change in the individual.* New York: Pergamon Press, Inc. 1976.

Kratochwill, T. R. (Ed.) *Single subject research: strategies for evaluating change.* New York: Academic Press, 1978.

Thomas, D. S., Loomis, A. M., and Arrington, R. E. *Observational studies of social behavior. Vol. 1: Social behavior patterns.* New Haven, Conn.: Yale University Institute of Human Relations, 1933.

SIMULATIONS

SIMULATIONS 5-1 AND 5-2

Topic: Concept and control

Background statement: The text has discussed the importance of what is known as the concept of control. This is a crucial factor in all research. Practice is one of the most effective means by which the concept of control becomes knowledge that is practical and functional. Try your hand at applying control in these simulations.

Tasks to be performed for Simulation 5-1

1. Refer back to the diagram that was presented in the feedback for simulation 4-4. This suggested a group study, using three groups with one experimental variable, teaching experience.
2. Apply the concept of control to attempt the formulation of equivalent groups other than the experimental variable. Make specific notes as to factors that might necessitate control attention. How would you control the factors you have noted?

For feedback see p. 326.

Tasks to be performed for Simulation 5-2

1. Refer back to the diagram that was presented in the feedback for Simulation 4-5. This suggested a study with two groups and one experimental variable, teaching method.
2. Apply the concept of control to attempt the formulation of equivalent groups, other than the experimental variable. Make specific notes as to factors that might necessitate control attention. How would you control the factors you have noted?

For feedback see p. 327.

SIMULATION 5-3

Topic: Basic design arrangements: time-series A-B

Background statement: Recall that the A-B time-series is one that has two phases, baseline and postintervention. Certain evidence concerning the strength or weakness of an experiment may be available merely by visually inspecting data displays.

Tasks to be performed

1. Inspect the hypothetical data display presented on the top of p. 112.
2. Comment regarding the strength of the design, noting as specifically as possible the rationale underlying your notes of strengths or weaknesses (for example, what about the concepts of control and phase change timing?).

For feedback see p. 327.

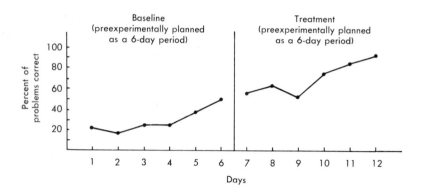

SIMULATION 5-4

Topic: Basic design arrangements: time-series A-B

Background statement: Several basic design arrangements form the basis for
most designs (in modified form) that are used by behavioral science researchers. These are rather easily portrayed by diagrams, which are helpful for the
beginning researcher in terms of identifying the appropriate design format.

Tasks to be performed

1. Diagram a study with the following characteristics:
   a. Difference question
   b. Time-series design
   c. A-B format

2. Insert hypothetical data on your diagram (indicating not only your hypothetical criterion measure but also the experimental variable). Explain the
   important decision point or points if there are any (e.g., timing for phase
   change).

For feedback see p. 328.

SIMULATIONS 5-5 AND 5-6

Topic: Basic design arrangements: time-series A-B-A-B

Background statement: Recall that the A-B-A-B time-series design is one that
has four phases. Several aspects of this design are crucial to its soundness,
and occasionally certain strengths or weaknesses are evident from visual inspection of the data.

Tasks to be performed for Simulation 5-5

1. Inspect the hypothetical data display presented on the top of p. 113.

2. Comment regarding the strength of the design and interpretation of the
   data, noting as specifically as possible the rationale underlying your notes
   of strengths or weaknesses.

For feedback see p. 328.

Tasks to be performed for Simulation 5-6

1. Inspect the hypothetical data display presented below.
2. Comment regarding the strength of the design and interpretation of the data, noting as specifically as possible the rationale underlying your notes of strengths or weaknesses.

For feedback see p. 328.

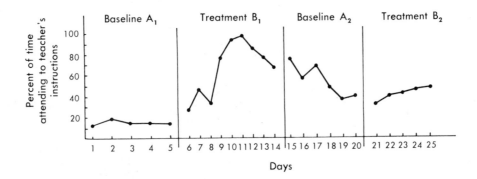

SIMULATION 5-7

Topic: Basic design arrangements: time-series A-B-A-B

Background statement: Several basic design arrangements form the basis for most designs (in modified form) that are used by behavioral science researchers. These are rather easily portrayed by diagrams, which are helpful for the beginning researcher in terms of identifying the appropriate design format.

Tasks to be performed

1. Diagram a study with the following characteristics:
   a. Difference question

  b. Time-series design

  c. Reversal format

2. Insert hypothetical data on your diagram (indicating not only your hypothetical criterion measure but also the experimental variable). Explain the
   important decision point(s) if there are any.

For feedback see p. 329.

SIMULATIONS 5-8 AND 5-9

Topic: Basic design arrangements: time-series multiple baseline

Background statement: The multiple-baseline design is one that involves several
  intricacies in terms of implementation and interpretation. Visual inspection
  of data displays provides a number of checks regarding how the experiment
  was accomplished.

Tasks to be performed for Simulation 5-8

1. Inspect the hypothetical data display below.

2. Comment regarding the points of concern and strength.

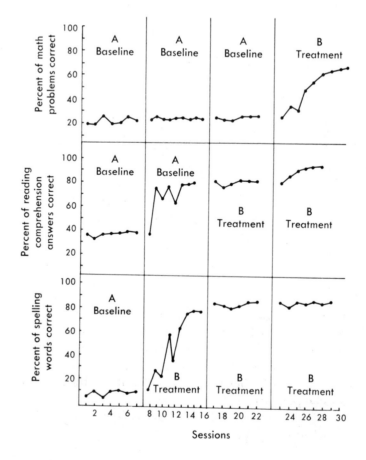

3. Suggest possible interpretations or reasons why the data may have appeared as illustrated.
4. If weaknesses are noted, how might these be addressed? For example, how could the problem be avoided, or how could the researcher's interpretation of results be confirmed or checked?

For feedback see p. 329.

Tasks to be performed for Simulation 5-9
1. Inspect the hypothetical data display below.
2. Comment regarding the points of concern and strength.
3. Suggest possible interpretations from the data.
4. If weaknesses are noted, how might these be addressed? For example, how could the problem be avoided?

For feedback see p. 330.

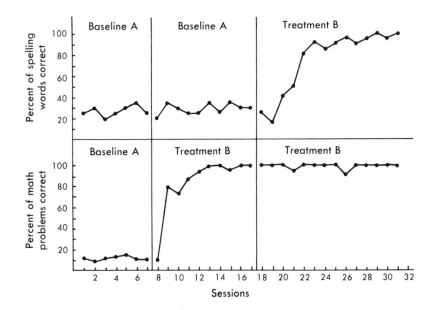

SIMULATION 5-10

Topic: Basic design arrangements: traditional experimental

Background statement: Traditional experimental approaches to designing research are considerably different from the time-series approach. Although the same type of data displays are not relevant (since continuous measurement is not involved), diagram inspection remains a useful approach to practicing knowledge application.

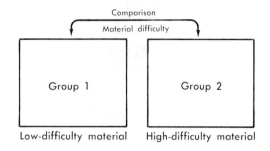

Tasks to be performed

1. Inspect the diagram above and answer the following questions:
   a. Is this a difference question or a relationship question? What is the rationale for your response?
   b. What is the experimental variable? Express this, keeping in mind the principle of generality.
   c. Is this a repeated-measures or an independent design? What is the rationale for your response?

For feedback see p. 331.

SIMULATION 5-11

Topic: Basic design arrangements: traditional experimental

Background statement: Inspection of diagrams permits application of design knowledge and skill from one angle. Frequently, however, one is required to generate diagrams from a set of information. This is essentially what is required when you are designing an investigation yourself. If you can diagram an experiment accurately, then you usually have a pretty adequate functional knowledge of research design.

Tasks to be performed

1. Diagram a study with the following characteristics:
   a. Difference question
   b. Traditional experimental design
   c. One experimental variable
      (1) Teaching method (three different types)
      (2) Independent groups
2. Label carefully the experimental variable on the diagram and be certain that it is evident where the comparisons are being made.

For feedback see p. 331.

SIMULATION 5-12

Topic: Basic design arrangements: traditional experimental

Background statement: Traditional experimental approaches to designing re-

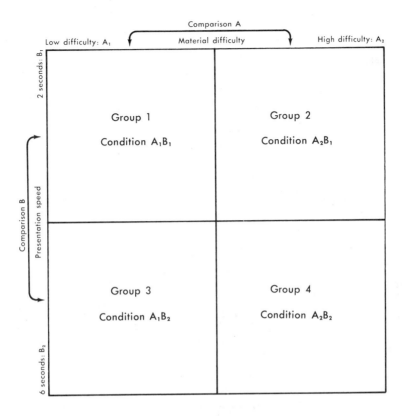

search are considerably different from the time-series approach. Although the same type of diagrams are not relevant, diagram inspection remains a useful approach to practicing knowledge application.

Tasks to be performed

1. Inspect the diagram above and answer the following questions:
    a. Is this a study that is asking a difference question or a relationship question? Why?
    b. How many experimental variables are involved? What are they? Remember the principle of generality.
    c. Is this an independent design, a repeated-measures design, or a mixed design? Why?

For feedback see p. 332.

SIMULATION 5-13

Topic: Basic design arrangements: traditional experimental

Background statement: Inspection of diagrams permits application of design knowledge and skill from one angle. Frequently, however, one is required to design an investigation rather than describe one that is already designed. Construction of a diagram from a set of descriptive statements is essentially the task that is required when designing an investigation and therefore is presented here to simulate such a task.

Tasks to be performed

1. Diagram a study with the following characteristics:
   a. Difference question
   b. Traditional experimental design
   c. Two experimental variables (both independent comparisons)
      (1) Teaching method (three different types)
      (2) Amount of practice (two amounts or levels)
2. Label carefully the diagram with respect to experimental variables, and be certain that it is evident where the comparisons are being made.

For feedback see p. 332.

SIMULATION 5-14

Topic: Basic design arrangements: traditional experimental

Background statement: Occasionally difficulty is encountered in moving from a general diagram of an experiment to the specific details that are involved. This simulation begins with your diagram from Simulation 5-13 and becomes a bit more specific.

Tasks to be performed

With the diagram from Simulation 5-13 performance in hand, answer the following questions:

1. What were the three different methods to be compared under the first experimental variable (what did you specify as method A_1, method A_2, and method A_3)?
2. What were the two levels that you will compare under the second experimental variable (comparison B)?
3. Now, write down a description of what the subjects will be doing in group 1. In other words, what is condition A_1B_1? Your description can be fairly short and can take the nature of: "Subjects in group 1 will receive condition A_1B_1, which means they will be taught with the _____ method and will receive _____ practice."
4. Now describe the conditions for the other groups in the same fashion.

For feedback see p. 333.

CHAPTER 6

Designing nonexperimental research

The previous chapter focused on designing experimental research, whereas this chapter will examine the process of designing nonexperimental research. Prior to beginning this discussion certain preliminary considerations need to be addressed.

The previous chapters have made it increasingly evident that many dimensions of research are somewhat fluid. Ethical considerations vary greatly depending on one's perspective, discipline, situation involved, and methodology used. The topics commonly studied and procedures used differ along the same lines. Likewise the language used to describe theoretical and methodological concepts is quite variable, again, depending on the perspective, discipline, and situation. Investigations using designs other than those in Chapter 5 certainly might be called experiments by some. In fact, it was noted at the outset that the "experimental-nonexperimental" categories are rather arbitrary and that others may use different classification systems (such as "survey and nonsurvey"). These classification schemes also reflect personal perspectives and disciplinary orientations. They are useful for communication and instructional convenience, but it must be remembered that they are somewhat artificial and the use of language is fluid, particularly as one crosses the boundaries of various disciplines.

The term "design" (used as a noun) has typically been associated with experimental research, one uses "this design" or "that design" to investigate a given topic. Regarding nonexperimental research, design, as a noun, begins to have less meaning. Nonexperimental research tends to focus on methods of investigation (e.g., survey, participant observation) that have not been labeled by the term design. There are a number of parallels, however, and the notion of *designing* a nonexperimental study is still very relevant. In the discussion concerning the designing of investigations, it has been clear that often what is actually being discussed is *planning*. (The term "planning" has even been used rather frequently.) In nonexperimental research, the idea of planning becomes more pronounced since there is no noun counterpart of "designing."

Despite the terminology differences, the general research process for nonexperimental investigations remains basically the same as what was discussed before. Certain procedural matters will change; some dimensions will be emphasized more, while others will be emphasized less. However, beyond these differences the fundamental process that began this book will ring familiar (Fig. 1-1). Initially there is a research question, the question is distilled into operational form, the study is planned, the data are collected and analyzed, and the results interpreted in terms of the original question. Because some different emphases, topics, settings, and methods are now involved, a brief examination of these processes is warranted in the nonexperimental context.

As was noted earlier, the initial idea for an investigation is often rather general and lacks specificity. To actually implement a study, it is very important to eliminate areas of vagueness through problem distillation. One of the first matters needing attention in the distillation process is a very precise specification of the problem or question to be studied. The researcher must be very clear and specific regarding what is being investigated and exactly what type of question is being asked. This leads to a particular point needing examination in nonexperimental research—the question.

Precise specification of the question is of obvious importance in all research. It is, however, particularly crucial in nonexperimental studies since there are a broader range of questions typically addressed. Three basic categories of questions were previously discussed: descriptive, difference, and relationship. Nonexperimental researchers work in all three categories, making it doubly important for the beginning researcher to know exactly what type of question is being investigated. As suggested by the design formats in Chapter 5, researchers using experimental designs tend to focus primarily on difference questions.

At the risk of being somewhat repetitive, it is important to remember the general distinctions between different types of research questions. The descriptive question basically asks *what is*. Descriptive research attempts to describe the existing behaviors, opinions, attitudes, or other characteristics of the group or culture under study. As you well know by now, difference questions ask *Is there a difference?* Investigations addressing difference questions may be comparing the opinions, behaviors, or characteristics of two or more groups or cultures. Lastly, relationship questions investigate *the degree to which two or more phenomena relate or vary together.* A researcher undertaking a study such as this may, for example, be interested in the relationship between marriage and annual net income. The question might read as follows: "As the length of marriage varies, what tends to happen to annual net income" (i.e., as length of marriage increases does annual net income tend to increase or decrease)? Rather than comparing groups (as in the difference question), the researcher records data (both length of marriage and annual net income) on a sample of subjects. With two measures on each subject, the investigator then computes a correlation coefficient, which provides an estimate of the degree to which the variables relate.

Any given study may involve more than one type of question. For example, the researcher may be investigating the relationship question noted above but at the same time may be interested in possible differences between geographic regions of the country. In this type of study, both a difference question and a relationship question are part of the same investigation. It is important for the beginning researcher to know that there are two questions to avoid confusion in the conceptualization of the study, its execution, and its interpretation.

As was discussed in Chapter 4, a second vital step in problem distillation is operational definition. This is as important in nonexperimental research as in any other type and definitely must be completed prior to beginning execution to avoid the need to make immediate (and potentially incorrect) decisions in the field. All terms, activities, measures, and other important factors must be specifically defined in a fashion that will permit someone to know exactly what is to be done, what is considered a complete response, and so on. (For example, what is meant by *net* annual income? Does this mean merely "after taxes income" or does it also include such cost items as necessary business expenses like union dues or membership dues to professional organizations?) Unless these matters are clarified, the investigation is likely to involve considerable error in the implementation process and the results will be less precise. If you can answer the question "What exactly do you mean by . . ."(e.g., net income), you probably have it operationally defined. If you cannot answer such questions, do not begin because it is guaranteed that you will be sorry later.

You will recall that the rest of the research process involves the data stage (planning for collection and analysis) and the inference or interpretation of results. These steps are vital for nonexperimental research just as they are for experimentation. In some cases they are more crucial. For example, it would be devastating to send out all your questionnaires and then find out that your instructions or questions were unclear. If your instructions were vague in an experiment, you may only loose the first subject or two. The designing of nonexperimental investigations *must* be undertaken with great care; your a priori decisions and questions must already be made and answered. Reviewing Chapter 4 will facilitate this process and is helpful for both the experienced and beginning researcher.

As was previously stated, the term "design" has less relevance to nonexperimental research than it does to experimentation. The labels typically attached to nonexperimental studies tend to reflect the methodology used for data collection (e.g., survey studies, observation studies). Consequently the planning of nonexperimental research will be discussed in this same fashion. It should be remembered that a variety of types of questions may be addressed within any given methodology. For example, a survey study may be descriptive, it may address a relationship question, or it may be undertaken for purposes of comparing groups.

SURVEY RESEARCH

Survey research involves asking questions of a sample of individuals who are representative of the group or groups being studied. As suggested above, such an investigation may have a variety of purposes (e.g., describing, comparing, correlating). The importance of problem distillation has already been emphasized, and certainly this must also be accomplished in a survey study. Assuming that this has been completed, the next step in designing a survey involves planning the procedures to be used in collecting data. This will include developing the instrument and determining the sample to be drawn. A variety of sampling techniques can be used and each involves very specific procedures that must be carefully planned and executed. These will be examined in detail in Chapter 8.

Surveys typically use two general procedures for data collection—questionnaires and interviews. Questionnaires might be distributed by hand (such as in a group meeting or class session), or they may be mailed to the respondents. Similarly, interviews may be undertaken on a face-to-face basis or by using the telephone. Each specific procedure has certain strengths and weaknesses that must be considered by the researcher in the process of selecting the one to be used.

The essential task of any survey is to obtain information from a sample of respondents that relates to the question(s) being studied. Although this sounds simple enough, it can often be a formidable undertaking. Great care must be exercised in planning a survey investigation to facilitate successful execution of the study. The factors to be addressed differ somewhat between questionnaire and interview research and will therefore be discussed separately.

Questionnaire investigations

If a questionnaire study is being designed, there is an obvious need to construct the instrument itself. This seemingly simple task has many pitfalls that may seriously threaten the investigation if they do not receive attention during the pre-execution planning. For example, the questionnaire must be constructed in such a manner that it will extract accurate information from the subjects. As a minimum, this means that the questions must be written clearly and in a fashion that minimizes the possibility of misinterpretation by respondents. There are also certain factors to be considered in construction of the questionnaire that can either encourage or discourage response by the subjects. This section will focus primarily on design issues other than the questionnaire itself. Questionnaire construction will be discussed in more detail in Chapter 9 which examines measures, instruments, and tasks.

Questionnaires may be personally distributed by hand or distributed to respondents through the mail. These two methods of distribution are clearly very different and involve different strengths and weaknesses that must be considered. Mailed questionnaires may represent a substantial savings of time and money and may also permit great accessibility to respondents that is simply un-feasible with questionnaires distributed by hand. The financial investment for a mailed questionnaire might be limited to the postage expense, the paper needed for the instrument reproduction, and the personnel costs involved in instrument development, reproduction, and mailing. No one would argue that each of these areas is becoming increasingly expensive, but they are still less costly than paying someone to personally distribute the questionnaire. (The other expense areas would remain constant since one still needs paper and has to pay personnel to develop and reproduce the instrument.) The accessibility of subjects may be a major consideration. Clearly if the respondents are geographically scattered, the mailed questionnaire may be the only option.

Problems with mailed questionnaires must also be considered carefully. Mailed questionnaire studies are often plagued with a low response rate (i.e., a small percentage of respondents completing and returning the questionnaire). In fact, this is often touted as being a major argument against mailed question-naires. Related to this difficulty is a problem of slow response. Subjects may take their own sweet time in returning the questionnaire, and the researcher has little means of controlling their behavior (which can really screw up the study). Ad-ditional difficulties include the lack of control regarding the nature of subjects' responses and particularly the potential of receiving information from a biased or atypical sample. It is difficult to argue against the idea that there is likely a difference between those subjects who respond and those who do not (and therefore the intended sample in general). Most of the factors involved in care-ful design of a mailed questionnaire are aimed at circumventing such problems as those noted here.

The planning of a mailed questionnaire study includes attention to a number of factors. Some of these may vary depending on the type of question being asked. Others are more specifically related to the procedures used in question-naire investigations. A synthesis of the problems that are particularly problem-atic with this type of study can be reduced to two major categories (1) low re-sponse rate and (2) the accuracy of subjects' responses. Clearly the researcher has limited means of controlling the respondent once the study is underway. Consequently all precautions possible must be taken before the study is initiated to circumvent both accuracy and response rate difficulties.

One of the questions that often plagues the beginning researcher concerns the issue of low response rate—just how low must it be before there is trouble. Of course answers to this question vary considerably, but the researcher must begin with the basic assumption that what he or she really wants is for all respon-dents to return their questionnaires completed. Whereas this would be the best of all possible circumstances, it seldom occurs. Some studies using mailed ques-tionnaires have response rates as low as 10 percent, which nearly everyone would agree is inadequate. Babbie (1973) suggests that a 50 percent response rate can be considered adequate, 60 percent return is good, and 70 percent or more should be viewed as very good. It should be noted, however, that such guidelines represent judgment statements and even Babbie states that ". . . they have no statistical basis . . .[p. 165]." They also do not represent wide consensus among researchers. For example, Bailey (1978) strongly suggests that researchers should not be satisfied with such low response rates and that the serious researcher should undertake several steps to substantially increase the return. From his point of view, with a properly constructed questionnaire and appropriate follow-up by the researcher, a 75 percent response rate should be achieved and return rates of 90 percent and above are quite possible.

A variety of factors are involved in the construction of an effective questionnaire, which will be discussed in more detail in Chapter 9. There are, however, certain factors that seem to relate to response rate that warrant examination here. One of these factors is the length of the questionnaire. Respondents are more likely to complete a one- or two-page questionnaire than they are one that is four or five pages long. There are no solid guidelines regarding optimum length for a questionnaire, but it seems clear that the shorter it is, the more likely the researcher is to obtain a satisfactory response rate.

Another consideration in planning relates to the ease with which a respondent can complete the questionnaire. Obviously this partially involves the length of the questionnaire, but there are other matters that also influence the effort required to complete the questionnaire. If there is little time and effort required, there will probably be a higher return rate (and perhaps more accurate and honest responses) than if the process is time-consuming and difficult. Part of this will be determined by the clarity of instructions provided for the respondent. Unclear instructions are likely to cause confusion regarding what is to be done and may even cause many subjects to place the questionnaire in the circular file. Open-ended questions may have the same effect if there are too many of them. Such questions take more time and effort since they require the respondent to write out the answers.

One of the best procedures for circumventing the difficulties mentioned above is to conduct a pilot test of the instrument. This was suggested earlier in the discussion of experimental research, and it is equally valuable in the present context. The pilot test would simply involve having a few individuals complete the questionnaire before the actual study is begun to be certain that the instructions and questions are clear and to assess the time and effort required on the part of the respondents. It is very important that the pilot test be conducted with individuals who are very similar to the respondents in the sample, otherwise the pilot will tell little or nothing concerning how the actual respondents will react.

A variety of other steps can be taken to improve the response rate in mailed questionnaire studies. For example, it is a commonly accepted practice to include a self-addressed, stamped envelope for subjects to use in returning the questionnaire. This obviously reduces the imposition on the respondent and substantially influences return rates. The nature of the cover letter may also be important. It is somewhat unclear whether or not a personal letter (i.e., Dear Mrs. Smith) is more effective than one that is rather impersonal (i.e., Dear Occupant). What is clear, however, is that the body of the letter seems important. A shorter letter results in higher response than one that includes long and involved statements. Additionally, a letter that has a firm or coercive tone is less effective than one that involves a somewhat more permissive appeal to respondents.

Respondents are more inclined to complete and return a questionnaire if they are convinced that the study is legitimate and of value. One factor that may influence this perception relates to organizational sponsorship of the investigation. A study that is being sponsored by a credible government agency (if you can find one), a university, or some other well-known and respected organization is likely to be viewed as more legitimate than one that is not. Subjects are generally more responsive to an investigation with such sponsorship than a study with no apparent organizational affiliation. It is important to note, however, that not all organizational sponsorships may be viewed favorably. The parenthetical comment concerning governmental agencies was only partially tongue-in-cheek. Certain sponsorships may be viewed with suspicion by respondents, such as those that may have a commercial motive (i.e., the salesperson appears at your door 2 weeks later). Although sponsorship of a questionnaire investigation is important in terms of response rate, the researcher must carefully consider the impact of the *particular* affiliation on the subjects being sampled.

Respondents are probably most likely to complete and return a questionnaire if they attend to it as soon as they receive it. Obviously the researcher cannot stand over the shoulder of each subject, but there are certain precautions that can be taken in terms of mailing. The response rate is substantially lowered if the questionnaire arrives just prior to a major holiday or vacation times. Questionnaire researchers should attempt to avoid such timing or any other periods that may have a similar effect. Subjects may be inclined to delay response until after the holiday has passed, and if it is an extended holiday, they may decide that it is too late to respond afterwards. Precise control is usually not possible because of many unknown influences (e.g., mail service). The researcher should, however, carefully consider the population being sampled to avoid potential timing problems. For example, if school personnel are involved, it is probably wiser to sample in September than it is in May.

It was mentioned earlier that follow-up contact is also a step that may improve the return rate in questionnaire studies. This seems to be an extremely potent procedure. Bailey (1978) cites evidence suggesting that response rates may be increased as much as 20 to 30 percent over those expected when no follow-up is involved. In general, three follow-up contacts seem to be about the optimum, with any more than that probably being viewed as harrassment by the respondent. Such follow-up often involves a reminder letter as the first contact, a second reminder letter with another questionnaire attached, and the third follow-up being a telephone call. A number of specific issues require attention in deciding the nature of follow-up procedures to be used (e.g., timing, protection of anonymity, content of the follow-up). The beginning researcher who anticipates undertaking a questionnaire survey should consult any one of the many volumes specifically devoted to this research method (e.g., Berdie and Anderson, 1974).

Turn to p. 135 and complete Simulation 6-1.

Interview investigations

Surveys using interviews have the same basic purpose(s) as questionnaire studies but simply use different data collection procedures. As noted earlier, interview investigations use personal contact and interaction to gather data necessary to address the question or questions being studied. Such contact may be made on a face-to-face basis or by telephone. Each procedure has its strengths and weaknesses that must be considered as the researcher decides which approach to use.

One of the difficulties already discussed in relation to interview studies is the high cost involved. If the interview is conducted on a face-to-face basis, costs can be extremely high. The basic expense of interviewer salary is often considerable; as travel and lodging expenses are added (if necessary), the financial outlay may become astronomical. This problem is one area in which the telephone offers a significant advantage over face-to-face procedures. Telephone interviews can be undertaken without travel expense and can be completed very quickly (when compared with face-to-face interviews). Both of these factors greatly reduce expenses, but there are problems involved in the telephone interview that may be so significant as to seriously limit its use.

Perhaps the most difficult problem involved in telephone interviews is one of sampling bias. Obviously the only respondents who can be contacted using this procedure are those who have listed telephone numbers. Immediately this makes the telephone survey less appealing for studies that need to sample a broad cross-section of the population. Certain segments simply may not be accessible–those persons with unlisted numbers. This problem must be carefully considered as one examines the telephone survey as a potential means of data collection.

Telephone interviews may also be plagued by the perception of the respondent regarding the motives and/or credentials of the interviewer. Everyone receives their share of telephone calls that they believe are suspect for one reason or another. The telephone has even become a major instrument of business for burglars who want to determine if a person is home, and they may even obtain information regarding personal possessions through a fake interview. There are many reasons to be somewhat suspicious of telephone calls from unknown persons. These same factors greatly influence the type of data that can be obtained using a telephone interview. Although it has certain advantages, these are often judged to be less compelling when balanced against the problems involved.

The face-to-face interview also has certain strengths and weaknesses that must be examined as the researcher considers its use. Generally speaking, the interview is a social interaction between people and is subject to all of the influences that affect such interchanges. (This is probably exaggerated with the face-to-face interaction.) Certainly the face-to-face interview is vulnerable to all of the potential biases that may be represented in the person of the interviewer. Data recording might be substantially altered to the degree that the interviewer has a personal investment or opinion regarding the outcome of the study. It may also be influenced by the perceptions of the interviewer in terms of the subject being interviewed. Suppose that the interviewer holds some serious and deep-seated biases regarding a particular religious group. If a respondent is encountered who belongs to that particular faith, it is not unreasonable to suspect that the interaction with that individual will be different than with individuals who are not so affiliated. Data may even be consciously altered in such circumstances.

Clearly the interaction involves at least two individuals—the respondent and the interviewer. Consequently the respondent must also be considered as possibly contributing to a bias problem. Even if I do not know you (the interviewer), I may have certain reactions to the way you appear. In reaction to such a perception, I may be cooperative, honest, open, or just the opposite of all those demeanors. Thus the personal interaction may be a significant factor in interview studies, both in terms of the interviewer and the respondent. It may cause problems, as most of these examples suggest, or it may contribute to an accurate and comprehensive investigation. At a minimum, it cannot be ignored as one plans an interview study or selects a procedure to be used.

The interaction between the interviewer and the respondent is very important, as suggested by the previous discussion. Certain considerations must receive attention by the researcher to maximize the effectiveness of this interaction and facilitate, to the degree possible, an accurate survey. One factor that is very important involves the characteristics of the interviewer. The interaction during an interview may be significantly influenced by a variety of personal characteristics in the same manner that any interpersonal interaction is affected. It is a commonly accepted fact that interactions between individuals of the same race or ethnic background are different than those that occur between persons of different races. This also seems to be the case regarding interview studies. If the study involves a particular racial or ethnic group, the researcher should be careful to use interviewers who represent the same population. Accurate and honest responses seem more likely to occur between individuals who share this personal characteristic. This rule of thumb also seems to hold for social status. Respondents seem to be more inclined to provide accurate and honest information to interviewers who are or appear to be from the same social class. Such influence seems to include matters of clothing and grooming. For the most part, interviewers should dress and groom themselves in a manner that will be similar to the sample of respondents, *but* the interviewers should maintain a balance between that perspective and one that legitimizes their role as professional interviewers. If interviewers are going to work in a lower class neighborhood, they should not be dressed in an elegant fashion, but at the same time they should be sufficiently "different" to provide credibility to their role. (Unless, of course, they are being deceptive in their activities as an interviewer, an issue that was discussed at considerable length in Chapter 3.)

Personal characteristics of age and sex may also be important, but there do not seem to be any clear guidelines regarding these areas. In some cases, it seems that same sex interviewers should be used, whereas in others the evidence is less conclusive and even confusing. The researcher must carefully consider the topic under study and the nature of the questions being asked when making this determination (for example, are sensitive questions being asked that would probably result in a same sex combination being more effective, or does it seem inconsequential). Age of the interviewer is also an unknown at this point. At times, and with certain topics, it seems that the most effective interview can be conducted with the interviewer and the respondent being about the same age. At other times, it appears that the interviewer should be older than the sample group to provide the credibility and maintain the legitimate role perception necessary for an accurate survey. Although these latter characteristics are currently somewhat unknown in terms of influence, they should not be ignored by the researcher considering an interview investigation. If there is a question in the investigator's mind, the topic should be examined at length, either by reviewing the literature or by undertaking a pilot study to provide empirical evidence relating to the methodology concern.

Interviewer behavior is also an influential factor in the success or failure of the data collection process. One of the first tasks that must be accomplished is the creation of a favorable impression on the respondent. Such initial perceptions may set the stage for a successful interview, or they may lead to a complete refusal to participate. The respondent must be immediately convinced that the interviewer is legitimate and the study is of sufficient value to become involved. If these phrases sound familiar, it is because this process is basically the same as was discussed previously regarding questionnaire studies. The task may, however, be somewhat more difficult since the interviewer is physically present and thus might represent more of a threat than the arrival of a questionnaire in the mail. The interviewer should always present credentials and identification papers and provide an explanation of the purpose and nature of the investigation. Although the respondent should not feel coerced, the interviewer will probably be more successful if the tone of the conversation "assumes" participation on the part of the person being approached. Clearly establishing rapport with the respondent is an extremely important factor in the success of the interview.

The actual conduct of an interview often involves the use of a questionnaire or standardized interview protocol. The obvious difference here is that the interviewer reads the questions or statements and records the subject's responses. As before, the construction of the protocol is crucial and it should undergo pilot testing prior to beginning the actual investigation. (Issues related to questionnaire and protocol development will be addressed in Chapter 9, which discusses measures, instruments, and tasks.) Interviewers using such procedures should be careful to systematically follow instructions in a consistent fashion to standardize the data collection process. There may be occasions when an interview study is conducted without a structured interview protocol. Such procedures, although useful in certain circumstances, do not provide the same caliber of objective and consistent data as those involving a standardized protocol.

Turn to p. 136 and complete Simulation 6-2.

OBSERVATION STUDIES

It was indicated earlier that observation may be used in a variety of investigations including experimental and nonexperimental research. It is being discussed in this chapter because it is clearly a data *collection* procedure and does not specifically involve a designed manipulation of treatments or an experimental variable. This, once again, illustrates a distinction that bears reemphasis. Investigations can be designed, which in many cases is conceptually similar to planning. The *procedures* for executing the study must be carefully *planned*, and many of those procedures involve data collection. Observation is a means of collecting data, and data collection is obviously an important part of the overall research process. However, the planning required for implementing the observation includes some separate and distinct considerations from the generic planning or design of an investigation.

Two factors become immediately important in planning the observation process: (1) the setting and (2) the structure exercised *on* the observations by the investigation itself. Both of these factors can be viewed in terms of a single concept—a continuum of structure. The *setting may be very structured,* such as a laboratory study, or it may be a *totally unstructured setting* in which the observer records information in a presumably natural setting (as in the traditional anthropology study of primitive cultures). The investigation may also involve a continuum of structure that is imposed by the investigation itself. In a fashion similar to the interview discussion, observations may be recorded using very structured categorization or counting of behaviors (e.g., a behavior checklist, rating scales) or they may be recorded without a specific guide for the observer (e.g., field studies in which the observer participates in the group and merely records whatever occurs). Specific operational procedures for conducting observation will vary considerably depending on the structure of the setting as well as the structure imposed by the investigation. In fact, each individual investigation may have certain features that are somewhat unique from other studies. Clearly an examination of all such possible variations is beyond the scope of this text. Consequently this discussion will be limited to certain generic considerations involved in developing a system of observation.

One of the first matters that must be addressed in planning an observational study is to identify *who is to be observed.* For some investigations, this may involve identifying the culture or group to be studied. In others it may mean a definition of the *types* of individuals to be observed (e.g., 12-year-old males with IQs between 70 and 85). Regardless of the type of study, the basic aim is to precisely describe the subjects who are going to be included for observation. Obviously without such a definition the study cannot even be planned, let alone executed.

Another factor that must be accomplished very early in the planning process is a determination of *what behaviors are to be observed.* This task will require an operational definition of the actual focus of the observations (assuming that *all* of the possible behaviors that might occur are not of interest). For example, the researcher may only be studying the "aggressive behaviors" between the 12-year-old males noted above. Even further in this context, aggressive behavior must be defined—is it physical, verbal, both? In another study, the researcher may wish to observe the verbal communication between 19-year-old female students. Likewise in this example, a number of factors must be defined and/or described (especially if the observation is to be more "structured"). The definition of behavior must be sufficiently precise so that the observer can reliably determine when or if it occurs, which, of course, means that the researcher must also attend to some other issues related to the behavior, such as defining any and all conditions under which the observations will be made. In what *setting* is the verbal communication between 19-year-old females to be observed? It was mentioned that they were to be students, but more details are still needed to implement the observation. Are they to be in small groups or large groups? Will the observation be in a natural setting such as the student union or will it be a contrived setting such as a class discussion (real or otherwise)? These latter points and questions raise still another factor that must be determined and described in detail. *What will be going on* in the setting? It is unlikely that any given study would be interested in all communication that might occur regardless of what was happening.

Most probably the researcher will be interested in studying communication (patterns, frequency, duration) under certain conditions that would include a particular type of setting and a particular type of activity.

It should be noted that some studies might be *specifically designed* to observe communication regardless of what was happening. *If* this is a part of the study, controlling the activities would not be a part of the procedure. This should, however, be determined from the outset (and the question should always be addressed during planning).

Time must also be a consideration in defining the conditions under which an observational study will be conducted. In this case time should be thought of in at least two fashions. One may want to define the time (of day, month, year) that the data are collected. For example, the researcher may want to study communication patterns in 19-year-old females as they first rise in the morning. Such a study might place a restriction on the time of day or time in terms of the first hour after rising. The second view of time may involve a time interval for observation and data recording. In this type of situation, the researcher may be interested in observing the "frequency (number of occurrences) per hour" of a given behavior. Time must be specified so that there is a constant frame of reference. If this is not done, the data may not be accurate and consistent (for example, two groups may interact the same number of times but one may generate 47 interactions in 30 minutes whereas another may generate 47 interactions in an hour).

Thus far behavior observations have been discussed without reference to methods of recording. In fact the discussion above may even suggest the "writing down" of each behavior—separately, completely, and in words. Although such procedures may be used in some circumstances, it is more likely that other means will be preferred for a number of reasons. Usually certain *types* of behavior (e.g., the "aggressive" behavior in the earlier example) or the different kinds of behavior exhibited by a particular type of subject will be of interest. Consequently one task that usually must be undertaken is the development of a *system for categorizing and coding* behavioral occurrences. For example, behavior might be roughly categorized into "aggressive" and "nonaggressive" with each being operationally defined. It might then be determined that certain specific behaviors should be observed in each category and are thusly coded to facilitate recording by the observer. Obviously there are a great many possibilities that would vary depending on the focus of the investigation. The subcategories might include both physical and verbal behaviors and those directed toward peers or those directed toward adults. A number of categories have already been provided (e.g., aggressive–physical–peer directed, aggressive–verbal–peer directed), but only a few possibilities have been suggested. The coding of behaviors would obviously become very important if there were many subcategories to be observed, otherwise the actual recording process may become extremely cumbersome. For example, in the rough outline above symbols such as A-P-P, A-V-P, and so on may be used to represent each possible behavior. In most cases, a carefully designed data sheet will be used so that the observer is only required to make a quick mark on the form if a particular behavior occurs. There are many possible approaches to coding behaviors, and the researcher must decide which best suits the study being planned. In some cases, an existing system will function very nicely (e.g., White and Haring, 1976), and in others the best approach may involve adaptation or development of one specifically suited for that particular study (e.g., Jackson, Della-Piana, and Sloane, 1975).

The researcher planning an observational study must attend to other issues regarding *how the data are to be recorded* prior to initiating the investigation. A variety of recording methods may be considered depending on the nature of the investigation. One of the simplest is known as the *tally* method, which may be preferred if the researcher is interested in the number of times that a particular behavior occurs. Once the behavior or behaviors of interest are clearly defined and coded, the observer tallies on paper, or with a hand counter, each time there is an occurrence. As always, the observations must be recorded in relation to a time frame such as a session or a prescribed interval (e.g., 5 minutes). This permits the determination of rate—the frequency per session. Another recording procedure that may be used is known as the *duration* method. The duration method is useful to determine how much time a subject spends engaged in the behavior of interest. In this case, the observer would probably observe an individual subject for a time, starting and stopping a stop watch as the behavior began and ceased. Observations may also be recorded using the *interval* method. This procedure might be used if you were interested in whether or not a particular behavior occurred during a given interval. Using such a method, the observer would simply mark the interval on the recording sheet if the behavior occurs during that period. The behavior might be continuous throughout the interval, or it may carry over from a previous period and cease halfway through the interval. In each of these conditions, the interval would be scored as an occurrence. The interval recording method may be useful for behaviors when it is difficult to count the individual occurrences. A subcategory of interval recording is known as *time sampling*. Time sampling is useful when the observer cannot watch the subject continuously and, instead, samples the observations by looking at the subject on a systematic basis (e.g., at the end of a time interval). Sampling may permit observations on a group of subjects simultaneously. If the target behavior is evident at the time the observer samples, it is recorded as an occurrence.

There are many variations in terms of recording observational data, and each has certain procedural matters that must be considered. Even from the limited discussion above, it is clear that different characteristics are involved in each and the data may differ substantially depending on the method chosen. Different research questions, subjects, and settings all influence the decision regarding which method will function most effectively. All of the specific considerations that may influence such a decision cannot be considered here as there are complete volumes that are devoted to the intricacies of this process (e.g., Jackson, Della-Piana, and Sloane, 1975). The primary purpose of this discussion was to sample some of these considerations and emphasize the importance of specifying which recording method will be used prior to beginning observation.

Another factor that must receive serious attention in observation studies involves the *reliability* of the data recording. Obviously any data collection procedure might include a certain amount of error whether the recording is accomplished by a machine or a human. A machine recorder may be calibrated incorrectly and thus not accurately represent what actually occurred. Clearly a human recorder may also be subject to error; some behavior might be overlooked and some may be noticed but recorded inaccurately. Consequently observation studies often (and should always) include certain precautions that attempt to determine observer reliability. This is typically accomplished by using two or more observers (either continually or on a periodic, spot-check basis) and calculating the degree to which they agree. Such procedures are known as determining interobserver reliability.

There are a variety of methods for calculating interobserver reliability, and the circumstances related to the investigation may suggest which should be used (Herbert, 1973; Jackson, Della-Piana, and Sloane, 1975). One type of procedure that has a considerable history of use involves *percentage agreement methods* (including simple percent agreement, effective percent agreement, as well as other variations). Percentage agreement methods are conceptually simple and easily computed, which has had certain appeal in terms of convenience and interpretation. Basically this type of procedure asks the question, how much of the time (what percent) did the two observers agree regarding the data recorded. Despite the advantage of simplicity, percent agreement methods have certain limitations that must be considered. One of the most serious limitations pertains to the number of observations recorded. In particular, if there are very few observations (opportunities for agreement), percentage agreement methods may provide a very imprecise picture of interobserver reliability. Herbert (1973) illustrated this dramatically as she reviewed the possibilities in examples in which there were *very* few observations. If, for example, there was only one opportunity or observation and both observers agreed, the reliability would be represented by a 100 percent estimate. On the other hand, if there was one agreement out of two opportunities the percent agreement estimate of reliability would be 50 percent. Thus there is a great deal of variation with small numbers of observations and the reliability estimates might be very misleading when compared with the same behaviors observed many more times. Additional problems with percent agreement methods also should be weighed by the researcher planning an observation study. These include limitations regarding further analysis, difficulties separating chance errors (or agreements) from those that are systematic, as well as others. The interested reader should consult any of the several publications that focus on these issues in depth (e.g., Hartmann, 1977; Herbert, 1973; Jackson, Della-Piana, and Sloane, 1975).

Correlational methods are also used to estimate interobserver reliability and, as expected, they also have certain limitations and advantages that warrant consideration by the researcher during planning. The use of correlation techniques for this purpose is conceptually similar to asking any relationship question; the purpose is to determine the degree to which factors relate or vary together. Thus if we have a positive correlation between two observers' recorded data, they tend to vary in the same direction. As observer A records an increased frequency, observer B also tends to record an increased frequency, which is some indication of the degree to which they agree or are reliable. The degree to which they agree is represented by the correlation coefficient. Correlation methods of assessing interobserver reliability have certain strengths not evident in percent agreement procedures. For example, correlation measures are not influenced by chance agreement in the same fashion that percent agreement methods are, and correlation coefficients have a definite mathematical interpretation regarding variation between observers. Correlations may also be used for further statistical analysis if this is desired in the particular investigation being planned. Correlation estimates are not, however, without problems: (1) they are more difficult to interpret to those who are not acquainted with statistical procedures, (2) correlation procedures also encounter problems when occurrences are infrequent (opportunity for agreement or disagreement), and (3) if there is little variation in the data recorded, the correlation coefficient obtained becomes less precise. Thus the correlation method overcomes certain problems but other limitations may present themselves. The researcher must determine the type of interobserver reliability method that will be used based on the specific characteristics of the study. It is important, however, that some reliability assessment be made to provide greater credibility to the results obtained.

A brief comment needs to be inserted at this point regarding the discussion of observation studies just presented. Much of what has been examined in this chapter applies primarily to observation research in which a certain amount of structure is imposed by the investigation. The chapter also discussed observational studies in which very little structure is exercised and the data may be recorded in the form of field notes such as with traditional anthropology research. Clearly the concerns for coding, categorization, and other structural matters change in such investigations and other factors must receive attention as well. The researcher must always be alert to those specific issues that require consideration in planning the particular type of study involved. This type of thoughtful decision-making is, of course, an evident need in all research regardless of approach.

REFERENCES

Babbie, E. R. *Survey research methods.* Belmont, Calif. Wadsworth Publishing Co., Inc., 1973.

Bailey, K. D. *Methods of social research.* New York: The Free Press, 1978.

Berdie, D. R., and Anderson, J. F. *Questionnaires: design and use.* Metuchen, N.J.: Scarecrow Press, Inc., 1974.

Hartmann, D. P. Considerations in the choice of interobserver reliability methods. *Journal of Applied Behavior Analysis,* 1977, *10,* 103-116.

Herbert, E. W. *Computation guide for interobserver reliabilities.* Salt Lake City: Bureau of Educational Research, University of Utah, 1973.

Jackson, D. A., Della-Piana, G. M., and Sloane, H. N., Jr. *How to establish a behavior observation system.* Englewood Cliffs, N.J.: Educational Technology Publications, 1975.

White, O. R., and Haring, N. G. *Exceptional teaching.* Columbus, Ohio: Charles E. Merrill Publishing Co., 1976.

SIMULATIONS

SIMULATION 6-1

Topic: Questionnaire studies

Background statement: Low response rate is a problem that has plagued survey researchers forever. This particularly becomes a problem when a questionnaire is mailed out to respondents. This simulation focuses on that difficulty and presents you with the task of advising your new employer, which may be a delicate situation.

Stimulus information: You have recently been employed by Monolith Oil Corporation as a Research Associate. Because of the energy crisis, Monolith executives have decided that they should become aware of the opinions of consumers. (This is definitely something new—since when do the opinions of consumers play an important role, particularly with oil companies?) As you arrive on the job, the first day you are *summoned* (now we are beginning to sound like an oil company) to the president's office regarding a questionnaire study that has been conducted regarding consumer views of the energy problem. By way of background, you are told that the problem is one of what appears to be a very negative reponse. (The consumers did not think that there was an energy crisis, but did believe that the oil companies were reaping unjustifiable profits from the public.) Obviously this is not what the president wants to hear, and so you are being asked to show how the study was conducted incorrectly. Disregard your personal opinions for the moment and consider the facts surrounding the study. The questionnaire was six pages long, it was mailed to respondents with no follow-up, and there was a ten percent response.

Task to be performed: Give the president advice, but do it tactfully. What information would you give the president? Was the study conducted correctly? If not, what would you suggest?

For feedback see p. 333.

SIMULATION 6-2

Topic: Interviews

Background statement: As you know from the material presented in this chapter, many influences may affect the success of an interview study. You have been asked to serve as a consultant with the Sociology Department of Northern Delta University, which is undertaking an interview study in a predominantly black neighborhood in Detroit. The researchers are relatively inexperienced in terms of interview studies and have asked your advice regarding the procedures that should be used.

Task to be performed: Since you have just completed "Research 32," you have considerable information concerning interview surveys. What will you suggest?

For feedback see p. 334.

CHAPTER 7

Potential design pitfalls

The previous two chapters examined certain fundamentals of designing both experimental and nonexperimental research. These discussions included some basic design formats and considerations for the initial conceptualization of an investigation. However, the designing of a study is far from complete with only the initial conceptualization considered.

It was mentioned earlier that the planning and execution of a study seldom, if ever, fits a particular "textbook" example. Often the specific study being planned will require slight (or even major) variations on the basic designs discussed so far. Each situation (i.e., setting, materials, subjects) presents a unique set of problems to be solved to execute a sound investigation. Some of these problems have been either mentioned or alluded to in previous chapters. In most cases, steps may be taken, *before* the study is actually begun, to substantially reduce the effects of such problems on the investigation. It is important to note the emphasis on "before" in this statement. Thorough planning is perhaps the most essential component in sound research. Although this has been emphasized earlier, it is so crucial that it will remain as a major theme throughout the text. Without a great deal of careful planning before the investigation is begun, there is a considerable chance that the study will fail or, at a minimum, have serious weaknesses. This chapter focuses on some of the potential problems that may be encountered in conducting research. Although these are also "textbook" examples, they represent crucial *types* of pitfalls that should receive consideration in planning and designing studies.

INTERNAL AND EXTERNAL VALIDITY

Two concepts, external and internal validity, are vital to a conceptual grasp of all research design. Use of the term "validity" in this context is somewhat different from its use in test and measurement areas. In the arena of research design, validity might be viewed as referring to the technical soundness of a study. As the researcher designs an investigation, attention must be given to both internal and external validity to safeguard against problems that may prevent meaningful implications being drawn from the results.

Speaking in the context of experimentation, Campbell and Stanley (1963) note that "*Internal validity* is the basic minimum without which any experiment is uninterpretable [p. 175]." An experiment that is internally valid is characterized by having successfully controlled (or accounted for) all *systematic* influences between the groups being compared, *except* the one under study. This, of course, is the core of the *concept of control* discussed earlier. If, for example, one were comparing two groups of children and the experimental treatment were teaching method, it would be desirable to have the only systematic difference between the groups be teaching method. Fig. 7-1 illustrates the type of design that might be involved. As indicated by the double arrow, the research question involves the effectiveness of teaching method 1 as compared with the effectiveness of teaching method 2. The differences between method 1 and method 2 are systematic differences in the sense that one group is systematically taught with method 1, whereas the second group is systematically taught with method 2. Any other *systematic differences* between groups 1 and 2 may result in performance differences that appear to be the result of the teaching method but really would not be. Consequently, to design an internally valid experiment, the researcher must eliminate all systematic differences between groups 1 and 2 *except* teaching method. This same basic principle for internal validity applies to nonexperimental research particularly when comparisons are involved. An example of such a situation may be found in a survey study in which the researcher wants to determine whether or not there is a difference between Democrats and Republicans in terms of annual income. In this case, the researcher would try to make the study internally valid by ensuring that the *only* difference between the groups was their political affiliation. More detailed discussion of such cases will be presented as they are encountered in the text.

External validity, as described by Campbell and Stanley (1963), "asks the question of *generalizability:* To what populations, settings, treatment variables, and measurement variables" can results obtained be generalized [p. 175]? In a basic way, external validity speaks to the issue of how much is the research setting (subjects, environment, measures) like the world about which the investigator wishes to say something. Is the sample sufficiently representative that the researcher can accurately say something about the population being studied? Fig. 7-2 illustrates the nature of external validity or generalizability questions. As before, the arrows represent the questions being asked. How well do the results of a given investigation represent or apply in terms of the population that is ostensibly being studied and the real world environment in which this population resides? Additionally, are the measures recorded representative of performance criteria that may apply in the outside world. If treatment variables (e.g., teaching method) are involved in the study, do they represent something that may serve as a treatment in the world outside the research setting? If a survey is involved, does the survey ask questions that are relevant to the world outside the interview or questionnaire setting? (Are the questions asked in a manner that the respondents answer in a manner that is similar to an "everyday" answer?)

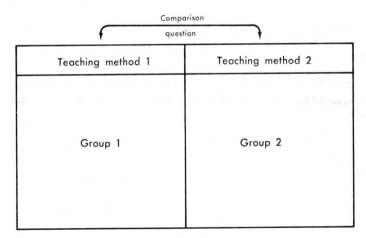

Fig. 7-1. Design comparing two methods of teaching.

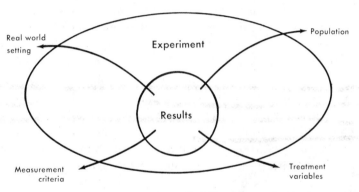

Fig. 7-2. External validity questions generalizability of results to the world outside the investigation.

To summarize, internal validity refers to the technical soundness of an investigation. A study is internally valid to the degree that influences, beyond that variable under investigation, have been removed or minimized as a systematic effect. External validity, on the other hand, speaks to the issue of generalizability. An investigation is externally valid to the degree that the arrangements, procedures, and subjects are representative of the outside setting, thus making results generalizable.

External and internal validity are sometimes at odds with each other. The logistics involved in designing an internally valid study occasionally mitigate against the achievement of as much generalizability as is perhaps desirable. This idea has already been encountered in the discussion of different research approaches. Approaches that exercise a great deal of environmental control (such as some experiments) may have great internal validity but may be less externally valid because of the artificial setting. Other approaches (e.g., participant observation) may have great external validity if the environment remains natural, but internal validity may be reduced to some degree. Thus the beginning researcher should realize that a given study may sacrifice some degree of either internal or external validity to achieve a greater degree of validity from the other perspective. Maximally meaningful research must thus be thought of in terms of *programs* of research that often involve a series of different but programmatically related studies. Studies conducted in the initial phases of a research program may sacrifice some degree of external validity to more precisely study the variables involved. Alternatively, later phases of a research program may sacrifice some degree of internal validity to achieve a better perspective of how the phenomena under study operate in the world outside the laboratory. Only the cumulative synthesis of evidence obtained in such a program of research will result in meaningful and precise changes in practice.

THREATS TO INTERNAL VALIDITY

Several types of influences threaten internal validity. Each type may be operative in a variety of designs. In the following discussion, the respective threats will be examined in the context of several vulnerable designs. As the reader continues through this chapter, two points should be kept in mind. First, it is important to avoid as many threats as possible to conduct the most rigorous study feasible under the circumstances. Second, it is difficult, if not impossible, to totally eliminate all problems; nearly every study conducted has some area in which it could be strengthened. After all threats that can be circumvented have been taken care of, those remaining are something that must be "lived with," so to speak, and interpretation of results must account for them.

History

The term "history," for design purposes, refers to *specific incidents that intervene between measurement points in addition to the treatment*. Since this is a different definition than that commonly used for the term, the definition is critical. As suggested by this definition, history is a threat to internal validity when the researcher is obtaining repeated measures or more than one observation on the same subjects.

History represents a threat to internal validity that is difficult to circumvent. One major cause of this difficulty is that the researcher may be unaware of historical events, and there is little that can be done in advance to prevent their occurrence. Several designs are vulnerable to this type of problem. Clearly, it may affect the pre-post design in traditional experimental research. History may also influence time-series experiments if the historical event occurs at about the same time as the intervention. Additionally, history may be a potential contaminator in nonexperimental research. For example, it may cause a problem when

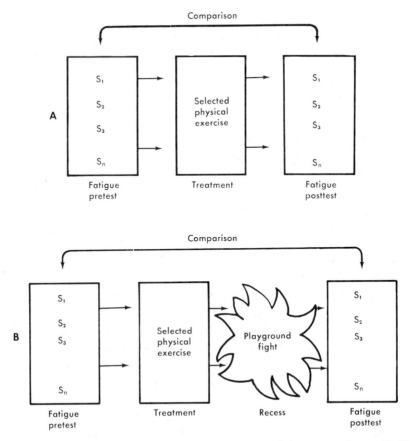

Fig. 7-3. A, Experimental design for a pre-post physical fatigue experiment. **B,** Experimental design for pre-post physical fatigue experiment with history as a threat.

an "incident" occurs between two interviews with the same subjects. Perhaps the factor under study was merely the passage of time between the two interviews (*but,* something traumatic also occurred during that time). To more fully discuss the history threat, some examples will be discussed in greater detail.

It was noted above that history may threaten pre-post design in traditional experimental studies. Suppose an investigator is conducting an experiment concerned with the effects of certain exercises on overall physical fatigue. The study is being undertaken with sixth graders and involves the administration of a pretreatment measure followed by the exercises, which, in turn, are followed by the posttreatment measure. Fig. 7-3, *A* represents a visual diagram of the experimental design. This investigation is asking a difference question. Represented by the double arrow in Fig. 7-3, *A,* the researcher will be comparing the pretest scores with the posttest scores to determine if there is a difference. Ostensibly the only major event between these two measures is the treatment, which in this case involves certain physical exercises. Assuming that the study is internally valid, any differences between pretest and posttest performance should primarily be a result of the treatment. This may or may not be the case. History might serve to threaten the internal validity of the study.

Suppose that the entire time required for this hypothetical experiment is about 2 hours. The experiment is initiated at 9:00 A.M. and proceeds through the pretest and the treatment by 10:30. At this time, recess is scheduled and the children go to the playground, where a serious fight erupts. The fight involves several children from the experiment and continues for nearly 10 minutes before it is broken up. At the end of recess, the children involved in the experiment return and take the posttreatment fatigue test. In analyzing the data, the researcher finds that the measures on the posttest show significantly greater fatigue than the pretest scores. If the experimenter is unaware of the specific event (playground fight), it might be logical to conclude that the physical exercises involved in the treatment seem to produce a significant general fatigue effect in sixth-grade children. Naive concerning the history contaminator, the experimenter assumes that the design in Fig. 7-3, *A* is operating when, in fact, the data are most probably being generated by the design represented in Fig. 7-3, *B*. There are two major experiences that the children encountered between the pretest and posttest. The resulting difference in scores could have been caused by either the treatment, the fight, or a cumulative effect of both. Inferences that the selected exercises generated the observed general fatigue may be in error.

How does one circumvent specific events, designated here as history, that may be operative *in addition to the treatment*? As was noted previously, this is difficult because history is often out of the control of the researcher. If the researcher *is* aware of these events, a judgment must be made whether or not the events have a high probability of influencing results. This type of judgment is subjective, but if the specific event is related to either the treatment or the measure, it probably has seriously weakened internal validity. The example given represents a situation in which the measures and treatment are most likely related to the specific event. In such a case the study is probably destined for a new start. If, on the other hand, the experimenter judges little or no effect as a function of history, the incident should be mentioned in the report and a rationale should be presented concerning why it was judged to have no substantial influence. (There is no way that the experimenter could legitimately conclude that the fight did not affect fatigue.)

There are some preventive measures that the researcher may take to lower the probability of history looming as a threat to internal validity. Naturally, when experimental logistics permit, a shorter period between pretest and posttest is desirable. This collapsing of the time span simply does not allow as much time for history to intervene. The study, however, may not permit such a short time

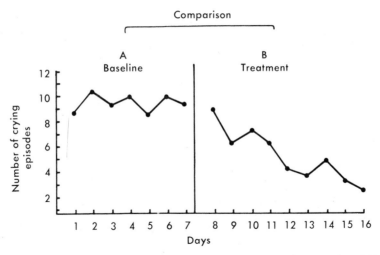

Fig. 7-4. Example of a data display from a hypothetical experiment using A-B design.

frame. The experimenter can also attempt to avoid times when there is a high probability of history intervening, such as recess or the lunch period.

History may also threaten the internal validity of a time-series experiment such as is often used in behavior modification studies. As noted in Chapter 5, this type of investigation is characterized by various data collection phases. Data are collected before the treatment or intervention to establish the baseline rate of the behavior being studied. After the experimenter is satisfied with the reliability of observation and stability of behavior frequency, treatment will be initiated in phase B. Fig. 7-4 illustrates a hypothetical experiment using the A-B design described in Chapter 5. Essentially this type of study is asking a difference question as suggested by the double arrow indicating comparison. Did the treatment make a difference? Is there a difference between baseline behavior frequency and that which was recorded after the intervention was initiated? The intervention or experimental variable may have been some aversive stimulus or reinforcement condition. The researcher, who is interested in the effect of the *experimental variable* (treatment), is assuming that the treatment under study was the cause of the change in behavior frequency. If some specific event *other than the treatment* occurs simultaneously with the intervention, history may be serving to threaten the internal validity of the study. The change in behavior frequency evident in Fig. 7-4 may be a result of the intervention, the specific history event, or a combination of the two. If the experimenter were to draw a conclusion that suggested the intervention as the cause of behavior changes, it might be in error.

Again, circumventing history as a threat may present serious problems. In this type of experiment, however, the researcher may do several things to guard against this threat. First and most important, this type of experiment is often replicated numerous times before the researcher begins to draw implications from results. The chances that any particular event might systematically occur in close proximity to the intervention over a series of studies is low. Thus the data will begin to center around the effects generated by the treatment over a series of replications. Often the researcher will reverse the experimental conditions (using the A-B-A-B design) after behavior has stabilized. Here again, the chances of the specific event either reversing or in some other way operating simultaneously with both intervention and reversal are low. Additionally, the use of multiple baseline procedures has resulted in lowering the threat of history. As mentioned in Chapter 5, the multiple baseline design serves as a means of studying the effect of a treatment on a given subject (but involving several target behaviors). (It has also been noted as a method of studying a particular treatment and a given behavior with more than one subject.) The probability of accidental historical incidents occurring at staggered intervals that coincide with all phase changes in a multiple baseline design is very low. However, once again the researcher should avoid (if possible) scheduling interventions close to high-risk times when history influences are probable.

History may also represent a contaminating influence in research in which repeated measurements are taken on the same subjects with only the passage of time between data recording sessions. In such a study, the researcher may be conducting an interview survey such as the brief example mentioned earlier. For example, the investigator was interested in respondents' attitudes regarding sex as a function of phases of the moon. This might mean that an interview would be conducted during the full moon and a second interview with the same subjects during the new moon period. It would be the aim of the researcher to attribute any attitudinal differences between the two times to the different phases of the moon (a *simple* comparison survey). This would be contaminated by a history threat if, for example, a nationally televised traumatic incident related to sex intervened between the two interviews. Differences in attitudes might be caused by the moon phases, the traumatic event, or both, making the results uninterpretable. Certainly the content of this example may seem rather remote, but the concept remains very important. A history threat may *seriously* influence results and make interpretation of results most difficult. (It should also be noted that this latter example is not restricted to nonexperimental research, it is also relevant to experimental studies of many topics such as memory or forgetting.)

History, in the form of specific intervening events *aside from the treatment or variable under study*, thus represents a grave threat to internal validity. As is evident from the preceding discussion, the potential for weakening an investigation is present in several research approaches. In all cases, the basic idea of research design is violated. To be internally valid, a study must permit attention to the question being asked (*the effects of the experimental variable*) without influences from factors that are not a part of that question *(influences other than the experimental variable)*. Once again, the concept of control is involved.

Maturation

Maturation represents a second threat to the internal validity of an investigation that serves to plague researchers working on several fronts in behavioral science. Distinctive from history problems, maturation refers to factors that influence subjects' performance because of time passing rather than specific incidents. Included in Campbell and Stanley's (1963) discussion of maturation influences are such examples as growing older, hunger, and fatigue. These processes become threats to internal validity in cases in which they operate *in addition* to the variable(s) being studied. This category of threat is of concern in longitudinal research such as is conducted in child development, in which the actual physiological growth process is involved. From the definition it also seems that maturation, in terms of hunger, fatigue, and similar such factors, may threaten myriad other types of research. It may be useful to explore some of the designs that are vulnerable to maturation as a threat to internal validity.

Researchers often wish to observe the effects of a treatment that requires a long time, long enough to be considered a longitudinal study. This is common, for example, in situations in which a school district is experimenting with a new type of program. Usually such a program evaluation is approached in a general fashion that includes a pretest, the program as a treatment, and a posttest with the time involved representing a full academic year. Such investigations are fraught with danger to internal validity. For the purposes of this discussion, however, maturation will remain the primary focus.

This type of study is essentially a pre-post design similar to the one diagrammed in Fig. 7-3, *A*, with a long treatment period. If the researcher proceeds with a single group, administering pretest, treatment, and posttest, a difference question is presumably being asked. This might be phrased, "Was there sufficient difference between pretest and posttest performance to be significant?" The inference basically involves the amount of change between the two measures. Because the assumption is that the study is not being conducted without a purpose in mind (although the frustrated teacher may wonder what the purpose was, since "nothing ever changes"), the effectiveness of the treatment would seem to be directly involved in that purpose. In short, the researcher is probably attempting to attribute any difference between the two performance measures to the treatment. The following is a brief explanation of why the researcher probably cannot attribute pretreatment versus posttreatment differences to the treatment.

Suppose, for the moment, that Fig. 7-5 represents a graph of the data obtained in this study. Assuming the difference in means is statistically significant, the researcher then must say something about the performance change. If the

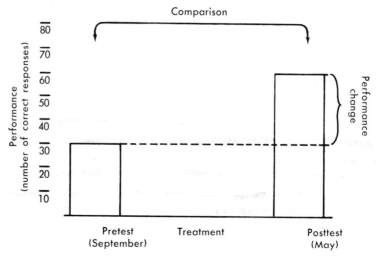

Fig. 7-5. Hypothetical data from a weak program evaluation.

inference is drawn that the performance change is caused by the treatment (experimental program) with no more information than the researcher has, that interpretation may well be in error. How does the researcher know that the performance change was caused by the treatment and not by the subjects' maturation? A full academic year is involved, and it would be expected that as the children grow older, they will probably perform better on most academic tasks as a function of maturation. This would be particularly true with younger children. Thus the performance change *might* be caused by the treatment, or the subjects' maturation, or both.

The question then arises as to how the researcher might avoid or circumvent the maturation factor, which threatens internal validity in the manner suggested. With only one group, this is indeed difficult. To be able to say much about the amount of change that is a function of the program, the researcher needs an estimate of how much change is expected as a result of maturation. If solid evidence exists concerning the amount of change *on the criterion measure* that can be expected if the children do nothing but grow, change in excess of this amount ought to be a result of the treatment. For example, if the children can be expected to improve by twenty correct responses merely as a function of maturation, improvement beyond this amount might be thought to be caused by the treatment. In the example, there was an average of forty more correct responses on the posttest than the pretest. If an average gain of twenty responses is expected as a function of maturation, about a twenty-response improvement may be thought to be a result of the treatment.

In reality, the approach to avoiding a maturation threat mentioned above is

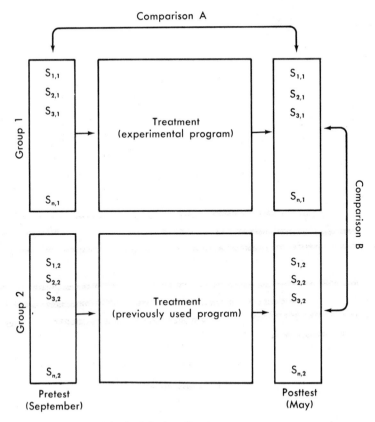

Fig. 7-6. Hypothetical design for 1-year program comparison.

generally not possible. First of all, solid evidence such as would be necessary is seldom if ever available. Even if it is available, what reason is there to think that the subjects in the study are like those from which the evidence was obtained? Basically little strength would be pragmatically available. There are more technically sound approaches to minimizing the maturation threat for this type of study.

In most cases, the nature of the research question suggests using multiple experimental groups. The study just discussed would probably compare the new school program with the program that had been serving the purpose previously. Certainly, the selection of the new program over what was previously used must be justified (just try to get the board of education to hand over the money without justification). Fig. 7-6 provides a visual representation of this design. In this type of design, difference questions are still being asked, but some additional elements have been combined.

The design represented in Fig. 7-6 has changed the question to a degree. It now would appear that the effects of two teaching programs are being compared. As indicated by the double arrows, pretest versus posttest performance differences are still of interest. If subjects are randomly assigned to groups 1 and 2, the two groups should not be different on the pretest. This should be checked just as a precaution after the pretest has been administered but before beginning the treatment. If the groups are different, they should be thrown back into the larger pool and the random assignment repeated. If the groups are not different on the pretest, the researcher is able to say much more about any differences that might exist on the posttest performance.

In a sense, the design portrayed in Fig. 7-6 is still vulnerable to maturation. If there is substantial change between the pretest and posttest scores (comparison A), it is still not known how much of that change was caused by maturation and how much was caused by treatment. There is a more solid basis, however, for saying something about the relative strengths of the programs being studied. Since both groups are involved in the treatment for the same length of time, both groups of children are assumed to have the same opportunity to mature. Therefore, if one group makes greater pre-post gains than the second group, other things being equal, that greater gain might well be attributed to a more effective program. Actually, to effectively assess the maturation question a third comparison group is probably necessary. This third group, as suggested by Fig. 7-7 would also be randomly generated but would not actually receive a treatment per se other than a placebo. *Placebo,* in this context, has the usual meaning, the sugar pill that makes patients think they are being treated when they are not.

The design represented in Fig. 7-7 is an efficient design because it compares the new experimental program with the previously used program and at the same time permits an estimate of how much change is caused by maturation. This is accomplished by using two types of difference comparisons: comparison A looking for pre-post differences within groups and comparison B looking for differences between groups on the posttest. For example, on comparison A for group 1, the differences between pretest and posttest performance may be caused by maturation, treatment, or both. If, however, the comparison A changes for group 1 are viewed in light of comparison A changes for group 3, more meaningful statements can be made. Group 3 receives a placebo as a treatment. The nature of this placebo activity is critical in that it must be *similar but unrelated* to the treatment. It is not desirable for the placebo to instruct in the sense that the programs under study do, since an assessment of maturation is wanted. For the moment, assume that there is an appropriate placebo. Comparison A differences that occur in group 3 can be assumed to be caused by maturation. Any comparison A differences that occur in excess of the group 3 changes might then be attributed to a treatment for either group 1 or group 2. Thus it is possible to begin to say how much change is caused by maturation and

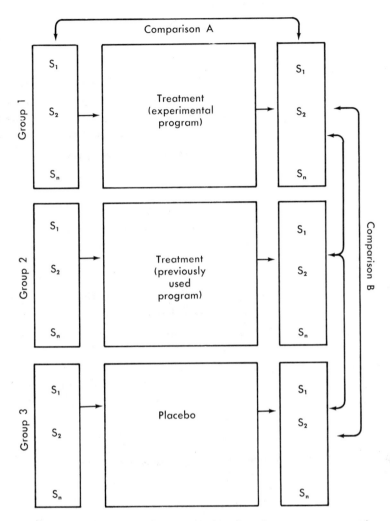

Fig. 7-7. Hypothetical comparison design that also assesses maturation.

how much is caused by the instruction (ignoring test practice for the moment).

The B comparisons then permit attention to another dimension. Comparison B between groups 1 and 2 provides some evidence as to the relative effectiveness of the two instructional programs. B comparisons between either group 1 or 2 and group 3 permit an assessment of how effective the respective instructional program is relative to the situation that would exist if no instruction per se were provided (group 3).

It seems necessary to deal with the pragmatic considerations of conducting such a study in the field. The value of randomly assigning subjects to the groups is obvious in that with this done, the researcher has a powerful technique for equalizing the groups before the experiment begins. In the school setting, this may not be possible. If not, the design is seriously weakened. A second problem might be generated if the three treatment conditions (experimental, previously used, and placebo) have to be implemented by three different teachers. In such a situation, the teacher differences are systematically tested, one in each group, and performance differences between groups might be a result of teacher effectiveness as much as the variables under investigation. (Imagine the difficulty in saying anything about treatment effectiveness if the teacher for group 1 is a star, the teacher for group 2 is average at best, and the one for group 3 is terrible.) It might be more advantageous to have all three groups taught by one person for the portion of each day involving the treatment. Even this approach would necessitate careful training to minimize differences between the person's preference for one treatment over the others. It becomes evident that this type of investigation is vulnerable to design problems on several fronts and requires careful attention and planning.

The study discussed above vividly represents the maturation difficulties encountered in a longitudinal investigation. Pre-post designs that involve even a period as short as a day also are subject to maturation problems such as hunger and fatigue. Their contaminating effects can be viewed from the same perspective used above for maturation in terms of growth. Control or comparison groups, which were suggested to estimate the effects of maturation for the longitudinal study, function in much the same fashion with a study of shorter duration.

Maturation also presents a threat to internal validity in studies in which a pre-post design is not used. In a traditional experimental design with only one test or performance measure, a serious difficulty might be presented in a situation in which two or more groups are being compared on some performance measure. The question being asked concerns "Is there a difference between these groups?" For whatever reason, the experimenter may find it most convenient to test one group of subjects completely and then to move to the next group for testing. By conducting the study in this manner the researcher may be systematically introducing a difference between the groups *in addition* to the experimental treatment. If, for example, group 1 is tested in the morning and group 2 is tested in the afternoon, maturation may be operative as a threat to internal validity. The members of group 2 may be systematically different from group 1 because they may be more subject to fatigue, since the testing is done in the afternoon. Regardless of whether it is fatigue, in the sense of being tired, or different in the sense of anticipating school dismissal, it is not unreasonable to assume that their psychological set may be systematically different from that of group 1. The point to be emphasized in this example is that maturation, with respect to fatigue, hunger, or a number of other variables, may be different between groups in addition to the experimentally imposed differences under study. As such, results from comparisons of the two groups may be interpreted as being caused by an influence (or absence of an influence) of the experimental treatment, when actually results are caused by maturation.

This type of problem would not be limited to experimental research. Clearly a survey might be vulnerable in exactly the same fashion as the example just presented. For example, a researcher wishes to conduct a survey on high school students' views regarding leisure time activities. In this case, sophomores and seniors are being compared. It is most convenient to use a questionnaire that can be distributed personally, completed, and returned immediately (such as in a study hall period). It is also convenient to collect data from the seniors during the Wednesday morning study hall and the sophomores during the Friday afternoon study hall. It is hoped that no one would execute a study in this fashion—the maturation threat to internal validity is so obvious. Differences between the groups could be caused by the intended comparison (seniors versus sophomores), the differences in views of leisure activities between Wednesday morning and Friday afternoon, or both.

Control for maturation threats in this type of study is relatively simple to implement. One probably cannot avoid the fact that subjects will perform differently under the influence of fatigue, hunger, or growth. What is important, however, is the elimination of the *systematic* way in which these variables influence one group differently as compared with another. In many situations, this may be accomplished easily in the field setting (such as a school, institution, or hospital).

To focus on the *systematic* dimension of influence, it is necessary to spread any effect of fatigue or hunger as nearly equally as possible among all groups. To do this, the researcher will want to gather data on about an equal number of subjects from each group in the morning and in the afternoon, or in the previous example, Wednesday morning and Friday afternoon. Thus whatever influence the differing times have is presumably spread evenly between the groups. Procedures for accomplishing this are simple. In the survey study, the researcher would simply have to sacrifice convenience and eliminate the practice of administering the questionnaire systematically to sophomores on Friday afternoon and seniors on Wednesday morning. Elimination of the maturation threat in the experimental example is equally simple. One technique that is both effective and convenient involves premarking all the data record sheets before beginning the experiment. Thus the data record sheet is already labeled as being for group 1 or 2 without the exact subject's name whose performance will be recorded on that sheet. The sheets are then placed side by side and shuffled together *thoroughly*. The order of testing as well as which group Johnny goes in is predetermined by the data sheet that is on the top of the stack. In this fashion it is also possible to go to the teacher and merely ask for any child (rather than specifically for Johnny). The ongoing class activities are thus disrupted much less than if one were to pull a subject, by name, out of reading, math, or some other activity. Since the order of testing subjects (and who will be in group 1 as opposed to group 2) is determined by shuffling, fatigue or hunger should influence both groups about equally. I have used these procedures for many years and have found them to be most satisfactory both in terms of assigning subjects to groups and controlling for maturation.

Studies using time-series designs, such as those often used in operant conditioning research, may also be subject to maturation as an internal validity threat. As was discussed under history, such investigations are generally asking a difference question such as, "Is there a difference between baseline and postintervention performance?" or "Does the intervening reinforcement contingency make a difference?" Maturation in a physiological growth sense may threaten the design if the duration of the experiment is sufficient that such growth might be expected. This is not often the case in operant research. When it is the case, however, maturation threatens in much the same fashion as has been previously discussed. If the duration of the experiment is sufficient to permit physiological growth (which may result in behavioral change), the researcher may incorrectly interpret this change as being a result of the intervention.

Many time-series studies are of sufficiently short duration that physiological maturation is not a problem. These studies are, however, subject to threats from maturation in the form of fatigue or hunger. If, for example, the experiment has a duration of a day with baseline being established in the first part of the morning, intervention and continued measurement might proceed throughout the remainder of the day but without sufficient time for contingency reversal. Fatigue, hunger, or some other influence, occurring merely as a function of time passing, may well affect performance *in addition* to the treatment. Thus an observed decrease in behavior might represent either fatigue or the intervening change in reinforcement conditions, and interpretation becomes difficult. Some strength would be added by reversing the treatment to baseline conditions. The reader will recall from Chapter 5 that this change is aimed at showing that the intervention was the influence that generated performance change. If the reversal is timed such that fatigue may be occurring in the subject, performance drop may be caused by fatigue as well as removal of the treatment. This type of situation highlights the necessity of performance stabilization before reversal. Even with stable data, however, maturation may threaten reversal designs.

The strongest safeguard against maturation difficulties in the experiment just mentioned would be replication. Additionally, replications should vary the time frame such that it would not be expected that the same maturation influences (probably unknown) would be operative. The data would thus be interpreted after a series of experiments in which maturation effects, if operative, would exert their influence at a different point during the experiment, providing a clearer picture of the actual effects of the treatment.

The sophistication of most time-series researchers is such that experiments are usually not designed in a fashion permitting the degree of vulnerability just exemplified. However, they too must be aware of maturation in designing investigations. The beginning student who is working without a vast experimental background must consciously plan a study to minimize maturation influences.

Testing or test practice

Testing or test practice also represents a threat to the internal validity of an investigation. Campbell and Stanley (1963) refer to this threat as "the effects of taking a test upon the scores of a second testing [p. 175]." From the nature of this statement, testing is obviously a threat in pre-post designs. Other types of designs, however, are equally vulnerable to testing weaknesses.

As noted, the threat of test practice is most obvious in investigations in which the researcher administers a pretest, a treatment, and then a posttest on the same subjects (or interviews, questionnaires, and the like). Presumably the researcher is assessing the difference between pretest and posttest performance with the intent of interpreting differences as being caused by the treatment. However, a portion of the change from pretest to posttest performance levels may be caused by test practice. This may be particularly true if the measurement represents a new and unique experience for the subjects so that they may have a great deal to learn just about how to perform. For example, if the subjects (e.g., rural children from Appalachia) have never encountered an achievement test before, their pretreatment performance might reflect to a great degree their lack of experience at taking such tests (as well as some reflection of their knowledge of content). Just taking the pretest may teach them a great deal, which would be reflected on their posttreatment scores. It is easy to see how this influence would serve to separate their pretest and posttest scores (generate greater differences) more than might be the case if only the treatment were operative. If the researcher viewing these results interprets these differences to be caused by the treatment alone, a serious interpretation error may have been committed. The differences may be a function of testing, treatment, or both.

Although the example above involves experimental research, the basic problem of "test practice" may very well threaten internal validity in nonexperimental research. Restating again, the threat of test practice is simply the effect of the first measure *on* the second. An interview (or questionnaire) may easily create the same type of situation. To the degree that respondents are sensitized, gain knowledge, or are changed in some other fashion by the first interview, data from a second interview may be altered.

To circumvent a test practice threat, the researcher generally may take one of two approaches. If the subjects clearly have a background including experience on the measurement instrument, the researcher might assume that test practice will generate less performance change and therefore be less of a threat. Another alternative for the researcher would be to induce experience with a pretest warm-up. Using this approach, the researcher provides practice on the task before the first measure, which serves to provide at least some pretest-posttest similarity in terms of the subjects' experience. Such procedures are still somewhat weak because they do not control or assess the amount of improvement caused by additional test practice. Although subjects have experience, they still may improve with more practice. A sounder procedure would involve a comparison group that does not receive the test practice, only the treatment.

To implement such a multigroup study, the researcher would initially draw a sample of subjects at random. If the plan involved having twenty subjects in each group, the sample would include forty subjects who would then be randomly assigned to the two groups (twenty to group 1 and twenty to group 2). Group 1 would then receive the pretest, but group 2 would not. Since group 2 subjects were randomly assigned from the same sample as group 1, there is little reason to believe that they are different (Fig. 7-8). Presumably the scores that group 2 would have obtained on the pretest, if one had been administered, would not differ from those obtained by group 1. From that point on both groups receive the same treatment and posttest. Any differences between the groups on the posttest should be a result of test practice, since the opportunity to learn from the pretest is the only difference between the two groups. Reference to Fig. 7-8 suggests that two questions may be addressed. Comparison A indicates performance change from the pretest to the posttest, whereas comparison B estimates the amount of test practice operative. The difference between the pre-post mean scores for group 1, minus the difference between groups 1

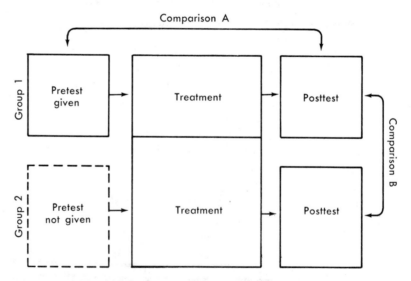

Fig. 7-8. Pre-post design controlling for testing.

and 2 on the posttest, presumably provides an estimate of the effect caused by treatment.

Testing is also a threat to repeated-measures research, which is not strictly defined as a pre-post design. Repeated-measures research includes studies in which three, four, or more test sessions are conducted with the same subjects. An example of such a situation might involve an investigation in which a pretest, two midtreatment tests, and a posttest are administered. There is considerable possibility for the subjects to learn from the test sessions themselves and thereby improve scores as a result of test practice rather than the treatment alone.

Classic examples of this type of threat have long plagued researchers who are studying memory or, more specifically, forgetting (Deese and Hulse, 1967; Belmont, 1966). Occasionally, in such studies the researcher may be interested in determining the amount of material that is forgotten over a period subsequent to the learning of the task. Often the passage of time is the variable of interest such that the researcher may want to determine how much material is remembered, say, immediately, 24 hours, and 7 days after the termination of learning. If subjects are tested for immediate recall and then after 24 hours and 7 days, the researcher may encounter difficulty assessing the amount of material forgotten. The problem arises because 24-hour performance does indeed represent the influence of the time passage since learning was terminated. However, it also includes the testing for immediate memory performance. The testing process per se may well have provided subjects with additional opportunity to learn. Similarly, 7-day performance (if repeated measures are obtained on the same subjects) represents time passage (presumably promoting forgetting), but it includes two additional opportunities for learning from the testing for immediate and 24-hour memory.

To circumvent the difficulty just described, the simplest procedure is to use multiple groups in a fashion not unlike that suggested for the pre-post design in Fig. 7-8. In one example, a sample of sixty subjects may proceed through the learning task, whereupon they would be randomly divided into three groups for testing memory. There is little reason to expect that the three groups are different, since they have been randomly assigned from the larger subject pool who experienced the same learning task. Group 1 might then receive an immediate memory test, whereas groups 2 and 3 would not. Group 2 would then receive a 24-hour test that group 3 would not and, finally, group 3 would receive the 7-day test. It can be assumed that the immediate memory performance for groups 2 and 3 (not tested) would be like that of group 1, and so on. Other things being equal, the 7-day performance of group 3 has only the passage of time, since additional opportunity to learn from immediate and 24-hour testing has been eliminated. By using staggered group measurement in this fashion, the researcher may attribute 24-hour and 7-day performance levels to forgetting rather than forgetting plus the possibility of additional learning.

Instrumentation

Instrumentation has also plagued researchers as a threat to internal validity. In this context, "instrumentation" is defined as "changes in the calibration of a measuring instrument or changes in the observers" that may influence the scores or measures obtained (Campbell and Stanley, 1963, p. 175). From the definition of the term "calibration," one of the first examples that comes to mind is the use of mechanical contrivances for data collection. For example, suppose that the researcher was using an audiometer to gather data. If something occurred midway through the experiment that changed the calibration of the instrument (such as adjustment by a well-meaning service representative), all the data collected from that point on would be systematically different than those data gathered before the change.

As noted in the definition, however, instrumentation problems are not confined to mechanical contrivances. In behavioral science as well as other arenas, much of the data are collected with human instrumentation such as observers and scorers. The same basic problem that was discussed with the audiometer example is present with human instrumentation. If something occurs during the study that alters the way responses are scored or recorded, data obtained subsequent to that point are systematically different (for reasons other than the variable under study). Factors that can alter human instrumentation were discussed earlier in Chapter 3 and have been given considerable attention by Rosenthal (1966) for the student interested in pursuing this topic in depth. From a generic standpoint, the earlier discussions of history, maturation, and testing become relevant if they are viewed as applicable to the observer rather than the subject. History, the specific event (somewhat like an audiometer adjustment), might occur at a given point and systematically alter the way in which the observer records data. Maturation and factors such as experimenter fatigue and hunger exert influence more slowly but may be equally systematic in the manner in which observations are changed by the human instrument. Testing, in the sense that the researcher becomes more adept at (or bored with) testing as the investigation proceeds, may also change the human instrumentation. These are merely examples of how the influence of instrumentation changes might occur. The way in which they serve to threaten internal validity depends entirely on the design being used in a given study. A variety of designs are vulnerable, including group comparisons, repeated measures on the same subjects, time-series experiments, and field studies using participant observation.

Time-series experiments have been discussed to a degree in the earlier portions of this text. Instrumentation as a threat to internal validity can be explored by again viewing the experiment using an A-B design in which baseline data are gathered for a period followed by an intervention and subsequent recording of observation data. The comparison of interest is, again, the difference in behavior frequency between baseline and the period after the intervention was introduced. It is desirable to be able to attribute any changes in behavior frequency to the intervention per se. If the researcher is inhibited in such inferences by systematic differences that occur *in addition* to the intervention, little can be said about the experimental variable.

The most serious problem is presented if the change *in addition* to the intervention occurs nearly simultaneously with the timing of the instrumentation change. Under these conditions the influence of the contaminating factor may appear to be a part of the experimental effect. In terms of instrumentation problems, the most obvious difficulty is presented by changes in the observer who is recording behavioral data. For example, perhaps the experimenter, either knowingly or unknowingly, alters his or her set for data recording because change is expected as a function of the intervention. As noted before, Rosenthal (1966) has explored this type of problem at great length. What occurs on the data sheet, then, is some change in behavior frequency as a result of the intervention per se, some change as a result of the observer's altered manner of recording data, and perhaps some change as a result of an interaction of the two. Since all that has been recorded is the behavioral frequency, no one knows how much of the difference may be attributed to the intervention, how much to the instrumentation changes in the observer, or how much to the combined influence of both.

Several approaches may be used to circumvent the potential problem noted above. Replication of experiments may help, although if the same observer is used, there is little reason to expect much assurance of control from this approach. Additionally, if other observers are used, they may also be subject to bias similar to that influencing the first observer. One approach, which may be more cumbersome but which may well provide more assurance of stable instrumentation, is a technique that can be borrowed in modified form from medical research. This approach (somewhat like the double-blind design) would involve a procedure whereby the person recording the data would not be aware of the time the intervention was introduced. Thus the contingency manipulation is performed by a person other than the observer. This would mean that the observer would not know precisely when intervention occurred except through actual changes in behavioral frequency. A difficulty with this procedure is, of course, that a research team is necessary instead of one person. Also, there may be situations presented in which it is not possible to double-blind the observer. Reversal and multiple-baseline designs provide some strength over the A-B arrangement. It is doubtful that specific or history-type observer changes will occur systematically at the same time as the various phase-changes. Instrumentation changes caused by conscious or unconscious bias, however, may still be operative in these designs. Observer training, multiple observer reliability checks, and the double-blind approach probably offer the most confidence concerning the avoidance of instrumentation threats to time-series designs.

Experiments in which groups are being compared may also be vulnerable to instrumentation threats. Actually the difficulty in this type of experiment is primarily a logistics consideration (that is, the manner in which the experiment is run) rather than an integral part of the study design. Since the objective is to compare group 1 with group 2, and so on, the concern must focus on minimizing systematic differences between the groups that are *in addition* to the experimental variable under study. Instrumentation presents the greatest potential threat of generating such differences when all the subjects in one group are tested and the experimenter then moves to the next group. Because of a variety of possible influences on the experimenter (e.g., fatigue, practice, or unconscious set), one group may be systematically treated differently than another. Thus the calibration of the instrument (the experimenter or observer) may change and cause systematic differences between groups in addition to the variable under study.

To control for this type of problem, the experimenter must focus on making such influences spread as evenly as possible among groups and thus remove the *systematic* dimension that may make groups different. Since there is little doubt that the experimenter will experience some fatigue or boredom regardless of what is done, a priori precautions must be taken to distribute such influence throughout the groups evenly. This may be done by randomly testing subjects from all groups such that the subjects in different groups alternate or counterbalance the order of testing. The result will be that about the same number of subjects from each group will be tested under all conditions of instrument calibration. The fashion in which this may be accomplished in the field is logistically simple and can involve shuffling premarked data sheets as was described earlier.

Instrumentation also serves to threaten the internal validity of pre-post and other repeated-measures designs. Changes in the calibration of either human or mechanical instrumentation that occur between measures generate differences between the data points being compared. Since this source of difference is in addition to the variable under study, interpretation may be clouded.

The researcher is not faced with a serious instrumentation difficulty if the data collection procedure entails techniques that involve little likelihood of calibration changes. This might be the case with a printed paper-and-pencil instrument (e.g., tests and questionnaires) used in pre-post or other repeated-measures studies. However, when human observers are used in data recording, much less assurance is possible that instrumentation is stable. One procedure that might be used (which exemplifies the difficulty in controlling this type of situation) concerns mechanical behavioral observation such as photography or videotaping. If the study involved a treatment, the pretreatment and posttreatment records could then be randomized with respect to order and rated by a panel of judges. In this fashion the data records obtained from taped behavioral observations are not identified as pretreatment or posttreatment measures. Since they need not be in order, they are less vulnerable to systematic calibration influences on the observer-raters.

Often such elaborate controls as in the example just given are not feasible. When they are not, researchers may have to be satisfied with careful scrutiny of the process so that they may be aware if instrumentation problems seem operative. This would represent a situation when the best the researcher can do is account for internal validity threats in the written report rather than actually control them.

Statistical regression

Statistical regression represents another threat to internal validity. Statistical regression, as an internal validity threat, is operative if subjects have been assigned to a particular group on the basis of atypical scores. Under such circumstances a subject's placement in, say, group 1 may be in error, since the score is atypical and that individual's more normal performance may be like that of the subjects in group 2. If the misclassified subjects then regress toward their average performance during the experiment, internal validity may be threatened seriously (groups thought to be equivalent turn out not to be; groups thought to represent certain differences actually do not).

From the nature of the above discussion, it can be seen that statistical regression may create a problem when group comparisons are being made. This should not be taken to suggest that all group comparisons are equally vulnerable. If the researcher forms two groups on the basis of random assignment, for example, to compare the effects of two treatment conditions, little threat is presented by statistical regression. Because subjects are randomly assigned to groups, there is little reason to expect more atypical scores in one group than the other. If, on the other hand, groups are being formed that represent preexisting subject classifications, statistical regression may well present a serious problem. For example, if the researcher wishes to compare performance on a given task by subjects representing two levels of intelligence, a regression problem may be encountered. For reasons unknown, there may be a portion of one group whose IQ scores are atypical. Results of the comparison, thought to be attributable to level of intelligence, may in fact be a function of some other factor. The researcher thinks two specified levels of intelligence are operating. In fact, because the scores on which the groups were formed are partially atypical for one group, the investigator may not actually have the types of groups expected. Consequently the performance or scores may appear more like that of the actual intellectual level at which the subjects usually operate rather than the atypical score. In this sense the performance may "regress" toward the average level of functioning.

Control for such a problem as the situation just described is difficult, particularly in the case of comparisons that may be made between preexisting subject classifications (for example, comparing levels of intelligence or emotionally disturbed compared with nondisturbed). (You will recall that these types of comparisons are what have been called "quasi-experiments.") Logistically, it is always somewhat unsafe to form such groups with only a single score or measure as a guide. It is helpful if the subject has several scores to give at least some general credibility to the most recent one, which is often used for group assignment.

The notion of statistical regression from an atypical score is also relevant as a threat to time-series research designs. A fairly common procedure called a probe is often used to establish the level of baseline skill or entry behaviors. This technique is usually characterized by presenting the subject with the task to be performed (or a part of the task) and assessing the ability to perform it. Based on the results of such a probe, the modification of behavior is planned and implemented. Essentially, the probe may be viewed in a fashion similar to the earlier discussed test scores used for group assignment. If, for some reason, a subject's response to a given probe is atypical (in terms of a usual or normal response), then the statistical regression problem presents itself. In somewhat the same fashion as the group design, a series of probes will provide some insurance against the atypical response being viewed as average. Time-series experiments are generally less vulnerable because of the greater number of data points usually recorded before an intervention or other phase change.

Statistical regression has primarily been discussed as a threat to internal validity in experimental investigations. For the most part, it has been most obviously a problem with this type of research. However, nonexperimental studies are by no means completely free of such difficulties. Certainly statistical regression could occur if one were conducting a survey in which groups were studied based on particular identifying data (and the data were incorrect or atypical).

Hawthorne effect

One threat to internal validity that has been widely discussed is the Hawthorne effect. In an abstract sense, the Hawthorne effect refers to the change in sensitivity, performance, or both by the subjects that may occur merely as a function of being in an investigation. This type of problem was discussed briefly in Chapter 2, particularly in terms of experimental research. Because of the experimental surroundings (e.g., laboratory), the change in routine wrought by the study, or any of a myriad of other fashions by which subjects are made to feel special, their performance may be different than it would if they were not subjects. Such an influence becomes a threat to internal validity with group comparisons, for example, when it is operative on one group and not the other. Under such circumstances, the members of group 1 might perform better because they feel "special," whereas the members of group 2 might not have the "special" feeling and might not perform as well because of this. This places a systematic difference between the groups *in addition* to the experimental variables. This is a big problem, since the researcher wishes to attribute differences between the groups to the treatment.

For the student beginning in research, the Hawthorne effect may become a problem because of a misconception concerning the idea of experimental and control groups. Perhaps by connotation derived from the terms "experimental" and "control" or perhaps because of a superficial understanding of these as functional concepts, the uninitiated may be led to the conclusion that an experimental group receives a treatment, whereas the control group receives nothing. If this approach is followed during the design of a study, the Hawthorne effect is likely to threaten internal validity. Assuming that the treatment somehow alters the subject's routine (besides the process under investigation), such alteration may increase, decrease, or in some other fashion modify the subject's sensitivity to the experimental task. If "nothing" is done to the control group, differences in performance between the groups might be attributed to the factor being studied, or to the fact that one group felt special but the other did not, or to a combination. At any rate, the researcher is in a difficult position to say much about why differences did or did not occur, since the Hawthorne effect may be operative in addition to the variable being studied.

As before, to control for the Hawthorne effect essentially means that the systematic *difference* between the groups (in addition to what is being studied) needs to be removed or minimized. It is difficult to imagine an experimental treatment that is not known in some way to the subject or that does not alter sensitivity in some fashion. Many years of studying the methods involved in research design have led most researchers to agree that it is difficult, if not impossible, to control the Hawthorne effect by removing it from the experimental group. Since the essence of the concept of control is to remove systematic differences (except the one under investigation) by making the groups as equal as possible, another approach to the Hawthorne effect is necessary. If the Hawthorne effect cannot reliably be removed from the experimental group, the most effective control method would seem to be to "Hawthorne" both groups equally. This might be distilled to mean that the members of the control group are treated in a fashion that should make them feel equally special, but they are not actually given the experimental treatment per se. Since the question focuses on the effects of the treatment, or differences between a group that receives the treatment and one that does not, Hawthorning both groups does not deter from this comparison. Thus the absolute level of performance by groups is not as important as the relative performance compared between groups. This type of control for the Hawthorne effect has perhaps contributed to an apparent decline in the use of terms such as "experimental groups" and "control groups." Many researchers have come to prefer the generic term "comparison groups" to avoid the misconceptions concerning what a control group adds to an experiment and how it ought to be treated.

As evidenced by the preceding discussion, the Hawthorne effect definitely is a concern when conducting an experimental study in which groups are compared. However, other types of research designs are also vulnerable to the influ-

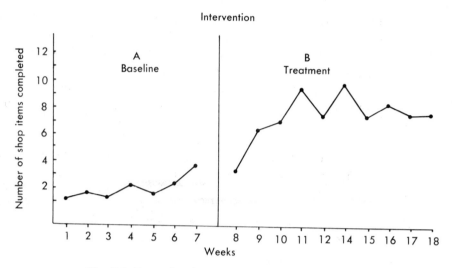

Fig. 7-9. Example of an A-B time series data display.

ences of the Hawthorne effect. A prime example is the continuous measurement or time-series experiment. For illustration, refer to the simple A-B pardigm exemplified by Fig. 7-9. As the intervention occurs, it is almost certain that the subject becomes aware that routine has changed. An observed change in postintervention performance may, therefore, be a result of the altered contingencies that are under investigation (e.g., reinforcement schedule); or the subject may have changed performance level because of the change in routine (Hawthorne); or, most probable of deductions, the performance change may be a result of a combination of the changed contingencies *and* the Hawthorne effect.

The question to be addressed, then, is how does one circumvent the possible influence of the Hawthorne effect in the type of investigation portrayed in Fig. 7-9? Some single-subject researcher may respond by saying, "Why bother?" This type of research has been characterized by a pragmatic immediacy philosophy. From that standpoint, one might simply contend that it is of no consequence whether the Hawthorne effect was operative in addition to the intervention. If the behavior can be modified, from an instructional point of view, that is important, and that should be the primary focus.

Many researchers from a single-subject background as well as from more traditional experimental design backgrounds would take a somewhat different stance on this issue. They would wish a more analytical approach that at least attempts to separate the influences of the Hawthorne effect from those of the intervention. Although it is difficult to be precise, a number of operations may be helpful.

One difficulty that is presented involves the collection of baseline data. As was noted previously, the question being addressed is essentially a difference question with the reference points being baseline performance compared with postintervention performance. If baseline data are gathered in a setting that primarily represents routine for the subjects (e.g., the classroom) and the intervention involves a nonroutine setting (e.g., another classroom or individualized instruction), the potential influence of the Hawthorne effect is immediately evident. The problem, of course, is focused on the difference created because baseline data are collected in a different setting than the intervention data. In some cases, the nature of the intervention necessitates a nonroutine environment (such as a small room with reduced stimuli). When this is the case, it is wise to also gather baseline data in the intervention environment. Additionally, since such a procedure would then influence the baseline performance, the baseline data collection should have sufficient duration to permit the subject to become acclimated to the changed environment. Most researchers require a stable behavior rate over a period before they will assume subject acclimation.

The Hawthorne effect still has a good probability of being operative when the intervention is implemented even if baseline and experimental settings are the same. There is little that can be done to eliminate the Hawthorne influence under these conditions, primiarily because the same subject is experiencing both the preintervention and postintervention conditions (e.g., change in reinforcement contingencies). Most researchers will, however, not assess the influence of their intervention until the behavior rate has stabilized. Reference to Fig. 7-9 reveals that the performance is much more erratic immediately after intervention than it is later. The Hawthorne effect is likely to be operative in its most potent form immediately after routine is disturbed. As suggested by the earlier discussion, the influence of the Hawthorne effect may be expected to decline as the subject becomes acclimated (i.e., as a new environment becomes routine). Thus the stable rate of performance is assumed to be reflective of the intervention at least to a greater degree than rates observed immediately subsequent to intervention. However, Fig. 7-9 indicates that even in the latter portions of postintervention data there are slight variations. The question that may then be raised relates to how one determines when the behavior is "stable." The generic approach to this problem is to avoid judging behavior as stable when the rate is either accelerating or decelerating. Different researchers are not in agreement on how close to horizontal the trend should be, however, and will put the general approach into operation in somewhat different specific fashions.

Turn to p. 178 and complete Simulation 7-1.

Most of this discussion has been couched in terms of experimental research. Clearly the Hawthorne effect could also seriously threaten the internal validity of nonexperimental investigations. The survey researcher and the field observer must remain just as aware of the potential problems of a Hawthorne effect as the experimenter.

Bias in group composition

Bias in group composition or in mode of subject assignment to groups is a threat to internal validity that reflects the core concept of internal validity. The use of the term "bias" in relation to groups connotes systematic differences between comparison groups *in addition* to the factor or treatment under study.

Use of the broader term "composition" is necessary because this threat is relevant to *quasi-experimental* designs as well as *true experimental* designs. You will recall that a true experimental design is generally considered to be one in which, initially, a single subject population is identified and sampled. Groups are then formed in some specified fashion (e.g., random assignment) that ostensibly ensures group equality before the initiation of treatment. Thus in an experimental design, the groups do not become different until treatment begins. The quasi-experimental design differs in the respect that the groups are not necessarily formed from the same single subject pool. In fact, the group composition, which is reflective of the research question, may be based on a preexisting condition such as levels of intelligence. Such an investigation might be portrayed by the diagram shown in Fig. 7-10. Quasi-experimental designs are particularly vulnerable to internal validity threats from bias in group composition, therefore, the example in Fig. 7-10 will be used to examine this problem. It should be noted from the outset, however, that quasi-experimental designs have been used and continue to be used in certain areas of behavioral science. They have considerable value, providing essential information to areas such as comparative and abnormal psychology and special education. In considering certain questions, a quasi-experimental design is the most obvious option, but the researcher must be aware of its relative strengths and weaknesses.

The basic problem involved in quasi-experimental designs centers around controlling systematic differences between groups *with the exception of the one under study*. In Fig. 7-10 the independent variable is intelligence, and to maximize internal validity it would be desirable to eliminate other systematic differences between the groups or at least to hold them to a minimum. Since this experiment is working with a preexisting phenomenon, it is necessary to be extremely cautious to avoid other differences that may be concomitant with the different levels of measured intelligence. For example, because of the nature of intelligence tests, there is substantial probability that the lower intelligence group (A) may have more minority children than the higher intelligence group (B). IQ tests are primarily verbal and are designed from the vantage point of white middle-class

Fig. 7-10. Example of a quasi-experimental design.

America. This would handicap other children with different verbal patterns to a greater degree than Caucasian children whose total language experience has been in the same framework as the test. If, because of this test bias, group A has more minority or linguistically different children than group B, performance on the experimental task may be more reflective of this difference than levels of intelligence. Similarly, subjects from lower socioeconomic levels may appear in greater numbers in group A than in group B. This may occur because of test bias or because of experiential background. Regardless of the reason, differences may reflect these other factors as well as intelligence. The researcher, to be precise in conducting the investigation, must decide if intelligence is the focus of the study, or racial differences, or socioeconomic status, or all of these in combination. To study all in combination would be a poor option if the researcher desires to do much specific interpretation of results.

The quasi-experimental design itself raises a red flag of caution because differences other than the one under study have a much greater probability of being built in. The presence of possible bias in group composition seriously deters the researcher from meaningful interpretation of results. There are certain precautions that may be taken, however, to minimize the probability of group composition bias in quasi-experimental designs. Initially the research question must be clearly and specifically articulated. If the independent variable is intelligence, then, by exclusion, factors such as socioeconomic status, race, sex, or age must be controlled or held constant between groups. If the question compares mentally retarded and nonretarded subjects on some learning task, the basis for such a classification must be specified. It may be retarded and nonretarded groups based on measured intelligence, which again activates the exclusion process of factors such as those noted above.

Working with the quasi-experimental design presents considerable challenge regarding controlling potential bias between groups. Since the researcher cannot make use of the power of chance in the form of random assignment, other alternatives must be used. In the absence of the power of random assignment, the researcher is faced with the unenviable task of determining which factors are important to control. This task is unenviable because of the error probability involved. Not only might the researcher inadvertently omit control for some factor that is known to be influential, vulnerability also exists from the multitude of variables that have not yet been identified as important to control. Thus, at the outset, the challenge presented in controlling potentially contaminating variables requires considerable experience of both a research and clinical nature. A checklist of what the researcher always wanted to avoid is usually not available.

The obvious question that may now be raised by the beginning researcher is, "How does one decide which factors need to be controlled?" These decisions are generally made based on both previous research and logic. In the case of previous research, one would probably choose to control any given variable that had been shown to influence performance on the task to be used. For example, if the task involved had been previously used, and if results had indicated that performance was substantially influenced by different stages of child development, the investigator would be remiss if chronological age were not held constant between groups. Similarly, if sex, socioeconomic status, or other factors had been previously shown to be influential in task performance, they certainly ought to be considered for control. For example, in the study portrayed in Fig. 7-10, intelligence was the variable under investigation. If the variables mentioned had been shown to influence performance on whatever task was being used, groups A and B should not be different in mean chronological age or socioeconomic status and should have about equal numbers of both sexes or only one sex in the total study.

It was also noted that a judicious use of logic and reason was helpful in determining what potentially contaminating variables ought to be controlled. Often previous research will not provide information directly related to the investigation being planned. In such cases the researcher must make control decisions based on information that is only tangentially relevant, laced together with logic and reason. In many instances, the researcher should just ask, "What is it that might influence performance on my task besides my independent variable?" In this type of situation, the investigator might decide that reading ability ought to be controlled and also that, since the hypothetical task requires visual input, visual impairment should be controlled. At this point there are two general approaches to control. With the objective of making both groups equal, a given variable might be removed from the total subject pool, or it might somehow be made equal between groups but left in the subject population. In the example noted above, it would probably be wise to define the subject population at the outset as having no identifiable visual impairments and to delete children with such conditions from consideration as subjects. Similarly with regard to reading level, all children who deviated, for example, more than a year from their age-appropriate reading level might be deleted from the potential subject pool. Even with this precaution the groups would have to be scrutinized before initiation of the experiment to ensure that they were not different in average reading level.

Operationalizing control in a quasi-experimental design has already been mentioned as being challenging. To facilitate this process, it is often useful to turn to the sampling procedure, since assignment is already somewhat predefined. Recalling the example in Fig. 7-10, the research question involved comparing the performance of two groups who had different levels of intelligence. Suppose for the moment that it has been determined that chronological age and socioeconomic status, as well as visual, central nervous system, and health impairments have been identified as being important for control. The question then becomes one of how to best accomplish such control.

With the quasi-experimental design, the researcher is essentially working with two subject populations distinguishable on the basis of the independent variable. In this example there will be one subject population defined by an intelligence range of 75 to 90 and a second population defined by an intelligence range of 100 to 115. One effective method of controlling the other identified factors is to define both populations as having the same characteristics on those given factors. Thus, although the subject population for group A is defined in different IQ ranges than group B, groups A and B should have a common age range and socioeconomic status. Additionally, both subject populations would not include any children with identifiable visual, central nervous system, or health impairments. Given these defined characteristics, the researcher can then randomly sample group A from subject pool A and group B from subject pool B. This is essentially the process known as stratified random sampling, so-called because the experimenter is randomly sampling from different strata or defined populations (see Chapter 8). Experience has shown that such procedures generally result in groups that are not different on the control characteristics that are defined in common terms between subject populations. Precautions should be taken, however, by comparing group means or in some other fashion assessing the group composition on these dimensions before initiating the experiment. If they are not equal, the groups should be resampled (recomposed) until pretreatment groups are not different on the variables being controlled.

As previously noted, the true experimental design involves a single subject pool from which groups are formed, ostensibly with no differences before the initiation of treatment. Bias in group composition does not present such a potential threat as in the quasi-experimental design because of the single subject pool and thus absence of preexisting systematic differences. Some of the initial considerations mentioned previously are also relevant for a true experimental design. As a precautionary measure during sampling, it is often wise to eliminate potential subjects who may encounter difficulties in performing the task (assuming such difficulty is not part of the normal deviation in performance). Of primary concern are substantial handicaps that are unrelated to the research question such as visual or central nervous system impairments. (Of course, if the researcher is investigating visual or central nervous system impairment, these conditions become a part of the study and are not eliminated.)

With the advantages offered by a single subject pool, group composition becomes predominantly a logistic consideration. The primary concern is to form groups that are essentially equal on a pretreatment basis. One of the most powerful procedures (also easily performed) involves randomly assigning subjects to experimental conditions or groups. Earlier methodological approaches often emphasized experimental matching as a means of equating groups. In addition to the many problems inherent in experimental matching (Stanley and Beeman, 1958; Prehm, 1966; Drew, 1969), the procedure does not take advantage of the fact that, with group comparisons, group performances such as means are compared rather than individual scores. Utilizing random assignment does acknowledge the fact that group performance is the focus and aims at making pretreatment *groups* equal rather than individual subject *pairs*. Using chance in this manner results in subjects varying at random on any antecedent factor (e.g., age or mental ability), theoretically resulting in random differences between groups that will approximate zero. Experience has substantiated the faith and theoretical base for random assignment equalizing groups. Often there is actually zero or nearly zero difference between groups on antecedent factors. Such faith should not, however, go unchecked in any given study. Groups should be compared on antecedent factors before initiating treatment merely to check the researcher's assumption of equality. Chance variation will, in a certain number of instances, result in significantly unequal groups before treatment. When this occurs, the groups should be placed back in the subject pool and reconstituted.

Turn to p. 179 and complete Simulations 7-2 and 7-3.

Experimental mortality

Experimental mortality is a threat to internal validity that has particular relevance to nonexperimental research despite the term "experimental" in its label. Experimental mortality becomes a threat to internal validity when there is a differential loss of subjects between comparison groups. It is not uncommon for a researcher to lose a certain number of subjects for a variety of reasons. Perhaps the subjects are absent from school on the test day, and timing is important, so they cannot be tested at a later time. On other occasions an error in research procedures might invalidate the data from a given subject, which necessitates deletion from the study. In general such experimental mortality presents no serious difficulty regarding internal validity as long as the loss is approximately equal between groups. The usual procedure that is used (as long as the group loss is approximately equal) involves randomly selecting replacement subjects from the same subject pool that was initially used to compose the groups. Experienced researchers will usually form their original subject pool so that a certain number of potential subjects remain as a replacement pool after groups are formed. In this fashion the composition of the replacement pool is presumed to not be different from that of the groups, thereby permitting replacement of lost or deleted subjects.

The threat to internal validity becomes a reality when groups lose subjects in different proportions. The researcher is often unaware of the exact characteristics of the subjects who are lost, in particular those characteristics that either related to or precipitated the loss. Consequently, whatever those characteristics are, they have been lost to a greater degree from some groups than others. If replacement is then initiated by randomly selecting from the replacement pool, the researcher may be building in systematic differences between the reconstituted groups. To elaborate further, an example may be useful.

Using a hypothetical situation from the psychology learning laboratory, suppose that the experiment involves white rats as subjects. Because of qualities in the subjects (unknown to the researcher), a substantially greater proportion of one group dies than in a second group. Although the exact reasons for death may be unknown, one reasonable possibility is that the subjects who were physiologically weak were more vulnerable to death. If replacement is accomplished by randomly selecting from the replacement pool, chances are that about as many strong rats will be chosen for replacements as weak rats. Thus the replacement subjects may include more strong rats than were in the group for which they are substituting. Since differential group loss would necessitate more replacements in one group than the other, the addition of more potentially strong rats to that group might well result in built-in differences between the groups. In such a situation, the researcher faces a serious problem. Excellent procedures for equalizing groups may have been implemented initially, but the mortality threat presents itself after the experiment is underway.

Circumventing experimental mortality as a threat to internal validity is extremely difficult. Depending on certain decisions of the researcher, several pragmatic questions and issues may be considered. First of all, the question arises as to just how different do the mortality rates have to be before the researcher ought to be concerned. This certainly varies from one type of research to another, and decisions are usually based on the experience and clinical judgment of the researcher. This is the type of decision that is best made before beginning the experiment. For example, based on what has been written in earlier research, an investigator may choose to say that any differential of 10% or more is going to be the point at which mortality is considered a threat to internal validity. Thus if group A lost 10% of the initial subjects, whereas group B lost 20% or 25%, the researcher would have the a priori caution point exceeded (that is, the differential would be 10% to 15%). The question then becomes one of what can be done about the threat. This may be one situation in which, after carefully examining the information available, the researcher may decide to proceed but to mention the loss as a potential weakness in the findings. The researcher may account for the potential threat by indicating that it existed, what effect it is believed to have had, but that, for whatever the reason, it is thought that no substantial influence on the interpretations possible was generated. If this choice is selected, the rationale sustaining the researcher's interpretations must have considerable strength.

A second decision might be in order if the differential mortality reaches or exceeds the a priori caution point. The researcher may decide that the internal validity threat is so imminent and potentially devastating to interpretation that the study should be discontinued with this sample of subjects. The researcher may choose to begin anew with a totally new sample of subjects.

Neither of the options just given is satisfactory. The first leaves the outcome in some question even with the most experienced researchers. The second is discouraging and expensive. The fact remains, however, that even if certain packaged approaches do not seem apparent to circumvent experimental mortality, the researcher must monitor each experiment to guard against it as a threat. The rigor of results is too valuable to sacrifice regardless of cost in dollars or frustration.

Experimental mortality presents difficulties in designs other than group comparisons. A design that is also vulnerable involves the investigation in which repeated measures are taken on the same group of subjects over a period. This, of course, speaks to the design that is often designated as the pre-post design. The pre-post design is more vulnerable under some conditions than others. Experimental mortality is not extremely problematic in situations in which the duration of the investigation is fairly short and the researcher actively implements both pretreatment and posttreatment measures. Such control is not always possible. For example nonexperimental investigations that are called "follow-up studies" often impose conditions on the investigators to a greater degree than they impose on the study. Follow-up investigations are extremely vulnerable to experimental mortality.

Follow-up studies are often used to evaluate the ultimate effectiveness of some treatment program. Areas frequently involved include clinical programs such as mental health treatment, vocational rehabilitation, and certain educational treatment programs. In these areas the acid test of program effectiveness is how well the clients (subjects) perform in a given environment after they leave the treatment program. Under these conditions the evaluation is often an afterthought in which the subject's status assessment on program entrance is recorded by the admitting clinician. Regardless of how well this assessment is accomplished, it may not have been completed with program evaluation as an objective. Records may be somewhat fragmentary with respect to the criteria ultimately chosen for follow-up assessment.

The follow-up investigation often is designed with the program entrance records serving as the first or pretreatment data point. Because of these circumstances, such studies are occasionally called "post hoc" in the sense that existing data are used. The researcher may or may not actually see the clients during their treatment and thus may have only the pretreatment records for identification of subjects. Experimental mortality becomes a serious issue when the investigator attempts to locate subjects for follow-up assessment. Experience has shown that this is perhaps the most difficult type of study to conduct, and experimental mortality is the primary source of difficulty.

Although the researchers have pretreatment description (plus the occasional assessment at the point of treatment termination), they may be able to locate only a small percentage of subjects for follow-up assessment. The difficulty focuses on the description of the subjects who cannot be located. Was the treatment program so effective for those subjects that they have blended into the environment to an extent that they can no longer be identified? An alternative might be that the program was not effective for them, and they essentially became so transient that location is impossible. Neither of these explanations is supportable by existing data. In fact they become speculations based on the absence of data; perhaps such speculations are so risky as to be meaningless.

The follow-up study is essentially a nonexperimental difference question comparing pretreatment and posttreatment measures. Experimental mortality threatens internal validity in that a different group composition is available at one data point than is available at the second. The researcher has little chance of knowing what the subjects look like who cannot be located. There is a rather substantial probability that those who cannot be located are different from those who can. Thus, if all the data are used from the pretreatment measures, the two data points are probably not comparable, since group composition may have changed. Any differences in, for example, group average scores may reflect the different composition as much as program impact.

One alternative is to use only pretreatment data from those subjects who can be located for follow-up. Although this circumvents mortality as a threat to internal validity, other problems are involved. From a pragmatic standpoint, using only this portion of data may not be an accurate assessment of program effectiveness. The questions posed previously concerning the unlocated subjects and why they cannot be located must be addressed again. There is good reason to suspect that the locatable subjects do not provide a representative sample of the clients going through the program. To use only a partial sample may therefore not be addressing the reseach question adequately if the question involves the effectiveness of the treatment on clients entering the program.

Circumventing the difficulties of follow-up studies discussed above seems to be primarily a logistics consideration. Ideally one would wish to sample all clients entering the program and then assess their change after they are out in their normal environments. To accomplish this the program evaluation must be planned in advance and a monitor system must be devised that will permit subject location.

Comments

After being exposed to threats to internal validity, the beginning student of research may be wondering if any investigation can be designed that controls or circumvents all possible weaknesses. The answer in the strictest sense is probably a negative one. Most studies can be improved in some fashion, which is representative of the behavioral science effort to constantly refine its scientific methodology. It should be kept in mind, however, that design changes often involve compromises or alternatives that trade improvement in one area at the sacrifice of another. Researchers must use their best clinical judgment when deciding exactly where it is most critical to implement the tightest control and where they can best afford to live with less rigorous control. Decisions of this nature are often dependent on experience as a practicing researcher.

It is also important to restate the necessity to control certain factors and account for others in the report. This is further evidence of the sacrifice in some areas to achieve tighter control in others. The process of accounting for some threats involves discussing their probable contaminative influence in the research report. Such discussion must be well grounded in logic. It is no longer acceptable to ignore the threat or even state that no effect occurred without specifying on what basis the statement is made.

Turn to p. 181 and complete Simulation 7-4.

THREATS TO EXTERNAL VALIDITY

As noted early in this chapter, external validity speaks to the issue of generalizability of results. As indicated by Fig. 7-2, external validity involves how well the results of a particular study represent or apply to the population, treatment variables, and measurement criteria presumably being studied in the real world.

Although internal and external validity are not in direct opposition to each other, each tends to operate to the disadvantage of the other. This is still another area in which the researcher must often decide to concentrate attention on one and perhaps sacrifice rigor with respect to the other. Such a situation does not necessarily demean the overall character of behavioral research, however. The value of research should not be assessed in terms of a given investigation but rather in terms of programs of research with a cumulative purpose. Early studies in a program of research may well represent pioneer efforts at knowledge acquisition. In these studies the researcher may be primarily concerned with determining how a given psychological variable operates. Since the focus is necessarily the microcosm of that factor, it probably will be desirable to make that focus as pure as possible, thus emphasizing internal validity control. As information accumulates establishing how the factor under study operates, the researcher then may become more concerned with its influence in the real world environment. This change in focus will necessitate an increasing attention to external validity, perhaps at the expense of internal validity controls. Ultimately as the scientist approaches the real environment he or she then has accumulated data not only on how the factor operates in a laboratory setting but also on its influence as it interacts with environmental contingencies. When generalizability becomes a concern of focus, the researcher will have a variety of threats to external validity to circumvent.

Population-sample differences

The entire population is seldom available to the researcher for study purposes. Even if the population were theoretically available, expense and time involved in recording data on the entire group are usually so great that it is unfeasible to do so. Consequently a researcher ordinarily works with a sample of individuals selected from the population.

One obvious dimension of external validity concerns the degree to which those subjects in the study are representative of the population to which generalization is desired. If there are significant differences between subjects and the larger population, it is likely that the subjects will respond differently (on the questionnaire, interview, or experimental task) than the larger group would. If the researchers are unaware of such differences, they may interpret the results as being applicable in the population when, in fact, they are not.

Population-sample representativeness relates directly to the way in which subjects are selected. Chapter 8 presents a detailed discussion of sampling techniques aimed at obtaining a representative group of subjects. However, since this is such a central issue in external validity, a brief examination seems warranted at this point. Bracht and Glass (1968) have discussed generalization issues concerning the accessible population and the target population. They suggest that "generalizing from the population of subjects that is available to the experimenter (the accessible population) to the total population of subjects about whom he is interested (the target population) requires a thorough knowledge of the characteristics of both populations [p. 438]." In this context Bracht and Glass are referring to the subject pool (accessible population) sampling arrangement discussed in Chapter 8. Using this approach, the researchers define the population in terms of the behavioral characteristics that are important in the research. They then identify an accessible population or subject pool that is presumably like the larger population with regard to those characteristics. It is from this subject pool that selection of the actual subjects occurs.

The central issue raised by Bracht and Glass relates to the researchers' knowledge concerning characteristics of the population and the subject pool. From this standpoint the researchers may find themselves in a somewhat difficult situation. As they proceed to define the population, it is probable that a thorough knowledge of all the characteristics of the population is not available. To the degree that there is confidence concerning the importance of those known characteristics (and the relative unimportance of those about which knowledge is not available), the researchers can control external validity. This speaks specifically to the approach the researchers take with regard to defining the population. Some maintain that it is better to define the population in a restricted fashion but to have more confidence in the knowledge concerning a restricted set of characteristics. Noting that Kempthorne (1961) maintains such a perspective, Bracht and Glass (1968) relate this position as the view that "it is better to have reliable knowledge about restricted sets of circumstances . . . and to have the uncertainty of extending this knowledge to the target population . . . than to define the experimentally accessible population so broadly as to be uncertain about inferences from the sample to the accessible population [p. 441]." The alternative position, as was noted earlier in the discussion of time-series research, requires a much less rigorous definition of characteristics. Generalization under these conditions is viewed as an inference from the subject(s) in the experiment to "a population similar to those observed."

Although I am inclined to favor the more rigorous population definition, the crucial factor is that the type of inference being made is kept clearly in mind. It is essential that researchers be aware of whether the population knowledge is reliable and that they be aware of the resulting level of confidence concerning generalization.

Artificial research arrangements

A second threat to external validity is embodied in the actual research arrangements chosen for the investigation. In one sense this phenomenon is the Hawthorne effect operating as a threat to external validity. To the degree that the research setting deviates from the routine the subject is accustomed to, it may be expected that the subject's responsivity is changed. If a group of children have their daily classroom routine altered by being tested in a "small distraction-free room", their performance may be either heightened or depressed as a result of the nonroutine setting. The subjects' performance on the research task may thus be different than it would be if they were to perform the task in a nonexperimental or routine setting.

The influence of research arrangements threatens external validity to the degree that the subjects' responsivity is altered. If subjects are responding differently because of the setting, their performance is not representative of the original subject pool from which they were drawn. The researcher may have initially gone to great lengths through sampling procedures to make the subjects representative of a given population to which generalization is desired. Although the subjects may have been representative at that time, they become a select, nonrepresentative group as soon as the investigation is initiated (if the arrangements are substantially artificial). The earlier discussion in Chapter 2 indicated that this type of problem was particularly evident in experimental research, especially in a highly artificial setting such as a laboratory. It should be emphasized, however, that nonexperimental research may be equally vulnerable to the degree that subjects are placed in a nonroutine situation. Certainly an interview may create a great degree of artificiality depending on how and where it is conducted. In all cases, experimental or nonexperimental, the researcher must judge the degree to which external validity is threatened by artificial research arrangements.

It has already been noted that certain phases of a research program may necessitate a sacrifice with respect to external validity. When subjects are individually treated, such as is often the case in many interviews (and psychological experiments), it is difficult to suppose that the research arrangements are routine. It may be that a change in routine is under study. The degree to which external validity is threatened, however, depends on the situation *to which generalization is desired.* If, for example, the researcher is studying a new method of individualized instruction, considerable generalizability might be possible. True, the results may not generalize to the classroom from which the child came, but it should be remembered that the researcher is exploring individualized instruction. Thus judgments concerning external validity must include consideration of the potential practical application to which the study is addressed rather than automatically making reference to existing settings. From the researcher's standpoint, if external validity is a serious objective, care must be taken to arrange the research setting as much like the target setting for generalization as possible. Such arrangements may include a variety of contingencies such as the physical setting, the interpersonal arrangements, the materials being used, and perhaps many others. Here again the researcher's experience and clinical judgment must be used in deciding priority contingencies necessitating attention.

Pretest influence

It is not uncommon to read reports of experiments in which the researcher used a pretest or warm-up task before initiating the actual experimental procedures. This is done for a variety of reasons, but in general the purpose is to ensure that when the subjects begin the experiment per se, the performance is reflective of the subject-task interaction and not the subjects' "learning to respond" behavior. Although it is a useful procedure for purifying the scrutiny of the subject-task interaction, such a pretest or warm-up may serve to threaten external validity. It is seldom that instructional and psychological procedures used in the field are preceded by a warm-up procedure. Consequently the "learning to respond" behaviors are usually a part of the subject's performance in a real world setting. In certain situations this represents a difference between the research task setting and the field setting that may be substantial, thereby diminishing the accuracy of generalization.

Pretest or warm-up procedures also threaten external validity in a similar but slightly different conceptual context than learning to respond. The pre-research activity may result in an increase or decrease in subjects' sensitivity to the variable under study. If this occurs, the results may not be representative of performance by subjects who are not pretested. Under such circumstances, perhaps resulting in increased or decreased attention, anxiety, or a number of other possibilities, generalizations to the population sampled (but not subjected to the pre-research experiences) may be in error.

As noted previously, the research program that is still identifying fundamental process operation may not be primarily concerned with generalization. However, if external validity *is* a central focus, the researcher must attend to pretest or warm-up as a threat. Assuming the research program has proceeded beyond the study of fundamental process, elimination of pre-research procedures may be in order to facilitate generalization. Since the initial learning to respond behaviors, as well as the initial changes in subject sensitivity, may be a part of performance in the field, inclusion of these influences in research concerned with generalization seems relevant. The actual impact of such pretest influence is often not known to the researcher. It may be expected, however, that the more unusual the overall task is for the subject, the more influence will result from warm-up or pretest.

Multiple treatment interference

The influence of multiple treatment interference as a threat to external validity is conceptually similar to that of pretest just discussed. It becomes operative when more than a single treatment is administered to the same subjects. Multiple-treatment investigations present obvious analytical internal validity problems since, beyond the first treatment, a subject's performance is difficult to attribute to any given treatment (e.g., treatment 2 or 3) because of the cumulative effect. Additionally, however, the generalizability of results from treatments subsequent to the first is also questionable. Because the effects of prior treatments are often not dissipated by the time later treatments are administered, the subjects may well have a depressed or increased sensitivity to a second or third research task. To the degree that such subjects' responsivity is altered for, say, treatments 2 or 3, the generalizability of results from these treatments is reduced. This, of course, assumes that a sequence of multiple treatments is not the usual setting in the population sampled.

Circumventing external validity difficulties in a multiple treatment experiment is probablematic to say the least. Since subjects approach the first treatment experimentally naïve (presumed free from systematic influences), results from that treatment are assumed to be externally valid if the setting is similar to that of the intended generalization. Because the subjects usually approach the second task not experimentally naïve (presumed under the systematic influence of treatment 1), they are not representative of the initial subject pool. The approach to circumventing this threat generally would require making reasonably certain that the subjects began treatment 2 also experimentally naïve. In some situations researchers may depend on the passage of time to accomplish this. Such an approach is of uncertain effectiveness, and the researcher may be depending on a fallacious assumption. Alternatively, if sufficient time passes between treatments for the first to dissipate, often the research appears more like two studies than two treatments within one.

Occasionally, the researcher may be able to determine that the effect of treatment 1 is negligible on the performance of treatment 2. To be certain of this, however, a study directly concerned with such influence may be required to provide empirical evidence. In lieu of expending the effort and expense necessary to provide such evidence for methodological purposes only, the researcher may decide to avoid a multiple-treatment design completely. This, of course, would be one fashion in which the researcher could be assured of avoiding the difficulties discussed above. The alternative might involve using a different randomly assigned group of subjects for each treatment.

Turn to p. 182 and complete Simulations 7-5 and 7-6.

Comments

This chapter has discussed problems and threats involved in the basic plan and execution of an investigation. The approach has been to focus on problems that may be encountered regarding both internal and external validity. The plan or conceptual design of an investigation is a core consideration in beginning a research effort. Many other decisions are also necessary as will be found in later chapters. It should be reemphasized, however, that the existence of a serious design threat may negate the worth of the most sophisticated or elegant measures, statistical analyses, and data interpretations.

REFERENCES

Belmont, J. M. Long-term memory in mental retardation. In N. R. Ellis (Ed.), *International review of research in mental retardation,* New York: Academic Press, 1966.
Bracht, G. H., and Glass, G. V. The external validity of experiments. *American Educational Research Journal,* 1968, *5,* 437-474.
Campbell, D. T., and Stanley, J. C. Experimental and quasi-experimental designs for research on teaching. In N. L. Gage (Ed.), *Handbook of research on teaching.* Chicago: Rand McNally & Co., 1963.

Deese, J., and Hulse, S. H. *The psychology of learning* (3rd ed.). New York: McGraw-Hill, 1967.

Drew, C. J. Covariate matching: a methodological note. *Perceptual and Motor Skills*, 1969, *28*, 799-800.

Kempthorne, O. The design and analysis of experiments with some reference to educational research. In R. O. Collier, Jr., & S. M. Elam (Eds.), *Research Design and Analysis: Second Annual Phi
Delta Kappa Symposium on Educational Research.* Bloomington, Ind. Phi Delta Kappa, 1961.

Prehm, H. J. Verbal learning research in mental retardation. *American Journal of Mental Deficiency,*
1966, *71,* 42-47.

Rosenthal, R. *Experimenter effects in behavioral research.* New York: Appleton-Century-Crofts, 1966.

Stanley, J. C., and Beeman, E. Y. Restricted generalization, bias, and loss of power that may result
from matching groups. *Psychological Newsletter*, 1958, *9,* 88-102.

SIMULATIONS

SIMULATION 7-1

Topic: Internal validity

Background statement: The ability to identify and circumvent internal validity
problems is essential for both the consumer of research and the person designing an investigation. Eliminating problems or potential problems is the
crucial behavior when one is planning a study. Identifying weaknesses permits research consumers to make their own decisions concerning how useful
the results might be. As with so many other skills, practice and related experience seem to greatly enhance the ability to use knowledge about threats
to research design.

Tasks to be performed

1. Read the following material.
2. Note any internal validity weakness(es) that is (are) evident from this report of the experiment. Suggest how data may have been contaminated if
   such contamination may have occurred. Suggest a way to circumvent any
   difficulty you note.

Stimulus material

Smith and Smith (1963) studied movement in an investigation that involved
two experimental variables. On one variable the experimenters were investigating subject naiveté about the fact that an experiment was underway. The second
experimental variable involved room color. The diagram on p. 179 illustrates
the fashion in which the study was designed.

These investigators varied the color of a contrived art gallery and found that
naïve subjects in a dark brown room took more footsteps at a faster pace than
subjects who were placed in a light beige room. The subject groups in the brown
gallery also covered nearly twice as much area, in a less dense movement pattern,
and spent less time in the room than those in the beige gallery. Under the second

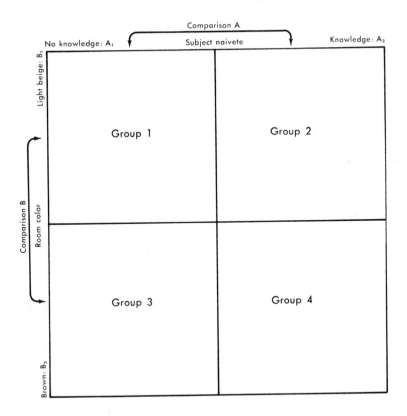

condition the subjects were aware that they were in an experiment, although the true nature of the investigation was camouflaged with information that another factor was under study. In this condition, subjects were run individually through the same rooms that the subjects had encountered as groups in the condition of no knowledge. Under this condition no difference in movement was evident between the brown and light beige conditions.

For feedback see p. 334.

SIMULATIONS 7-2 AND 7-3

Topic: Internal validity

Background statement: The ability to identify and circumvent internal validity problems is essential for the consumer of research as well as for the person designing an investigation. Eliminating problems or potential problems is the crucial behavior when one is planning a study. Identifying weaknesses permits research consumers to make their own decisions concerning how useful the results might be. As with so many other skills, practice and related experience seem to greatly enhance the ability to use knowledge about threats to research design.

Tasks to be performed for Simulation 7-2

1. Read the following material.
2. Note any internal validity weakness (es) that is (are) evident from this report of the experiment. Suggest how data may have been contaminated if such contamination did occur. Also be alert for other weaknesses, if any, such as logic weaknesses or inferences that may not be supportable from this study.

Stimulus material for Simulation 7-2

Simulation 7-2 from Drew, C. J. Research on the psychological-behavioral effects of the physical environment. *Review of Educational Research,* 1971, *41,* 477-465.

Rohles (1967) reported a series of experiments conducted on the effects of manipulating the thermal environment. Results indicated that a temperature of 98° F with a relative humidity of 70% did not produce thermal stress, whereas 105° F with 70° relative humidity did. Following the line of reasoning that anxiety might be related to this finding, the author identified high- and low-anxiety individuals and asked them to participate as subjects. None of the highly anxious subjects would volunteer.

Rohles (1967) also described an investigation of crowding and thermal stress. One group of subjects was composed primarily of juvenile delinquents, parolees, high school dropouts, and those awaiting the draft. A second group was composed of graduate students of a similar age. In crowded conditions with high temperatures, the first group exhibited a great deal of aggressive behavior. This behavior diminished, however, in smaller groups or lower temperatures. The subjects who were students did not exhibit aggressive behaviors even under the highest temperatures and most crowded conditions. It was hypothesized on the basis of these findings that "if individuals who are prone to exhibit aggressive behavior are exposed to high temperatures under crowded conditions, the threshold for exhibiting this behavior will be lowered."

For feedback see p. 335.

Tasks to be performed for Simulation 7-3

1. Read the following material, which is a contrived subjects section in the method part of a research article. Note that the study involves a two-group comparison, which is the context within which you must look for internal validity problems.
2. Note any internal validity problem (s) that is (are) evident from this description of group composition. Suggest how data may have been contaminated if you think that such contamination did occur. Suggest a way to design the study that might circumvent the problems you have identified.

Stimulus material for Simulation 7-3

Thirty mentally retarded subjects were selected randomly from an institutional population with IQs ranging from 55 to 75 and chronological ages (CAs) 20 to 26 years. A nonretarded sample was selected in a similar fashion from a college-student population with CAs 20 to 26 years. Subjects evidencing a speech, hearing, chronic health, or behavior problem that might interfere with experimental performance were eliminated from the population before sampling procedures were initiated.

For feedback see p. 335.

SIMULATION 7-4

Topic: Internal validity

Background statement: As noted in the text, internal validity is as much a concern with time-series designs as it is with traditional experimental studies. This simulation presents a time-series situation and asks that you criticize and circumvent any difficulties noted.

Tasks to be performed

1. Read the following material. Note difficulties as well as the experimenter's explanation.
2. Determine the soundness of the experimenter's inference. Do you agree with the explanation or not? Why?
3. What would you suggest as a means of circumventing any internal validity problems noted?

Stimulus material

A time-series experiment was conducted on a young boy who was identified as being hyperactive. The experimenter believed that the hyperactive behavior could be brought under control by positively reinforcing the child for remaining in his seat and "on task" while ignoring (thereby not reinforcing) any out-of-seat occurrences or "off-task" behavior. Since the experimenter suspected that the hyperactive behavior was being reinforced and maintained in the classroom, it was decided that an A-B-A reversal design would be used. The data collected appeared as in the illustration on p. 182.

In viewing the above data display, the experimenter became excited, since it appeared that the treatment (reinforcement contingencies) were effective in reducing inappropriate behavior. Baseline appeared to be stable (stable high rate) and evidenced a change under phase B. The rate stabilized nicely and showed a somewhat gentle but convincing reversal under phase A. Thus the experimenter was prone to suggest that the treatment affected change in inappropriate behavior.

Then some new information came to the attention of the researcher. The mother had long been frustrated by the child's behavior and had consulted the local Dr. Spock (more appropriately, the family physician), who prescribed medication to control the hyperactivity. This medication was begun on the day that phase B was initiated. The medication rather than the reinforcement contingencies could have generated the behavior change in B. The researcher, however, maintained that the treatment was effective as evidenced by the reversal when the reinforcement contingencies were changed back to baseline condition.

Do you agree or disagree with the interpretation? If so, would you use it for the same or different reasons? If not, why not? How would you change the design or in some other way test the interpretation?

For feedback see p. 337.

SIMULATION 7-5

Topic: Internal validity

Background statement: The ability to identify and circumvent internal validity problems is essential for the consumer of research as well as for the person designing an investigation. Eliminating problems or potential problems is the crucial behavior when one is planning an investigation. Identifying weaknesses permits research consumers to make their own decisions concerning how useful the results might be. As with so many other skills, practice and related experience seems to greatly enhance the ability to use knowledge about threats to research design.

Tasks to be performed

1. Read the following stimulus material, which is a sketch of an investigation that was concerned with the treatment of acne.
2. Note any potential internal validity weakness(es) and suggest how they could be circumvented. What about external validity?

Stimulus material

An investigation was conducted at a famous research center in the East on the treatment of acne in teenage boys and girls. A sample was drawn randomly from volunteers who, by self-admission, had moderate to severe acne problems. Two comparison groups were formed by random assignment with careful precautions taken to ensure equal distribution of sexes between the groups. One group received the new acne treatment, while the second group received an identically packaged placebo of innocuous material. Exactly the same instructions were given to both groups by the same experimenter. Diet was controlled between the groups.

After a 4-week treatment period, the same experimenter individually interviewed each subject in both groups and assessed the severity of the acne after treatment. Data were collected by the clinical judgment of the experimenter using a standard checklist carefully designed to maintain objectivity.

For feedback see p. 337.

SIMULATION 7-6

Topic: Study design
Tasks to be performed
1. Read the following stimulus material.
2. What type of research question is asked?
3. What is the experimental variable?
4. What type of general design approach seems appropriate?
5. Diagram the study as you see it.
6. What variables need to be controlled?
7. Now design the study in detail.
8. In relation to item 7, note categories of details that require your attention.

Stimulus material

You have been asked to compare the effectiveness of two types of visual instruction. Both methods use filmed presentations. One presents the information in animated form (cartoon-like characters such as those used in *Sesame Street*). The other approach presents the same information in the same sequence with actual people performing the same operations that the animated characters do. The manufacturers of the films are concerned that the animation, although of high interest, may be sufficiently removed from reality that the effectiveness of instruction is reduced.

For feedback see p. 338.

CHAPTER 8

Subject selection and assignment

This chapter explores certain topics that are frequently called logistic dimensions of research. Logistics, used in this context, is defined broadly and essentially refers to various activities that are involved in implementation of a research study. Use of the term "logistics" should not be taken to mean that the topics of discussion are of secondary importance. Instead of taking an attitude that it is *mere* logistics, the researcher must remain alert during study execution. Errors during this phase may destroy the worth of the most carefully laid plans. Additionally, a complete articulation of each implementive step before actually beginning a study is of vital importance. Only by accomplishing this level of detail in planning can pitfalls be avoided before they threaten the soundness of an investigation.

SUBJECT SELECTION

Since behavioral science is involved in the study of organisms, the selection of those organisms for a given experiment is of vital importance. Several questions arise in selecting the subjects for an investigation: (1) Are the subjects appropriate for the research question? (2) Are the subjects representative? (3) How many subjects should be used? From a conceptual soundness standpoint, the researcher must be assured that the subjects are appropriate for assessment of the topic being studied. Child development (in the usual sense) is hardly being investigated if the subjects are college sophomores. Likewise, if the intellectual status of schizophrenic adults is the topic, the subjects certainly ought to fit that definition. Consideration regarding such subject variables is a part of defining the population operationally and includes a multitude of factors to which the researcher must attend.

An integral part of the subject selection issue is the representativeness of the sample. Assuming that the researcher wants to know something about how a given population responds, the subjects should "look something like" that population. Since it is doubtful that the entire population can be tested, a sample will have to be used that presumably will provide results similar to those that would have been obtained if the entire population had been studied. The degree to which results are generalizable, or are externally valid, is vitally influenced by subject selection.

Closely related to the generalizability issue is the third concern of how many subjects should be used. This question is repeatedly asked by beginning research students and is difficult to answer to their satisfaction. Sample size presents a problematic question because no set answer or rule may be given. Several contingencies impinge on decisions as to what is an adequate sample.

Defining the population

Defining the population under investigation is essential both with respect to identifying subjects appropriate for the research question and obtaining a representative sample. A population refers to all "members of any well-defined class of people, events, or objects" who, for research purposes, are designated as being the focus of an investigation (Kerlinger, 1964, p. 52). The population may be large (theoretically infinite) or it may be limited, depending on the researcher's definition. For example, a population might be defined as "all third-year nursing students in the United States who are enrolled in degree programs" Such a population would include a rather large number of individuals who are potential subjects. One additional defining restriction, however, would dramatically reduce the size of this population. If the population were to be defined as "all third-year *male* nursing students in the United States who are enrolled in degree programs," the number of potential subjects would be much smaller. The essential factor in population definition involves the *units* or *restrictions* that are used to describe the set. In the first example, four restrictions were used in definition: (1) nursing students, (2) third year of study, (3) in the United States, and (4) enrolled in degree programs. Unless the population is clearly defined, the researcher does not know what units or restrictions to use when selecting the sample of subjects. In addition, without a clearly defined set of characteristics it is unclear to whom the results are generalizable.

The descriptive characteristics used in defining a given research population must relate to the topic under study. If one is investigating some aspect of measured intelligence, then it only makes sense that the population definition include some unit(s) that reflect(s) intelligence specifications. In addition to defining the population for purposes of inclusion, definition restrictions also serve to exclude subjects with unwanted characteristics. Often this is important in terms of the precision of the study, and it certainly should involve a priori rather than hasty field decisions. In the example concerning nursing students, the population was defined as being enrolled in degree programs. By this definition the researcher is not interested in students who are enrolled in diploma programs (degree versus diploma is a distinction made in the professional training of nurses), and such students are not eligible as potential subjects. In this case the exclusion restriction was an integral part of the population inclusion definition.

Often additional restrictions are added to population statements, such as, "Individuals with marked visual, hearing, or emotional deviancies that are judged as potentially interfering with task performance will be eliminated before sampling." Such restrictions involve subject properties that are not a part of the investigation and would contribute only error variance to the results.

After the population is defined, the researcher must obtain or construct a complete list of all the individuals in the population. This list is known as a *frame*. Constructing the frame can be an extremely difficult and laborious task unless such a listing is already available. In fact, as Cochran (1963) notes, it is occasionally impossible to construct a complete frame as defined by the population (such as listing all of the fish in a given lake). Pragmatic considerations often necessitate certain procedural deviations from what would be involved in the construction of a theoretically precise frame.

If it becomes logistically impossible (or economically unfeasible) to construct a precise population frame, the researcher may find it necessary to work with a truncated or more restricted list. For example, resources may not permit the construction of a population frame for "all fourth-grade students in the state of Oregon." The experimenter may then decide to form what is known as a subject pool by selecting a number of districts throughout the state that are representative of the larger population. From this subject pool a sample of subjects can be drawn who will actually participate in the study. Fig. 8-1 represents a pictorial example of such a procedure.

This procedure certainly weakens the confidence with which sample results

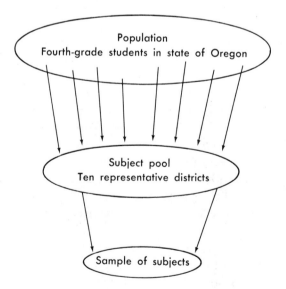

Fig. 8-1. Subject selection using a subject pool.

can be directly generalized to the initially defined population. Some would maintain that if the frame is compiled from the subject pool, then this is, in fact, a redefined population that is presumably representative of a theoretically larger but not actually formed population. From a pragmatic standpoint, it is of little consequence what term is applied. This is a field procedure that is not uncommon, and, if it is implemented with care, it can provide acceptable results. The subject pool arrangement portrayed in Fig. 8-1 has certain advantages beyond economics. An investigation is seldom conducted without an occurrence of subject mortality. When subjects are lost from the sample, the subject pool can then be used as a replacement pool for selecting alternative subjects. Since the original sample was drawn from this same source, there is little reason to believe that replacement subjects will not approximate those who were selected initially.

Occasionally a researcher will form a subject pool even when a complete population frame is available. Usually this is done specifically for purposes of replacement of subjects who are lost or deleted from a study because of procedural or other error in the investigation. Such an arrangement may facilitate the field operation, since return to the larger population frame is made unnecessary.

Turn to p. 212 and complete Simulation 8-1.

Representativeness of the sample

Once the researcher has a frame from which to sample, the next task is that of actually selecting those subjects to serve in the study. Since the knowledge that the investigator will obtain about the population is to be based on a sample, the degree to which that knowledge is accurate depends on how well the sample represents the population. This highlights the importance of the sampling procedures that are used. If the sample does not accurately represent the population, interpretations of the results may not be accurate for individuals other than those actually used as subjects. If the researcher is unaware that the sample is unrepresentative, incorrect inferences may be drawn concerning the population.

In the subject pool procedure noted above, the issue of representativeness is crucial at two points during the process of selecting subjects. Initially the construction of the subject pool must receive careful attention for representativeness. The previous example concerning fourth-grade students will illustrate this point well. If the ten districts selected for the subject pool are *not* representative of the state population, there is little reason to believe that a sample drawn from that pool can produce results that are generalizable to the population. The second point at which the researcher must be cautious regarding representation is when the sample is selected from the subject pool. Identical issues are involved here; simply stated, the sample must be representative of the pool if results are to generalize to that pool, and if the subject pool is representative of the population, then results should be somewhat generalizable to the population at large.

Various sampling approaches

Several different sampling procedures have been used in behavioral science over the past years. Determination of which procedure should be used is often based on the conditions under which the study is conducted. The crucial nature of subject selection demands that the researcher use the most appropriate and rigorous technique possible.

Simple random sampling. Random sampling is probably the best known method of selecting subjects in the attempt to form a sample representative of the population. Simple random sampling (occasionally called unrestricted random sampling) is a selection process whereby *each individual in the frame has an equal chance of being chosen*. Because each person has an equal chance of being selected, it is presumed that the population characteristics will be represented essentially to the degree that they exist in the population. It should be noted that a random sample does not *totally* ensure that all the population characteristics *will*, in fact, be represented in the sample. However, since chance is used to construct the sample, random sampling substantially reduces the possibility that a biased or unrepresentative group will be selected. More confidence may be placed in the representativeness of the sample when the population is homogeneous with regard to its characteristics. This simply makes less diversity to be represented. Likewise, the more heterogeneous the population is, the greater the chance that all aspects of characteristic diversity will not be represented.

Procedures for accomplishing a random sample are simple and easily implemented. Any technique that actually makes all units in the frame equally vulnerable to selection will suffice. For example, drawing names from a fishbowl will effect a random selection process. It is necessary to have the names on individual slips of paper and to mix them well. Similarly, the names might all be placed on cards that are shuffled, after which the desired number of subject cards is selected from the deck. The shuffling procedure must be conducted carefully, however, if a random sample is to truly be approximated. The essential element involves the thoroughness with which the cards are shuffled. Studies have indicated specifically that *casual* shuffling *does not* approximate a chance mixing of cards. (Remember this point the next time the poker game does not seem to be giving you your fair share.)

The most effective procedure for random sampling is also probably the most easily implemented, using a table of random numbers. This technique requires the researcher to assign consecutive numbers to each individual listed in the frame. Once this is accomplished, a table of random numbers is used to select those who will serve as subjects. (Tables of random numbers or random units are found in appendices of many statistics books, or one might use specially prepared books of tables such as *Tables for Statisticians* by Arkin and Colton or *Standard Mathematical Tables* published by The Chemical Rubber Company.) To use the random number table, the researcher merely begins at any point in the table and reads systematically in any direction (vertically or horizontally). When a number is encountered that matches one of the assigned numbers in the frame, that individual becomes a subject. Numbers that are not a part of the frame list are ignored (for example, if the number 386 appears in the table when the frame includes only 300 individuals, it is ignored). Similarly, numbers already selected are ignored once they become part of the sample (such as the second or third time that 46 appears in the table). This procedure continues until the desired number of subjects is obtained. A random number table with specific instructions for use may be found in Simulation 8-2 at the end of this chapter.

Turn to p. 213 and complete Simulation 8-2.

Stratified random sampling. Stratified random sampling is a useful technique when the type of investigation being conducted does not permit subject selection from only one population. Such circumstances may exist if the researcher wishes to study two or more groups of individuals who are distinctly different on the basis of some variable important to the research (the quasi-experimental design discussed earlier). An example of such a situation might involve a developmental study in which three different age level groups are being compared on a given learning task. Since developmental level is a part of the investigation, formulation of the three groups at different age levels must be forced or ensured by purposeful contrivance. Certainly one cannot expect to obtain three distinct age level groupings by random sampling from a single population.

The different developmental levels in this example actually form three different subpopulations known as *strata.* Each subpopulation or stratum constitutes a group to which the researcher may wish to generalize results. In a sense then, for sampling purposes, each stratum must have subjects selected from it as if one were conducting three miniature experiments. The subject group for each age level will therefore have to be sampled in a fashion that makes that group representative of the age level subpopulation being studied. An effective way to accomplish this is to use stratified random sampling from each of the respective subpopulations.

Implementation of stratified random sampling is accomplished in much the same way as simple random sampling. Once each of the strata is defined clearly, a subpopulation listing or frame is constructed of the individuals who are potential subjects. In this example of a developmental study, three frames would be necessary, one for each age range (e.g., group A, 3 to 5 years; group B, 6 to 8 years; group C, 9 to 11 years). The researcher then randomly samples from strata A, B, and C, until the desired number of subjects is obtained for each.

This procedure provides a convenient method of attending to the issue of representative samples from the subpopulations. Additionally, other variables may be held constant with considerable effectiveness in an attempt to equalize groups on variables other than that under study. Using the developmental investigation as an example, it is usually desirable to have the different age groups similar on factors such as measured intelligence. To accomplish this, the variable of measured intelligence is defined in common across groups. One would then randomly sample from all the individuals who were 3 to 5 years of age who had a measured intelligence between, say, 90 and 110; likewise from those 6 to 8 years of age who had measured intelligence between 90 and 110 and so on. There is little reason to expect intelligence differences between groups using this procedure. It is prudent, however, to check on this assumption before initiating the experiment. Such a precaution would simply be accomplished by computing group IQ means and statistically testing for differences. If groups are different, the sample should be redrawn from each subpopulation until the IQ variable is constant. I have used such a procedure many times over the years and, to date, I have not encountered a stratified sample that required redrawing even once. Often the control variable means are so similar that equality is obvious even before statistical testing.

Stratified random sampling is also useful in situations other than those suggested above. Occasionally the logistics of a large investigation may make simple random samples from the total population difficult. An example of this use is found in a national survey being conducted with field offices located throughout the nation. Administrative convenience may suggest that the regional responsibility of a given field office should be defined as a stratum and a sample drawn randomly from that subpopulation. If the sample is drawn with care, there is little reason to expect unrepresentativeness with regard to the stratum, and, in fact, the composite sample of all strata should represent the larger population.

Proportional sampling. Certain situations exist that generate unrepresentative samples if either simple or stratified random sampling is used. Such a condition might be found if a particular subgroup of the defined population were present as, say, a 10% proportion of the total population. In the previous discussion of stratified sampling, although not actually mentioned, it was implied that the subpopulation samples would be the same size. This approach would overrepresent the 10% group, since subgroups carry equal weight. To avoid such an error in representation (particularly when the groups are to form a single composite sample), it is often useful to sample from subgroups in the same proportion that they exist in the larger total population. This procedure is known as proportional sampling.

Implementing proportional sampling is accomplished in somewhat the same fashion as is used in the stratified approach. Subpopulation frames are constituted, after which a sample is drawn from each. The difference is simply that each subgroup sample is drawn only in the proportion that it exists in the larger population. For example, if two subgroups exist in the population, one constituting 90% (e.g., female nurses) and the second only 10% (male nurses), then the composite sample from both subpopulations would represent a 90% to 10% split in proportional representation. This would be achieved by randomly selecting subjects from one frame (female nurses) until 90% of the total sample had been obtained and then for the second group (male nurses), which constitutes the remaining 10%.

Proportional sampling is used for investigations that have a different purpose from those using equally represented strata. For investigations such as the earlier developmental study example, equal-sized stratified samples are most appropriate. The developmental example is the type of study in which the subsamples are to be maintained separately and perhaps compared. This type of investigation is much different from the national survey example, in which the strata samples are ultimately to be combined in a composite sample to be totally representative of the national population. In the latter case the subsamples are not to be compared as any major purpose of the study. Since the inference is aimed more at describing the total national population, representative proportions are more important and probably would warrant proportional sampling. This would prevent male nurses from being overrepresented in describing the population.

Systematic sampling. At times conditions are such that methods other than chance sampling techniques may be used to draw from the population. Systematic sampling is a logistically convenient procedure that may be expected to result in a representative sample *if the frame is arranged appropriately*.

Imagine, for the moment, that a sample of 100 subjects is to be drawn from a population frame of 1000. The first task to be performed is the establishment of what is known as the sample interval. This may be done by dividing the population frame by the size of sample to be drawn. In this example, 100 would be divided into 1000, resulting in a sample interval of ten. Now the researcher must determine where in the frame to begin drawing subjects. This is accomplished by selecting randomly any number from the first interval. After this has been done, subjects are selected by choosing *every kth* individual from the frame until the desired sample size is obtained. Suppose the randomly identified beginning number in the example was 7. The first subject would be the individual numbered 7 in the frame; then using the sample interval of ten, numbers 17, 27, 37, 47, and so on would be drawn until there were 100 subjects.

Systematic sampling is easily executed and is therefore desirable for field operations. The precision with which a systematic sample represents the population may be expected to at least equal random sampling, *if and only if*, the population frame list is arranged in an unbiased fashion. A variety of precautionary checks are necessary to avoid sample problems. The major point of difficulty involves possible trends that may exist in the frame list that would result in systematic bias. If, for example, the frame is constructed in a fashion whereby individuals are listed in an order of increasing age, considerable bias may result. Because of the systematic progression through the list, two separate samples may be different depending on the beginning number. The earlier example that began at 7 would be substantially older than a sample that began at 2 or 3. In either case the sample mean age may be considerably different than the population mean age, raising questions relating to the representativeness of the samples. Similarly an alphabetically constructed frame may result in a biased sample if influential variables related to surname are operative in the population. Examples of this type of problem may include concentrated pockets of minority groups having characteristic surnames. The precision of systematic sampling thus is essentially determined by the degree to which the population frame is arranged free of influential trends. As with many decision points in research, determination of problems is usually based on logic and experience. Other than a few example trends, such as those noted above, there is no check-list of problems to avoid that is functionally relevant in all the situations that the researcher may encounter.

Sampling, as with other aspects of research design, often requires the investigator to combine component techniques to achieve a desired outcome. At times it may be effective to combine the concepts of stratified and systematic sampling. Cochran (1963) calls such an approach "stratified systematic sampling." As the label suggests, this approach would be used when definably different population frames are available without biasing trends evident in the way they are listed. Systematic sampling procedures, as described above, may then be implemented within these frames.

Cluster sampling. Occasionally the researcher will not find it feasible to list all the individuals who are potential subjects when formulating a frame. It may be that the individuals are already grouped in some fashion into clusters of elements (for example, a school or a geographical region would constitute a cluster of students, people, or elements). Cluster sampling is a procedure whereby the researcher lists all the clusters and takes samples from this list. Thus, instead of sampling the individual members of the population, a sample of clusters is initially selected from which the subjects are then obtained. For example, suppose the researcher were conducting a study involving junior high school students in a large metropolitan area. Rather than formulating the population frame by listing all the junior high students in the area, the investigator lists all the junior high schools (clusters). From this list a random sample of schools may be drawn from which the actual subjects will be selected. The researcher may elect to use all the students available in the selected clusters or only a sample from those clusters.

Cluster sampling is similar to the subject pool arrangement discussed earlier in this section. As with subject pools, a critical concern must be the representativeness of the clusters that are initially selected from the total population. If the clusters are drawn in a manner that promotes confidence in generalizability, similar confidence should be warranted regarding the performance of subjects sampled from those clusters.

Double sampling. Double sampling or two-phase sampling is a procedure that is often useful for survey research. Essentially, the term is descriptive of the process; the investigator probes the subjects twice. Reasons for using double sampling techniques vary. Basically two situations represent the most frequent usage. The first involves what is essentially an intense follow-up with part of a larger primary sample. Such an investigation may be initiated with a rather large sample using an inexpensive survey instrument. With the results of the first instrument in hand, the researcher may then elect to sample a smaller group from the first round of subjects for purposes of obtaining more in-depth data. The second phase, because of procedures under these circumstances, is usually more costly, which makes using the total first-phase sample unfeasible. Second-phase subjects are usually sampled in a fashion that will attend to representativeness with regard to the first-phase subjects and, in turn, the population. It is not unusual for second-phase sampling to be accomplished using random procedures.

The second use of double sampling is essentially an attempt to gather missing data. Again used most often in survey research, this procedure is aimed at gathering the information that is absent because of subjects who do not return questionnaires during the first phase. The missing data may alter the results of the investigation if those who fail to complete the questionnaire are, in some fashion, different than subjects who do return the instrument. By virtue of their failure to respond, it is probable that these subjects *are* somehow different (e.g., attitude or motivation). To preserve the integrity of the first sample, the researcher may implement phase 2 by drawing a second sample from nonrespondents. Usually phase 2 involves procedures that are somehow more persuasive in eliciting responses (such as interviews or threats). Caution must be exercised in assuming that second-phase data are the same as that obtained in phase 1. Certainly the subjects are from the same first sample, but the research conditions have, by definition, changed. It *is* the second probe, and further differences are involved if the instrumentation is changed. Double sampling may, however, preserve the sample integrity to a greater degree than selecting new subjects from the replacement pool. Judgments regarding this must be based on the researcher's assessment of the population and sample characteristics.

Sample size

One of the questions frequently asked by beginning students in research is, "How many subjects do I need?" This question is also one of the most difficult to answer simply because there is no set sample size required under all conditions. Given different circumstances, larger or smaller samples may serve adequately. The reader interested in more depth regarding appropriate samples may wish to refer to one of the books that is totally devoted to this topic and that present several formulas for estimating size (e.g., Cochran, 1963; Sudman, 1976).

One primary concern with regard to sample size is that an adequate sample of behavior be obtained. Certain characteristics of the population have a great deal to do with how large the sample must be to accurately predict population factors. *If there is little variation in the population (i.e., if the population is homogeneous), then a much smaller sample will suffice than if more variation is present.* One consideration, then, in determining sample size has to do with the population variance. If the population under investigation is highly variable, the sample must be larger to permit more of that variation to be represented in the subjects selected. Behavioral science is plagued by considerably more variance than, say, agriculture or biology. Consequently, samples in behavioral science usually require a larger proportion of the population for accurate generalization than the "harder" sciences.

A logical question at this point is, How does one determine population variability? The answer to such a question is often unsatisfying. Obviously, one is going to obtain only an estimate of population characteristics. If the researcher is conducting an investigation on a given population, it can be assumed that there are some unknowns relative to that population. Often there will be some clues available in previously published research. Some populations have been shown to be more variable than others over the years. Greater variability is evident, for example, in populations that are deviant on some psychological dimension than in those that are within the normal range. Even in areas not directly related to mental functioning, mentally retarded persons are more variable than nonretarded individuals. Knowing this, the researcher can expect more error variance in any group of retarded persons, making an adequate sample necessarily larger. Information concerning such variability can often be gleaned from the published literature in an area of investigation, and samples can be drawn accordingly (e.g., Prehm, 1967, 1968). For many investigations the published articles provide several clues regarding implementing the research. In the absence of specific clues or information (such as in the case of a pioneering effort in an area), it is usually prudent to proceed cautiously. A pilot study may be useful for obtaining guidelines, or the first phase of a double sampling design may similarly provide initial information concerning subject characteristics. Often the early stages of a program of research are conducted with a conservative attitude that leads the researcher to take larger samples to ensure adequate power.

Experimental studies asking difference questions often are designed so that the total sample of subjects is divided into two or more treatment groups. One factor that must be kept in mind is that when treatments are applied to these smaller groups, they essentially become subsamples of the larger group. Therefore, the researcher must consider the number of treatment groups involved rather than the total number of subjects in the experiment. For example, the investigator may select sixty subjects for an experiment in rote learning. Suppose the study is designed so that six experimental conditions are required. If these are independent conditions, such an experiment would require the total sample (N) be assigned in some fashion to six different groups, resulting in a cell size (n) of 10. A cell n of ten subjects is a rather small sample of behavior that may prove to be inadequate. With only ten subjects per cell, the treatment mean is much more vulnerable to change by an atypical performance than if the group were larger. If researchers do not consider cell size from the outset, they may be dissatisfied with such small subgroups. Probably the most prudent approach to circumventing this difficulty is to determine a priori the desired cell n and let the total N be established in this fashion. Appropriate cell size is plagued with the same uncertainties that have previously been noted regarding generic sample size. Even in areas of known error, I am somewhat nervous with cell n's less than 15 (although at times other logistic concerns force deviation from this personal rule of thumb). More confidence may be placed in cell sizes of 20 to 25, which results in rather large sample N's in more complex experiments.

Clearly nonexperimental investigations also ask questions where subgroups may be formed for comparisons. Bailey (1978) discusses this in relation to survey research and essentially takes the same position noted above for experiments. The subgroups in any study simply must be of an adequate size to provide a credible sample of behavior, opinions, or other such data as are being collected.

As this discussion began, it was evident that no clear agreement exists concerning the "magic" minimal number of subjects necessary for a study to be sound. For example, Sudman (1976) reviewed several hundred survey studies and found considerable variation between surveys that sampled nationally and those that were regionally oriented. In general, he found that national surveys used samples of 1000 or more, whereas regional studies varied considerably (50 to 1000+) but tended to use smaller samples. The earlier discussions suggest that experimental studies tend to use much smaller samples than these numbers noted for survey research. Perhaps the best specific guidance can be found by reviewing recent literature in the area being studied. Current research in, say, medical surveys or cognitive development will provide the clearest indication of "present professional practice" for those substantive areas.

The researcher must also remain cognizant of certain statistical considerations when determining sample size. Frequently, limited subject availability will necessitate samples that are somewhat smaller than is desirable. Under such conditions it may be necessary to alter the statistical analyses that can be used. A more complete discussion of this aspect of research design is found in Part III of this book. It is important to note at this point, however, that sample size considerations must also include statistical plans. If this is not accomplished during the planning phases of an investigation, the experimenter may encounter disappointing problems when the time comes to analyze the data.

Subject selection for different purposes

Topics of discussion regarding subject selection have thus far been generic. There remain, however, a few brief concerns that need examination, which relate specifically to the type of question being asked.

Comparative or difference questions. As was noted in earlier chapters, the two basic concerns of comparative investigations are internal and external validity. To recount briefly, internal validity refers to the technical soundness of a study, whereas external validity has to do with generalizability of results. The researcher who is selecting subjects for a comparative investigation must remain cognizant of both internal and external validity as the study proceeds. At times, concerns of internal validity tend to diminish the generalizability of results. In Chapter 5 this dissonance was mentioned in relation to experimental procedures, but similar conditions exist regarding subject selection. As was noted in earlier sections, the subjects selected for a study must be appropriate for the construct under investigation. If the research question involves the study of developmental trends in learning math facts, it is probable that several age-level groups will be compared. To accomplish this, it has already been suggested that one might form stratified age groups with an implied (if not explicit) break or gap between groups. By forcing the composition of such groupings, the generalizability of results may be somewhat restricted.

The statement concerning restrictions on generalizability should not be interpreted as meaning that results do not generalize at all. Indeed, if adequate stratified sampling procedures have been employed, there is reason to believe that the within-group results will generalize. The point being made is that the broad spectrum of children does not exist in strata; the children progress somewhat continuously through a sequence of ages. It is doubtful that the results of such a stratified experiment will generalize well to children who fall between the experimentally contrived strata. Thus results are somewhat *restricted* with regard to external validity by the nature of experimental arrangements that are necessary for constructing an internally valid study for this example.

It was noted in Chapter 5 that the researcher may wish to sacrifice some rigor in either internal or external validity to emphasize the other dimension. Depending on the stage of a program of research, it may be expedient to concentrate on one dimension at the expense of the second. Early in a program of research the investigator may be more concerned with internal validity to ensure a more pure examination of fundamental constructs. As the research program progresses and data begin to accumulate concerning these variables, more attention may be addressed to the broader generalizability of results. Such alterations in emphasis regarding internal and external validity will most likely be reflected in subject selection procedures. As the program of research progresses, it is more likely that the researcher will attend more closely to the broadest possible generalizability—thus to the representativeness of the sample. This is somewhat different than sampling concerns that may be operative early in a research program. At these initial stages the researcher is more likely to be most concerned that the subjects are appropriate to the construct under study, with generalizability perhaps being limited in terms of the broader population of possible individuals to whom results might apply in the future.

Relationship or correlation questions. Subject selection for investigations of relationship questions is somewhat different than for comparative questions. In the absence of comparisons, different concerns related to study design are operative. Correlational questions have the primary purpose of demonstrating the degree to which phenomena relate. Practically speaking, the reasons for investigating such relationships usually involve the prediction of one variable or set of variables on the basis of measurements taken on the other variable. One example of such prediction is the use of entrance exam scores to predict college achievement (grades). This prediction is based on correlations between entrance exam scores and college grades that were obtained on previous students.

Applications of prediction must be vitally concerned with the accuracy of those predictions, which immediately leads to issues of external validity. If the relationship that is observed in an investigation does not generalize to a given group for which prediction is desirable, the study itself has lost much of its value. Thus, in subject selection, the researcher must be vitally concerned with the representativeness of the sample with regard to the population on which prediction is desired.

Beyond the mere representativeness of subjects in relationship studies, there are some characteristics of correlational methods that tend to relate results rather critically to samples. One specific factor relates to the variation that is present in the sample. With a more heterogeneous group of individuals the correlation coefficient will be higher than with a more homogeneous group. Thus, if the sample that is drawn is more heterogeneous (more variable) than the population, the predictive power demonstrated in the investigation will not obtain for the population. Likewise if the sample is more homogeneous than the population, the demonstrated relationship (predictive power) may be lower than actually is possible in the population at large. This highlights the importance of drawing representative samples in all phases of relationship research programs.

Descriptive questions. The third general type of research question has been discussed repeatedly as being one that asks "What is?" The researcher investigating this type of question essentially intends to provide a description of the characteristics, opinions, or behaviors of a given group, culture, or setting. Subject selection for a descriptive study must emphasize one concern in a preeminent fashion—*accuracy* of the description (external validity, if you will). A descriptive investigation that does not accurately characterize the group being studied is not only worthless, it is likely to be misleading. This places the representativeness of the sample in a position of crucial importance, and all the steps described earlier related to defining the population and ensuring a representative sample must be very carefully undertaken.

Other questions. The discussions thus far have focused on sampling procedures in the context of research. A variety of sampling approaches may be used effectively for questions that are not primarily of a research nature. For example, sampling for studies that have a research purpose of prediction (relationship research questions) have been discussed. Prediction is also undertaken in nonresearch settings such as forecasting election outcomes on election day. Election prediction has become very sophisticated recently, and many people are often amazed when winners are selected accurately with only one percent (often less) of the returns counted. Certainly such a small sample would make researchers very nervous, particularly if it were a random sample. However, the procedures used in election prediction today are extremely accurate and you cannot argue with success. One of the reasons for such accuracy is that the election sample is not undertaken randomly. A procedure known as *purposive sampling* is used, whereby the predictor obtains data from a particular district that has consistently voted for winners. Because of this consistency, that district serves as a better prediction than a random sample of several districts.

A complete examination of sampling is far beyond the scope of an introductory design text. There are complete volumes that focus solely on sampling (e.g., Cochran, 1963; Sudman, 1976) for both research and nonresearch questions. The reader interested in a more comprehensive discussion of sampling theory and procedures should consult one or more of these references.

SUBJECT ASSIGNMENT

A variety of research designs that are asking difference questions have been examined. Such investigations may involve survey studies that compare groups or experiments that focus on comparison between two or more performances of groups assigned to experimental conditions. For the most part, the process of assigning subjects to groups is a procedure used in experimental research, particularly traditional experimental studies. Consequently this discussion will be couched primarily in terms of experimentation. The researcher involved in nonexperimental comparisons should attend to those issues in this section that may be generalized to such an approach. The main focus of subject assignment is the concept of control that has relevance to all comparisons—experimental or non-experimental.

As noted above, experiments often are addressing difference questions that involve comparisons between two or more performances. These performances may be the result of a variety of designs such as baseline versus postintervention comparisons in time-series research or pretreatment versus posttreatment comparisons with a single group of subjects, as well as comparisons of two or more groups on a single-performance test. It is this latter example, in which multiple group comparisons are conducted that involve different groups of subjects for the conditions and also require subjects being assigned to those groups. This process is the primary concern of this section.

Subject assignment in multigroup experiments is of central importance to internal validity. The problem, of course, is one of how to divide those individuals who are a part of the sample into groups that will receive the different treatments. In Chapter 7 several examples were given in which the researcher was comparing the effectiveness of teaching methods (e.g., method A, B, or C). The teaching methods in these examples represent conditions of the type that are often compared with different groups for each condition.

Recall that the concept of control refers to the notion that groups are assumed to be essentially equal in all respects *with the exception of that variable under investigation.* Thus, if teaching method A were being compared with method B, the difference in teaching methods should be the only way in which the two groups are not equivalent. The notion of control is the central issue with regard to internal validity, and subject assignment to groups is the primary technique a researcher has for ensuring control. Subject assignment is therefore of vital importance and must be accomplished in a carefully planned fashion.

Assignment by chance

Assignment of subjects to different treatment conditions is frequently accomplished using chance procedures. Although this does imply that subject assignment is "left to chance," so to speak, it in no means that the procedure is unplanned or haphazard. In fact, chance assignment refers to a carefully planned and executed technique in which the researcher uses randomness to form the groups for the study.

A brief note needs to be made concerning random assignment and random sampling before proceeding with assignment approaches. It is not uncommon for the beginning research student to become only vaguely aware of random procedures. One source of confusion is a lack of distinction between sampling and assignment. Random sampling is, indeed, a separate and different procedure than random assignment and has a different purpose. *The use of random techniques in sampling is aimed at obtaining a representative sample from the population.*

This is important for purposes of generalizing results to the population, which is the essence of external validity. Random assignment of subjects, on the other hand, is a different procedure with a different purpose.

Random assignment of subjects to different conditions is a technique used by researchers in an attempt to form equivalent groups. The aim of random assignment is *group* equivalency, since individual variation or individual differences within groups will remain. Another concern is equivalence of subject properties (e.g., motivation or intellect) that exist on a pretreatment basis. Hopefully, this will permit any posttreatment differences that may appear to be attributed to the treatment. Definitions of random assignment are reminiscent of definitions of random sampling, primarily because it is the same fundamental process being used. Basically, random assignment involves a procedure by which subjects are assigned to groups in such a fashion that each subject in the study has an equal chance of being placed in any of the treatment groups. Within this general procedure there are several techniques for actual implementation.

Captive assignment. Occasionally a researcher will have the total sample identified and available at the outset of the investigation (as opposed to situations in which all subjects are not present at one time). Underwood (1966) has called this type of situation one in which the subjects are *captive*. This makes it possible to actually know which subjects, by name, will be in which experimental group at the outset. Consequently, somewhat different operational techniques are used to randomly assign subjects than in other situations.

When the researcher has the total sample captive, procedures for random assignment to conditions are simple. Individuals in the sample are listed by name, forming a frame much like that accomplished with a population for sampling purposes. Once this is completed, the experimenter effects what is essentially a miniature random sample for each of the treatment groups. This might be done using the fishbowl arrangement as before. Subjects are assigned consecutive numbers from 1 to N. These numbers are then written on individual slips of paper, placed in a fishbowl, and mixed thoroughly. This is also done frequently by placing the subject's name on the slip rather than a corresponding number. Once either names or numbers are in the receptacle, the subject groups may be drawn randomly. If, for example, the study involved two conditions, the first half of the total sample that is drawn from the fishbowl might form the first group n, and the remaining sample constitutes the second group. Thus if the sample N equaled fifty individuals, the first twenty-five slips of paper drawn would constitute the group for treatment A, whereas the remaining twenty-five would be assigned to treatment B. The researcher may choose another procedure to achieve the same end. For example, the decision may be to use the first subject for group A, the second for B, the third for A, the fourth for B, and so on in an alternating fashion until both groups are complete. In either case, there is little reason to suspect that bias has been systematically introduced that would make the groups different.

Random number tables may also be used effectively to assign subjects to groups. As before, it is necessary to formulate a list of the subjects in some sort of order. This process may conveniently be accomplished with an alphabetical listing. Once this is completed, the random number table is used to assign treatment to the subjects in consecutive order beginning with the first name and proceeding through the list. Using the previous example in which there were two experimental conditions, the researcher would be interested only in the digits 1 and 2 as they appeared in the table. As before, he or she would begin at any point in the random unit table and proceed systematically in any direction (horizontally or vertically). If the first digit encountered is 2, the subject in the first list position is assigned to group 2. If the second and third digits are 1, those individuals occupying the second and third list positions are assigned to group 1. This procedure is continued until group n's are completed. The researcher ignores irrelevant digits (those other than 1 or 2 in this example) and similarly ignores either 1 or 2 after that respective group n is completed. Therefore, after the twenty-fifth subject is assigned to group 2, the remaining encounters with 2 in the table are ignored. Using the random number table is frequently more convenient than drawing from a fishbowl, particularly when large numbers of subjects are involved (unless, of course, you really enjoy cutting up all those little slips of paper).

Turn to p. 214 and complete Simulation 8-3.

Sequential assignment. There are occasions when the researcher does not have the entire sample captive (the actual names are not all present before beginning the procedures). Under such conditions, a different assignment procedure is obviously necessary. The term "sequential assignment" is used specifically by Underwood (1966) and describes the method involved. This type of situation is one that, in reality, frequently presents itself. The researcher often does not have the exact sample drawn. Instead, with the population defined, he or she may be operating from a subject pool (drawn in a representative fashion) and not know exactly which individuals from that pool will ultimately serve as subjects. Additionally the experimental procedures may be being conducted over a period of time rather than at a single sitting. Under these conditions, the researcher may gather data on three or four subjects one day, another three or four the second, and so on. Individuals from the subject pool are then presented for the study on a sequential basis. When they do present themselves, the subjects must be assigned to one of the treatment conditions in such a fashion that will guard against the formulation of biased or unequal groups. Such a setting is not at all uncommon in studies in which subjects are tested or interviewed individually, since, if there are many subjects in the study, it is usually impossible to test all subjects in a day (even a week or month may easily be involved).

A slight modification of the fishbowl procedure may be used nicely. Suppose a researcher were again conducting a study with an N of 50 and two experimental conditions (cell n of 25). The researcher may simply place fifty slips of paper in the fishbowl, twenty-five with condition A written on them and twenty-five with condition B. After thoroughly mixing the slips in the bowl, they may be extracted one at a time. As the first slip is drawn its specified condition (A or B) is listed and likewise until all slips have been drawn and their respective conditions listed in order. Once this step is completed, the experimenter is ready for the first subject to appear. As this occurs, that subject is assigned to the group indicated by the first slip drawn, the second subject is assigned to the second slip drawn, and so on. Using these procedures, it is not likely that the subject groups will be systematically different.

A similar procedure may be implemented using shuffled cards or data sheets premarked by condition. Following the example study just given, twenty-five cards would be marked with condition A and twenty-five with condition B. These cards are then shuffled thoroughly (recall the importance of a *thorough* shuffling; casual shuffling is often not random). Once completed, the first subject to appear simply is assigned to the condition appearing on the first card. As before, the sequential testing of subjects corresponds with the sequence of shuffled conditions.

Alternative procedures for sequential random assignment are also available, of course, through the use of random number tables. One way in which this may be done is to assign digits to represent each of the conditions for which groups are to be formed. If, for example, six experimental conditions were being studied, then the digits 1 through 6 would become relevant for use in the random number table. Suppose it has been determined that cell n's will be 20; this would result in a sample N of 120 subjects. The sequence of assignment may be determined by using the random unit table as before with digits 1 through 6 being relevant. If the first number encountered is 5, then the first subject to appear will be assigned to condition 5. Likewise the second may be assigned to 3 and so on until the total of 120 subjects with twenty per group has been obtained. Also in the usual fashion, if group 5 is completed with twenty subjects, then subsequent encounters with digit 5 in the table are ignored. Usually a complete list is made of the group sequence (e.g., 5, 3, 1, . . .) including the full complement of subjects to be assigned before the experiment begins. This way the sequence of assignment is predetermined randomly before each subject appears for testing.

Occasionally a researcher will wish to exert a bit more control than is possible with the randomized procedures described above. As an illustration, take the six-condition experiment just described. Table 8-1 presents an example of the sequence of subject assignment to conditions. For convenience of example purposes, however, only a portion of the assignment sequence is provided (recall that the entire subject list will include an N of 120). Despite the fact that this is

Table 8-1. Example of assignment sequence list for six-group study

Subject number	Group assigned	Subject number	Group assigned	Subject number	Group assigned
1	5	24	4	47	1
2	1	25	3	48	3
3	6	26	1	49	4
4	3	27	6	50	5
5	2	28	5	51	1
6	3	29	2	52	2
7	6	30	3	53	6
8	2	31	1	54	6
9	1	32	2	55	1
10	5	33	4	56	4
11	5	34	5	57	3
12	6	35	6	58	5
13	3	36	2	59	2
14	1	37	3	60	5
15	2	38	1	61	4
16	2	39	4	62	2
17	1	40	5	63	6
18	6	41	6	64	1
19	5	42	2	65	3
20	3	43	6	66	5
21	3	44	4	67	4
22	4	45	5	68	1
23	6	46	3	69	3

only a partial list, a potential bias problem is evident in only this portion. Note that there is no individual assigned to condition 4 until the twenty-second subject appears. Although the groups will most probably even out by the time the 120th is reached, the cell n for condition 4 must be obtained in greater proportion from the later subjects than other groups. The problem would be more pronounced if a smaller total N were involved in the study. It is not unreasonable to suspect that certain subject variables may be operative in the promptness with which subjects appear for experimentation (e.g., motivation, interest, or compulsiveness). These variables, which are essentially unknown but highly probable, may well be influential in the way in which a subject performs the experimental task. If in fact such influences are operative in, say, the first thirty or so subjects to appear, condition 4 is likely to be systematically different than the other groups (by the time the thirtieth subject appears, the group count is as follows: group 1, five subjects; group 2, five subjects; group 3, seven subjects; group 4, two subjects; group 5, five subjects; group 6, six subjects).

One method of circumventing the problem exemplified above is known as *block randomization*. This procedure considers a block to be a sequence in which

Table 8-2. Example of randomized block assigned sequence list for six-group study

Subject number	Group assigned	Subject number	Group assigned	Subject number	Group assigned
1	5	24	6	47	4
2	1	25	5	48	2
3	6	26	2	49	3
4	3	27	4	50	5
5	2	28	1	51	2
6	4	29	3	52	1
7	5	30	6	53	4
8	3	31	6	54	6
9	2	32	1	55	5
10	4	33	4	56	2
11	1	34	3	57	3
12	6	35	2	58	1
13	2	36	5	59	4
14	6	37	4	60	6
15	1	38	1	61	6
16	4	39	2	62	5
17	5	40	6	63	2
18	3	41	3	64	1
19	5	42	5	65	4
20	2	43	3	66	3
21	1	44	1	67	1
22	4	45	6	68	5
23	3	46	5	69	6

each condition appears once. The researcher draws subjects at random within a block, ignoring all digit repetitions until each condition has appeared once (the completion of a block). As soon as each condition has appeared, a new block is begun, and this procedure is repeated until the sample N is totally assigned to conditions. Table 8-2 presents an example of the previously assigned subject pool that has been sequenced using block randomization. Each block in the table is set off by horizontal lines under the condition digit that completes that respective block. The subject assignment to conditions is considerably different than was exemplified in Table 8-1. Because of the control imposed by block randomization, the group proportions existing by the time the thirtieth subject appears are substantially changed. Beyond this control, however, the assignment within blocks is random, presenting little reason to expect systematic bias between group characteristics.

Turn to p. 215 and complete Simulation 8-4.

Comments on chance assignment. It is evident from the preceding discussion that all random assignment procedures do not absolutely ensure the absence of bias between groups. The use of what has been called free random assignment procedures (those without nonchance controls such as were imposed in block randomization) is vulnerable to the generation of nonequivalent groups occasionally. Although such bias occurs infrequently, the statistical theory on which random procedures are based says that atypical groups will appear a certain percent of the time by chance.

There are precautions that may be taken by the researcher to circumvent such occurrences. Captive assignment may permit the researcher certain checkpoints that are not possible with sequential assignment. By virtue of the actual identification of all subjects before beginning the study, the researcher may be able to determine equivalency of groups on a preexperimental basis. To accomplish this, relevant measures must either be available or administered before the initiation of experimental procedures. Since the exact composition of groups is known, groups may be compared on these preexperimental measures before administering the treatments. If the groups are statistically different, they may be thrown back into the sample pool and reassigned until they are equivalent. Such procedures are not possible with sequential assignment, since the exact individuals serving as subjects in each group are not identified preexperimentally. Although this is a useful safeguard, its function certainly depends on the relevance of the preexperimental measure. If the measure is not related to the experimental task (for example, if the task involved discrimination learning and the preexperimental measure is shoe size), it may be of little use in estimating group equivalency with respect to related subject variables. The preexperimental group comparison also presumes that other unmeasured, experimentally related variables are not different. One must remain cognizant that precise equivalency may not be determined in a "money-back–guaranteed" fashion. However, the use of certain controls in combination with random procedures greatly enhances the confidence one may have that the groups are probably not different in a significant manner.

As was mentioned previously, sequential assignment does not permit the same type of preexperimental checkpoints that captive assignment does. Certain precautions may be taken, however, to circumvent total experimenter helplessness. Despite the fact that researchers do not have actual subject names available, they do have the information necessary to scrutinize the sequence of assignment. It is always prudent to carefully examine the assignment sequence list to identify possible idiosyncrasies that may result in biased assignment of subjects to conditions. Such an atypical sequence was evident in Table 8-1. If a potential problem is noted, the investigator may then exercise some control options. One possibility may be to specify some a priori rules and reassign in a free random fashion. Such rules may be that no more than three (or some specified number) consecutive subjects may be assigned to any one treatment condition. Likewise the block randomization procedure may be a desirable option to control for extremes in assignment sequence occurring by chance.

An additional procedure that might be used does not actually facilitate equivalent groups but does more to guard against flagrant misinterpretation of results. Recall the previous discussion of preexperimental measures on subjects that are related to the experimental task. Since complete groups are not identified, such data are not useful before instituting the treatment. These measures may, however, serve for a group comparison on a post hoc basis or after the study has been completed. Such comparisons would provide the researcher with information concerning the pretreatment status of the groups. If the groups are not different, the researcher might then proceed to interpret the data as if group equivalency were in effect (at least assumed) before the treatment. If, on the other hand, the groups appear different on a pretreatment basis, considerable care must be exercised in results interpretation (if the data are amenable to meaningful interpretation at all). An alternative to this last possibility may be found through specific statistical procedures. Analysis of covariance is a method whereby statistical equivalency may be imposed to facilitate interpretation of results if pretreatment differences exist. This procedure, however, in no way offsets the desirability of group equivalency that exists as a part of actual group composition.

The importance of subject assignment procedures cannot be overemphasized in studies in which group comparisons are being made. Obviously in group studies this is a central concern in the technical soundness of an investigation. It therefore demands the researcher's careful attention both in terms of planning and implementation.

Assignment by controlled methods

We have previously discussed subject assignment procedures in which the researcher exerted certain controls in contrast to using free random assignment. Those procedures did, however, rely *primarily* on chance with the controls or restrictions being imposed as added modifications. This section explores methods that primarily rely on control and, in some cases, use chance procedures as secondary modifications.

Probably the first method that comes to mind under controlled assignment is experimental matching. There are several specific procedures that generically fall under the matching method. Generally speaking, experimental matching differs from random methods in that the researcher attempts to *force* group equivalency on a given dimension using data that are available on a preexperimental basis. For example, suppose it had been determined that measured mental age was an important variable related to subject performance on a given task. Under such circumstances the researcher may wish to have groups that are equivalent on mental age. Using experimental matching, the researcher would see to it that the groups involved were not different on mental age.

As was noted earlier, there are some alternatives in the way an experimental match may be implemented. The researcher may decide to perform a group match, in which case the only concern is that group means and variances are equal. Since the primary concern with a group match involves the composite representation of the control variable (i.e., means and variance), those are the focus of monitoring during group formulation. Usually the entire sample is listed in rank order on the control measure (mental age in the earlier example). With this completed, the highest subject is usually arbitrarily assigned to one of the conditions (e.g., treatment 1). The second highest student is then assigned to treatment 2, the third to treatment 3, and so on until one subject has been assigned to each condition. Once that has been accomplished, the usual procedure is to then reverse the order, for example, beginning with treatment 3, then 2, then 1, for purposes of assigning the second subject in each group. This procedure is continued until a complete cell n has been constituted for each treatment and the total N assigned. Although this procedure will usually generate little difference in group means, it is frequently the case that the researcher will carefully monitor group means to ensure similarity. If statistically different means do occur in following such procedures, it is not unusual to find group mean adjustment's being made. Since the group mean is the concern, adjustments may be made by subject substitution. The use of such procedures to control means occasionally makes it difficult to achieve equal variances between groups at the same time. Although this difficulty has been noted by experimental psychologists (e.g., Underwood, 1966), methods for avoiding the difficulty have not received serious attention to date. It is not uncommon for group matches to primarily focus on means.

A second approach to conducting an experimental match involves what is usually called assignment of matched pairs. Assignment of matched pairs, as the label suggests, is a procedure whereby a subject-by-subject match is accomplished, again, for purposes of formulating presumed equivalent groups. To perform such a subject assignment, the researcher, as before, has a preexperimental measure that is related to performance on the experimental task. He or she then scrutinizes all the scores in the sample in search of subjects with equal or nearly equal scores. If three groups are to be formed, three subjects must be drawn with "matched" scores. Such subjects are usually then assigned to the three conditions. This procedure is continued until cell n's are completed.

One basic requirement for either group or subject-by-subject matches is the preexperimental measure on which the control dimension is based. The match measures are usually implemented in one of two fashions: (1) using a task that is separate but highly related to that which is involved in the treatment, or (2) using the initial performance level on the treatment task itself. The first source of match data seems self-explanatory, but there are certain specific concerns that must be addressed. Probably the most pressing area involves the strength of the relationship between scores on the control measure and performance on the experimental task. It is usually prudent for the researcher to have statistical evidence of such relationship either from previous research or pilot correlations computed in preparation for the experiment. If the researcher merely assumes a relationship, the design is seriously weakened in terms of control.

The second source of match data mentioned above involved initial subject performance on the experimental task itself. This is frequently a convenient method of obtaining control dimension data. Inherent in this procedure, however, are certain requirements concerning the logistic characteristics of the experimental task. First, it is obvious that the task must be constructed in a fashion that requires multiple trials or responses from the subjects. Some learning tasks are designed in this way and permit a series of trials until the subject's performance reaches a given criterion level. To implement the match, the researcher provides each subject a few trials on the experimental task. After this has been accomplished, performances on these trials are scrutinized and the match is performed. Then the remainder of the experiment is conducted with the difference in treatments being implemented at this point.

Beyond the logistics of the task, using initial performance for match data has an additional concern that must not be ignored. This involves the strength of the relationship between performance on the initial trials (match data) and total performance. It seems likely that performance on a given task ought to be highly related to subsequent performance on that same task. This may not be the case in all circumstances, however. In fact, on some experimental tasks the initial phases of performance are different from the later performance and occasionally the total performance scores. It is not wise, therefore, to assume a relationship in the absence of some evidence, even on the same task.

Experimental matching enjoyed considerable popularity in the earlier years of behavioral science. However, there are several difficulties that were encountered with experimental matching that have led researchers to move more in favor of random techniques as a means of equating groups. Perhaps the primary work that began this move was Fisher's classic work published in 1925 entitled *Statistical Methods for Research Workers.* Although the move has been gradual, it has been of sufficient magnitude to generate statements such as that of Campbell and Stanley (1963) who suggest that "matching as a substitute for randomization is taboo even for quasi-experimental designs [p. 185]." The nature of difficulties with experimental matching has been discussed widely (e.g., Stanley and Beeman, 1958; Prehm, 1966; Drew, 1969), and these difficulties are of sufficient importance that the beginning researcher needs to be at least introduced to them. Since there are situations in which it is not possible to effectively use random assignment, knowledge concerning the pitfalls of experimental matching becomes doubly important when it must be used.

From the outset certain logistic restrictions are evident with experimental matching. Using either group or matched pairs procedures, it is necessary to have preexperimental data available on subjects before assignment to groups. To have these data available, it is obviously necessary that the sample be captive (in the earlier sense of actually having individuals identified). If the exact individuals were not identified (such as was described under sequential assignment), the researcher could not obtain match data and perform the preexperimental match.

One of the most perplexing problems with experimental matching involves the control variable itself. Because any given variable is chosen as the one on which groups are matched, it is assumed to be an important factor for control. It has been repeatedly stated that such a variable should not be used based only on assumptive evidence of importance, although it is not unusual to find this to be the primary basis for choice. In both group and paired matching procedures, it is important that sound evidence of the relationship between the match variable and experimental task performance be available. Beyond the relationship question, however, are some additional implicit assumptions that concern the match variable.

Although it is not uncommon to encounter match design studies with more than one control variable, for the moment examine the case in which subjects are matched on one dimension. By the selection of *that* variable for matching or control, the researcher is explicitly indicating its perceived importance. At the same time one must ask certain questions concerning the other variables on which subjects were not matched. (Remember, the focus is momentarily on the case of matching on a single dimension.) Since there is no match on the multitude of other possible dimensions, the assumption may be made that they are not important for control. The reasoning here is highly tenuous. The point being made is that the logic used in selecting the match variable (that it is important) is not easily reversed (those not selected are not important). Yet by ignoring other variables, the design itself may suggest such reasoning.

By exploring this issue just a bit further, it becomes evident that the unattended variables may indeed create problems. In the process of matching subjects, the researcher is, in fact, placing subjects in groups in a fashion that is systematic. A serious unknown is the degree to which this process introduces systematic bias between the conditions on the unmatched (perhaps unknown) variables. In fact, there is reason to suspect that this may have occurred. Random assignment, on the other hand, gives little reason to expect systematic differences between groups. The very process involved is aimed at creating groups that are unbiased on both known and unknown variables. This is a strength that is built into random assignment and that is essentially absent in matching procedures.

It has been mentioned that the researcher using matching procedures for subject assignment frequently selects more than one variable for control. It is not uncommon to encounter reported matching studies in which several dimensions are controlled ("subjects were matched on sex, IQ, socioeconomic status . . ."). At least two concerns need to be addressed under such circumstances. Despite the addition of more control variables, the issues discussed previously remain as design concerns. Human subjects are extremely complex. It is almost inconceivable that *all* the possible dimensions that may influence subject performance can be considered and controlled. The unknown or unattended influences are still highly suspect with regard to being potential contaminators. The second concern is one of pure logistics. As the number of match variables increases, the difficulty of implementing a match is also increased greatly. It is enough of a task to simply find matched subjects on a single dimension. The magnitude of the problem is increased severalfold, for example, just by adding one additional control. Finding an adequate match with more than two becomes a task that creates several additional problems. Because of the difficulty in performing such a match, the precision with which it is accomplished is frequently sacrificed. Such sacrifices usually begin with rather small deviations (e.g., subjects were matched on measured IQ within ±5 points) but often are necessarily increased as the subject pool nears exhaustion.

The difficulties discussed above are generally more prevalent in pair-match procedures than group matches. The fact remains, however, that these are pitfalls that are encountered in using any experimental match designs. Random subject assignment provides a more powerful procedure when it can be used. Additionally, the use of random assignment with analysis of covariance has also been suggested as preferable to experimental matching on a number of dimensions (Stanley and Beeman, 1958; Prehm, 1966; Drew, 1969).

SUMMARY COMMENTS: SUBJECT SELECTION AND ASSIGNMENT

After discussing different procedures for subject selection and assignment, a frequent question that remains unanswered is, "Which procedure is the best?" This question cannot be answered in a general way that speaks to all conditions. Under different contingencies, different procedures are most appropriate. Likewise the convenience often required in a field setting may alter the exact procedures required. Despite my preference for random assignment procedures, there are times when matching may be more practical. The one factor that should be kept in mind, however, is that convenience or pragmatic considerations ought not be permitted to intercede to a degree that rigor is sacrificed. Although the press of difficult situations often makes this tempting, if such sacrifice is permitted, the study probably is reduced in terms of meaningfulness, and perhaps the worth of conducting it is in question.

The replacement of lost subjects frequently presents a difficult problem. It was previously mentioned that many researchers operate from a subject pool drawn from the larger population. This is an appropriate manner in which to replace lost subjects, assuming that the subject pool is constructed in a careful manner that will permit reasonable generalizability. Certain precautionary statements need mention, however. First, subject mortality may present a serious problem in group studies (previously discussed in detail in Chapter 7). If subjects are lost differentially from groups, the replacement of subjects may create an internal validity problem. It is not unusual to be faced with considerable lack of information about lost subjects. In particular, the question is raised about why they were lost and, if replaced randomly from a subject pool, whether the replacements are similar to those who were lost. If, for example, lack of subject vitality is a prime reason for mortality (e.g., the weaker rats die), randomly sampled replacements will most likely be different, since random sampling will probably include strong as well as weak subjects. Since the lower subject vitality is (hypothetically) the reason for mortality, the group composition has a good probability of being changed by the replacements (if all subjects lost are weak and replacements are equally divided, weak and strong, the group as a whole is stronger). As noted in Chapter 7, the differential loss (and replacement) of subjects from groups may well result in internal validity bias. Likewise, replacements may alter the generalizability of results if the representativeness of the group has changed. Subject replacement is frequently necessary, and therefore it is vital that the researcher be aware of potential problems that may be generated in the process.

REFERENCES

Arkin, H., and Colton, R. R. *Tables for statisticians.* New York: Barnes & Noble, Inc., 1950.

Bailey, K. D. *Methods of social research.* New York: The Free Press, 1978.

Campbell, D. T., and Stanley, J. C. Experimental and quasi-experimental designs for research on teaching. In N. L. Gage (Ed.), *Handbook of research on teaching.* Chicago: Rand McNally & Co., 1963.

Cochran, W. G. *Sampling techniques* (2nd ed.). New York: John Wiley & Sons, Inc., 1963.

Drew, C. J. Covariate matching: a methodological note. *Perceptual and Motor Skills,* 1969, *28,* 799-800.

Fisher, R. A. *Statistical methods for research workers* (1st ed.). London: Oliver & Boyd, 1925.

Kerlinger, F. N. *Foundations of behavioral research* (1st ed.). New York: Holt, Rinehart and Winston, Inc., 1964.

Prehm, H. J. Verbal learning research in mental retardation. *American Journal of Mental Deficiency,* 1966, *71,* 42-47.

Prehm, H. J. Rote learning and memory in retarded children: some implications for the teaching-learning process. *Journal of Special Education,* 1967, *1,* 397-399.

Prehm, H. J. Practical implications of research on the learning and retention performance of the retarded. Paper presented at the International Conference on Mental Retardation, Montpelier, France, 1968.

Stanley, J. C., and Beeman, E. Y. Restricted generalization, bias, and loss of power that may result from matching groups. *Psychological Newsletter,* 1958, *9,* 88-102.

Sudman, S. *Applied sampling.* New York: Academic Press, Inc. 1976.

Underwood, B. J. *Experimental psychology* (2nd ed.). New York: Appleton-Century-Crofts, 1966.

SIMULATIONS

SIMULATION 8-1

Topic: Population definition

Background statement: This simulation represents one part of a hypothetical population frame construction for sampling purposes. The population is defined as "all third-year male students enrolled in West Rebew State." Computer printout material was generated for all students and coded with the digit 1 for first-year students, 2 for second-year students, and so on. Below is a reproduction of one page of that printout.

Task to be performed: Construct a portion of the population frame from the list presented. Do so by placing an X by each name that will become a part of the population frame.

Bacco, F. Donald	1		Barclay, Robert B.	1
Bach, Jay T.	3		Bardin, Robyne Anne	3
Bachman, Thomas	4		Barker, James R.	3
Back, Donald R.	2		Barker, Sara	4
Back, Laura J.	6		Barnes, Linda F.	2
Backer, Jane Z.	3		Barnes, Mike L.	3
Backman, Fred	1		Barnes, Scott	2
Bacon, R. Myrtle	3		Barnhart, Cyrus F.	1
Bacon, Robert F.	3		Barnumm, Daniel	4
Badger, Mike	3		Bennett, Ellen	6
Bagley, David	6		Berg, William J.	3
Bagley, Penny	2		Bernard, Clifford	4
Bailey, Bob Jo	3		Berrett, Colleen	3
Baird, James V.	6		Best, Sandy	4
Baird, Sally Jo	1		Bigelow, Randy L.	3
Banks, Vernon L.	4		Bigelow, Robert W.	3
Bannon, Diane	2		Bragg, Raymond J.	3
Barber, Anne L.	2		Brassiere, Newland	1
Barber, George	3		Burns, Sallie	2
Barber, Jeanne	1		Burton, Archibald	4
Barclay, Larry	3		Butkus, Lowell Tom	1

For feedback see p. 338.

Random number table

For the next few simulations you will be needing a random number table. A short table is therefore provided on p. 213. Random number tables are simple to use. Specific instructions will be included with each simulation concerning how it is to be used in the particular task presented.

Line	Column					
	1	2	3	4	5	6
1	10480	15011	01536	02011	81647	91646
2	22368	46573	25595	85393	30995	89198
3	24130	48360	22527	97265	76393	64809
4	42167	93093	06243	61680	07856	16376
5	37570	39975	81837	16656	06121	91782
6	77921	06907	11008	42751	27756	53498
7	99562	72905	56420	69994	98872	31016
8	96301	91977	05463	07972	18876	20922
9	89579	14342	63661	10281	17453	18103
10	85475	36857	53342	53988	53060	59533
11	28918	69578	88231	33276	70997	79936
12	63553	40961	48235	03427	49626	69445
13	09429	93969	52636	92737	88974	33488
14	10365	97336	87529	85689	48237	52267
15	07119	61129	71048	08178	77233	13916
16	51085	12765	51821	51259	77452	16308
17	02368	21382	52404	60268	89368	19885
18	01011	54092	33362	94904	31273	04146
19	52162	53916	46369	58586	23216	14513
20	07056	96728	33787	09998	42698	06691
21	48663	91245	85828	14346	09172	30168
22	54164	58492	22421	74103	47070	25306
23	32639	32363	05597	24200	13363	38005
24	29334	27001	87637	87308	58731	00256
25	02488	33062	28834	07351	19731	92420

SIMULATION 8-2

Topic: Random sampling

Background statement: You have been assigned the task of evaluating a piece of instructional material. The group for which the material is designed is defined as those children who range in age from 5 to 7 years. Your subject pool (presumably representative of all children in that age range) has been listed, and corresponding numbers have been assigned to each child's name. The numbers run from 1 to 85.

Tasks to be performed

1. Using the random number table provided, draw a sample from the subject pool to be used in the study. The size of the sample that has been determined as sufficient is thirty.

2. Construct the subject list using the code numbers that appear in the table.

Use of the random number table: For purposes of this simulation, begin in the upper left corner of the table (column 1, line 1). Place your ruler vertically on column 1 in such a way that it covers all but the first two digits in each line. When you have done this, you should see the following digits for lines 1 through 5: 10, 22, 24, 42, and 37. You are using the first two digits in each number because your population frame has 85 individuals in it, and 85 is a two-digit number. If your population frame had 120 individuals, you would cover all but the first three digits.

Now proceed down the column and list all the relevant numbers for your sample. Recall from the text that relevant numbers include those in the frame, and you ignore a given number the second time it appears. When you reach line 25, begin in the same fashion in column 2 until you have your thirty subjects.

For feedback see p. 339.

SIMULATION 8-3

Topic: Random assignment: captive

Background statement: You are conducting a study that involves two comparison groups. Your total sample is fifty subjects, and they are to be assigned to the two groups. The individuals are already identified by name so you can implement a captive random assignment.

Task to be performed: Using the random number table provided, assign the following subjects to groups A and B using captive random assignment.

1. Robert	14. David	27. Carole	40. Virginia
2. Myrna	15. Earl	28. Phil	41. Sonia
3. Ralph	16. Lorraine	29. Don	42. Anita
4. John	17. Maurice	30. Walt	43. Bruce
5. Sally	18. Terry	31. Bonnie	44. Suzanne
6. Sherry	19. Carl	32. Doug	45. Alice
7. Lois	20. Ken	33. Steve	46. Barbara
8. Andy	21. Wilmer	34. George	47. Clyde
9. Joel	22. Anne	35. Mary Ann	48. Karle
10. Thomas	23. Alan	36. Sandra	49. Kent
11. Eugene	24. Kevin	37. Larry	50. Travis
12. Dennis	25. James	38. Rick	
13. Anna	26. Kay	39. Joy	

Use of the random number table: For purposes of this simulation the technique is similar to that in simulation 8-2. First, begin in the upper left corner of the table (column 1, line 1). Place your ruler vertically on column 1 in such a way that it covers all but the first digit in each line. When you have done this, you should see the following digits for lines 1 through 5: 1, 2, 2, 4, and 3. You are using only the first digit in each number because you only have two groups, for these purposes identified as 1 and 2. Both are single-digit designations, and you therefore need only single-digit options for assignment.

Now proceed down the column and assign the subjects to the respective groups 1 and 2 in the order that they appear. Ignore irrelevant digits. Begin again in column 2, 3, and so on until you have completed your assignment. Review the text pages if further direction is necessary.

By the way, you will run out of columns on this one (that is, you will not have twenty-five subjects in either group when you finish column 6). When you get to this point, change ruler positions so that only the last digit shows in each column and begin again in column 1. You could begin again anywhere, but for feedback purposes use the last digit (which will result in 0, 8, 0, 7, and 0 for lines 1 through 5).

For feedback see p. 339.

SIMULATION 8-4

Topic: Random assignment: sequential

Background statement: You are conducting a study that involves two comparison groups. Your total sample is fifty subjects, and they are to be assigned to the two groups. The identity of the individuals, however, is not specifically known to you. They will appear at the lab in an undetermined order, which will require that you use sequential assignment to form your groups.

Task to be performed: Using the random number table provided, assign the following subject positions to groups 1 and 2 so that when the actual subjects appear they may be sequentially assigned to a group.

1.	11.	21.	31.	41.
2.	12.	22.	32.	42.
3.	13.	23.	33.	43.
4.	14.	24.	34.	44.
5.	15.	25.	35.	45.
6.	16.	26.	36.	46.
7.	17.	27.	37.	47.
8.	18.	28.	38.	48.
9.	19.	29.	39.	49.
10.	20.	30.	40.	50.

Use of the random number table: For purposes of this simulation, use the random number table in exactly the same fashion as you did in simulation 8-3. The only difference in this case is that you will be assigning the subject positions (represented by the numbers just presented) to groups, since you do not know what the names are yet.

For feedback see p. 340.

CHAPTER 9

Measures, instruments, and tasks

There are many details in conducting a research investigation that must receive attention even after the basic design or plan is determined. As previously suggested, the totality of a piece of research involves a series of interrelated parts. This chapter, midway in that series, relates directly to what has gone before (problem and design) and will vitally relate to what follows (analysis and interpretation). Although some procedural issues have been discussed previously, this chapter will specifically address measures, instruments, and tasks.

SELECTION OF CRITERION MEASURES

One of the tasks that faces the researcher during the completion of an investigation plan is the selection of a criterion measure. The "criterion measure" is synonymous with the term "dependent variable" and refers to *that which is being measured in the study.* At the outset it may be useful to reemphasize the distinction between dependent variables and the independent variable or experimental variable used in experimentation.

The "independent variable," as noted earlier, refers to the "experimental variable" in experiments (treatment), meaning that factor being studied. If the researcher is comparing the effectiveness of two instructional techniques (e.g., method A versus method B), the experimental variable is method of instruction. There are two levels or conditions within that variable, A and B. In this example the researcher is *not* measuring method of instruction; method of instruction is being studied as an independent variable. What is being measured has not been mentioned yet. It has been alluded to, however. The measure will somehow have to assess *effectiveness.* If the instruction methods were designed for teaching reading, the immediate task would be to determine how the effectiveness might be assessed. One approach might be to measure reading comprehension by the number of correct responses made by subjects on a test. In such an example the number of correct responses would be the criterion measure.

Criterion measure thus refers to that which is measured, that which is to be counted, the metric that is to be used to assess the impact of the independent variable or treatment. If a researcher were conducting a descriptive study of the height of a particular group of individuals, the criterion measure might be specified in terms of inches (as number of correct responses was the measure in the previous example). Many students are somewhat confused by the term "criterion" used as a modifier for measure. The term is primarily a result of traditional usage. In the example of reading comprehension, the criterion or acceptable method for assessing this construct was the number of correct responses. The term "criterion" is not used in the same sense as a performance goal to be achieved (such as the idea that students must reach a certain performance level or criterion before they are certified as having passed a course). Instead it is a means of measuring the actual level of performance that a subject accomplished.

To say that the researcher must select a criterion measure in the process of designing a study may sound somewhat pedantic to the informed reader. Many times, however, the beginning researcher is frustrated in attempting to identify a criterion measure for thesis or dissertation purposes. Often the frustration and difficulties arise from confusion in the areas discussed above.

Amid the confusion regarding independent and dependent variables, there is also a conceptual concern that must receive attention. This consideration involves the level of specificity regarding the criterion measure selected. Nunnally (1967) has made a useful distinction concerning those factors that can and cannot be measured. He uses the terms "objects" and "attributes." Objects are constructs that cannot be measured directly. Their existence (or the degree to which they exist) must be inferred from the measurement of certain attributes that are observable and are believed to indicate something about the object. An example of an object is learning. It has long been acknowledged in experimental psychology that one cannot measure learning directly. One can, however, infer that learning exists or has occurred through observation of certain performance dimensions. In this example, learning is considered the object, whereas the performance (e.g., number of correct responses) is an attribute of the object.

Because objects are not directly measurable, they cannot be considered for use as criterion measures. The attributes of the object, because they are observable, countable, or in some fashion amenable to having a metric applied, achieve the level of specificity that must be present in a criterion measure. The object usually represents a more global construct (e.g., self-concept, intelligence, or anxiety), whereas the attribute is a more specific, definable, observable type of factor that presumably reflects something about the nature of the object.

Obviously the relationship between a criterion measure and the construct under investigation is critical. To use Nunnally's terminology, one must be assured that the criterion measure selected is indeed an attribute of the object being studied. Although this is an apparent and important consideration, it is one that is frequently troublesome for the beginning researcher. There are no prescribed rules for determining that the presumed relationship between criterion measures and constructs being studied is sound. Frequently, previous research has pioneered the establishment of accepted criterion measures. If this is true, the researcher has some guideposts that will facilitate the process. When such guidance is absent, however, the researcher must rely on experience, judgment, and intuition to assess the logical relationship between a given criterion measure and the factor being studied.

Perhaps a few examples of what is meant would be helpful. In the previous example involving a descriptive study of a selected group's height, the suggested criterion measure was inches. This is a logical criterion measure, since the inch is the primary unit for determining length in the United States. It would be foolish, however, to attempt to describe a particular group's height using a criterion measure of ohms. Even beyond the matter of accepted measurement units, a criterion measure of ohms does not hold an intuitive or logical relationship to the purpose of a study that involves a description of height. Likewise, if the purpose of an investigation was to test a particular dimension of a psychological theory, the criterion measure selected should have a logical or established relationship to that psychological construct. Usually, one would not want to use performance on mathematical computation problems as a measure of self-concept. The behavior that is observed or counted as a criterion measure must have a stronger intuitive relationship to the construct being studied than is evidenced between computation of mathematics problems and that elusive construct of self-concept.

Many other concerns must also be addressed in selecting criterion measures. Assuming that the researcher has attained a measurable level of specificity and that the relationship of the measure to the topic is acceptable, he or she may still be faced with other decisions. It is not unusual to be faced with two or three possible criterion measures that are acceptable with respect to specificity and the relationship to the construct under investigation. Under such circumstances, the choice may be based on several considerations.

One characteristic that may suggest the selection of a given measure over other alternatives involves the communication efficiency of the measure. Which measure is the most efficient means for investigating and communicating about a given problem? In the earlier example concerning the descriptive study of height, it was suggested that the criterion measure of inches might be appropriate. Of course, the inch is not the only measure for height. People who are horse enthusiasts are well acquainted with another measure of height known as hands. For a descriptive study of human height, however, hands would seem to be a less efficient measure than inches. Because nearly everyone who might read a report concerning the height of humans is accustomed to using inches, hands would probably have to be translated into the more orthodox measure. Since such a translation is cumbersome and unnecessary because of the availability of inches as an alternative, there is good reason to prefer the use of inches in the first place. This choice is predicated on the assumption that the hands measure does not have other properties that make it more desirable.

Other considerations are also involved in the selection of criterion measures. One important factor is the *sensitivity* of the measure. It is possible that one measure might be more sensitive to subject performance differences than the alternative being considered. In the interest of precision, it is usually preferable to use the most sensitive measure available, assuming that other considerations do not make its use undesirable (such as subject reaction or other logistic difficulties). For example, in cognitive psychology a great deal of research has been conducted on the learning of verbal material. Because of the extensive work in verbal learning, a sophisticated technological base has been developed with specific subareas of investigation. A substantial amount of research has been conducted that focuses on the rate at which subjects acquire knowledge. Two possible criterion measures for rate of acquisition serve well to exemplify the sensitivity issue.

For example purposes, say that the subjects are required to learn a list of eight paired words (e.g., dog-fist, lion-water, baby-sky). One attempt at each of the eight pairs is defined as a trial. For criterion measure purposes one might record the number of trials that it takes a subject to make three correct responses on each pair. An alternative criterion measure might involve counting the number of errors a subject makes in reaching the three-correct-response level of proficiency. In this example the number of errors is the more sensitive measure, whereas trials represents a more gross measure. This is the case since a subject may make a variable number of errors (reflecting variations in acquired knowledge) within a list trial. Consequently, the number of trials may be the same for two subjects, but rather substantial differences may exist in the number of errors committed. Because errors seem more reflective of the knowledge being acquired, it is the more sensitive measure and therefore is probably preferred as a criterion measure. Although this example comes from experimental research, the same issue is equally important in nonexperimental investigations as will be seen in future sections.

To summarize regarding the selection of a criterion measure, there must be a logical relationship between the measure and the topic being studied (it must be an attribute of the object), it must be specific and observable (one must be able to determine its existence either by counting or in some fashion certifying its existence or absence), and it should be efficient and sensitive to performance differences. Although this discussion of criterion measures follows the chapters concerned with design and planning, at least some attention is usually given to measurement in the later stages of problem distillation.

Turn to p. 236 and complete Simulations 9-1 and 9-2.

INSTRUMENTS AND TASKS

Hand in hand with discussion of criterion measures is the issue of the instrument or task to be used. Instruments or tasks presented to subjects must generate behavior that may be recorded in the form of the criterion measure. Therefore, there must be a logical relationship between the instrument the researcher selects and the constructs being studied. The instrument or task (usually contrived, constructed, or selected from some that exist) must be so designed as to generate behavior that is presumed to be an attribute of the object-topic under investigation. For example, suppose a researcher were conducting a survey aimed at ascertaining the political affiliation of a particular group of people. To determine a subject's political affiliation, the researcher must generate some response from the subject that will identify to which political party he or she belongs. An efficient way of obtaining this type of data might involve simply asking the subject either through the use of a mailed questionnaire or by personally interviewing the subjects. In the first case the questionnaire is the instrument that generates the subject's response, and in the latter example the subject's response is given directly to the interviewer. Either of these approaches could serve the purpose of providing an acceptable criterion measure for the study. The selection of which to use would depend on many considerations related to the investigation being planned.

Instruments and tasks vary greatly as one reviews the various approaches to research. Some experimentation may actually include a task that the subjects perform and their performance results in the criterion measure. Others may involve the administration of a test instrument of some type. Nonexperimental research, as has been discussed, may be undertaken by means of surveys (questionnaires or interviews) and observation studies (although observation may be the data collection technique used in experimentation as well). In each, there is some instrument that is used to generate the data and the researcher must give careful attention to its characteristics, advantages, and potential problem areas.

The process of generating the actual data in an investigation may be conceived as an interaction between certain subject characteristics and the properties of the task or instrument. This, of course, implies that once the subject perceives the stimulus of the task, it in some fashion may alter his or her responsivity. For example, it is likely that a subject's responsivity is altered somewhat if a part of the treatment or task involves receiving an electric shock. It seems reasonable to expect that such an experience may result in, perhaps, a bit of anxiety, a heightened sensitivity, or any number of changes in subject properties.

The researcher must be doubly concerned about altered subject properties in situations in which the same subjects are administered more than one treatment or measure. In the strictest sense, the subject cannot be assumed to be the same after the first measure has been taken. This was exemplified in several sections in Chapter 7. There are times, however, when it is not feasible to do anything but administer multiple measures. In fact, certain investigations make it a desirable part of the design. However, the present discussion does not consider it as a desirable or built-in part of the study. When multiple measures are administered, the researcher seems to have two basic options, to systematically administer one before the other or to rotate the order of administration in some fashion.

If one of the measures is obviously less sensitive to subject changes, then that measure should be administered after the other. An example might involve a situation in which teachers were supposed to evaluate certain instructional materials and the researcher also wanted to know how much information the subjects had about the material. With these two example measures, one is the obvious first measure that should be administered. The evaluation measure is probably more sensitive than an information recall test. If the teacher did not do well on the information test, the evaluation might be systematically lowered. It is doubtful, however, that subjects will do less than their optimum on an information test because of the evaluation rating. Therefore it seems reasonable that the evaluation measure should precede the information test.

If there is little apparent difference in measure sensitivity, priority of administration is not relevant. Under these circumstances, the researcher usually desires some assurance that neither measure systematically comes before the other, thus creating an unaccounted-for influence. To accomplish this, measures are generally counterbalanced (i.e., measure A then B; B then A) or randomly ordered. All that these latter procedures do is mask or mix the influence of each respective measure on the other equally.

The types of instruments and tasks that can be used in research are nearly endless, limited only by the researcher's imagination and the specific nature of the study. Differences are clearly evident between tasks even when several investigations are part of a program of research on the same topic. Researchers are constantly attempting to refine their instruments or perhaps study a slightly different dimension of the same construct. Because these types of variations are a routine part of science, it makes little sense to present a list of specific tasks or instruments as being representative or desirable. Researchers must become well acquainted with the literature in their particular area of investigation to identify those that may be useful or could be modified to function effectively. There are, however, certain potential difficulties that are somewhat generalizable to various types of tasks and various types of instruments. These problem areas should be carefully considered as one selects a task or adapts one that already exists.

Performance range and experimental tasks

One of the most frequent difficulties encountered in task selection, particularly with regard to experimentation, involves the range of performance that the task will permit. The performance range of a task refers to the *variation in responses possible within the limits imposed by uppermost and lowest possible performance scores on the task.* Take the example of a hypothetical achievement test that is being used as a task. Suppose the number of correct responses is being scored as the criterion measure. If the total number of questions on the test is 25, the performance range would have a ceiling of 25 and a floor of zero (if the subject made no correct responses). The desirable situation, of course, is to have the task designed so that the subjects can perform without being limited by the task itself. Unless this is the case, the level of performance probably reflects the task limits rather than the experimental treatment (e.g., method of instruction). In many cases it is difficult to select or contrive a task that will permit subjects to perform fully to their ability without being hampered in some fashion by task performance range.

Ceiling effect. If the subjects in an investigation (or a subgroup of subjects) perform the task so well that they "top out," this is what is known as a ceiling effect. A ceiling effect occurs when *the performance range is so restricted or limited on the upper end that subjects cannot perform to their greatest ability.* Such results would be called an experimental artifact, since they represent an artificially determined performance level generated by constraints of the experiment rather than constraints of ability. The term "ceiling effect" accurately describes what happens to the subjects. This may be aptly illustrated by an analogy. Suppose a researcher were to conduct a descriptive study concerning the jumping ability of a professional basketball team, using as the criterion measure the upper height reached (in feet and inches) on a wall by each subject's right hand while jumping as high as possible. The results would look rather strange if the study were conducted in a room with an 8-foot ceiling (the usual height of ceilings in residences). Not only would the ballplayers be restricted in their performance by the ceiling, the researcher might end up with some brain-injured subjects (certainly the seven-footers).

More in the realm of behavioral science, Fig. 9-1, *A,* provides a visual example of results in which a ceiling effect was probably operative. In this hypothetical experiment, mentally retarded subjects were compared with nonretarded subjects to assess the effectiveness of two teaching methods. The number of correct responses on a test served as the criterion measure with a task performance range of 0 to 25. If the researcher is not alert to the apparent ceiling effect, an interpretation may be made of these results that is in error. One interpretation might suggest that there is a differential effectiveness between teaching methods for some subjects but not all. Method A seems superior to method

B for retarded subjects, but that difference is not evident with nonretarded subjects. This would be a logical interpretation if the nonretarded subjects had not performed at or near the upper limit of the performance range. Because their group means are so close to the task ceiling, one might suspect that their performance represents task limitations rather than the effectiveness of teaching methods. This possibility becomes even more likely when one considers the fact that the results are in terms of group means. Because the means for the nonretarded

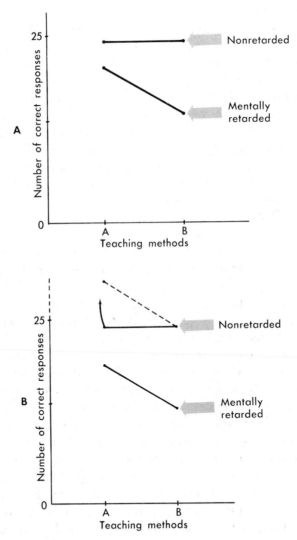

Fig. 9-1. A, Graphed data showing probable ceiling effect. **B,** Possible results without task-generated ceiling effect.

group are so near 25, there were undoubtedly a large proportion of those subjects who made correct responses on all test items. One has no way of knowing how many correct responses they might have made if the task ceiling had been raised.

Fig. 9-1, *B*, portrays hypothetical results that might have been obtained if the task performance range had been expanded in terms of upper limits. Interpretation of these data may be much different than was previously suggested under the conditions of the ceiling effect. One aspect of the interpretation that would certainly change would be the absence of differential effectiveness between teaching methods for nonretarded subjects. The data presented in Fig. 9-1, *B*, suggest that teaching method A is more effective than method B for both retarded and nonretarded subjects. This represents important information that was not evident in Fig. 9-1, *A*. It is also information that is not obtainable since the imaginary study in Fig. 9-1, *A*, would not permit its observation. Thus with a ceiling effect operative, one does not know whether there was no difference between method A and B with nonretarded subjects because (1) the methods were not differentially effective, or (2) the range of task performance was so restricted that these subjects could not perform to the best of their ability. The situation represented in Fig. 9-1, *A*, is often referred to as a result in which possible differences are "masked."

Floor effect. Task restrictions may occur at the lower end of the performance range as well as the upper end. In situations in which *variation in subject performance is restricted by the lower limit of the task,* results are influenced by what is called a *floor effect.* In the previous example, zero correct responses was the lower limit of possible subject performance. Since zero responses is the floor with any task, the difficulty of the material itself becomes a primary determiner of lower limit.

Fig. 9-2, *A*, presents results of a hypothetical investigation in which a floor effect would seem to be operative. Using the same research variables as before, the number of correct responses serves as the criterion measure for a comparison of teaching methods with retarded and nonretarded subjects. Since the mean correct responses for the retarded groups are so near zero, one suspects the task floor is limiting possible performance variation. Again, unless the researcher is alert to this apparent artifact in the data, the interpretation may well be in error. If the floor effect were ignored, the data in Fig. 9-2, *A*, might result in an interpretation that method A was more effective than method B for nonretarded subjects but not for retarded subjects. One does not know whether the absence of differences between methods A and B with retarded persons is caused by the fact that they are not differentially effective or that the task itself was so difficult that possible influence of the methods is masked.

Fig. 9-2, *B*, portrays hypothetical results from this same study that might have been obtained if the task performance range had been expanded with re-

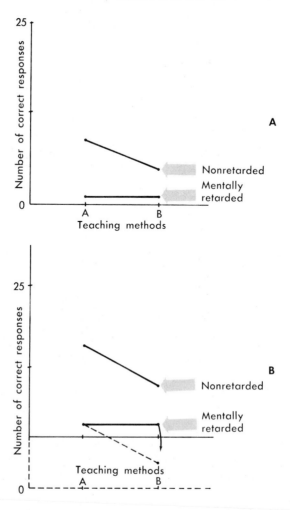

Fig. 9-2. A, Graphed data showing possible floor effect. **B,** Possible results without task-generated floor effect.

gard to lower limits. In this case such a change might have been accomplished by using less difficult material for the test. Easier items might have permitted the retarded groups to exhibit some performance variation. Although the floor is still zero correct responses, one has reason to believe that variation of the retarded subjects with less difficult material (Fig. 9-2, *B*) is more representative of their ability to perform than was the case when the lower limit was masking performance. Interpretation of these data, as before, would probably be different from the interpretation for data in Fig. 9-2, *A*. It would now seem that method A was more effective than method B for both groups of subjects.

Alteration of task performance range. It is desirable to find a task performance range that does not itself limit the response variation of subjects. Since the objective is to study subjects (their behavior, physiological sensitivity, ability, etc.), logically the subject must be permitted to perform. As the experimenter progresses in a program of research, it is not at all uncommon to find that alteration of the task range is necessary. Usually *determination of the need to expand the performance range is based on results that involve an apparent floor or ceiling effect.*

As was suggested earlier, expanding the performance range of the task may be accomplished in a number of different ways. What actually occurs in an experimental setting is that the subject interacts with the task. The task presents a certain set of properties, and the subject uses a certain set of abilities (e.g., visual perception, auditory perception, or physiological maturity). These two components of subject and task combine in some fashion to generate the results observed. To obtain nonartifactual data with respect to performance range, researchers may alter either of these two components. Thus far it is the task that has been altered. Depending on the circumstances, they may elect to use different subjects (e.g., younger or brighter) to avoid performance range problems. Younger subjects, for example, may circumvent a ceiling effect if performance level is related to age. Experimenters must, however, be somewhat cautious in using a subject change to alter performance range problems. If there is a substantial change in the subject description, it is probable that a different organism is being studied (i.e., developmental differences). This is a particularly delicate matter if the primary focus of the research is the subject (e.g., response properties of the subject). It is not always the case, however, that the subject is the central focus. There may be investigations in which the primary interest is the task (e.g., stimulus properties of a given instructional material). Under such circumstances the researcher may be more willing to change subject characteristics than task properties.

Subject characteristics are more commonly the focus of investigation than task properties. Therefore alteration of task properties represents the most common approach to circumventing a floor or ceiling effect. The fashion in which this may be accomplished was clearly exemplified in a series of studies that investigated the effects of organizing material on subjects' recall performance (Simpson, King, and Drew, 1970; Drew and Altman, 1970; Freston and Drew, 1974). The initial study compared mentally retarded and nonretarded subjects' recall on two lists of words, one that was organized by conceptual category (e.g., fruits and trees) and another that was randomly organized (conceptually unorganized) (Simpson, King, and Drew, 1970). Table 9-1 summarizes the results in terms of mean correct responses by group and experimental condition. The total number of words (and possible correct responses) was 25. Inspection of the group means in Table 9-1 suggests strongly that the nonretarded subjects' performance was limited by the task ceiling. These results represent essentially the

Table 9-1. Retarded and nonretarded mean correct responses by list organization*

Subject classification	List organization	
	Unorganized	Organized
Nonretarded	23.73	24.00
Retarded	12.67	17.20

*Adapted from "Free recall by retarded and nonretarded subjects as a function of input organization" by R. L. Simpson, J. D. King, and C. J. Drew, *Psychonomic Science*, 1970, *19*, 334.

Table 9-2. Mean correct responses as a function of list difficulty and organization*

List difficulty	List organization	
	Unorganized	Organized
Low	23.73	27.47
High	15.80	17.27

*Adapted from "Effects of input organization and material difficulty on free recall" by C. J. Drew and R. Altman, *Psychological Reports*, 1970, *27*, 335-370. Reprinted with permission of publishers.

same type of data contamination earlier evident in Fig. 9-1, *A*. Thus the researchers were not able to determine from this study whether organization of material has an influence on the recall of nonretarded individuals. This lack of information then became the central question for a subsequent study.

For the second study a change in task was necessary to circumvent the ceiling effect. Only nonretarded subjects were used in the second study. The age was lowered slightly but not sufficiently to be concerned about the problem of studying a different developmental level. To expand the performance range, two levels of material difficulty were used. Additionally, the list of words that each subject received was lengthened to thirty words. The easier list had a difficulty level that approximated that used in the Simpson, King, and Drew study. A second set of words was then constituted with a difficulty level substantially above the first. Table 9-2 summarizes the results in terms of mean correct responses by list difficulty and organization (Drew and Altman, 1970). Analysis of the data indicated that a significant difference did occur between performance on organized and unorganized material. At least from this it is evident that a ceiling effect had been circumvented sufficiently to permit differences to appear. Inspection of the means, however, suggests that performance on low-difficulty material was approaching the ceiling, although not nearly as much as in the previous work. This was expected, since the low-difficulty list was essentially at the same level as that used by Simpson, King, and Drew (1970) with the exception of being slightly longer.

The Drew and Altman (1970) study exemplifies well the variety of minor adjustments that may be made to influence the interaction between subjects and the task. The age level of subjects was slightly different from that in the first study (range of 19 to 24 years, whereas the first study had an age range of 21 to 27 years). This probably had little or no influence, considering the age of the subjects. It is a technique that can be used, although, as noted previously, a dramatic change in subject age may result in a developmentally different subject. This would be more of a problem with subjects who were younger than those used in these studies. A second minor adjustment was made by increasing the list length from twenty-five to thirty words. Lengthening the task must also be done somewhat cautiously, since extremely dramatic changes may also alter the nature of the study. Caution must be exercised to avoid letting the lengthened task become a test of endurance instead of accomplishing the actual purpose of the investigation. Usually this problem is avoided by running a quick pilot test of the task.

Adjusting the performance range thus may be accomplished in a number of fashions. Decisions are usually made on the basis of clinical experience and inspection of previous task-subject interactions. For example, further adjustments were made in a third study conducted subsequent to those just described. A different population was under investigation that had some unique properties causing concern. Notably this third group was diagnosed as having learning disabilities and therefore was expected to have greater variation than had been experienced in either of the previous studies. Great variability in performance seems characteristic of this population. Additionally, this variation was expected at both ends of the performance range. Consequently, three levels of material difficulty were used to ensure that subject performance would fall within the task limits. These were designed as follows: (1) a low-difficulty list, which was easier than even the low-difficulty material in Drew and Altman, (2) an intermediate-difficulty list that fell approximately between the high and low lists in Drew and Altman, and (3) a high-difficulty list that had a difficulty level above that in previous studies. As the results were analyzed, it was apparent that the judgment had been correct. All means were nicely plotted well within the performance limits imposed by the task (Freston and Drew, 1974).

Performance range: quasi-experimental designs. Task performance range difficulties present a particularly challenging problem in quasi-experimental designs. The reader will recall from Chapter 7 that a quasi-experimental design is one in which the experimenter is comparing groups that are different on the basis of some preexisting condition. Examples of quasi-experimental studies are found throughout the research literature in sociology, psychology, education, medicine, and many other disciplines. The previously cited studies in which mentally retarded subjects were compared with nonretarded subjects represent a classic situation of a quasi-experimental nature. Likewise, investigations comparing different cultural groups or physiologically different groups and developmental studies comparing several age level groups are all examples that would be considered quasi-experimental.

The problem arises in attempting to contrive a task with sufficient performance range to cover the broad range of response variation present in all groups. For example, studies in child development may necessitate a minimum of three levels of chronological age to obtain even a rough picture of developmental trends in performance. It is somewhat difficult to ascertain much developmental information from only two levels in many cases. Three or more levels permit a more complete developmental picture. Even with three age levels, the performance range may be extremely problematic. Imagine the difficulty in designing a task that will permit performance of groups with mean ages of 4, 6, and 8 years. Likewise, the problem is equally challenging for groups that are deviant on other dimensions. Such preidentified subject classifications as "high, average, and low achievement" bring with them vast differences in background information and likely wide performance ranges. When planning an investigation, the researcher must be doubly cautious in selecting the task if a quasi-experimental design is involved. A pilot test of the task with each type of subject group will probably be necessary to determine the degree to which the task will serve appropriately. This is more advisable than investing resources in a full-blown investigation that obtains results contaminated by performance range restrictions.

Turn to p. 236 and complete Simulations 9-3 and 9-4.

Questionnaires

To the beginning researcher, questionnaire studies may seem to be the easiest type of investigation to undertake. All one does is put the questions to be asked on paper, mail them out, then sit back and wait for the data to roll in. This simplicity, however, is deceptive as was shown in Chapter 6. There are many intricacies to questionnaire studies that are not apparent on the surface, and some of them relate directly to the instrument itself. This section will provide a brief examination of some issues pertaining to the construction of the questionnaire instrument.

As was noted earlier, the questionnaire represents the link between the researcher and the data. It must, in large part, stand on its own since the researcher is not usually present to prompt a response or clarify areas where the subject may be confused. This leads to a point of departure for designing the instrument. Since the researcher cannot personally work with each respondent, it is important to solve as many problems as possible as the questionnaire is being constructed. One procedure that is very useful is to mentally anticipate the difficulties that may arise. This type of process was previously encountered in the planning of experiments. Quite simply, the researcher's task is to keep Murphy's Law from ruining the study and this can be partially accomplished by asking a series of questions.

Generally speaking the researcher wants to know what factors might make a subject fail to respond and/or what might lead a subject to give inaccurate responses. Some of these issues have already been discussed. First and foremost, the respondent must be convinced that the study is legitimate and worth the effort of response. Part of this task may be managed through appropriate sponsorship and a well-written cover letter. However, the questionnaire itself must also contribute to this effort. The amount of effort required on the part of the respondent is also important—the less effort, the better. This leads to certain points that must be considered. The questionnaire should not be so lengthy that it requires a great deal of time and effort to complete. This same type of guideline pertains to the type of questions asked. If there are many open-ended questions, the respondent may not be willing to take the time to write out all the answers (whereas the same information might be obtained by questions for which the subject can merely check alternative responses). These brief examples illustrate the importance of the manner in which the questionnaire is designed and lead directly to some of the more specific issues involved in instrument construction for this type of study.

Obviously the questions being asked in a questionnaire are central to the data collection process. They must be clearly worded so that there is minimal chance for the respondent to be confused. As noted before, the best protection against problems such as this is a limited pilot test of the instrument prior to beginning the study. This is a crucial step and should always be conducted to avoid serious inaccuracies and inconsistencies in the data. However, in addition to the pilot test there are several points that need attention as the questions are being written.

One problem that must be avoided involves items that actually have two questions included in one. Bailey (1978) illustrates this type of problem with the following example: "Does your department have a special recruitment policy for racial minorities and women [p. 97]." This type of question is very typical of verbal conversation but causes serious difficulties on a questionnaire. The problem lies with the word "and," which may cause confusion for the respondent. What response should be given if the department has a policy for minorities but not for women? If the question is read literally, a "yes" answer can only be given if policies exist for both groups. A negative response might result if there is no policy for women, minorities, or both. This question might be worded more clearly by substituting "or" for "and," or it might be separated into two questions. Items should always be reviewed carefully to ensure that only one question is involved in each.

All possible precautions should be taken to avoid ambiguous questions. Certainly the example presented above was vague in terms of what response was really desired. There are, however, other types of ambiguity that the researcher should avoid such as terminology. Certain words may not be well known to the respondents and may therefore be ambiguous. (Researchers should not expect respondents to use a dictionary unless they are willing to settle for a very low response rate.) On the other end of the continuum, there may be some terms that everyone thinks they know but which have been used so much and so loosely that the meaning has become very fluid (as in the case of slang terms or phrases). Such terms or phrases may generate very inconsistent responses simply because they have different meanings to different people. Thus the researcher must be cautious regarding the use of uncommon terms as well as those that are commonly used. The best safeguard against ambiguity in a questionnaire is a pilot test of the instrument or at least a critical review by an independent but alert group of colleagues.

The points mentioned above alluded to potential problems related to the level of wording used in questionnaires. However, wording level warrants reemphasis. A delicate balance must be maintained between precise and colloquial language. After the researcher avoids the obvious problems of "four-bit" words and slang, attention should be turned to the general level of wording of the questionnaire. For this consideration, the primary concern must be the sample of subjects being studied in the survey. If the respondents are considered "well educated," the language level may be somewhat higher than if they are less educated. At times there may be an inclination to use slang phrases to establish rapport with the respondents (e.g., studying adolescents' opinions of music). Here again, caution must be exercised because of the problems with slang terminology. The same slang phrases may have widely varying definitions for adolescents in California and South Dakota.

Particular care must be taken when a survey involves sensitive topics (e.g., sex, drinking habits, use of drugs). Such topics raise the probability that respondents may not return the questionnaire or respond inaccurately. Although this is a persistent problem there are some precautions that can be taken in questionnaire construction that may help. One of the difficulties mentioned above was the possibility of inaccurate responses. Subjects may be inclined to answer in a manner that they think is "socially appropriate" rather than being completely honest. Questions may be worded in a fashion to partially offset such tendencies. For example, the same item could be phrased two different ways:

1. Do you smoke marijuana?   Yes ☐ No ☐
   If yes, how often?   Once a week ☐ Once a month ☐ Every day ☐
2. How often do you smoke marijuana?   Once a week ☐ Once a month ☐
   Every day ☐ Never ☐

Subjects may give "socially appropriate" (or "legally appropriate") answers in either case but there is less chance of this happening in question 2. The wording in number 1 makes it very easy to say "no" whereas the second wording makes it somewhat more difficult. Other approaches to sensitive topics include wording the question in a manner suggesting that the practice is either widespread or that there is no consensus regarding what is socially appropriate. Some might suggest that sensitive topics such as those noted above should simply be avoided because of the response problems involved. Certainly other less sensitive topics do not present as many difficulties, but researchers cannot avoid an area of investigation just because it may be troublesome to study. Often it is just such topics that really need to be investigated.

The order in which questions appear may also have an influence on subjects' responses. For example, it is usually best to place the easily answered questions first. In this fashion, respondents may become more committed to completing the questionnaire as they proceed since they have already spent time on the task. Similarly, if there are sensitive questions or open-ended items requiring more effort, these are best placed at the end of the questionnaire. Even if the subject refuses to answer these specific items, the responses to the other questions have already been provided and there is greater likelihood that the instrument will be mailed back.

Clearly there are many considerations involved in the construction of a questionnaire. Only a few have been examined here. Beginning researchers who anticipate undertaking such an investigation should consult reference volumes specifically focusing on these types of studies and instruments (e.g., Bailey, 1978; Berdie and Anderson, 1974). Many of the issues discussed in this section are also relevant to constructing structured interview protocols. As was mentioned previously, such interview studies are similar to questionnaire surveys except that an interviewer personally reads the questions to the subjects and records responses.

Turn to p. 238 and complete Simulation 9-5.

Observation

Observation studies were examined in Chapter 6. It is clear from this earlier discussion that the *observer* is the most central factor in such data collection. This is somewhat different from other types of research in which an instrument or task is of central importance (e.g., as the questionnaire is in questionnaire surveys). There are, however, certain instrument considerations that also must receive attention in observation research. Observers must have some means of recording the data. This section will provide a brief examination of data recording instruments that can be used for observation studies. As was mentioned in

Chapter 6, there are certain types of observation that impose very little structure on the data recorded whereas others involve a great deal of structure. This latter type of observation is the primary focus of this discussion, since the data recording instrument is a major source of structure.

Observation recording instruments may be very simple, or they may be quite complex depending on the nature of the study. The data sheet will probably be quite simple if an investigation is aimed at recording information on only a few behaviors. More complex instruments are obviously necessary for studies involving many behaviors or many subjects who are being observed simultaneously. One important guideline in developing an observation instrument pertains directly to this complexity factor. The instrument should never be more complex than is necessary to serve the purposes of the study. Complex instruments require more effort from the observer than those that have simple formats. As more effort is required there is a greater likelihood that errors will be committed during data collection. This obviously generates more inaccurate data and may contribute to reduced interobserver reliability. *A delicate balance must be struck between a format that is sufficiently precise to meet the needs of the study and one that is as simple as possible* (thus convenient to use).

Formats for observation instruments will vary depending on the data recording method being used. For example, the format might be very simple if the researcher is merely counting the occurrences—the tally method. Fig. 9-3 illustrates a data recording format using the tally method for the aggressive behavior study discussed in Chapter 6. Note that the categories of behavior are provided on the form for the observer.

The data instrument might look quite different if the observer were using a duration recording method. Recall that duration data involve the amount of time that the subject is engaged in the target behavior. In this case the observer will note the time that the behavior begins (i.e., by starting a stopwatch) and when it terminates (i.e., by stopping a stopwatch). This process of starting and stopping the stopwatch would likely continue (without resetting the watch to zero) for a specified period such as a one-hour reading lesson. The data, then, would be the total amount of time that the subject was engaged in the target behavior (e.g., self-stimulation) during that one-hour observation session. Fig. 9-4 illustrates a data form for the duration recording method.

As was noted in Chapter 6, observation studies may also use the interval method of recording data. Such procedures focus on whether or not a particular behavior occurred during a given interval. Basically the observer would simply place a check mark or a code symbol on the recording form if the behavior occurred during the specified interval. Fig. 9-5 illustrates an interval recording form. The codes in this example are simple: *P* represents physical aggressive behavior, *V* represents verbal aggressive behavior, and a blank interval box means that neither of these target behaviors occurred during that interval.

	Subject: David	
Aggressive behavior	Session 1	Session 2
Physical		
Peer	HHT	//
Adult	/	
Verbal		
Peer	HHT //	HHT ///
Adult	//	/
Nonaggressive behavior		
Physical		
Peer	/	
Adult	/	///
Verbal		
Peer	//	/
Adult	/	////

Fig. 9-3. Observation data sheet using the tally recording method.

Subject:_____ Target behavior:_____

Observer:_____ Date:_____

Location:_____ Activity:_____

Session number:_____

Time ended:_____

Time started:_____ Total behavior_____
                              duration (read
Total session   from watch)

Length:_____   hr.   min.

Fig. 9-4. Data form for duration recording method.

Subject: _____David_____   Observer: _____Mary_____

Date: _____5/16_____   Activity: _____Playground recess_____

Session number: _____12_____   Time started: _9:15 a.m._

Target behaviors and codes: _____Physical aggression = P,_____

  verbal aggression = V

Interval length: _____15 seconds_____

1 VP	2 P	3 V	4 PV	5 V	6
7	8 V	9 P	10 P	11 P	12 VP
13 V	14	15	16 V	17 V	18 P
19 VP	20 V	21	22	23	24
25	26	27 P	28 P	29 V	30 VP

Fig. 9-5. Data form for interval recording method.

Observation instruments can obviously take many forms as indicated by the examples presented above. As with most research, the specific format must often be tailored to fit the investigation being planned. The beginning researcher may find it helpful to review current literature in the area being studied or consult volumes that focus in greater depth on observational recording systems (e.g., Jackson, Della-Piana, and Sloane, 1975).

REFERENCES

Bailey, K. D. *Methods of social research.* New York: The Free Press, 1978.

Berdie, D. R., and Anderson, J. F. *Questionnaires: design and use.* Metuchen, N. J.: Scarecrow Press, Inc., 1974.

Drew, C. J., and Altman, R. Effects of input organization and material difficulty on free recall. *Psychological Reports,* 1970, *27,* 335-337.

Freston, C. W., and Drew, C. J. Verbal performance of learning disabled children as a function of input organization. *Journal of Learning Disabilities,* 1974, *7,* 424-428.

Jackson, D. A., Della-Piana, G. M., and Sloane, H. N., Jr. *How to establish a behavior observation system.* Englewood Cliffs, N.J.: Educational Technology Publications, 1975.

Nunnally, J. C. *Psychometric theory.* New York: McGraw-Hill Book Co., 1967.

Simpson, R. L., King, J. D., and Drew, C. J. Free recall by retarded and nonretarded subjects as a function of input organization. *Psychonomic Science,* 1970, *19,* 334.

SIMULATIONS

SIMULATIONS 9-1 AND 9-2

Topic: Criterion measures

Background statement: The data that are collected in a study represent the researcher's evidence of how the subject interacted with the task. Specification of the measure to be taken is therefore a crucial part of planning any investigation. It is also a frequent area of difficulty for the beginning researcher.

Tasks to be performed

1. Read the following stimulus material, which is a summary statement about a hypothetical study.

2. Suggest a criterion measure that might be appropriate for the investigation.

Stimulus material for Simulation 9-1

A teacher in your school wishes to compare the effectiveness of two reading programs. The study has been designed in a traditional experimental framework with two groups of subjects, one receiving one program and the second receiving the other program. Suggest the criterion measure(s) that may be appropriate.

For feedback see p. 340.

Stimulus material for Simulation 9-2

A study is to be initiated with a young girl who has been in preschool for 6 months. The teacher is extremely concerned because the child is withdrawn and does not interact with the other children much. This has become a problem because much of the daily activity involves spontaneous or free play in small groups. It has been determined that this behavior will be the target for modification through reinforcement contingencies in a time-series design. Suggest a criterion measure(s) that may be appropriate.

For feedback see p. 341.

SIMULATIONS 9-3 AND 9-4

Topic: Performance range

Background statement: The performance range in an experimental task is a crucial issue if the data obtained are to truly represent the subjects' ability to perform. Certain studies are particularly vulnerable and require considerable ingenuity on the part of the experimenter to design an appropriate task. The simulation you are presently performing involves an investigation that is developmental in nature and focuses primarily on a subject question concerning the development of classification concepts in children. One study has been conducted before yours, and you are using it as a point of departure for designing your own. The study is focusing on the cognitive development of classification concepts and does not involve instruction per se as an experimental variable. Your study is intended to be a follow-up on the previous work. The data presented in the stimulus material are to be used as a point of departure.

Tasks to be performed for Simulation 9-3

1. Inspect the following data table from the earlier study.
2. Graph the data to facilitate inspection.
3. Do you see anything in particular that should receive your attention in planning your own study?
4. If there are problems, what changes seem in order to circumvent those problems?

Stimulus material for Simulation 9-3

Mean correct responses on classification task performance*

Subject age group (years)	Material difficulty	
	Low	High
3 to 4-6	22.0	12.7
5 to 6-6	28.6	16.3
7 to 8-6	29.2	22.8

*Thirty items on the classification task.

For feedback see p. 341.

Tasks to be performed for Simulation 9-4

1. Inspect the following data table from the earlier study. Note the criterion measure (different from that in Simulation 9-3).
2. Graph the data to facilitate inspection.
3. Do you see anything in particular that should receive your attention in planning your own study?
4. If there are problems, what changes seem in order to circumvent those problems?

Stimulus material for Simulation 9-4

Mean trials to criterion on classification task performance*

Subject age group (years)	Material difficulty	
	Low	High
3 to 4-6	6.1	29.2
5 to 6-6	3.0	16.7
7 to 8-6	1.5	6.3

*The task will permit one trial performance to reach criterion. Therefore the best possible performance is one trial to criterion.

For feedback see p. 342.

SIMULATION 9-5

Topic: Questionnaire construction

Background statement: One very important factor in questionnaire construction involves the manner in which questions are worded. This has been a continuing problem for survey researchers and must receive careful attention in the planning process. The simulation you are presently performing focuses on questionnaire wording.

Tasks to be performed

1. Inspect the wording of the questions presented below.
2. Identify any wording that may cause response problems.
3. Rewrite the questions to circumvent the difficulties.

Stimulus material for Simulation 9-5

1. Do you mow and trim your lawn regularly?   Yes ☐ No ☐
2. Is your yard florous?   Yes ☐ No ☐

For feedback see p. 343.

PART III

Data analysis and results interpretation

CHAPTER 10

Research design related to statistics

The research process should be thought of as a series of vitally interrelated parts. It becomes necessary to highlight this fact once again by noting that there is a crucial relationship between the design of a research study and the statistical tools used. Frequently this relationship is not clearly conceptualized by the beginning student. Consequently it is not uncommon to find an investigation that is designed to ask a particular type of question and statistical techniques used to analyze the data that are more appropriate for a different type of design. The purpose of this chapter is to examine the relationship between research design and the statistical techniques used. Additionally, several topics involve preliminary considerations to the selection of the appropriate statistical tool.

Throughout the portion of this book that deals with statistics it will be necessary to keep in mind the scope of the text. It is not the intent to provide a detailed discussion of how to use statistical tools. This has been accomplished in a variety of textbooks that focus solely on statistical methods (e.g., Bruning and Kintz, 1968; Winer, 1971). Neither is it the intent, nor would it be possible, to examine all the specific techniques that are available for data analysis. Rather it is the purpose of this portion of the text to provide an introduction to the area of statistical analysis, to indicate how these techniques fit in the overall scheme of the research enterprise, and to suggest generally some of the analyses that may be applied in certain situations.

STATISTICS: WHAT AND WHY

Glass and Stanley (1970) noted a "mixture of awe, cynicism, suspicion, and contempt" evident in general attitudes concerning statistics [p. 1]. Such views, both openly and subtly expressed, are commonly encountered by most researchers. Why do such attitudes prevail concerning the statistical aspects of research? I have noted an additional reaction to those mentioned that may shed some light on this question. A high proportion of beginning students are fearful of the area of statistics. (Recognize it? The sweaty palms, tight stomach, and high frequency of nervous laughter?)

241

This fear is often accompanied by an absence of knowledge concerning what statistics are. It may be that the fear, "awe, cynicism, suspicion, and contempt" are related to this lack of knowledge and understanding about what statistics are and why they are useful. An example of such a lack of knowledge came to my attention recently when a student asked if a statistical test was an instrument to be administered to the subjects in an experiment. Admittedly, this student was just beginning to learn about research, but the question still was a red flag concerning the entering knowledge of some individuals who have little background. Statistical methods are procedures for *analyzing the data* (scores), which have already been obtained from administration of the research task or instrument to the subjects. This section will discuss briefly the whats and whys of statistical methods.

Once the data are collected it is the researcher's task to scrutinize the scores, draw certain conclusions concerning the subjects' performance, and interpret the data in terms of the original research question. To interpret the data it is necessary that the researcher have a way of looking at the scores that will provide a clear picture of what happened in the experiment. It is seldom* that this can be reliably accomplished by merely inspecting the numbers or performance scores. Visual inspection usually permits attention to only loose questions, and answers to such questions are frequently vague. It may be possible to determine that George scored about as well as most subjects, or that Sally obtained the highest score in all groups, but little can be said about group performance. Groups are often the basis for the research question (such as "How well can this group be expected to perform on task X?" or "Which is more effective, teaching method A that group 1 received or teaching method B that group 2 received?") The researcher has to be able to speak in terms of group performance if the group represents the basis for answering the research question. Statistics represent summary and analysis procedures that permit the researcher to determine group performance characteristics in a manner that is far more precise and convenient than visual inspection of the raw data.

There are statistical tools available for nearly every conceivable research purpose or question. Two broad categories of purpose are generally involved in behavioral research—descriptive and inferential. Descriptive studies, as the name indicates, have the primary purpose of describing a sample or group of individuals. The description may involve annual yearly income, average height, educational achievement, or any of a number of different dimensions. Descriptive studies usually do not intend to go beyond the process of providing a picture of the group that is being investigated.

---

*It is particularly difficult to obtain a clear picture of the results by merely inspecting the scores when groups of subjects are involved. Graphed raw data from time-series experiments using only one subject are much more amenable to interpretation by visual inspection, although even in these circumstances certain statistical procedures are useful.

Inferential research, on the other hand, has a substantially different purpose. An inferential investigation, although it may describe a group, also has the purpose of drawing implications from the data with regard to a theory, a model, or a body of knowledge. It may be that the researchers are testing the soundess of some psychological theory, making some predictions with regard to student success, or determining which of several teaching approaches is more effective. In accomplishing this purpose, they are inferring beyond the behavioral facts of the data to some abstract concept or to some generalized situation. This inference beyond a reporting of "what is" is the characteristic of inferential research that distinguishes it from descriptive research. In reality the distinction between inferential and descriptive studies may be somewhat blurred. It is not difficult at all to find examples of investigations that involve both purposes to some degree. The distinction is being made here for instructional convenience in examining different statistical methods.

Different statistical procedures are designed to facilitate the functions of descriptive and inferential studies. These general categories of statistical techniques are generically identified as descriptive statistics and inferential statistics. The former provide a summary of the data from which a description can be made (e.g., average height or range of intelligence). Descriptive statistics make it possible to conveniently scrutinize characteristics or performance. Inferential statistics have a different purpose (see Chapter 12).

Statistics are used to perform research functions that cannot be accomplished without them. In descriptive research, statistics provide a convenient and precise summary of the data that permits the researcher to describe "what is" or "what happened" in situations in which mere visual inspection of the data would be insufficient. Far from being an academic exercise or hurdle (designed to generate hives, poor complexion, and general ill health in students), statistics serve practical purposes in research.

WHICH STATISTIC? FOUNDATIONS OF TOOL SELECTION

That statistics play an important role in the overall research process is not meant to contradict earlier statements, which attempted to deemphasize them. Previously, statistics were characterized as *"just* tools." This characterization intended to emphasize to the beginning researcher that the research process involves a *series* of important segments, with statistics representing only one. This is the perspective that has been maintained throughout the text and is an accurate perspective of research and its components.

Many statistical tools are available to the researcher for different purposes. To select the appropriate technique, certain considerations must receive attention. The remainder of this chapter will examine one of the basic factors that the researcher must consider in selecting the statistic to be used—the different types of data that may be collected.

The nature of the data

The importance of selecting an appropriate criterion measure was previously discussed. The decision is crucial. The researcher must now consider several factors that relate both to the research question and to the type of statistical tools that may be applied.

Criterion measures represent a means of describing real world events or occurrences (such as a child's behavior). It is essential that the criterion measure or data accurately represent or parallel the events, otherwise the research question intended for investigation may not be what is actually being studied. For example, numbers have the property known as *identity*. A number is unique and is not exactly the same as any other number. If a number is used as the criterion measure representing an event, the event should also have the property of identity. That is, there should be reason to believe that the event so designated is unique from other events. Numbers also have the property of *order*. One number is less than or greater than another on some continuum. Occurrences to which such a type of measure is applied should also have order. If one event is represented by a given number (e.g., 6) and a second event is represented by a higher number (e.g., 7), there should be a sound basis for believing the second event to be larger or greater on some continuum than the first. This may be exemplified by ranking the relative heights of basketball players. By lining the team up in order from the shortest to the tallest, it is possible to rank each individual in terms of height relative to the others on the team. Numbers are also characterized by the property of *additivity*. By adding together two numbers, one can obtain another number, which is different or unique. This last property is important for most of the arithmetic operations performed in analyzing data.

Not all of the events that are studied in behavioral science have all the properties of identity, order, and additivity. Different events have certain properties but not others. This does not mean that they are not legitimate topics for investigation or that data cannot be recorded on them. It does, however, emphasize the necessity of specifying a criterion measure that parallels the observed phenomenon. Different types of data are amenable to different types of analysis. It is crucial that the beginning researcher become acquainted with measurement scales to make appropriate decisions in selecting the statistical tool needed.

Nominal data. The first type of data to be discussed is called nominal data, occasionally referred to as categorical or classification data. Nominal data represent the most primitive type of measurement. They are useful when all that can be accomplished is the assignment of events to categories. For example, an item on a questionnaire may require a "yes" or "no" response from the subject. Under such circumstances all that can be determined from the data is whether a subject's response falls into one or the other of two categories. Other examples are found in biological classification systems, psychiatric diagnostic categories, and many other areas both in and beyond the boundaries of science.

The essential element to be noted with regard to nominal data is that the information, whether in the responses, attributes, people, or characteristics, is in the form of categories that are distinct and mutually exclusive, without an apparent underlying continuum. If numbers are used to designate categories (e.g., response type 1 or response type 2), they serve only as identification labels. Such numbers would not represent any magnitude or order continuum and could be replaced with any symbol that would conveniently and effectively discriminate one category from another (e.g., group A or group B). Nominal data have the property of identity, since presumably each category is completely different from the other categories.

Ordinal data. The second type of data to be discussed is known as ordinal or rank order data. Ordinal data move measurement from the qualitative discrimination between events, which is characteristic of nominal data, to a more quantitative basis of assessment. Ordinal measurement is characterized by the ability to rank order events on the basis of an underlying continuum. Thus the ranks denote "greater than" or "less than" on the dimension being assessed.

A variety of situations exemplify ordinal data. The earlier ranking of basketball players with regard to relative height would result in ordinal data. Likewise, ordinal data may be generated by the frequently used Likert or 1 to 5 scale. Recall the yes-no questionnaire response example mentioned under nominal data. It is possible that this dichotomous response option might be transformed to a Likert scale with an underlying continuum representing relative degree of agreement. This could be accomplished by following the stimulus statement with a response format such as:

Highly disagree	Disagree	Neutral	Agree	Highly agree
1	2	3	4	5

The respondents could provide considerably more information as to how they viewed the stimulus statement with this type of format than be merely selecting a dichotomous response of yes-no or agree-disagree. With this type of data the researcher is able to discriminate between those subjects who are only mildly in disagreement with the statement and those who are firmer in their position. The relative firmness of the viewpoints is all that may be determined, however. The actual amount of difference beween any two response possibilities is not known. One cannot say that the difference between any two responses represents an equal interval (for example, the amount of difference in agreement between 1 and 2 is not known to be the same as that between 3 and 4). Thus the serial order of responses may be determined so that a response of 4 is relatively more in agreement with the statement than a response of 3, but one does not know what the actual interval is. Ordinal data have both the properties of identity and order but, since the interval is unknown, additivity is not present.

Interval data. The third type of data to be examined is called interval data. Interval data have all the properties of nominal and ordinal data plus added information concerning the interval units. When an interval measurement is possible, the researcher is working with known and equal distances between score units. With interval data it is not only possible to determine greater than or less than but also the magnitude of a difference in the underlying continuum of what is being measured. If, for example, the differences between scores are equal (that is, the difference in score units generated by subtracting 10 from 25 and 20 from 35 is 15), then there is a corresponding equivalence in property magnitude differences. Interval data are characterized by all three number properties: identity, order, and additivity.

Common examples of interval data include calendar time and temperature as measured on centigrade and Fahrenheit scales. Differences in the score units on these measures represent known and constant magnitude differences in the factor being measured. The example measures also involve a property that is characteristic of interval data, an arbitrary zero point. Temperature perhaps exemplifies this characteristic most vividly. Temperature measured as 0° on the centigrade scale reads 32° on the Fahrenheit scale, whereas 0° F is the same as −17.8° C. Thus the zero point is arbitrary, attained at different points depending on which scale is used, and in neither case does 0° indicate the complete absence of temperature. (Absolute 0° in temperature is on the Kelvin scale.) Likewise the calendar time or numbering of years was rather arbitrarily begun on the Christian calendar with the birth of Christ.

Measurement in behavioral science does not achieve interval status as frequently as it does in the physical sciences. For example, data generated in cognitive psychology and education are often recorded in the form of the number of correct responses or the number of errors committed (as measures of, say, learning or forgetting). The researcher seldom knows whether the units represented by such measures are equal, making it difficult to say with certainty that interval data are being obtained. Usually the behavioral researcher will assume that the units approximate equality unless the data are obviously ordinal or nominal. This assumption, if reasonably in harmony with the properties of what is being measured, provides more latitude in terms of statistical methods that can be used.

Ratio data. The fourth and final type of data to be discussed is known as ratio data. Ratio data have all the properties of interval data but are distinguished in that the zero point is not arbitrary. A zero score on a ratio data scale *does* signify total absence of the property being measured.

Examples of ratio data are primarily found in physical measurement and seldom if ever in behavioral science. As noted in the previous section, temperature measured on the Kelvin scale (also known as the absolute zero scale) conforms to the characteristics of ratio measurement. Likewise height, weight, and time (to perform) are examples of ratio scale data. Occasionally behavioral scientists will be interested in time (such as response latency) or some other measure that appears to be a ratio scale. This type of measure, however, is not frequent. Work is primarily conducted in the nominal, ordinal, and interval scales. Fortunately, there are few statistical procedures that require ratio data characteristics, and consequently the primary focus in this text will be the first three types of data.

> Look below and complete Simulations 10-1, 10-2, 10-3, and 10-4.

REFERENCES

Bruning, J. L., and Kintz, B. L. *Computational handbook of statistics.* Glenview, Ill.: Scott, Foresman and Co., 1968.

Glass, G. V., and Stanley, J. C. *Statistical methods in education and psychology.* Englewood Cliffs, N.J.: Prentice-Hall, Inc., 1970.

Winer, B. J. *Statistical principles in experimental design* (2nd ed.). New York: McGraw-Hill Book Co., 1971.

SIMULATIONS

SIMULATIONS 10-1, 10-2, AND 10-3

Topic: Nature of the data

Background statement: In many cases you will be presented with data that have already been collected. Frequently it is up to you to determine what type of data is involved in the study. This will require knowledge and experience with different data types so that you can make subsequent decisions concerning data analysis.

Tasks to be performed

1. Review the following stimulus material, paying particular attention to the nature of the data collected.
2. Answer the following questions concerning the data that are being recorded:
   a. What type of data is involved in the study?
   b. What properties do the data have and why?

Stimulus material for Simulation 10-1

The feedback for simulation 4-4 suggested one approach to having teachers evaluate instructional material. This suggestion included an example of a 1 to 5 scale such as:

Excellent		Average		Poor
1	2	3	4	5

In view of what was discussed in Chapter 10, respond to the two questions under part 2 of the task to be performed above.

For feedback see p. 344.

Stimulus material for Simulation 10-2

Suppose you are faced with the situation in which teachers are predicting job success for their high school students. In accomplishing this task they are asked to categorize their pupils into groups of "successful" and "unsuccessful." In view of what was discussed in Chapter 10, respond to the two questions under step 2 of the task to be performed.

For feedback see p. 344.

Stimulus material for Simulation 10-3

In this simulation suppose that you have been asked to serve as a consultant for a medical research program investigating the use of certain drugs with infants. One of the topics of interest is possible side effects of the medication. The project director suspects that the child's temperature may be seriously elevated when the drug under study is administered. The criterion measure here, then, is temperature. In view of what was discussed in Chapter 10, respond to the two questions under step 2 of the task to be performed.

For feedback see p. 344.

SIMULATION 10-4

Topic: Nature of the data

Background statement: As noted, both in this chapter and previous simulations, the nature of the data is something that a researcher must be able to determine to complete later tasks in the investigation. Occasionally different types of data may be generated even though the same phenomenon is being assessed.

Tasks to be performed

1. Review the following stimulus material, which involves the assessment of age.
2. Identify the type of data involved in each of the examples (A, B, and C).

Stimulus material

A. Ten subjects are classified and placed in one of three categories:

Classification 1	Classification 2	Classification 3
Young	Middle-aged	Old

B. Ten subjects are ranked from youngest to oldest.
C. The ages of ten subjects are recorded.

For feedback see p. 344.

CHAPTER 11

Statistics for descriptive purposes

Once the data have been collected and recorded in the form of raw scores, the researcher usually has several operations to perform. In nearly all cases, the first process is data compilation in some form that describes the group performance. Compilation or data summary in descriptive form, as noted previously, involves the use of descriptive statistics. Two general categories of descriptive statistics are commonly used—measures of central tendency and measures of dispersion. Measures of central tendency provide an index of where the scores tend to bunch together or of the typical score in the group of scores. Measures of dispersion, on the other hand, "describe the 'spread' or extent of difference among" the scores in the group (Hays, 1963, p. 157). Both measures of central tendency and dispersion will be discussed in this chapter.

A preliminary note should be made regarding the researcher's objective in compiling a descriptive data summary. If the investigation has the primary intent of describing the group, the researcher may well terminate analysis with the compuataion of descriptive statistics. Such statistics will provide the information necessary for the goal of group description. It is possible, however, that the investigation has an inferential purpose beyond mere group description. If this is the case, the descriptive statistics represent preliminary computations necessary to perform further data analysis. Thus descriptive measures are commonly computed regardless of whether the investigation is a descriptive or inferential study. In the first case, the descriptive statistics are probably terminal operations, whereas in the latter case, they are preliminary operations in preparation for further analysis.

CENTRAL TENDENCY MEASURES

Data may be summarized and presented in a number of ways. Frequently it is desirable to be able to characterize group scores with a single index that will provide some idea of how well the group performed. This requires a number that is representative of the distribution of scores that were obtained. One type of index commonly used for such group description involves numbers that represent the concentration of scores, known as central tendency measures. Three measures of central tendency are generally discussed, the *mean*, the *median*, and

249

the *mode*. Each measure has slightly different properties and is useful for different circumstances.

The mean

Probably the most familiar measure of central tendency is the mean. The mean or arithmetic average is obtained by simply adding the scores for all subjects together and dividing this total by the number of individuals in the group. In a spelling test, the mean might be twenty-five correctly spelled words. These data might appear like the example in Table 11-1. At the top of the table is an X over the column where scores appear. This X is frequently used as a conve-

Table 11-1. Hypothetical raw scores on spelling test

Subject	X
1	33
2	6
3	25
4	35
5	10
6	30
7	25
8	32
9	35
10	19
	TOTAL = 250

Table 11-2. Hypothetical example of grouped data approach occasionally used in computing means

Score interval	X	f	fX
60 to 64	62	2	124
55 to 59	57	1	57
50 to 54	52	6	312
45 to 49	47	10	470
40 to 44	42	20	840
35 to 39	37	18	666
30 to 34	32	19	608
25 to 29	27	16	432
20 to 24	22	13	286
15 to 19	17	9	153
10 to 14	12	2	24
5 to 9	7	3	21
0 to 4	2	1	2
		N = 120	TOTAL = 3995

nient shorthand symbol to represent the score of the individual subjects (number of words spelled correctly in this example).

The example just given involves a mean calculated on actual raw data scores. This procedure becomes somewhat laborious if many individuals are serving as subjects. In such circumstances, the researcher may wish to compute what is known as a grouped-data mean. Using this approach, the data are grouped into intervals as in the example in Table 11-2. Because each score does not have to be summed individually, the computation is considerably easier. In Table 11-2, X is the midpoint of the respective interval. Any score that falls into a given interval is assigned the value of the midpoint (for example, a score of 63 would be given a value of 62 in Table 11-2). The f refers to the frequency with which scores fall into a given interval (for example, there were eighteen individuals with scores in the interval of 35 to 39). Each X is then multiplied by its respective f to obtain fX (e.g., 6 times 52 is 312), and the fX values are then totalled. The mean is then obtained in the same manner as before, by dividing the total scores (fX total) by the number of individuals (N can be obtained by adding the fs, since each f represents a subject). The mean for this example turns out to be 33.29.

As might be expected, using the grouped-data approach for calculating means introduces a certain amount of error into the computation. This error occurs when scores are assigned the interval midpoint value and, although not serious in most cases, must be kept in mind when data are being summarized. Because of this error, it is usually preferable to compute raw data means unless the number is so large that the process is simply too cumbersome. If grouped data means are used, the researcher must remain cognizant that some error may be present in the means.

One additional factor to be considered with regard to this error involves the size of score intervals used. Greater error is likely with larger intervals than with smaller intervals, since the midpoint of the smaller interval is likely to be closer to a given exact score. Of course, if intervals are reduced considerably, the computation task becomes more laborious in a manner approximating the use of raw data.

The mean has occasionally been likened to the fulcrum on a seesaw. This analogy places the mean at what Hays (1963) calls the center of gravity in a distribution of scores. Consider the first example of a mean as presented in Table 11-1. If this distribution of scores were placed on a seesaw, it might appear somewhat like Fig. 11-1. The mean of 25 is positioned as the fulcrum with the individual scores represented as weights placed at the appropriate distances from the center. The score deviations away from the mean are then noted as plus and minus values on their respective sides of the fulcrum. These deviations are then summed for each side, and the total minus deviations are equal to the total plus deviations (+40 and −40). This is characteristic of means as a measure

Fig. 11-1. Center of gravity effect of deviations around mean.

of central tendency and is essentially the formal definition of a mean: *the total signed deviations around a mean equals zero* (+40 added to −40 equals zero).

The median

A second measure of central tendency is the median. The median is *a point in the distribution that has exactly the same number of scores above it as below it when all scores are arranged in order.* The specific point at which the median exists in a given distribution is slightly different depending on whether the number of individuals in the group is odd or even. If N is odd, then the median is the middle score in the distribution. If N is even, then the median is a hypothetical score value midway between the two scores that occupy the midpoint in the distribution. Suppose one wished to determine the median in the series of scores that follows:

3,   5,   6,   9,   10,   12,   14

Since there is an odd number of individuals ($N = 7$), the score that occupies the midpoint in the distribution becomes the median; in this example it is 9. In another series of scores, determining the median is slightly different. Consider the following:

3,   5,   6,   9,   10,   12,   14,   16

There is now an even number of scores ($N = 8$), which places the median midway between the two middle scores. In this case, the interval between 9 and 10 is one unit on the scale. Midway between the two would involve half of that interval or 0.5. The median is therefore 9.5.

The examples and discussion of medians thus far have involved raw data scores. Medians may also be obtained with data that are grouped by interval. The process is essentially the same. For example purposes, turn to Table 11-3. Since N is 32, the median will be at a point where sixteen scores fall above and sixteen below. Counting individuals up from the bottom in the f column yields $2 + 2 + 9 + 10 = 23$, which is beyond the median point. To obtain exactly 16, some but not all of those cases that fall into the score interval of 15 to 19 must be taken. Looking at the next lower interval, $2 + 2 + 9 = 13$, which is only 3 short of the 16 needed for the median. Therefore, take 3 of the 10 cases in the score interval of 15 to 19. For computation purposes, those ten scores must be

Table 11-3. Illustration of grouped data for median determination

Score interval	f
30 to 34	2
25 to 29	1
20 to 24	6
15 to 19	10
10 to 14	9
5 to 9	2
0 to 4	2
	$N = 32$

assumed to be spread evenly throughout the interval even though they may not be in reality. With this assumption, the median point can be determined by proceeding $^3/_{10}$ of the distance into the interval. Since the interval distance is 5 units, $^3/_{10}$ of that equals 1.5 units. This 1.5 units must now be added to the lower limit of the score interval of 15 to 19 to obtain the median.

At this point a note needs to be made concerning interval limits. The *exact* limits of any interval are actually midway between the intervals that are usually specified. In Table 11-3, the exact limits for the specified median interval (15 to 19) would be 14.5 and 19.5 (29.5 and 34.5 for interval 30 to 34, 24.5 and 29.5 for interval 25 to 29, and so on). Thus if 1.5 units are added to the lower limit of the median interval (14.5), a score of 16 is obtained, which is the median for this example. (Note that in this example the median *score* was 16 and that it was also necessary to find the *point* at which 16 scores were above and 16 below—the definition of a median. The two 16s are a coincidence and obviously other examples might result in differences between the median score and the number of cases needed to obtain that median.)

The grouped-data procedure for determining the median is particularly useful when a large N is involved in the study. This approach is considerably easier than ordering the actual scores for many individuals.

The mode

The third measure of central tendency to be discussed is the mode. The mode is simply an indicator of *the most frequent score or interval*. For raw data or actual score distributions, the mode would be defined as that score that occured most frequently (that is, more subjects obtained that score than any other score). For data grouped into intervals, the midpoint of the most frequently occurring interval is considered to be the mode. For example, in the distribution of scores illustrated in Table 11-3 more scores fell into the interval of 15 to 19 than any other interval. Since the midpoint of that interval is 17, this would be considered to be the mode.

Occasionally more than one score or interval will appear with modal frequencies. If two scores (or intervals) occur more frequently (and with equal frequency) than other scores, the distribution is said to be "bimodal." This term is used somewhat loosely on occasion when the two modes are not precisely equal, although the score that occurs most frequently (between the two) is distinguished as the "major mode," whereas the less frequent score is called the "minor mode." This distribution with only one most frequently occurring score is "unimodal."

Comments on selection

As might be expected from the foregoing discussion, the mean, median, and mode have a variety of different properties and are useful in different situations. From the outset the type of data collected has considerable influence on which measure is preferred. If nominal data have been gathered, the mode is the only central tendency description that may be used. Ordinal data, on the other hand, will permit the use of the median as well as the mode. Interval and ratio data, since they both include additivity, permit the computation of a mean in addition to the other central tendency measures.

Some difference of opinion exists regarding such "cut and dried" statements as those just presented. In all cases the researcher must be concerned about the meaningfulness of the central tendency measure that is selected. It makes little sense to present a median or mean when categorical data are being scrutinized. Even if numbers are used to designate the categories, they are merely serving as labels and could easily be replaced by letters (e.g., A, B, C) or by any other convenient designation that would permit discrimination. The numerals thus do not say anything about the properties being observed except that they have identity and are discriminable. Certainly one could perform arithmetic operations on the label numbers, but such manipulation would have no meaningfulness with regard to the property. For example, suppose there are two categories, male and female, designated with numbers 1 and 2. It makes little sense to obtain an arithmetic mean. (What does 1.5 mean in terms of these categories?)

Ordinal data do not present such a clear situation as nominal data. Mean ranks found in research literature may or may not be appropriate depending on the situation. Ordinal data varies considerably in terms of how nearly the ranks represent magnitude as well as order. In some cases the data fit into a lower-level ordinal scale and represent only gross directionality. On other occasions the ranks may suggest considerably more concerning magnitude even though exact interval equivalence is not a certainty. Under such circumstances the use of the mean is meaningful in terms of the property being measured to the degree that magnitude statements may be approximated. Again, researchers must remain cognizant of their purpose, that of being able to say something meaningful about the topic. Mere manipulation of numerals does not fulfill this purpose.

Depending on the shape of the distribution, the three central tendency mea-

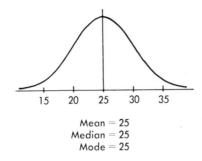

Mean = 25
Median = 25
Mode = 25

Fig. 11-2. Example of a unimodal symmetrical distribution of scores.

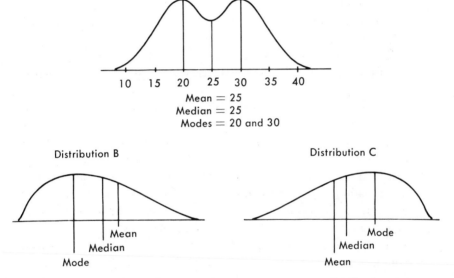

Fig. 11-3. Central tendency measure placement in various distribution shapes.

sures may have the same score values or different values in a given set of scores. If the distribution is shaped like the example in Fig. 11-2, the mean, median, and mode will have the same score value. This unimodal, symmetrical distribution results in all three central tendency measures being at the same point in the curve.

Distributions that are not unimodal *and* symmetrical result in a somewhat different picture of the central tendency measures' placement. For example, distribution A in Fig. 11-3 is symmetrical but *not* unimodal. In fact, this distribution appears to have the double-hump appearance of a bimodal distribution.

Distribution A therefore is characterized by two modes, which makes it impossible for the three central tendency measures to have the same score value. However, the median and mean in distribution A still have the same score value. This is to be expected when symmetry exists in the way that the scores are distributed.

Distributions B and C in Fig. 11-3 represent a different central tendency picture than either of the other examples. Both of these distributions are characterized by being asymmetrical in shape. When distributions are asymmetrically shaped, they are known as *skewed* distributions. Distribution B illustrates what is called a postively skewed distribution, whereas distribution C is an example of a negatively skewed set of scores. The direction of the skewness is referenced toward the tail or point of the curve. Since measurement scales commonly read from left to right in an ascending fashion, the term "positive" is used when the tail is toward the upper end of the scale and "negative" when the tail is toward the lower end. Note the positioning of the central tendency measures in skewed distributions B and C. Such skewness in distributions tends to generate different score values for each of the measures. The mode, as usual, is positioned at the hump or most frequently occurring score. The median is positioned at the middle of the score distribution, whereas the mean tends to be nearer the tail than the other measures.

The mean is by far the most frequently used measure of central tendency in behavioral research. There are several reasons why this occurs. One important reason involves purposes of research other than description. If the researcher is conducting an inferential study, it is likely that he or she will wish to compute additional analyses on the data. The mean is amenable to further arithmetic manipulation and is thus more useful for many of the additional operations necessary in inferential statistics.* The median and mode, on the other hand, are more frequently terminal descriptive statistics.

It is evident from the previous discussion that all three measures of central tendency may vary from sample to sample with regard to the exact score value that each represents. This will occur as a result of the way in which the scores are distributed as well as individual differences in the scores regardless of distribution shape. The mean tends to be somewhat less likely to substantially change position than the median and mode. This greater stability increases the desirability of the mean as a measure of central tendency in most samples. There are, however, occasions when this is not the case. If a particular sample includes a few atypical or extreme scores, the mean may give a distorted picture of the distribution. For example, suppose a sample of individuals is being described in terms of annual income. Say the sample includes primarily those individuals in the middle income bracket, with the exception of one person who has a multi-million-dollar yearly income. In this case the mean is likely to suggest a much

---

*The mean is not the *only* measure used in inferential studies. This will become evident in later sections, when nonparametric and parametric inferential techniques are discussed.

higher average income than is actually typical. If such extreme scores are involved in a distribution, the median may well provide a more adequate description of central tendency than the mean. It is frequently advisable to provide more than one measure of central tendency if accurate description is essential. This is particularly important if distributions are skewed as in illustrations *B* and *C* in Fig. 11-3.

The choice of which measure of central tendency to use depends entirely on what the researchers want to do and in what fashion they wish to describe their sample. If the researchers want to guess a given subject's score and to be *exactly correct* most often, the mode is the best score to pick. This is simply because more subjects got that score than any other score in the distribution, which raises the probability that the researchers would guess exactly right. For purposes of purely descriptive research, Hays (1963) notes that "the median is a most serviceable measure [p. 165]." Despite the fact that it is somewhat less stable than the mean, the median is not so affected by extreme scores and thus is often more descriptive of the typical score. Additionally, it is easily communicated. Beyond the realm of descriptive research, for inferential purposes the mean is usually the preferred measure over the median or mode. As with other areas of the research process, selection of a central tendency measure must be accomplished on the basis of research purpose. Rigid adherence to a particular measure at all times is inappropriate.

Turn to p. 263 and complete Simulations 11-1 and 11-2.

DISPERSION MEASURES

Describing a set of scores in terms of central tendency furnishes only one descriptive dimension of the distribution, where the performance levels tend to be concentrated. In performing this function, the central tendency measure, whether it is the mean, median, or mode, attempts to characterize the most typical score with a single index.

A second important way of describing scores involves measures of dispersion. Dispersion measures provide an index of *how much variation there is in the scores,* that is, to what degree individual scores depart from central tendency. By determining where the scores concentrate and to what degree individual performances vary from that concentration, a rather complete description of the distribution is available. In fact, in the absence of a dispersion description to accompany the central tendency measure, knowledge about a given set of scores is limited. An example will serve to illustrate this point. Assume that two members of a bowling team are practicing seriously for a tournament. During the last month of practice before the tournament, they maintain a cumulative record of their scores to determine averages with their newly acquired skill level. Fig. 11-4

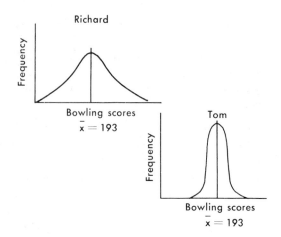

Fig. 11-4. Hypothetical distributions of bowling scores for two bowlers.

illustrates the distribution of scores for both of the bowlers. Note that both individuals have the same average (mean) score of 193, yet their bowling performances are considerably different. Tom is an extremely consistent bowler. He can be relied on to fill most of the frames and hit for a reasonable number of strikes. He seldom shoots below 180 but likewise seldom has bowled above 206. Richard's score, on the other hand, is all over the place. Although he has the same average score of 193, his ball placement is erratic. When he is hitting well, his score runs well up into the 200's, but during an off night he is fortunate to break 100. During the last month when scores were recorded (for purposes of this book, of course) he bowled a 282 the first game on one night and followed with a second game of 104.

Information provided by the central tendency measure in the above example is limited. Much more is known about the two bowlers' performance by also viewing the distributions of scores with respect to variability in performance. One may wish to make some decisions concerning next year's bowling team based on such information. In discussing variability indices, three measures of dispersion will be examined, the *range,* the *semi-interquartile range,* and the *standard deviation.* Each provides somewhat different information.

The range

The range is the simplest and most easily determined measure of dispersion. As suggested by the term, the range refers to *the difference between the highest and lowest scores in a distribution.* If Richard's highest score during his month of bowling practice was 282 and his lowest score was 96, the range for the month's performance would be 282 minus 96, or 186 pins.

The above example illustrates the ease with which the range in a set of scores

Fig. 11-5. Hypothetical symmetrical distribution of scores divided into quarters using quartiles.

may be determined. This provides a quick index of variability, which provides additional information beyond the central tendency measure. Unfortunately, the usefulness of the range is somewhat limited because it uses little of the data available in a set of scores. It is determined entirely by the two extreme scores. Since the extreme scores may be capricious, the range may fluctuate a great deal. Its usefulness is primarily limited to preliminary data inspection. After all, an extreme score may be generated by a number of factors that are not particularly representative of the subject's usual performance (e.g., physical or emotional trauma or irregularities in materials or instrumentation).

The semi-interquartile range

The second measure of dispersion to be examined is the semi-interquartile range. Before exploring this measure, however, certain related items require attention. Initially, it is necessary to distinguish between *quartiles* and *quarters*. The hypothetical distribution illustrated in Fig. 11-5 is divided into four sections or quarters. The points used for accomplishing this division, designated Q_1, Q_2, and Q_3, are known as quartiles. Thus the quartiles are *points on the measurement scale that serve to divide a distribution of scores into four equal parts*. A subject's score may fall *in* a given quarter or *at* a given quartile, but not in a quartile, since the quartile represents a point on the scale.

Strictly defined, the semi-interquartile range is *half the range in scores represented by the middle 50% of the scores*. Turn again to Fig. 11-5 to examine this definition more closely. The middle 50% of the scores in the distribution represents those scores between Q_1 and Q_3. To establish the first and third quartiles, a simple counting procedure is involved. Q_1 may be determined by counting up from the bottom of the distribution until a fourth of the scores have been encountered. If there were forty-eight subjects in the total group, then 12 would be a fourth of 48. The twelfth score up from the lowest would be at the first quartile. Similarly, the twelfth score down from the highest would be at the third quartile. Midway between these two points is the second quartile or Q_2. Note that since Q_2 is the midmost score in the distribution, it coincides with the median. The semi-interquartile range is represented by the difference between Q_1 and Q_3 divided by 2, or

$$\frac{Q_3 - Q_1}{2} = \text{Semi-interquartile range}$$

For example, if Q_1 was at 36 in the hypothetical distribution of scores and Q_3 was at 92, then the semi-interquartile range would be $92 - 36 = {}^{56}/_2 = 28$ score units. The semi-interquartile range is generally represented by Q, thus in the example $Q = 28$.

If the distribution is symmetrical as in the one in Fig. 11-5, the semi-inter-quartile range is the same as either $Q_2 - Q_1$ or $Q_3 - Q_2$. This changes, however, if an asymmetrical or skewed distribution exists. This is exemplified by Fig. 11-6.

The semi-interquartile range is a measure of dispersion that, like the total range, is easily determined and does not involve complicated computational operations. It is, however, superior to the range as a dispersion index. It is a more stable measure, primarily because it uses much more of the available data than the range. As such it provides a much more complete picture as to how the scores are distributed along the scale of measurement.

The standard deviation

The third measure of dispersion to be discussed is the standard deviation. By far the most commonly used index of variability, the standard deviation involves somewhat more complicated computational procedures.

The standard deviation may be thought of as *a measure of variability in the scores around the mean.* The mean is therefore the reference point, and the standard deviation provides a description of the distribution of individual scores around that point. In fact, the actual deviation of each score from the mean $(\overline{X} - X)$ is used in calculating standard deviation. Standard deviation (SD), in one sense, might be thought of as an average of all the deviations from the mean. Let us turn to Fig. 11-7 for an illustration to facilitate this discussion.

Standard deviation is expressed in score units and represents a width index along the measurement scale. The width of this index becomes greater when the scores of a distribution are more variable and more narrow as the scores are more concentrated around the mean. Referring back to the example concerning bowlers, the standard deviation of Richard's scores will be considerably larger (wider) than that of Tom's scores. Richard's distribution looks much like the hypothetical illustration in Fig. 11-7, whereas Tom's scores are much more concentrated. Although this example involves a distribution of scores in a single individual (intraindividual variability), it is obvious that a single measure taken

Fig. 11-6. Hypothetical skewed distribution of scores divided into quarters using quartiles.

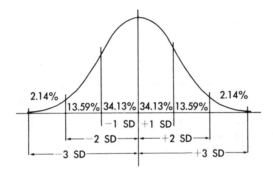

Fig. 11-7. Normal distribution with standard deviation divisions.

on a group of individuals would also result in a distribution of scores and can be conceived in the same fashion. This is called interindividual variability.

Fig. 11-7 represents a hypothetical set of scores that are normally distributed. The term "normal" in this context should not be viewed literally with other distribution shapes being thought of as abnormal. It is actually defined in terms of certain mathematical properties that determine its shape and was not developed as a description of actual events in the real world. A more descriptive term might be "bell-shaped" distribution.

Note the percentages indicated for each standard deviation in Fig. 11-7. These percentages remain constant for any set of normally distributed scores. Thus for a normal distribution one can expect that about 68% of the scores will fall between +1 and −1 standard deviations. (This also translates into 68% of the area under the curve.)

Comments on selection

Several issues are involved in the selection of which measure of dispersion is preferable. Certainly if a quick and easily computed index is needed, the order of preference is range, semi-interquartile range, and standard deviation. Using convenience as the sole criterion for selection is questionable, however. The most stable and reliable index of dispersion is the standard deviation, followed by the semi-interquartile range, with the range being the least stable measure. Likewise, if additional statistical computation beyond mere description is in order (e.g., inferential studies such as group comparisons), the standard deviation should be the choice.

Somewhat like the mean, the standard deviation is affected by a few atypical, extreme performances (highly skewed distribution). When such a situation exists, the standard deviation does not provide as accurate a description of score dispersion as the semi-interquartile range. Thus when an extremely skewed distribution is obtained, Q is preferable over standard deviation. Q is frequently viewed as a natural dispersion companion when the median is used for central tendency.

Consideration must also be given to the type of data collected when selecting the measure of dispersion. If standard deviation is to be used, the data must certainly have the property of additivity. This would limit the use of standard deviation to interval and ratio data. Range and semi-interquartile range may also be used with interval and ratio data, but standard deviation requires at least interval data. If ordinal data are collected, range and semi-interquartile range may be used. Nominal data, however, present a rather different situation, since the only property present is identity. Measures of dispersion, since they assess variability along some assumed continuum, are not usefully applied to data without such a continuum. Therefore, when working with categorical data, descriptive summaries are best accomplished using modal statements for determination of which category(ies) received the concentration of responses. Beyond this, description can probably best be facilitated by frequency graphs for each category.

Although guidelines have been presented concerning which dispersion measure may be used under what conditions, it is evident that considerable judgment is required on the part of the researcher. As in other areas of the research process, rigid rules are not applicable in all situations. If the semi-interquartile range will provide a more accurate description than standard deviation (despite the availability of interval data), then Q should be used. The basic purpose of *accurate description* must be kept in mind in determining which tool to select.

Turn to p. 264 and complete Simulations 11-3 and 11-4.

REFERENCE

Hays, W. L. *Statistics for psychologists.* New York: Holt, Rinehart and Winston, Inc., 1963.

SIMULATIONS

SIMULATIONS 11-1 AND 11-2

Topic: Central tendency measures

Background statement: Descriptive statistics are frequently useful for summarizing group performance. Central tendency measures provide a single index that is representative of the concentration of scores or where the scores tend to be bunched. One of the determining factors in the choice of which central tendency measure should be used is the type of data collected.

Tasks to be performed for Simulation 11-1

1. Review the following stimulus material.
2. Answer the following questions:
   a. What type of data are involved in the example?
   b. What central tendency measure should be used and why?
   c. What score represents the central tendency measure?

Stimulus material for Simulation 11-1

You are a coach for a university golf team. The Department of Health, Physical Education, and Recreation has developed an instrument that is supposed to assess your team members in terms of their probability of tournament success. This instrument involves a pencil and paper test that has a score possibility of 1 to 7. The best possible score is 1, and 7 is the worst. These scores are based on ratings of performance by a highly qualified judge who has several years of experience as a golf coach. Your varsity team takes the test and scores are transmitted to you in the following form.

Name	Score
Peggy	2
Joseph	5
Roberta	7
John	4
Judy	1

Respond to the three questions in the previous section on task to be performed.

For feedback see p. 345.

Tasks to be performed for Simulation 11-2

1. Review the following stimulus material.
2. Answer the following questions:
   a. What type of data are involved in the example?
   b. What central tendency measure should be used?

Stimulus material for Simulation 11-2

You are working on a research program for a large drug firm. The laboratory has developed a new formula for use with tiny infants that will presumably reduce the vulnerability to pulmonary problems. One concern, however, is the possibility of side effects that may be undesirable. A serious elevation in temperature is suspected as a potential problem. The criterion measure here, then, is temperature. Respond to the questions under part 2 of the task to be performed.

For feedback see p. 345.

SIMULATION 11-3

Topic: Dispersion measures

Background statement: Dispersion measures provide an index of how much variation exists in a set of scores. Such information is an important addition to the description provided by central tendency measures.

Tasks to be performed
1. Review the following stimulus material and all of Simulation 11-1, including the feedback.
2. What dispersion measure is appropriate for this situation and why?

Stimulus material

You have been asked to consult with a group of students who are conducting their first research project. The data involve ratings on fifty-two golf students in terms of their probability of tournament success. The same instrument is being used as in Simulation 11-1.

Respond to the question in step 2 of the task to be performed above.

For feedback see p. 345.

SIMULATION 11-4

Topic: Dispersion measures

Background statement: Dispersion measures provide an index of how much variation exists in a set of scores. Such information is an important addition to the description provided by central tendency measures. Selection of a given dispersion measure may be influenced by a number of factors.

Tasks to be performed
1. Review the following stimulus material.
2. What dispersion measure is appropriate for each of the situations presented?

Stimulus material

You have been serving as a scout for a professional basketball team. You have just returned to your office late one evening after watching two potential recruits. You were able to observe both players during seven different games each, so you have considerable data on them. Suddenly the head coach calls and wants a quick summary of the players' scoring. Both individuals had the same mean points scored during the seven games (22.3). What measure of dispersion might you give the coach on such an immediate basis (you don't even have your pocket calculator with you)? What measure of dispersion might you give on your written scouting report, which you can submit after a bit more time?

For feedback see p. 346.

CHAPTER 12

Statistics for inferential purposes

THE INFERENTIAL PURPOSE
General background

It was noted in earlier chapters that certain investigations have a purpose beyond mere description. Commonly called "inferential" studies, they have the purpose of drawing implications from the data to some setting, subjects, or materials other than those that were directly involved in the completed study. In some cases such studies are testing the applicability of a theory, model, or body of knowledge in a new setting or with subjects that have not previously been used. In other cases studies may be investigating the effectiveness of one or more treatments or teaching techniques. Such studies are usually considered inferential by virtue of the suggestions that are generated from results. Certain preliminary issues that are similar to those examined with descriptive statistics also warrant discussion in terms of inferential statistics. One of the first involves what they are and what they do. Inferential statistics, like those used for descriptive research, are tools for analyzing data in a fashion that will address the question being asked.

It was noted very early in this volume that three general types of questions are typically explored in behavioral research—descriptive, difference, and relationship. Chapter 11 described statistical procedures often used for descriptive studies. This chapter will focus on the two remaining types of questions—difference and relationship. These general categories of research questions are often involved in inferential research. As is evident from the material in earlier chapters, a broad spectrum of specific research questions may be examined within these two general types.

The statistical techniques used for inferential research essentially tell the researcher whether the results obtained are different from chance, that is, what is the probability that chance could have generated the result? This is an important piece of information since the researcher would like to *infer* that the treatment generated the observed performance. For example purposes, suppose that the researcher is comparing the effectiveness of three instructional methods, A, B, and C. Students in the group receiving method C performed better on the test than did those receiving either A or B. It is important to know whether the difference was probably caused by the treatment or whether it represents normal variation in performance as a result of chance. If the differences are sufficiently dramatic that the probability of this result being caused by chance is low (5% or less), then the differences are called statistically significant. Since the probability of chance is low, the researcher is inclined to infer that the differences are results of the effectiveness of instructional methods. To determine what the probability of chance is, the researcher applies a statistical test to the data. Thus for inferential research, statistics are the means by which researchers scrutinize their data to ascertain whether chance or the treatment probably generated the results. This certainly cannot be determined by merely inspecting the raw data visually.

It was noted that a chance probability of 5% or less is usually considered to be statistically significant. A brief expansion on this statement is appropriate at this point. Particularly, some explanation of significance notation is in order. The reader may have encountered such symbols as $P < .05$ and $P < .01$ in reading research reports. The *P* refers to probability, and the statement as a whole means that the probability is less than 5% (or 1%, depending on which is used) that the obtained results are caused by chance. Strictly speaking, *only 5 times out of 100 would results such as these be expected due to chance influences.* Thus *95 times out of 100 when results such as these are obtained, they will be due to the treatment.*

Use of 5% as the cutoff point for statistical significance is actually arbitrary. This level was used early in the development of statistical procedures and has continued more out of tradition than because of any specific logic. Some researchers have maintained that a more logical basis should exist for determining what is and is not considered statistically significant. Despite these arguments, however, the 5% probability level of chance persists as the generally accepted upper limit for results to be considered statistically significant.

Several statistical techniques are used in inferential studies. At times it seems that the multitude of different statistical tests is never-ending, particularly to the beginning researcher. Although there *are* many different statistical tests, they do not exist merely to initiate ulcers in graduate students. Since there are many different research questions that may be asked, many different tools are necessary to apply to these problems. Just as the mechanic cannot make a screwdriver turn a nut, the researcher cannot make an inappropriate statistical test fit the question. Additionally, the mechanic cannot *only* remove screws and expect to disassemble an automobile. Likewise researchers cannot *only* ask the research questions for which they have statistics and expect to fully investigate the problem. In both cases a full range of tools must either be in hand or within reach (whether it be the toolbox or the textbook).

For the most part, the various statistical tests merely represent variations on a few basic themes. This chapter will essentially focus on the basic themes of statistical tests and attempt to indicate what types of variations are appropriate under what conditions. Only the more commonly used analyses will be explored. The interested student may consult any one of many advanced statistical texts for specifics regarding a particular technique that is not fully detailed in this volume.

Parametric and nonparametric issues

Most beginning researchers feel somewhat intimidated by the whole idea of dealing with statistics in general, let alone a breakdown into categories of statistics. Yet the topic just discussed leads into such a categorization. A given research question and situation, like a $^9/_{16}$-inch bolt, requires a specific tool, in this case, a statistical tool.

Two general types of statistics have been developed and used in inferential research over the years, *parametric* and *nonparametric* tests. Both types of analyses serve the purpose of determining whether the results obtained are likely to be due to chance or to the variable(s) under study. Essentially the same types of research questions may be served by both parametric and nonparametric statistics. Either parametric or nonparametric analyses may be used in studies that investigate relationship questions or ones that investigate difference questions. This provides the researcher with a broad range of statistical tools that may be used. Selection of the appropriate type of statistical analysis depends on a number of factors including the nature of the data being gathered, the size of the sample, and certain assumptions about the population. This section will expore those factors in preparation for subsequent sections, which will present a variety of specific tests.

Assumptions. When a researcher collects data on subjects, the data involve recording one or more scores on each individual. These scores represent a sample of all such possible scores in the universe. For example, recording the heights of thirty different subjects would result in thirty different scores. These thirty scores represent a sample of all the possible different heights in the population. The population scores have certain characteristics or values such as a mean and a standard deviation, and they are distributed in a particular way.

Parametric statistics require a number of assumptions about the nature of the population from which the sample scores were drawn. For example, a given parametric statistic may require that the scores be normally distributed in the population. For that particular statistic to be appropriate, this assumption must be valid or the results of computation may not be accurate. The population values (e.g., mean, distribution, and standard deviation) are known as parameters, and since this category of statistics requires assumptions about these values, they called "parametric" statistics.

Since all the scores in the population are not recorded, the researcher has no way of verifying what the parameter values are specifically. Consequently parameters or population values usually exist only in theory. Unless there is other information available (such as some massive study that previously recorded scores on the entire population), these values are truly assumptions. They are assumed to exist in a particular form that is in harmony with the requirements of the statistic that the researcher wishes to use. If, however, there is reason to believe (either by logic or previous information) that the population values do not conform to the requirements of a given statistic, the researcher would be in error to use that analysis.

The above statements should not be taken to mean that the researcher may capriciously choose a statistical analysis and decide that the assumptions are met by the data. These assumptions must be not only reasonable but supportable. If the soundness of any assumption is questionable, then a given statistical analysis should not be used. It is this reason that has generated the development and use of nonparametric statistics. Nonparametric statistics require fewer assumptions regarding the nature of the population from which the scores are drawn. This category of statistics has sometimes been referred to as "distribution-free." This term may be misleading. It is *not* the case that no assumptions at all are involved, rather that the nature of the population from which the scores were sampled is less frequently important. Requirements for nonparametric statistics more often involve the type of data and make fewer references to the population than parametric analyses.

Thus one of the differences between parametric and nonparametric statistics involves the assumptions that must be met. For parametric statistics to be appropriate, the researcher must be able to reasonably assume that certain characteristics are true about the population from which the scores were drawn. (Specific assumptions that are necessary for given analyses will be noted later in the chapter as selected tests are presented.) Nonparametric statistics do not, in general, require as many nor as rigorous assumptions.

Nature of the data. An additional difference between parametric and nonparametric statistical analyses involves the nature of the collected data. Four types of data were discussed in Chapter 10: nominal, ordinal, interval, and ratio. Each of these types of data were described as having different measurement properties. Nominal data have the property of identity, ordinal data have identity and order, and interval and ratio scales have identity, order, and additivity. These properties are important in terms of what statistical analyses can be performed. Table 12-1 presents the four data types with their respective measurement properties and indicates the appropriate application of parametric and nonparametric analyses.

As indicated in Table 12-1, the application of parametric statistics is limited to data that are either interval or ratio in nature. This limitation is dictated by the mathematical operations involved in the computation of parametric statistics. These analyses require arithmetic manipulations such as addition and subtrac-

Table 12-1. Summary of four types of data, their respective measurement properties, and statistical application

Type of data	Relevant measurement properties	Statistical application
Nominal	Identity	Nonparametric statistical analyses
Ordinal	Identity Order	
Interval	Identity Order Additivity	Parametric as well as nonparametric statistical analyses
Ratio	Identity Order Additivity	

tion, as well as others that necessitate the property of additivity. Without this property such manipulations are meaningless, since they are not an accurate representation of real world events (i.e., if the digits 1 and 2 designate apple and orange categories, they cannot be added and result in a meaningful representation). Nonparametric statistics can be used with ordinal and nominal data, since they do not require such mathematical manipulation. They may also be used with interval or ratio scales, since these data types *more* than satisfy the computational requirements of these analyses. *If,* however, other necessary characteristics are present in interval or ratio data samples (e.g., distribution assumptions, an adequate sample size), parametric statistics are generally preferred, since they are more powerful and make more efficient use of data.

Thus the type of recorded data help to determine selection of the statistical analysis to be used. If the researcher collects data that are of the nominal or ordinal scale (e.g., yes-no or male-female categories; ranking or 1-to-5 rating scales, respectively), nonparametric analyses should probably be used. If interval or ratio data are available, either parametric or nonparametric statistics may be used. The decision in the latter case is made on other factors such as distribution assumptions (previously examined in a general fashion) and sample size.

Sample size. As suggested by previous brief comments, the size of the sample must also be a consideration when selecting a statistical analysis. If few subjects are used for experimentation (e.g., $N = 6$ to 8), there is little alternative. Nonparametric analyses are more appropriate. This is particularly true unless "the nature of the population distribution is *known exactly*" (Siegel, 1956, p. 32). Despite knowledge about population distribution, such a small number of subjects does not represent much of a sample of behavior. With such a limited sample, the mathematical operations required by parametric statistics (e.g., computation of means) become highly questionable as to accuracy. Unless replicated several times with only six subjects, there is the distinct possibility that an atypical sample has been drawn and that the performance is not at all representative. Although this is always a problem, the use of parametric statistics may suggest a false sense of security regarding the accuracy of the portrayal.

This raises an immediate and practical question. What is an adequate sample size for using parametric statistics? If a definitive answer were available, this section could have been much shorter, perhaps one or two lines. Judging from the massive amount of literature available in the statistical area, such an answer is not possible. It has been my general rule of thumb that groups of less than twelve to fourteen are questionable in terms of using parametric statistics. This means that if two groups are being compared (treatments A and B, traditional by now in this text), then each group should contain minimally twelve to fourteen subjects before parametric tests may be used confidently. Certainly fifteen and even twenty per group increases the comfort with which the parametric mathematics may be performed, but the concern here is minimums. "Rules of thumb" are, of course, not hard and fast rules. Researchers must use their best judgment and consultation resources. The fact remains that with n's much less than those noted above, the confidence in parametric analyses is substantially reduced, and nonparametric statistics are preferred.

Parametric-nonparametric statistical analyses have primarily been discussed in terms of group studies that use traditional experimental designs. This type of research has historically made greater use of statistical analysis than have investigations using single-subject experimental designs or nonexperimental studies. There is, however, an increasing interest in the application of statistical procedures in studies that are not traditional experimental in nature (e.g., Gottman and Glass, 1978; Glass, Willson, and Gottman, 1975; Gentile, Roden, and Klein, 1972; Hartmann, 1974). In most cases, the same factors require consideration in selection decisions between parametric and nonparametric analyses.

Comments on parametric and nonparametric statistics. As noted above, three general areas are involved in selecting parametric versus nonparametric analyses: assumptions about the nature of the population distribution, the type of data that are collected, and the size of the sample. In all of these areas, parametric statistics have been the standard and more rigorous in terms of requirements. *Parametrics require more stringent assumptions about the population distribution of scores, necessitate more sophisticated data, and require larger sample sizes.* This does not, however, imply that nonparametric analyses are a panacea for researchers who do not wish to attend to these factors. Nonparametric statistics do not represent tools that may be applied in a capricious manner, with an expectation of the same outcome. The advantage of nonparametric statistics involve the characteristics already described. They may be used in situations in which knowledge is lacking concerning the population distribution or in which the necessary assumptions for parametrics cannot be met. They may be used in studies in which small samples are drawn and with more primitive types of data. If, however, *the necessary requirements for parametric statistics are met, they are preferred over nonparametric analyses* for a variety of reasons. Parametric statistics are more powerful than nonparametric analyses when they can be used (Keppel, 1973). Additionally, they make more efficient use of data. If the data are of an interval or ratio scale, nonparametrics are wasteful in terms of the information used versus that which is available in such measurement (Siegel, 1956; Keppel, 1973). One further advantage offered by parametric statistics involves greater flexibility in terms of the types of research questions to which they may be applied. This is particularly evident with more complex studies in which more than one variable is under investigation. Thus when it is possible to satisfy the requirements for parametric analyses, they should be favored over nonparametric statistics. When this is not possible, the use of nonparametrics provides the researcher with an alternative that is more powerful than mere visual inspection of the data.

Turn to p. 296 and complete Simulations 12-1, 12-2, and 12-3.

DIFFERENCE QUESTIONS: WHICH STATISTIC AND WHEN

Early in this text, a distinction was made between difference and relationship questions. By way of review, difference questions are involved in studies that *compare*. Such comparisons may be between the performances or answers of two or more groups (e.g., where the groups receive different treatments or where the groups are compared on a survey regarding annual net income), within a group but between different conditions (e.g., pretest-posttest experiments or answers to questions before and after an election), or within a single subject but between different treatment conditions (e.g., baseline-treatment-reversal comparisons). Relationship questions, on the other hand, explore the degree to which two or more phenomena relate or vary. This type of investigation might ask, "As intelligence varies, what *tends* to happen to reading ability?" As intelligence increases, does reading ability tend to also increase, or does it tend to decrease? (Another example discussed earlier involved length of marriage and annual net income.) Relationship studies involve recording data on a sample of subjects (e.g., both intelligence and reading scores). With two measures on each individual, the researcher then computes a correlation coefficient to determine how the two variables relate in the group, rather than comparing them.

Difference questions and relationship questions require two distinctly different types of statistical approaches. The purpose of the present section is to discuss difference questions and briefly examine the type of statistical techniques that may be employed for data analysis. Relationship statistics will be presented in a subsequent section in this chapter.

Many variations and combinations of difference questions may be asked. For nearly any type of difference question that may be contrived, there are statistical techniques that may be appropriately applied. In the course of this discussion, both parametric and nonparametric analyses will be noted.

Comparing two data points   _Difference_

The first type of difference question that will be examined involves comparing two data points. In this context, the term "data point" refers to a performance record, score, or summarization of scores such as a group mean. The two data points could be performance records on two groups (such as the mean correct responses by groups A and B), two performances by the same group (such as in a pre-post investigation), or two performances by a single subject (such as baseline performance compared with postintervention performance in a behavior modification experiment). There could be several variations on these types of arrangements. It has been my experience that, with the basic design and statistical frameworks in mind, the researcher can apply appropriate variations on these themes for a given research problem.

Independent comparisons. Throughout this text examples of two group comparisons with one experimental variable have been used. (Group A receives one teaching method, group B receives a second teaching method, and the experimental variable is method of instruction.) This is one of the simplest types of experiments to conceptualize with essentially a single focus question, "Is there a difference in effectiveness between teaching method A and B?" Other things being equal, this question becomes, "Does group A perform differently than group B?" The term "independent" indicates that the scores under condition A are not affected by or do not affect those under condition B. For practical purposes this means that the two groups are constituted from different subjects (which is not the case with, say, a pre-post situation). Thus there is no reason to believe that the performances are not independent.

Two groups may be compared under circumstances in which the researcher is faced with a weaker data scale (nominal or ordinal measurement) or few subjects per group or both. As was noted earlier, either of these conditions would require the use of nonparametric statistics. Under other conditions in which interval data are approximated, the required distribution assumptions are reasonable, and if a more adequate sample is tested, parametric analyses are appropriate.

Parametric analysis. For comparisons in which interval or ratio data are recorded, it is common to compare the mean of the scores obtained by group A with the mean of group B. This process is testing for differences between two independent means. Since means are being specified, it is assumed that the appropriate data have been recorded that will permit the necessary mathematical manipulations.

Two parametric statistics are available for this situation, the $\bar{z}$ *test* and the *t test for differences between independent means*. The $\bar{z}$ test is useful for samples with more than thirty individuals in a group. The *t test* is similar to the $\bar{z}$ test except that it is also applicable for groups equal to or less than thirty. Since the *t* test is more flexible in terms of the number of subjects ($n = 12$ to 30 or above), it is almost universally used in comparisons of two means.

As suggested by its inculsion as a parametric statistic, the *t* test requires interval or ratio data and group samples of about twelve or above. In addition to these requirements, the *t* test assumes that the criterion measure is normally distributed in the populations from which the means are drawn and that both also have equal variation in terms of the criterion measure. If these assumptions are reasonable (or if there is little reason to believe that they are drastically violated), the *t* test for differences is a powerful and convenient analysis for comparing two independent means. It is simple to compute, and formulas may be found in nearly any introductory statistics text. For step-by-step procedures, the reader is directed to the volume by Bruning and Kintz (1968). Remember that the test to be used is the *t* test for differences between *independent* means. The reason for this emphasis becomes evident later as a variation of the *t* test is examined.

Nonparametric analysis. Nonparametric statistical analyses may be used under certain conditions in which parametric statistics cannot be applied. For situations in which two independent data points are to be compared, there are analyses that can be used with both nominal and ordinal data.

Two nonparametric analyses will be mentioned for investigations in which nominal data have been recorded. The reader will recall that nominal data are characterized by categorical representation of events. For example, yes-no responses on a questionnaire and performances that are scored as pass-fail or successful-unsuccessful would be considered nominal data.

If a small number of subjects are used (total N less than 20), a useful statistic for comparing two groups is the *Fisher exact probability test.* This test might be used in comparing, say, groups A and B if the data that were collected involved categories such as pass versus fail. Table 12-2, illustrates diagrammatically how such a comparison might be made. Fisher's test is simple to compute, and procedures may be found in Siegel (1956). If the sample is large, however, the computation becomes laborious. In situations in which N is greater than twenty, it is much easier to use the *chi-square (χ^2) test for comparing independent samples.*

The chi-square test for two independent samples, like Fisher's exact probability test, may be used with nominal data. The previous example (groups A and B that had performance categorized as either pass or fail) will also serve satisfactorily for the chi-square test. The question is essentially, "Does group A differ

Table 12-2. Example of how comparisons might be made
using Fisher's exact probability test

Groups	Performance categories	
	Pass	Fail
A	*n*	*n*
B	*n*	*n*

from group B in terms of how many subjects passed as opposed to how many failed?" The chi-square test is preferred when *N* is greater than twenty. This test requires a cell size *(n)* of at least 5. Thus in Table 12-2 none of the categories (e.g., group A, passed; group B, failed) should have less than five individuals so categorized if the chi-square test is to be used. If this occurs, such as group B having only three individuals who passed, Fisher's test should be applied instead. Computational procedures may be found in Siegel (1956).

Two nonparametric analyses will also be mentioned briefly for studies in which ordinal data have been collected. Again, by way of review, ordinal data are characterized by the ability to rank order events on the basis of an underlying continuum. The ranks denote greater than or less than on the dimension being assessed, a property that is not necessarily characteristic of categories. The example of a rating scale of 1 to 5 was used in Chapter 10. The reader may wish to refer to this chapter for additional review and examples.

When data are of at least an ordinal scale, two groups may be compared using the *median test*. Using the previous example, this analysis addresses the question of whether there is a difference between the medians of group A and group B. The median test may be used with a variety of sample sizes. Individuals interested in computational procedures should, again, consult Siegel (1956) or other texts that provide details on this technique.

A second nonparametric analysis that is useful for comparing two independent samples of ordinal data is the *Mann-Whitney U test*. This is a powerful nonparametric analysis for comparing two groups for which rank-order data have been collected. This test also may be used with a variety of sample sizes and with different sample sizes in each group (e.g., group A, $n = 1$, and group B, $n = 3$, up to group n's of 20). Beyond group n's of about 20 the Mann-Whitney U test becomes somewhat laborious to compute. Readers who need to use this test in such situations should consult Siegel (1956) for appropriate procedures.

Nonindependent comparisons. Nonindependent comparisons of two data points represent a considerably different situation from that of independent comparisons just discussed, although they are variations on the same theme. The nonindependent comparison is almost defined by characteristics that are *not* the case for independent comparisons. In the latter situation, the scores in condition

A are not affected by or do not affect those under condition B. In practice this has generally meant that the two groups (conditions A and B) are constituted from different subjects. In the nonindependent situation, on the other hand, there is some reason to believe that scores under condition A have some effect on those under condition B. This might be the case if repeated measures were taken on the same subjects. For example, Fred's performance is measured under condition A and then again under condition B. Since Fred's performance is recorded under both conditions, there is reason to believe that the two scores are not independent because his score in one condition may well have some influence on his score in the other. (There is *no* way that his reading ability in one performance test is not going to have some relationship to his performance on another test.) Similarly, if two groups of subjects are constituted by experimental matching (see Chapter 8), the two groups are not considered independent. The characteristics of subjects in group B are determined by those in group A.

In either of these situations, repeated measures on the same subjects or matched subjects, a different set of statistical procedures is appropriate for data analysis. These procedures are the topic of this section.

Parametric analysis. Probably the most frequently used parametric statistic for this type of comparison is the *t test for differences between nonindependent means.* As the name suggests, this analysis is a computational variation on the *t* test previously discussed under independent comparison. Since it is a parametric statistic, at least interval data and a sample size of twelve or above are required. Additionally, the assumption of a normally distributed criterion measure should be reasonable if the *t* test is to appropriately applied. This test could be used in situations in which a pretest mean was to be compared with a posttest mean (the same group being tested under both conditions). The question would essentially be, "Is there a significant difference between the pretest mean and the posttest mean?" Remember that for comparing two nonindependent means, the *t* test to be used is different than that used for independent means. Computational procedures may be found in nearly any introductory statistics text (e.g., Bruning & Kintz, 1968). Several name variations commonly appear with this analysis including *t* test for nonindependent means, correlated *t* test, and *t* test for related means. These terms are used interchangeably and all designate the same analysis.

Nonparametric analysis. Recall that nonparametric statistics are useful in situations in which parametric analyses are inappropriate. A variety of nonparametric analyses may be used to compare two nonindependent data points. When nominal data have been collected, the *McNemar test for significance of changes* is a useful analysis. Siegel (1956) characterizes the McNemar test as being "particularly applicable to those 'before and after' designs [p. 63]." This type of situation might well be found in the form of a pretest-posttest study.

If ordinal data have been recorded, two nonparametric analyses are available—the *sign test* and the *Wilcoxon matched-pairs signed-ranks test.* Both of these tests, once again, are used for situations in which performance is assessed on the same subjects at two different times.

The sign test is so named because the signs + and − are used as integral parts of computation. This test is easy to use and may be applied with rather small samples (e.g., $N = 6$). One assumption must be reasonable for appropriate application of the sign test—this analysis does require that the variable being assessed and scored in terms of ranks must have a continuous distribution. An example may serve to clarify what is meant by this assumption. Suppose all the students in a given group are being ranked in terms of height. The continuous distribution requirement simply assumes that there is a continuum of heights possible that underlies the ranks of 1 through 15 (if there are fifteen in the group). No other assumption is required.

The Wilcoxon matched-pairs signed-ranks tests is the second nonparametric statistic to be mentioned for ordinal data. This analysis is more powerful than the sign test because it takes into account the magnitude of differences between scores rather than merely indicating in what direction the change occurred. (Using the sign test, the direction of change is all that is considered. A change in one direction is denoted by a +, whereas a change in the other direction is designated as a −.) Because the Wilcoxon test makes a greater use of the actual ranks, it does require that the experimenter be able to judge the magnitude between ranks. When this is possible, the Wilcoxon test is perferred over the sign test. Computational procedures may be found in Siegel (1956).

It should be kept in mind that both of the above analyses ask the question, "Is there a significant difference between two sets of related performances?" This question may take the form, "Is there a difference in this group's performance on the pretest as compared with the posttest?"

Turn to p. 297 and complete Simulations 12-4, 12-5, and 12-6.

Comparing more than two data points

One experimental variable. The discussion of statistical analyses thus far has focused on comparing two data points (e.g., comparing performances of two test situations such as two means or two medians). This discussion has examined, if only briefly, comparisons that were independent as well as those that were not independent. In all cases the comparisons were between two groups or performances with one experimental variable involved. Return for a moment to the classic example of groups A and B in which two teaching techniques are compared. There is one experimental variable, method of instruction, with two types (conditions A and B) representing the specific conditions compared. Likewise if a time-series study is conducted, baseline performance is compared with performance under treatment. In this case the experimental variable may be desig-

Fig. 12-1. Independent comparison design with one experimental variable and five specific conditions.

nated as level of positive reinforcement. The two specific conditions within this experimental variable are the absence versus presence of the treatment (baseline versus treatment). In a similar fashion a pre-post experiment may be conceived as a comparison of absence versus presence of the treatment with a single experimental variable.

Frequently a researcher wishes to conduct a study in which one experimental variable is involved, but more than two specific conditions exist within that variable. Expanding the previous example, a study may be conducted that investigates method of instruction but compares three or more specific types (groups A, B, C, etc). Experiments of this type are merely variations on the previous basic theme with *one experimental variable under study.* The only change represented is that more than two specific conditions are compared within that experimental variable. Instead of two drug dosages, the researcher may wish to compare performance under five levels of dosage (amount of drug treatment being the experimental variable). These variations do, however, require use of different statistical analyses than those previously discussed.

Independent comparisons. Independent comparisons of three or more data points, with one experimental variable, should be viewed in much the same fashion as independent comparisons are in general. Independence, once again, means that the scores under condition C are not influenced by those under conditions B, A, and so on. As before, this usually takes the form of different groups of subjects for each condition. Fig. 12-1 illustrates how five conditions might be designed to test the effects of variation in level of drug dosage. For the present purpose, twenty different subjects have been assigned to each of the five different experimental groups, making this an independent comparison design.

If the researchers have collected interval or ratio data, they are in a position to consider the use of parametric statistics. Perhaps the most commonly used statistic for this type of comparison is the *one-way analysis of variance for comparing independent means.* Shortened to one-way analysis of variance or ANOVA, this test is a powerful technique for comparing three or more means. It is important to emphasize that this discussion is about a *one-way ANOVA for independent comparisons.* Variations of the basic ANOVA will recur in later discussions with different types of designs. One of the reasons for the popularity of ANOVA is its great flexibility for different designs.

The ANOVA provides a convenient analysis for making a simultaneous test for differences among the five means of performance scores by the subjects in Fig. 12-1. As noted ealier, ANOVA is a parametric statistic. Several assumptions must be reasonable before it can be appropriately applied. The type of data must be suitable for this type of analysis, interval, or ratio. Additionally, four other assumptions are usually considered as being required: (1) the scores recorded are normally distributed in the population, (2) the variation in scores is approximately the same for all groups in the experiment (i.e., the score variation in group A is about the same as that in group B, C, and so on. This is commonly referred to as the assumption of equal variance or homogeneous variances), (3) the observations or scores are independent, and (4) the performance variation in the total sample is a result of additive influences. Although these assumptions may appear overwhelming to the beginning researcher, in practice it is obvious that they are not. ANOVA is simply used too frequently for them to present an insurmountable problem. In reality some latitude is possible in terms of how rigorous one must be about meeting these assumptions strictly. Considerably more detail regarding these assumptions is needed before the ANOVA is applied. Information concerning assumptions as well as computational procedures may be found in most statistical texts that present inferential analyses (e.g., Guilford and Fruchter, 1973).

As with other research situations, there are occasions when nominal or ordinal data are recorded with the intent to compare more than two data points (still within the realm of one experimental variable). Under these conditions, of course, one must turn to nonparametric statistics for analysis purposes. Using the same basic design arrangement that was presented in Fig. 12-1, suppose for a moment that there are nominal data with which to work. This might be the case if there were some sort of dichotomous categories regarding the subjects' health status (e.g., "cured" versus "not cured"). The different groups can be statistically compared under this type of situation by using the *chi-square test for k independent samples.* The chi-square test for this comparison is a simple expansion of the analysis that was mentioned previously for comparing two groups. The term "k" is used to designate the number of groups being compared. For the example in Fig. 12-1, k would be equal to 5, since there are five groups. However, as a part of the general title of the analysis, k is used to indicate "several, depending on the exact number of groups in the experiment." As before, the cell size *(n)* needs to be at least 5 or larger. Thus this test would not be appropriate if there were only four or three in any cell. The discussion presented previously for chi-square remains appropriate for its use here and, as before, computational procedures may be found in a variety of statistical text-books (e.g., Siegel, 1956).

Two statistical analyses are appropriate for comparing more than two independent data points if ordinal data have been collected—the *median test* and the *Kruskal-Wallis one-way analysis of variance by ranks*. The median test for this situation is an extension of the median test that was previously mentioned for comparing two data points (in fact it is frequently designated as the *extension* of the median test). Computational procedures may be found in Siegel (1956) as well as other texts that deal with nonparametric statistics.

The Kruskal-Wallis one-way analysis of variance by ranks represents a second statistical technique that is useful for comparisons of k independent data points when ordinal data have been collected. The requirements of this analysis are essentially the same as those for the extension of the median test presented above. The Kruskal-Wallis, however, is more efficient because it makes use of more of the available information than does the median test. Consequently, when the experimental situation permits use of either test, the Kruskal-Wallis is preferred.

Nonindependent comparisons. Occasionally the researcher may wish to compare three or more data points that are not independent. Such a situation might arise if, for example, the same subjects were tested three times with some treatment or event occurring between the measurements. Fig. 12-2 illustrates how

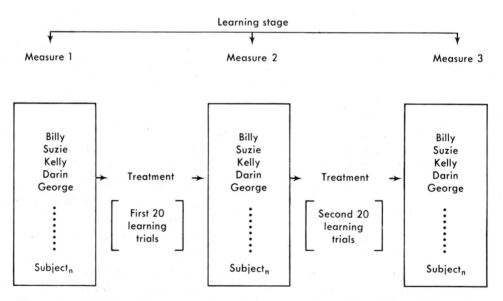

Fig. 12-2. Nonindependent comparison with one experimental variable and three data points.

such an investigation might be designed. The same subjects are given a pretreatment measure (measure 1), then the first twenty practice trials of the learning task are administered. This is then followed by a midexperiment assessment (measure 2), the next twenty practice trials and, finally, the third test (measure 3). This type of study can easily be viewed as an extension of the pre-post design mentioned previously with the addition of a third test. Expansions may, of course, involve more than three data collection points (e.g., four, five, . . . k). On occasion the treatment that intercedes between measurements may involve only the passage of time rather than application of an active treatment. In all cases in which multiple measurements are administered, the researcher must be cautious about the effects of the testing itself as noted in Chapter 7.

If the researcher has collected nominal data and wishes to compare three or more nonindependent data points, a useful analysis is the *Cochran Q test*. Such a situation might occur if the design involved testing the same subjects under three different drug dosages. The data might be recorded as "cured" versus "not cured," thus falling into the categorical type of measurement. This example is merely used for illustrative purposes, and it is necessary to remain aware of the design problems that would be presented by such an experiment. One obvious difficulty would be the multiple treatment interference problem, which was noted as affecting both internal and external validity in Chapter 7. Certainly there would have to be some assurance that the effects of drug dosage 1 were not still operating when the dosage 2 condition was implemented. Computational procedures for Cochran's Q may be found in Siegel (1956).

If the recorded data are ordinal in nature, three or more nonindependent data points may be statistically compared using the *Friedman two-way analysis of variance by ranks*. Although the title includes the term "two-way" (usually suggestive of two experimental variables), this analysis is appropriately discussed here because it actually makes a one-way comparison. To illustrate, suppose that the study concerning drug dosage was arranged as in Table 12-3. The Friedman analysis compares the ranks between the dosage conditions, which, since there is one experimental variable (level of drug dosage), is a one-way comparison despite what the analysis title suggests. Because the same subjects are tested under all conditions, this situation falls into the nonindependent data point comparison category. The Friedman technique may be used with small samples (Siegel provides tables for situations in which $N = 2$) and is relatively simple to compute.

If the researcher has collected interval or ratio data, parametric statistical techniques may be considered for analysis purposes. With this level of data and assuming that other factors are present such as an adequate sample size and a reasonable assurance that assumptions are approximated, the task at hand is essentially one of comparing three or more nonindependent means. Probably the most commonly used statistical test for such a comparison is the *analysis of variance for repeated measures* (with one experimental variable—thus a one-way

Table 12-3. Example of nonindependent comparisons between three drug dosage conditions

	Dosage conditions		
	2 ml.	**6 ml.**	**10 ml.**
Subject 1			
Subject 2			
Subject 3			
Subject 4			
.			
.			
.			
Subject n			

ANOVA with repeated measures). The distinction is important to highlight. Previously a one-way ANOVA for comparing independent means (resulting from different groups' performance) was discussed. The present description is of a one-way ANOVA for comparing three or more *nonindependent* means (resulting from repeated measures on the same subjects). The computation procedures are somewhat different and may be found in most statistical texts that focus on inferential statistics.

Turn to p. 299 and complete Simulations 12-7 and 12-8.

Two experimental variables. The discussion of statistical procedures has thus far focused on situations in which one experimental variable is being investigated. (The term "experimental variable" is being used generically here as before; it essentially refers to comparisons that may be made whether the study is an experiment in the true sense or a comparison between data points in a nonexperimental study such as a survey.) Hypothetical studies in which two or more data points are compared (such as performance under three different teaching techniques) within the single experimental variable (method of instruction) have been examined. Frequently studies are conducted in which more than one experimental variable is of interest in the same investigation. This section will discuss statistical data analysis in situations with two experimental variables under study. You may wish to review the sections on this type of investigation in Chapter 5.

Note that there is less emphasis on nonparametric analyses than in previous

Fig. 12-3. Hypothetical independent comparison with two experimental variables.

sections, a reflection of a point made earlier in this chapter. Parametric statistics offer greater flexibility in terms of the types of questions asked, particularly with regard to more complex designs involving more than one experimental variable. Do not interpret this as freedom to apply parametric analyses under all conditions in which two or more experimental variables are studied. Restrictions concerning the type of data, sample size, and assumptions are still operative.

Independent comparisons. An investigation with two experimental variables that involves independent comparisons merely represents a conceptual combination of more simple designs. Fig. 12-3 illustrates a hypothetical investigation with two experimental variables, material difficulty and amount of practice. Comparison A, which represents the material difficulty variable, has two specific levels, high-difficulty material and low-difficulty material. Comparison B, the amount of practice variable, has three levels of ten trials, twenty trials, and thirty trials. Thus there are six different data points to be compared. This is an independent design, since there is a separate group of subjects for each condition (randomly assigned).

An investigation such as that in Fig. 12-3 is usually designed for situations in which parametric analyses can be applied, since nonparametrics are so cumbersome with complex studies. This, of course, means that interval data are collected, cells include twelve or more subjects, and the researcher is reasonably sure that the assumptions of normal distribution and equal variance are approximated. If these elements are present, the most popular statistical technique for this situation is the *two-way analysis of variance for comparing independent means.* This analysis is an extension of the independent ANOVA noted previously under independent comparisons with one experimental variable. By now it should be evident that the ANOVA is an extremely flexible statistic that may be computationally modified to fit a variety of research designs. This is an important factor in its great popularity and contributes to its frequent appearance in the research literature. In addition to its flexibility, however, the ANOVA is an extremely powerful analysis, often viewed as the standard against which other techniques are compared. Computational procedures for this analysis are really rather simple and certainly less formidable than many beginning researchers think. They are found in most statistical texts under titles such as two-way ANOVA, two-factor ANOVA, and ANOVA for double-classification experiments.

If the requirements are not met for parametric statistics, the researcher will have to resort to nonparametric analyses. In an experiment such as that exemplified above, data analysis becomes cumbersome, Common nonparametric techniques previously reviewed constitute the main choices from which selection may be made. In such a situation the experimenter has little choice but to analyze one comparison at a time while ignoring the second experimental variable. This would mean, in the example just given, that two independent data points would be compared (high versus low difficulty) by combining the performances of groups 1, 3, and 5 for high difficulty and groups 2, 4, and 6 for low difficulty (refer to Fig. 12-3). The second variable would then have to be analyzed comparing the three amounts of practice, ten trials (by combining the performance scores of groups 1 and 2) versus twenty trials (groups 3 and 4) versus thirty trials (groups 5 and 6). Such an approach is obviously more laborious and does not provide as much information. It may, however, be the only option if parametric analysis is not appropriate.

Mixed comparisons. Mixed designs have previously been introduced in Chapter 5. Review of this material will alert the reader to the fact that mixed designs involve a study, with at least two experimental variables, in which *independent comparisons are made on one variable and repeated measures are used on the second.* For

Fig. 12-4. Hypothetical mixed comparison with two experimental variables.

the purposes of this section, use the example in Fig. 12-3. This independent design would be altered to a mixed design if it were set up with different groups for each level of variable B that received both high- and low-difficulty material. The different groups for each level result in three *different* groups of subjects, the independent variable. Receiving both high- and low-difficulty material constitutes repeated measures on the difficulty variable. Such a design is illustrated in Fig. 12-4.

As noted earlier, investigations that are designed in this fashion are usually planned with the intent of using parametric statistical analysis. If the requirements for such computation are met, the *two-way mixed analysis of variance* would be an appropriate analysis for this type of experiment. This is another variation on the basic ANOVA theme, which further illustrates its great flexibility. Computational procedures are somewhat different from those presented before and essentially combine the components of independent analysis with those for repeated measures. "Mixed" ANOVA is used in the same sense as the "mixed" design described earlier. Details for computing this analysis may be found in a variety of statistical texts that include discussions of inferential statistics.

Investigations that will not permit the use of parametric analysis (e.g., inappropriate data, small samples, or drastic assumption violation) would, again, require the application of nonparametric techniques. Basically the same approach as that described in the previous section would be applied. Data from one variable at a time would be analyzed using the appropriate nonparametric statistic (e.g., either two or k data points, independent or nonindependent, depending on the situation). As with two factor studies or more complex experiments, nonparametric analyses are considerably more cumbersome.

Turn to p. 301 and complete Simulation 12-9.

Logical extrapolations: more complex designs

The phrase "more complex designs" has been used in this chapter in a relative sense and generally as a means of referring to studies with more than two experimental variables. The term is not meant to connote complex in the sense of "difficult." It has been my experience that some of the most "difficult" experiments are really made difficult by virtue of ill-defined problems that have not been distilled to operational form. On the other hand, some of the "easier" pieces of research often involve several experimental variables ("complex" in the sense of the number of variables) but are made easy in the sense that they are clearly and operationally defined.

Using more complex designs. For purposes of the present discussion, the phrase "more complex designs" is used to generally refer to studies asking dif-

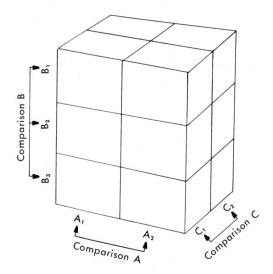

Fig. 12-5. Diagrammatic representation of a hypothetical study with three experimental variables.

ference questions with three or more experimental variables. Such designs have already been introduced in Chapter 5 and considered briefly. This type of study is conducted when the researcher wishes to examine three or more experimental variables simultaneously. Diagrammatic representations of such studies are somewhat more difficult than with two variables. Fig. 12-5 illustrates an experiment with three variables. This diagram, although totally hypothetical, involves variable A (with two levels, A_1 and A_2), variable B (with three levels, B_1, B_2, and B_3), and variable C (with two levels, C_1 and C_2). This experiment might be labeled a $2 \times 3 \times 2$ design in a research report with the numerical designations referring to the specific levels in each variable.

If the experiment illustrated in Fig. 12-5 involved different subjects for each cell group, it would be considered a totally independent design. This would mean that twelve separate groups of subjects would be used. As before, the term "independent" is used to indicate that the scores in any given cell do not have an influence on the scores in any other cell. This, of course, precludes repeated measures on any variable. Using this example, suppose for the moment that the basic requirements for parametric analyses are met. This would mean that interval or ratio data had been collected, that each cell had twelve or more subjects, and that the assumptions of normality and equal variance were reasonable. If these elements were present, data could conveniently be analyzed using a *three-way analysis of variance for independent comparisons*. This analysis will yield a great deal of information and, as before, merely involves computation extensions of the more simple ANOVA procedures discussed earlier. Computation proce-

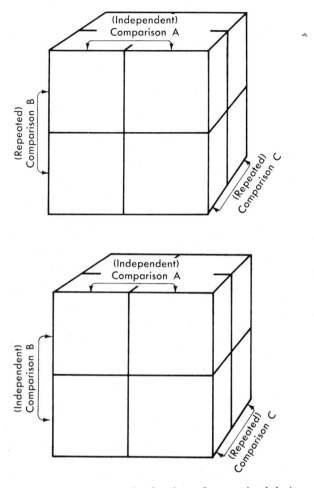

Fig. 12-6. Option examples for three-factor mixed design.

dures are not difficult but do become increasingly laborious as the design becomes more complex.

Now examine this same design assuming that it is not possible to use parametric statistics. As noted during the discussion of studies with two experimental variables, such a situation makes data analysis cumbersome, since nonparametric statistics are not nearly as flexible in terms of application to more complex designs. Probably the best approach under such conditions would involve analyzing the comparisons separately (e.g., comparison A, then B, and finally C). The basic nonparametric approaches to perform such analyses have been described earlier in this chapter. Hopefully the researcher would plan ahead sufficiently and either ensure the appropriateness of the study for parametrics, *or* design a simpler investigation.

Reconsider the three-factor experiment that was illustrated in Fig. 12-5. It may be that the researcher will want to obtain repeated measures on one or more of the experimental variables. If this is the case, the design becomes a three-factor mixed design, since it combines independent comparisons on some experimental variables (i.e., different groups for variables A and B) and repeated measures on others (e.g., variable C). This type of design was introduced previously in Chapter 5 and is illustrated in Fig. 12-6. Note that two examples are shown in Fig. 12-6. One indicates comparisons A and B as being independent, and comparison C is the variable on which subjects receive repeated measures. For this experiment four different groups of subjects would be necessary, and they would all be measured twice under the two C conditions. The second example in Fig. 12-6 indicates only variable A as independent, and repeated measures are obtained on both variables B and C. Only two groups of subjects would be used in this example, and both groups would be measured under all B and C conditions. Both of these examples are considered mixed designs.

If the studies in Fig. 12-6 include the appropriate elements for parametric statistics, the data can be analyzed using the *three-way mixed analysis of variance.* This technique is an extension of the mixed ANOVA discussed earlier. Slight computational modifications are made depending on whether one or two variables are independent.

Problems with more complex designs. The last section described more complex designs that may be used to investigate difference questions and statistical procedures that can be applied for data analysis purposes. Studies were discussed that included three experimental variables. The researcher may wish to conduct an investigation that includes even more experimental variables (e.g., four, five, or more). Such studies may be implemented and data analyzed using logical extrapolations of what has been discussed previously. There are analysis of variance procedures that can be computed for such designs, both totally independent as well as mixed (e.g., four-way ANOVA). In fact, as computer use has become increasingly sophisticated, there have been a number of sophisticated analysis procedures developed that make the computational capability nearly limitless. There are, however, some serious problems involved in using such complex designs.

As the complexity of an investigation increases, it becomes more difficult to create and maintain a mental image of the various components included in the study. It has been my experience that one of the most effective means of conceptualizing a study is to draw a picture of it much like the diagrams that have appeared throughout this text. Most people are accustomed to visualizing phenomena primarily in a two-dimensional fashion (particularly as they illustrate on paper). It is possible to draw three-dimensional designs such as those in Figs. 12-

5 and 12-6, but, when presented with additional factors to illustrate, the task becomes difficult. This results in a conceptualization problem, particularly for the beginning researcher. Related to this difficulty is the task of interpreting results from a complex experiment once the data are analyzed. Remember, analysis of data is *not* the end product of research. There is little reason to conduct an investigation unless the *results can be meaningfully interpreted.* Such interpretation frequently becomes overwhelming when the design is complex. Thus, although the design and analysis capability exists for highly complex experiments,

Table 12-4. Summarized inferential statistics for difference questions

	Type of comparison		
	Independent	**Nonindependent**	**Mixed**
Two data points			
Parametric	$\bar{z}$ test	t test for	
	t test for	nonindependent	
	independent means	means	
Nonparametric	Nominal data		
	Fisher exact	McNemar test for	
	probability	significance of	
	Chi-square (χ^2)	changes	
	Ordinal data		
	Median test	Sign test	
	Mann-Whitney U	Wilcoxon matched-pairs	
	test	signed-ranks	
More than two data points			
One experimental variable			
Parametric	One-way ANOVA	One-way ANOVA (for	
	(independent)	repeated measures)	
Nonparametric	Nominal data		
	Chi-square (χ^2)	Cochran's Q	
	for k		
	Independent		
	comparisons		
	Ordinal data		
	Median test	Friedman	
	Kruskal-Wallis		
Two experimental variables			
Parametric	Two-way ANOVA		Two-way
	(independent)		mixed
			ANOVA

the interpretation of simpler studies is far easier and more straightforward. More importantly, this may well result in a more meaningful outcome in terms of practice and theory.

Another area requires brief comment before leaving the topic of inferential statistics for difference questions. It was noted earlier that time-series experiments that use one subject have not used statistical analysis to any great degree. A variety of factors have contributed to this state of affairs, most of which relate to the assumptions necessary for using certain techniques that were discussed briefly in various parts of this chapter. Edgar and Billingsley (1974) have examined the use of statistical analyses with single-subject experiments and clarified many of the issues involved. Various approaches have been suggested for analyzing data in time-series experiments, some involving such dramatic departures from tradition as the application of analysis of variance to studies using A-B-A-B designs (Gentile, Roden, and Klein, 1972). At this time, however, the use of statistical analyses in time-series experiments is not a fully developed component in behavioral research. Many issues remain to be clarified, and there is a great deal of interest in this topic (e.g., Gottman and Glass, 1978; Glass, Willson, and Gottman, 1975; Gentile, Roden, and Klein, 1972; Hartmann, 1974; Kazdin, 1976; Kratochwill, Alden, Demuth, et al., 1974; Thoresen and Elashoff, 1974). With the growing interest in this area, it is likely that many developments can be expected in the future.

A variety of statistical procedures have been discussed thus far in this chapter. The questions and conditions under which each might be most appropriately applied have been examined. Obviously these are general considerations; specifics may alter somewhat the analysis chosen. However, these general guidelines may be very helpful to the beginning researcher and are summarized in Table 12-4.

RELATIONSHIP QUESTIONS: WHICH STATISTIC AND WHEN

Thus far focus has been on statistical procedures that may be applied to a variety of difference questions. The purpose of this section is to briefly describe techniques that may be used for data analysis when the researcher is investigating a relationship question.

By way of review, relationship questions are involved in studies that explore the *degree to which two or more phenomena relate or vary together.* Such an investigation might examine the relationship between height and weight *(as height varies, what tends to happen to weight?).* For this type of study the researcher records both height and weight on a sample of subjects. With two measures on each subject, the data are then analyzed by computing what is known as a correlation coefficient. The correlation coefficient provides an estimate of the degree to which the variables measured relate. The coefficient itself is the outcome of the computation and may range from $+1.00$ to -1.00. (Most results fall between these extremes, such as .70, $-.50$, etc.) Correlations that result in coefficients with a plus sign are known as positive correlations. Such results indicate a positive relationship, which means that the two variables tend to vary in the same direction (as height increases weight also tends to increase, or as height decreases weight also tends to decrease). Coefficients with a minus sign are known as negative correlations. Negative correlations indicate inverse relationships between the two variables. They tend to vary in opposite directions; as one increases the other tends to decrease. (For example, as the frequency of cardiac arrest increases in a population, longevity tends to decrease.)

A correlation that results in a $+1.00$ coefficient indicates a strong positive relationship between the two variables being measured. Sometimes known as a "perfect positive correlation," a $+1.00$ coefficient indicates that each time one variable either increases or decreases, the second variable also exhibits an increment change in the same direction. *(Each time height increases, weight also increases.)* Similarly, a -1.00 correlation is indicative of a strong relationship of an inverse nature. In such a situation, each time there is an increase in one variable there is a decrease in the second.

Correlation coefficients that are closer to zero indicate a much weaker relationship between the two variables being measured. A zero correlation suggests that there is no systematic variation at all between the two variables, either positive or negative.

Statistical significance in relationship studies essentially means the same thing that it does in comparative investigations. Once the sample is selected and the measures recorded, the data are then analyzed using one of a variety of computational formulas. This results in a correlation coefficient such as has just been discussed. The researcher then checks this coefficient with statistical tables to determine whether it is statistically significant. If the correlation obtained is significant ($P < .05$ or $P < .01$), it is doubtful that the relationship observed is a result of chance. The researcher is then likely to interpret the data as suggesting that a relationship does exist between the two factors measured.

A word of caution is in order concerning the interpretation of correlational studies. A high correlation coefficient, even if it is statistically significant, should *not* be taken to mean that variation in one factor (e.g., height) *causes* variation in the second factor (e.g., weight). Causation should *not* be inferred from correlational data. A high correlation coefficient merely indicates that the two variables tend to vary systematically, either together for positive correlation or inversely in the case of negative correlation. Such a relation permits the prediction of one variable from knowledge about the second but does not permit statements about causation. Many factors that may vary systematically in this world do not actually act on one another.

A second note is also appropriate at this point in terms of interpretation of correlation coefficients. It was noted above that 1.00 correlations (either + or −) rarely occur and that coefficients such as .70, .50, and so on are more frequent. Perhaps because of the way the correlation coefficient is presented, a .70 correlation is occasionally *misinterpreted* as representing the percent of variation in common between the two variables being measured. This is an inappropriate interpretation and, in most cases, inaccurate. A .70 correlation does *not* mean that 70% of the time when one factor varies, the second measure also changes. In fact, if one is interested in the percent of variation in common, the obtained correlation coefficient should be squared. Using the previous example, a correlation of .70 actually indicates less than 50% variation in common between the two measures (.70 × .70 = .49 or 49%). This presents a different picture than the previous misinterpretation of a .70 coefficient. There are certain formulas that include correction factors in computation (primarily reliability formulas used in test construction). In general, however, a correlation should not be taken as representative of percent.

The term "correlation" is a general label for the type of analysis used in relationship investigations. Actually several specific techniques are used in different situations, much as was encountered with statistics for difference questions. In selecting the appropriate correlational technique for analysis purposes, the researcher must pay close attention to the type of data that have been collected on both variables (i.e., nominal, ordinal, interval, or ratio). The reader may wish to review the discussion concerning different types of data found in Chapter 10.

Perhaps the most commonly known correlation technique is the *Pearson product-moment correlation.* This analysis may be used when *both of the measures recorded* (variable 1 and variable 2, height and weight in the previous example) *are either interval or ratio data.* The symbol for the product-moment correlation is *r,* which is occasionally used to refer to correlation in general. This use of the symbol is actually incorrect, since it specifically denotes the product-moment analysis. The product-moment *r* is a highly popular correlation technique, primarily because it provides a stable estimate of relationship. When the data permit its use, this is definitely the preferred analysis. Computational procedures may be found in most standard statistical texts (e.g., Guilford and Fruchter, 1973; Bruning and Kintz, 1968).

Two correlational techniques may be used if the *data collected are ordinal* (that is, the measures on *both variable 1 and variable 2 are in the form of ranks).* The more widely known analysis is the *Spearman rank-order correlation,* which is also known as ρ *(rho).* The second technique is *Kendall's tau,* which may also be used when both measures are in the form of ordinal data. Kendall's tau is preferred over the Spearman correlation when only a small sample is available (*N* less than 10). It is, however, somewhat more difficult to compute, and, when the sample size permits, the Spearman rho should be employed. Computational procedures for Spearman's analysis may be found in most statistical texts (e.g., Guilford and Fruchter, 1973; Bruning and Kintz, 1968). Computational procedures for Kendall's tau are somewhat less available but may be obtained from Siegel (1956) as well as Bruning and Kintz (1968).

Data in the form of a dichotomy (e.g., successful-unsuccessful) may also be submitted to correlational analysis. Because a dichotomy represents categories, data of this type fall into the nominal level of measurement. Two correlational techniques may be used with this type of data.

If the data on *both variables* represent an *artificial dichotomy,* the analysis to be applied is the *tetrachoric correlation.* A note of explanation is in order regarding artificial dichotomy. An artificial dichotomy would exist if the experimenter arbitrarily divided performances into two categories. This might be the case with the "successful-unsuccessful" example above, in which someone has rather arbitrarily defined what is successful and unsuccessful performance. If such data are recorded on both variable 1 and variable 2, the experimenter can obtain a correlation using the tetrachoric procedure.

A second type of dichotomous data may also be correlated. When data on both variables represent *true dichotomies,* the analysis of choice is the *phi coefficient.* A true dichotomy exists when the categories are relatively clear-cut and are not determined arbitrarily. An example of this type of situation might be the absence versus presence of a student's response. Assuming that the determination of whether the student responded is clear-cut, such data would be considered a true dichotomy. When such data are recorded on both measures, an estimate of relationship can be obtained with the phi coefficient.

The discussion thus far has examined correlational techniques that may be used with nominal data and ordinal data as well as interval and ratio data. In each case, however, the procedure was designed for the *same type of data on both of the measures being correlated.* That is, if the analysis under discussion was appropriate for rank data (Spearman's rho, Kendall's tau), this type of data was required on both variable 1 and variable 2. A limited number of techniques are available that permit correlation when data on one variable are of one type and data on the second variable are of a different type. The remainder of this section will present two such correlational procedures.

The concepts of artificial and true dichotomies have already been encountered. Consider for a moment a situation in which the researcher has data in the form of an *artificial dichotomy on one variable and interval or ratio data on the second variable.* Recall that the artificial dichotomy data will be the result of two arbitrarily defined categories. If the researcher wishes to correlate two measures such as those above, this may be accomplished by using a technique known as *biserial correlation.* This type of situation might be encountered if, for example, the researcher wanted to determine the relationship between success or failure in a physical fitness test and the speed in a 100-yard dash. In this example the time to run the 100-yard dash is literally ratio data. The other measure, recorded as pass-fail on the physical fitness test, is artificial dichotomous data, since the cutoff point is arbitrarily determined. After all, someone's judgment is involved in deciding what is or is not physically fit.

A precautionary note is in order in terms of use of the biserial correlation. It was previously noted that the extreme limits for any correlation are +1.00 and −1.00. In computation of the biserial correlation, it is mathematically possible to exceed these limits, particularly if the measures are not normally distributed. This is a characteristic of this particular formula of which the researcher should be aware. Otherwise a correlation of 1.15 might result in wasted searching for a computational error that really is not there. Such a result is generated by the relative lack of precision in the technique, emphasizing the preference of measures other than the artificial dichotomy when possible.

If the data involve a *true dichotomy on one variable and interval or ratio data on the second variable,* an estimate of relationship may be obtained by using the *point biserial correlation.* Recall that the true dichotomy is the result of clear-cut categories such as male-female. This is a different situation from that presented by the artificial dichotomy. The point biserial correlation is frequently used in investigations that relate sex categories to performance on tasks that generate at least interval data. Modifying the earlier example, the point biserial procedure

Table 12-5. Summarized inferential statistics for relationship questions

	Parametric conditions	Nonparametric conditions
Same type of data on both measures		
Interval or ratio data	Pearson product-moment correlation	
Ordinal data		Spearman rank-order correlation ($N > 10$)
		Kendall's tau ($N < 10$)
Nominal data		Phi coefficient (true dichotomies)
		Tetrachoric correlation (artificial dichotomies)
Different types of data on the two measures		
Nominal (artificial dichotomies) and interval or ratio		Biserial correlation
Nominal (true dichotomies) and interval or ratio		Point biserial correlation

might be used to correlate sex categories with performance in a 100-yard dash. This analysis is closely related to the powerful product-moment correlation and does not have the mathematical idiosyncrasy noted for the biserial technique (exceeding the ± 1.00 range). Computation procedures for the point biserial correlation may be found in Bruning and Kintz (1968).

Examination of statistical procedures for relationship questions has been limited to situations in which two variables are of interest, such as the classic examples of height and weight as variables 1 and 2. More complex techniques are available to permit correlation of more than two variables. These analyses, however, generally require a knowledge of and degree of comfort with statistics that are frequently not present in the beginning researcher. Consequently, these procedures have been omitted to maintain the conceptual integrity of an introductory presentation.

A variety of statistical procedures have been discussed here for relationship questions. The conditions under which each might be most appropriately applied have also been examined. Clearly these are general considerations and the particular conditions of an investigation might alter the analysis used. These general guidelines, however, may prove useful to the beginning researcher and are summarized in Table 12-5.

 Turn to p. 301 and complete Simulations 12-10 and 12-11.

COMMENTS

The discussion of inferential statistics presented in this chapter has by no means been comprehensive. Not all of the myriad statistical tools have been discussed, nor has any single technique been explored in great depth. The purpose of this chapter was simply to provide an introductory description of selected analyses that might be applied under a variety of research circumstances. The nature of the presentation was intended to give the reader an overview of various types of statistical tools and to provide a guide as to when they might be used. Certainly more comprehensive knowledge will require consultation of a variety of texts that have the sole purpose of presenting statistical analyses. Likewise, information on computational procedures and formulas has intentionally been omitted from this chapter. This was done on the assumption that such inclusions might detract from the student's necessary grasp of the purposes and uses of various analyses. The result has been a frequent reference to other sources for computational information. Without fail an attempt has been made to consider these references carefully to select those that are elementary and clear yet accurate in their presentation. Hopefully the student now has a general knowledge (or can refer back to this chapter) of what statistic to use where. Armed with this background, it will be a much simpler task to make sense of and apply the basic statistical tools used in behavioral research.

REFERENCES

Bruning, J. L., and Kintz, B. L. *Computational handbook of statistics.* Glenview, Ill.: Scott, Foresman & Co., 1968.

Edgar, E., and Billingsley, F. Believability when N = 1. *The Psychological Record,* 1974, *24,* 147-160.

Gentile, J. R., Roden, A. H., and Klein, R. D. An analysis-of-variance model for the intrasubject replication design. *Journal of Applied Behavior Analysis,* 1972, *5,* 193-198.

Glass, G. V., Willson, V. L., and Gottman, J. M. *Design and analysis of time-series experiments.* Boulder, Colo.: Colorado Associated University Press, 1975.

Gottman, J. M. and Glass, G. V. Analysis of interrupted time-series experiments. In T. R. Kratochwill (Ed.), *Single subject research: strategies for evaluating change.* New York: Academic Press, Inc., 1978, 197-235.

Guilford, J. P., and Fruchter, B. *Fundamental statistics in psychology and education* (5th ed.). New York: McGraw-Hill Book Co., 1973.

Hartmann, D. P. Forcing square pegs into round holes: some comments on an analysis-of-variance model for the intrasubject replication design. *Journal of Applied Behavior Analysis,* 1974, *7,* 635-638.

Kazdin, A. E. Statistical analyses for single-case experimental designs. In M. Hersen and D. H. Barlow (Eds.), *Single case experimental designs: strategies for studying behavior changes.* New York: Permagon Press, Inc. 1976, 265-316.

Keppel, G. *Design and analysis: a researcher's handbook.* Englewood Cliffs, N.J.: Prentice-Hall, Inc., 1973.

Kratochwill, T., Alden, K., Demuth, D., et al. A further consideration in the application of an analysis-of-variance model for the intrasubject replication design. *Journal of Applied Behavior Analysis,* 1974, *7,* 629-634.

Siegel, S. *Nonparametric statistics for the behavior sciences.* New York: McGraw-Hill Book Co., 1956.

Thoresen, C. E., and Elashoff, J. D. An analysis-of-variance model for intrasubject replication design: some additional comments. *Journal of Applied Behavior Analysis,* 1974, *7,* 639-642.

SIMULATIONS

SIMULATIONS 12-1, 12-2, AND 12-3

Topic: Parametric versus nonparametric statistics

Background statement: Selection of the appropriate statistical tool is an essential first step before the data are analyzed. It will do no good to perform computations correctly if the incorrect analysis has been used. The choice between parametric and nonparametric rests on three factors as noted in the text: assumptions, nature of the data, and sample size. Since the assumptions exist primarily in theory (unless evidence exists that suggests a problem) your practical decision may have to be based primarily on the latter two.

Tasks to be performed

1. Review the following stimulus materials.
2. Indicate whether you would be inclined to use parametric or nonparametric statistics and why.

Stimulus material for Simulation 12-1

You are conducting a study in which two reinforcement techniques are being compared to determine which is most effective. Two groups of children have been formed by random assignment with twenty subjects in each group. The data are collected on a scale that rates behavior on a scale of 1 to 7 with 1 representing nondisruptive and 7 representing highly disruptive behavior.

For feedback see p. 346.

Stimulus material for Simulation 12-2

You are working as coaching assistant for the varsity basketball team at Southern Grant University. The coach is planning a defense strategy for the year. To accomplish this task, you have been asked to analyze the scoring patterns of players who are 6 feet 5 inches or less in height as compared with those 6 feet 6 inches or above. The league tends to be rather evenly distributed in height. When you break it out, the league has sixty players in the shorter group and sixty in the taller group. Your measure is the number of points scored. What type of statistical test will you use, parametric of nonparametric? Why?

For feedback see p. 346.

Stimulus material for Simulation 12-3

You are conducting a study for a research laboratory on a rare eye disease. This is a progressive ailment, and the project director is interested in any differences between individuals who are in the early stages versus those in the late stages of the disease. One of the symptoms is an atypical flutter of the upper lid. The question, then, is whether a difference exists in the frequency of upper lid flutters between early- and late-stage patients. The criterion measure is the frequency of upper lid flutters per 2-minute observation period. Since the disease is so rare, there are only three subjects in each group. What type of statistical test will you use, parametric or nonparametric? Why?

For feedback see p. 346.

SIMULATIONS 12-4, 12-5, AND 12-6

Topic: Comparing two data points

Background statement: The actual determination of which statistical test should be used depends on several factors. As was noted earlier, the type of data and the sample size are important general considerations. The specific test selection will then be further narrowed by the question being addressed (e.g., comparing two independent groups or comparing pretest and posttest scores). Such a selection process frequently involves considering several alternatives. I have found it unnecessary to try to memorize all the possible alternatives. Consequently you are encouraged to refer to the relevant portion of the chapter in responding to this simulation. Such reference is realistic in terms of the actual research process, since many researchers do not believe it is worth the effort to memorize the alternative statistical tests and the specific situations in which they are appropriate. The more frequently used tests become easily remembered after they are used a few times.

Tasks to be performed

1. Review the following stimulus materials.
2. Indicate which statistical test you would select for data analysis and why.

Stimulus material for Simulation 12-4

Suppose you are back at your previous job as coaching assistant for the varsity basketball team at Southern Grant University. Recall that in Simulation 12-2 you were asked to compare the scoring of those players 6 feet 5 inches or less with those 6 feet 6 inches or above. This, then, is a study that compares two groups of sixty subjects each. Your criterion measure was the number of points scored, which represented at least interval data.

Now walk through a few of the preliminary steps before you get to the actual test selection.

1. The first step is to determine what summary or descriptive statistic will be used. Do you want to compare group means (mean points scored for group 1 as compared with mean points for group 2), medians, or modes? Since you have interval data, group means are most likely appropriate. So, the first decision is made; you are comparing two means.

2. Are these independent means or are they nonindependent? Since two different groups are involved (as opposed to the same group measured twice as in a pre-post situation), you have little reason to believe that the performances are not independent. Therefore, in the absence of any compelling argument otherwise, these are probably independent groups.

3. Now, what statistical test would you suggest? Review the relevant chapter pages if you wish. Recall that the feedback for simulation 12-2 suggested the general type of statistic (parametric) because of the sample size and the type of data.

For feedback see p. 346.

Stimulus material for Simulation 12-5

You have been asked to work in a psychology laboratory. The topic of your first investigation involves comparing the effectiveness of two reinforcement techniques. Two groups of children have been formed by random assignment with fifteen subjects in each group. Treatment is administered and measurements are then taken. The data are collected on a scale that rates behavior on a scale of 1 to 7 with 1 representing nondisruptive behavior and 7 representing highly disruptive behavior.

Review briefly what is involved in this study by asking a few specific questions.

1. Is this an independent or a nonindependent comparison?
2. What type of data are being collected, and what does this suggest relative to the selection of parametric versus nonparametric analyses?
3. What is the size of the sample, and what does this suggest?

Now, what statistical test would you suggest? Review the relevant chapter pages if you wish.

For feedback see p. 347.

Stimulus material for Simulation 12-6

You have been asked to serve as a statistical consultant for an environmental research team that is studying certain aspects of pollution control. A new facility that has been constructed in the valley has proved effective in reducing pollution in other parts of the country. One expected result is a reduction in the frequency of sinus infection symptoms as the pollution is reduced. A sample of 100 individuals has been randomly selected for study. The subjects will be examined three times during the first 15 days of the month (pollution device not operative) and three times during the second 15 days of the month (pollution device operating). The data will involve recording the number of symptoms for each subject, computing an average for all subjects on the first 15 days, and comparing that with the mean for all subjects during the second 15 days.

Review briefly what is involved.

1. Is this an independent or a nonindependent comparison?
2. What type of data are being collected, and what does this suggest relative to the selection of parametric versus nonparametric analyses?
3. What is the size of the sample, and what does this suggest?

Now, what statistical test would you suggest? Review the relevant chapter pages if you wish.

For feedback see p. 347.

SIMULATIONS 12-7 AND 12-8

Topic: Comparing more than two data points

Background statement: See background statement for Simulations 12-4, 12-5, and 12-6.

Tasks to be performed

1. Review the following stimulus material.
2. Indicate which statistical test you would select and why.

Stimulus material for Simulation 12-7

You are working as a research consultant for a well-known drug firm in the East. The laboratory has developed a new formula for use with tiny infants that will presumably reduce the vulnerability to pulmonary problems. One concern, however, is the possibility of undesirable side effects. A serious elevation of temperature is suspected as a potential problem. Consequently three different compounds have been developed in an attempt to circumvent this difficulty.

The laboratory wishes to conduct a study comparing the three compounds to determine whether any of them will be less influential on temperature elevation. Three groups of infants will be randomly constituted with twenty subjects each. The data will be recorded in degrees Fahrenheit.

Review briefly what is involved.

1. How many experimental variables are indicated in this study, and what is it (what are they)?

2. Is the study independent, nonindependent, or mixed?

3. What type of data are being collected, and what does this suggest relative to the selection of parametric versus nonparametric analyses?

4. What is the size of the sample, and what does this suggest?

Now, what statistical test would you suggest? Review the relevant chapter pages if you wish.

For feedback see p. 347.

Stimulus material for Simulation 12-8

You have been employed by a health spa to direct a new weight reduction program. Since this is a new program, the owner has asked that you conduct a careful evaluation to monitor its effectiveness. As you ponder your assignment, you come to the conclusion that you will assess your enrollees over a period of time, taking a measurement before they acutally begin, one midway through the program, and a final measure at the end of the 4-month course. Since this program is conducted as a group endeavor, all of the first participants will begin at the same time and move through the 4-month sequence simultaneously. You have thirty individuals in your group, and your criterion measure is weight.

Review briefly what the problem involves.

1. Identify the experimental variable or variables.

2. Is the study independent, nonindependent, or mixed?

3. What type of data are being collected, and what does this suggest relative to the selection of parametric versus nonparametric analyses?

4. What is the size of the sample, and what does this suggest?

Now, what statistical test would you suggest? Review relevant chapter pages if you wish.

For feedback see p. 348.

SIMULATION 12-9

Topic: Comparing more than two data points

Background statement: See background statement for Simulations 12-4, 12-5, and 12-6.

Tasks to be performed

1. Review the following stimulus material.
2. Indicate which statistical test you would select and why.

Stimulus material

Once again you are serving as a consultant for that well-known drug firm in the East. The laboratory has refined a new medication that influences heart rate, but it still needs to test two forms of the drug (compound A and compound B). The laboratory director also needs information on dosage and wants to test the effects of a 5 ml. dose versus a 10 ml. dose. Four groups have been constituted by random assignment with thirty subjects in each. The criterion measure is heart rate per minute.

Review briefly what is involved.

1. How many experimental variables are indicated in this study, and what is it (what are they)?

2. Is the study independent, nonindependent, or mixed?

3. What type of data are being collected, and what does this suggest relative to the selection of parametric versus nonparametric analyses?

4. What is the size of the sample, and what does this suggest?

Now, what statistical test would you suggest? Review the relevant chapter pages if you wish.

For feedback see p. 349.

SIMULATIONS 12-10 AND 12-11

Topic: Relationship between two measures

Background statement: See background statement for Simulations 12-4, 12-5, and 12-6.

Tasks to be performed

1. Review the following stimulus material.
2. Indicate which statistical analysis you would select and why.

Stimulus material for Simulation 12-10

You have been asked to serve as a consultant for a major research firm in a large metropolitan area. One of the initial studies involves investigating the relationship between certain variables that are thought to be important. The project director has obtained height and weight measures on a random sample of 500 individuals residing in the area. You have been asked to suggest a correlational analysis that is appropriate for use in estimating the relationship between these measures. What analysis will you suggest? You may wish to review the relevant chapter pages.

For feedback see p. 349.

Stimulus material for Simulation 12-11

George Simpson, the superintendent in your school district, has been conducting some investigations on pupil achievement during the past year. He gathered preliminary data on a small sample of students last year ($N = 8$), particularly focusing on reading and mathematics. In this small study, he had the teacher rank each student in terms of performance in reading and math. He then correlated the ranks using the Spearman rank-order correlation. He wants to follow up this year with a much larger sample ($N = 50$) also using ranks and has asked your advice. Initially he wants to know if he used the correct analysis last year, and secondly he wants to know whether the same analysis is appropriate with the larger sample that has been proposed. What is your advice? You may wish to review the relevant chapter pages.

For feedback see p. 349.

CHAPTER 13

Completing the research process: results related to behavior

Many beginning researchers labor through the development of a research question, through the design and implementation of a study, and even through data analysis, only to find themselves confronted with serious difficulty in terms of interpreting results. The frequency with which computer printouts are discarded in frustration is appalling but not at all surprising. The intuitive leaps from data to behavior are difficult at best, but in fact these leaps are representative of a broader problem related to acquisition of a Gestalt-like concept of the research process. It should not be surprising that difficulties are encountered, since the process of interpretation, in fact the total process of research, is rarely taught formally. More often than not college instructors have mastered and are usually involved only in the instruction of segments of the research process. Indeed the segments generally taught lend themselves well to rote memorization but are not placed in the context of research as a thinking activity. Consequently, students may be well equipped with library research information, statistical computation skills, or 3×5 card details, but they are virtually unable to even approach the implementation of a study. The absence of an overall concept of the total research process not only impedes implementing research but often reduces the effective acquisition of even the segment skills.

This chapter will discuss the relationship between various segments of the research act with the intent of providing a Gestalt of the process and hopefully placing these segments in functional perspective. Additionally, attention will be given to interpretation of results, which is a factor of vital importance to progress in behavioral science.

RESEARCH AS AN INTEGRATED PROCESS

Several roadblocks appear to deter research from being viewed as an integrated process. Perhaps the primary impediment is the previously mentioned segmenting of the overall research act. This segmenting is generated in a variety of fashions, the most powerful of which may be the approach to teaching. Courses on statistics are usually taught with little or no attention as to how statistics relate to either the research question or the meaning of results. Similarly, writing is taught primarily from a term paper framework with little attention focused on how to build a logical, reasoned case or how to articulate intuitive leaps from datum A to datum B to resulting conclusions. Since little effort is exerted to synthesize these disjointed parts, the beginning researcher is often handicapped by the conceptual gaps existing between the various segments of the research act. This may result in a limited perspective of research that is inharmonious with actual implementation of an investigation. As has been noted previously, research actually represents a continuous process beginning with a theoretical construct or body of knowledge that generates a research question. The nature of the research question, in turn, dictates to a considerable degree the method to be employed. All that has preceded relates to the interpretive discussion of results. The gaps in conceptual continuity will be addressed in the following discussion in an attempt to highlight the relationships between various segments of the research act.

The conceptual gaps in the research process represent points where the student has a high probability of encountering difficulties. Often these problems are extremely frustrating. Because the difficulty is one of a conceptual nature it is not easily remedied. Were it, instead, one of a mechanical nature (e.g., computation decision or error), a remedy might easily be found in the form of advice from a consultant.

One of the first high-risk points encountered in the research process involves the intuitive (and actual) relationship between the theoretical construct and the research question. A second high-risk problem arises during translation of the research question into the method (which includes study design, data collection, and analyses). Finally, certainly of no little importance, are the conceptual relationships between results and inferences or interpretations back to behavioral terms. These problematic areas represent vital and logical relationships that must be well understood if the researcher is to have the functional capacity to work in a variety of settings.

Theory related to the research question

As noted previously, one of the first conceptual problem areas is represented by the relationship between the research question and the theoretical model or body of knowledge. Many people experience difficulty determining what an abstract theory or model means in behavioral terms. Essentially this is a deductive reasoning process that moves from the general statement of a theory to the specific behavioral performance.

A theory or model is an abstract framework that generally provides an overview of the inferred processes (e.g., learning) and how they operate. Since the theory functions at an abstract level, it usually does not include specific statements as to how the subject will behave under given conditions. In the absence of exemplars, the beginning student (and often the experienced researcher) may encounter difficulty in visualizing how the theory postulates relate to a specific behavioral instance. Yet this process is vital to the development of a related research question.

One source of the translation difficulty is that students tend to view a theory as a total entity that must be related to behavior. Yet a model or theory often encompasses a rather broad area of behaviors that, when viewed as a whole, does not intend to predict behavioral specifics. A model is generally a composite concept such as learning and as such, it should be translated in terms of the various parts or dimensions of behavior that are included. Each behavioral dimension should be treated somewhat apart from the total model. By considering only one part of a theory or one statement within a total theory at a time, the specific contingencies of a situation may be more easily described and behavior under these more limited circumstances may be predicted. After the results are obtained, to test the behavioral dimension under study, the findings are usually related back to the larger theoretical construct. To attempt to consider the total theory from the outset, however, seriously impedes the statement of a researchable question. This process may be compared to eating a pastrami sandwich. If a person tries to swallow the sandwich whole, he or she will invariably choke and certainly not derive pleasure from it nor be efficient in eating. On the other hand, one bite at a time from the sandwich is an approach that is easily translatable into operational terms and represents a manageable procedure.

Translating this analogy into the context of research, several steps may be profitable. The student initially must hold the totality of the theory in storage while concentrating on one facet or dimension. Then with this segment of the model under focus the question seems to be, "What does this postulate mean in terms of behavior?" The answer to such a question needs to be situation specific if it is to predict behavior. For example, the part of the theory under study may suggest, "Under variable reinforcement conditions a child who is socially immature should perform in a particular way." Since theory represents an abstraction, the empirical test of such a prediction becomes the task of research.

Continuing the process of asking progressively more specific questions, the researcher moves closer to a manageable research question. "If, under *these* (hypothetical) *conditions, this particular type of child* is expected to perform in a certain way, *then* how could I observe the behavior to either confirm or deny the prediction?" This question leads rather directly to the initial stages of study design and the specifics involved in the method to be used. It really represents several questions and resulting decisions that need attention. For example, how may the conditions specified by the statement be set up in the real world (or at least in a laboratory approximation of the real world)? How is the researcher going to know whether these conditions have exerted an influence? What is going to be measured to represent the behavioral performance? (What is the researcher going to count, the number of correct responses?)

As suggested by the preceding discussion, the leap from a theory to a research question represents a dramatic increase in specificity. Intense implementation of deductive process is involved as the researcher moves from the total theory or model to the particular facet under study and, in turn, to the research question. This funnellike process may be hidden between the two visible end points, the generalized model and the specific, often molecular, research question.

For clarity it may be useful to proceed through a sequence of events from the beginning to the culmination of a piece of research. At the first stage, a possible researchable question could be, "What are the effects of a variable reinforcement schedule as compared with continuous reinforcement on the learning performance of socially immature children?"

The question related to method and analysis

The next gap to be bridged is between the research question and the experimental method. Because of the specificity of the example research question above, translation to a tight, crisply articulated problem should not present great difficulty. The method basically must permit measurement aimed at answering the question posed. More specifically the method can be approached in terms of describing subjects, materials, and procedures. In terms of the example question, the subjects must in some fashion be determined to be "socially immature children." This gives us at least two dimensions to consider. First of all, who are "children"? This term would seem to suggest a chronological age range of people who are young enough to be considered children but probably not old enough to yet be thought of as adolescents. For these purposes it is sufficient to say that chronological age needs to be specified. The second dimension suggested by the above phrase is the necessity of determining that the subjects are "socially immature." How is this to be accomplished? It may involve some standardized evaluation instrument, or it may mean that children are so classified by observations. At any rate, on some logical basis, if subjects are to be obtained who are relevant to the research question, they must be sampled from a group who will fall within the framework of "socially immature" children.

The next area of focus that relates experimental method to the research question is represented by the materials to be used. Materials or apparatus for the example question may include one or two factors depending on how the study will be implemented. Certainly it will be necessary to specify the materials to be used that relate to the phrase "learning performance." What is it that the children are going to learn? Even more specific on this point, how are these materials going to generate the criterion measure? If, for example, mathematical problems that require written responses are to be used, then is the researcher willing to contend that the number of correct responses represents learning? In fact it should be noted that the phraseology of the example research question is somewhat naive. Learning and performance generally should not be used together. Actually mathematics performance is being used to infer learning. The point to be made here is simply that the materials chosen must also relate to the research question. In this example, the materials or experimental task must relate to what is considered to be learning.

The second dimension of materials discussion relates to reinforcement. If the subjects are going to be reinforced with tangible rewards (e.g., candy and tokens), reinforcement probably is best discussed under "materials." On the other hand, if verbal praise is to be used, the reinforcement part of the question receives attention under "procedures." Also, if tangible rewards are to be dispensed by machine or some other apparatus, this should be described. These types of details need to be specified and their choice must relate to the research question being explored.

The third area of focus that relates experimental method to the research question is represented by the procedures that are actually put into operation. As with subjects and materials, the procedures must be relevant to the research question. This means that how the experimental conditions are to be implemented must be conceptualized in terms of the research question.

The next intuitive relationship requiring discussion is that which links the research question to the analysis of data. It is not uncommon among beginning students to pose a relationship question, whereas their design and analysis are appropriate for a difference problem. The example research question suggests that the effects of variable versus continuous reinforcement are being compared. This is a difference question, which should be reflected by the design and the analysis technique used. More specific information on the analysis segment has been presented in earlier chapters. The difficulty that often represents a conceptual gap involves the logical relationship between the research question and the selection of *which* analysis technique to use. It simply is not appropriate to approach a difference question with a correlation or a relationship question with a *t* test.

This section has emphasized the fact that the research process involves a series of highly interrelated segments. The relationships between these various areas are crucial and require specific focus because they are often overlooked in instruction and frequently are not included in the conception of research held by the beginning researcher. In review, this section has been a miniature replay of much of what has been discussed in greater detail in earlier portions of this text. Hopefully the overall view of research is no longer like a prism that distorts the relevant perspective of any activity area.

One important area of the research process remains to be discussed—interpretation of results. This area is strongly related to other activities in research and should not be viewed apart from the total research enterprise. It is highly dependent on all that has gone on before.

INTERPRETATION OF RESULTS

Perhaps the most difficult conceptual gap to bridge is the relationship between the numbers obtained as results and the inference to behavior. This may result in part because many people without research experience glean little meaning from numbers and, in particular, statistical statements such as $P < .05$. Interpretation concerned with the meaning of results in terms of behavior requires that the individual must at least know what such statements mean. Assuming this level of knowledge is present (or amenable to acquisition), the relationship of results to inferences about behavior may begin with a series of questions. If, for example, the study involved a comparison of groups (a difference problem), the first question is usually, "Did the groups perform differently?" This question may be answered by reviewing the results of the statistical test. (Was there a significant difference? If they were different, which group had the higher performance?) This latter question can be answered by simply inspecting the group means if mean scores are being used.

The next step really initiates the process of inference. What do the performance differences mean in terms of behavior? The researcher cannot get by with merely answering this question by saying that group 1 made more correct responses than group 2. That is evident in the results and adds no interpretive information. Inference requires attention to the psychology of behavior. The researcher must make some intuitive leaps as to *why* "group 1 made more correct responses than group 2." Would these differences have been predicted by the model that was discussed in the introduction? If so, in what fashion is the model supported? Would these data suggest that some particular psychological construct is operative in the process of learning? These questions exemplify the process of inference from results to behavior. Research that has a maximal impact on both theory and practice will attempt to push back the frontiers of understanding by the use of inference in this fashion.

An even greater challenge is represented by results that would not have been predicted by the model or theory being tested. Here again it is not enough to merely say, "These data would not support the theory of. . . ." The question must be posed as to *why* the data do not support the theory. Do the data, instead, suggest that an alternative model is probably operating in the learning process? If so, this is an important and exciting finding. Perhaps the data suggest a modification of the model. This type of finding exemplifies the process of empiricism as it serves to shape models and theories. Fully interpreted results should include other possible explanations for the data if they do not support the theory under study.

Last but not least, the researcher may choose to interpret what the results might mean for practice or clinical application. This process is particularly important in applied research endeavors. Do the data suggest that teachers might more effectively instruct if they were to use a particular reinforcement technique? Do the data suggest that instructional materials might be more effective for certain children if they were designed in a particular way? Results may suggest that a given counseling technique might be effective with a particular group of students. The point to be emphasized is that research results that are interpreted for application require the same intuitive inference processes relating data to the real world that were involved in inference from data to theory.

Interpretation for practice has not always been a respected activity in which researchers may engage. There has, however, been a substantial shift in philosophy regarding interpretation for practice in recent years. Not only is it given less of a peripheral status than was previously the case, it is being expected by journal editors under certain conditions. Whether interpretation for practice is attempted depends primarily on the audience for which the report is intended.

Drawing implications for practice and inference in terms of alternative models are two activities that represent a process that may be difficult for experienced researchers as well as the beginning student. Teaching these skills is an area about which little is known as well. One serious roadblock to such interpretation might be called "conceptual rigidity," which can be illustrated by an example.

As noted, research often is launched from the framework of a theory, model, or some other explanatory conceptual framework. The relevant dimensions of this model are discussed in the introduction, which gives the researcher a mental set to proceed with the study. This set may also work against the researcher when it comes to the interpretation of results. If he or she does not conceptually explore beyond the boundaries of the model, the set may become too rigid to permit alternative inference. The confinement of oneself strictly to the boundaries of the model is what I refer to as conceptual rigidity. The framework of the model is indeed useful and necessary to launch an investigation. The limits of such a framework, however, may become somewhat like conceptual fences. If researchers never go beyond those conceptual fences once the study is designed, they will find themselves less effective in terms of data interpretation. There are several resulting difficulties.

Initially, difficulty is encountered when the data do not fit between the conceptual fences. A quick examination of nearly any professional journal will indicate that this often occurs as evidenced by the frequency with which "results do not support . . ." whatever model is being tested. When data do not fit within the conceptual fences of a model, a statement that "these data do not support . . ." will not alone suffice. It is at this point that the researcher must go beyond the explanations provided by the model and either suggest an alternative theory that the data *will* support or modify the model being tested.

Since the theory being tested seldom involves practice, implications in this area frequently involve the conceptual fence notion. Often implications for practice are even more difficult because researchers are not generally in the field practitioner role on a continuing basis. Thus in a real sense, the current set of experiences that are temporally and conceptually close to the researcher often do not involve clinical application or practice. Implications for practice therefore may require an even more dramatic assault on conceptual rigidity than model alternatives.

Researchers who are either unable or unwilling to inferentially explore beyond the boundaries of a model will reduce their impact even if the data were predicted by the model. At face value their discussions of results will appear somewhat sterile and unexciting to read. It should be emphasized that one must stay within the legitimate boundaries of the *data*. The researcher should, however, be willing to watch the subjects beyond the pure criterion measure level. Such observation often is revealing in a clinical sense and is not infrequently discussed during the interpretation. These observations should always carry a qualifying statement such as "Subjective experimenter observation suggested. . . ." Science moves back the frontiers of the unknown at an incredibly slow pace. Without the help of such observations and their interpretation related to the data (which often generate further research), the movement would be even slower.

This chapter has emphasized some of the lesser known processes of research, primarily the judicious use of intuition and logic. I do not intend to give the impression that all researchers must do is gather data and then say whatever their imagination suggests. At all times the researcher must stay in close touch with what the data indicate in terms of logical leaps and inferences. The use of logic and conceptual relationships is, however, one of the most important processes in research. This chapter also highlights research as a dynamic, even creative act. Research does not always carry such a connotation for the uninitiated. Beginning researchers must, if they are to achieve the impact possible and desirable, learn to incorporate creative thinking into their repertoire of behavior.

How does one acquire the skills discussed in this chapter? As mentioned previously, the pat formula for such instruction is not presently known, at least to most professionals involved in research training. What is known is that with some prerequisite level of information acquired, most students progress most rapidly from practice. Once one begins to break down conceptual fences, the divergent thinking necessary seems best nurtured by experience at asking the additional questions. What are other psychological or theoretical explanations for the same results? What are modifications of the theory being tested that would predict the data obtained? To what practical setting might these results be relevant: curriculum planning, student diagnosis, counseling, placement, or educational progress?

It is not necessary for students to wait for their first study to practice the process of inference and data interpretation. In fact it is desirable to gain some experience before beginning the first study. I have used a simulation technique with my own students that has shown considerable success. Simulations have been presented with each of the previous chapters in this text. Simulations for interpretation, however, require material of such length that presentation in this volume is not possible. If you are interested in such practice, you are encouraged to try the following procedures:

1. Select a journal article (report of a study) that is in an area familiar to you; if possible, let it be one in which you have done considerable reading, have considerable experience, or both.

2. The initial study should have a fairly simple design. As you become more experienced, more complex studies can be used (for example, select a simple study that compares two groups for the first try).

3. Tape a piece of paper over the author's discussion section.

4. Read the article carefully up to the discussion section.

5. Now, write your own discussion of the results. Interpret the results in terms of the theory or literature reviewed in the introduction and in terms of what the results might mean for practice and future research. Be thoughtful during this process and review Chapter 13 of this text.

6. Remove the paper from the article, and compare your discussion with that of the author. Did you hit the main points? Do not be concerned about the polish of your writing or differences in style. After all, the author probably has been working in the area considerably longer than you and has also been writing a good bit longer.

7. Practice.

COMMENTS

It is evident that research is more than statistics. It is, in fact, a series of parts that have specific relationships and that strongly involve the use of mental exploration and intuition as well as logic. Hopefully, the beginner will see research not as sterile and mechanistic, but as the dynamic process that it is.

Glossary

A-B design A time-series design that involves two phases: A, in which the baseline data are collected before treatment is implemented, and B, in which data are recorded while treatment is under way. This design is not widely used, since more sophisticated designs have been developed that provide stronger evidence.

A-B-A-B design A time-series design that involves four phases. The first A represents baseline before treatment is implemented. The first B represents initial application of treatment. The second A designates removal of treatment and return to baseline conditions, whereas the second B represents a return to treatment conditions. This design is also known as a reversal design.

analysis of variance Also known as ANOVA; a parametric statistical analysis used for comparing three or more means simultaneously. This is a popular procedure in behavioral research in which group designs are used. The ANOVA is highly flexible, and variations may be used for comparisons of independent groups, repeated-measures comparisons, experiments with one experimental variable (one-way ANOVA), two experimental variables (two-way ANOVA), and more complex experiments.

attributes A term used by Nunnally (1967) referring to the observable, countable, or measurable dimensions of an object. For example, one cannot measure learning directly, but it is possible to infer that a certain amount of it has occurred by observing performance on a task. The performance is the attribute by which one infers that learning has occurred (such as number of correct responses on a test).

baseline The phase or phases of a time-series experiment in which data are recorded on the subject in an untreated state. Frequently this is the first phase in which data are recorded before treatment is initiated. Performance under this condition is compared with performance of the subject during the treatment phase or phases.

bias Any influence that distorts the experimental results and thereby causes error in the findings. For example, the researcher may subconsciously favor one group of subjects over another and score them somewhat higher than a truly objective observer would. This would be experimenter bias and would threaten the soundness of results.

bimodal distribution A distribution that has two modes. If two scores occur more frequently than other scores (and with equal frequency), the distribution is said to be bimodal.

captive assignment Assignment of subjects to experimental treatments when the total sample is identified and available at the outset of the investigation. This makes it possible to know which subjects, by name, will be in which experimental group at the beginning of the experiment.

ceiling effect An effect that occurs when the performance range of a task is so restricted or limited on the upper end that the subjects cannot perform to their maximum ability.

cell A particular experimental condition in a multigroup study. For example, in the diagram at the top of p. 314 there are four conditions (A_1B_1, A_2B_1, A_1B_2, and A_2B_2) and four corresponding cells.

central tendency measures Descriptive statistics that are used to summarize a group's performance in terms of where the scores tend to be concentrated. Three central tendency measures are commonly used, the mean, the median, or the mode, depending on the circumstances.

cluster sampling A type of subject selection that is useful when every individual in an entire population cannot be listed to form a frame but the population exists in groups or clusters (such as school districts, regions, or states). Instead of listing the individuals, the frame is formed by listing the clusters, and a representative sample of clusters is drawn. Subjects are then selected from the clusters.

control, concept of The process of holding all pos-

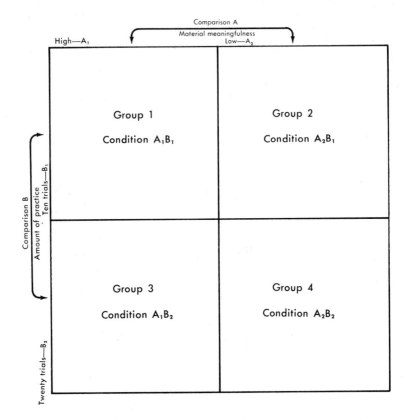

sible influences constant except the experimental variable, which is what is being studied. For example, if the researcher is comparing the effectiveness of reading programs A and B, the reading programs should be the only factor that is different between groups. All other influences (such as intelligence or age) should be equivalent between groups.

correlation A general term for the type of statistical analyses used in relationship studies. Correlational studies investigate the degree to which two variables (such as height and weight) vary together in a population. Such an investigation would be asking the question "As height varies (increases or decreases), what tends to happen to weight?"

criterion measure That which is being measured in a study. If, for example, a study were focusing on the height of a particular group, the criterion measure might be inches. Criterion measure is synoymous with the term "dependent variable."

data Generally, the information gathered during the course of a study to answer the question being investigated. The term "data" covers all information that may be recorded on subjects, such as age, intelligence, or performance scores (which are probably the criterion measure). Usually the term is used with reference to the criterion measure or performance scores.

dependent variable *See* criterion measure.

determinism The assumption of science that there is a lawfulness in the events of nature rather than capricious and chaotic incidents. Events are assumed to have causes, and if all influences could be exactly duplicated, the event would recur in the same form.

dispersion measures Descriptive statistics that are used to summarize a group's performance in terms of how much variation there is in the scores, that is, to what degree individual scores depart from the central tendency. Three dispersion measures are commonly used, the range, the semi-interquartile range, or the standard deviation, depending on the circumstances.

double sampling A type of subject selection, sometimes called two-phase sampling, that is often useful for survey research. The term is descriptive of the process in that the investigators probe their subjects twice (for example, as a more intensive follow-up on a cursory initial probe or as a follow-up for those subjects not responding to an initial questionnaire).

empiricism An approach to enquiry emphasizing knowledge that comes through factual investigation, with the facts being obtained from sources external to the investigator. The primary means by which information is obtained involves direct experience or objective observation through the senses.

experimental matching The assignment of subjects to experimental treatments in a manner that attempts to force group equivalency on a given factor (e.g., age or IQ) by matching subjects on that factor.

experimental mortality A threat to internal validity that occurs when loss of subjects changes the composition of the sample initially drawn. When this occurs, particularly if more subjects are lost from one group than from another group, the researcher may not have groups that are constituted in the same way that they were when the study was initiated.

experimental variable That phenomenon that is under study, that factor that the researcher manipulates to see what the effect is. For example, if the researcher were interested in determining which of two teaching methods was more effective, the experimental variable would be method of teaching. "Experimental variable" is synonymous with the term "independent variable."

external validity The generalizability of results from a given study. External validity involves how well the results of a particular study apply to the world outside the research situation. If a study is externally valid or has considerable external validity, one can expect that the results are generalizable to a considerable degree.

finite causation The assumption of science that natural events have a limited number of conditions that are responsible for its occurrence and that these conditions are discoverable. Finite causation essentially presumes that everything in nature is *not* influenced by everything else.

floor effect An effect that occurs when the performance range of the task is so restricted or limited on the lower end that the subjects' performance is determined by the task rather than by their ability to perform. Under such conditions the task is so difficult that the researcher is unable to obtain any evidence about how the subjects can perform.

generality, principle of A characteristic of a correctly stated experimental variable. If an experimental variable conforms to the principle of generality, it is stated in terms of the abstract variable being manipulated (e.g., method of teaching) *rather than* the particular conditions being studied (teaching method A compared with teaching method B).

Hawthorne effect A change in sensitivity or performance or both by subjects merely because they are in a study. This may occur when an experimental situation is sufficiently different from routine that subjects are somehow made to feel "special." The Hawthorne effect becomes a threat to internal validity when one group receives such a "special" treatment and another does not, thereby introducing a systematic difference between groups in addition to the experimental variable. This same effect is a threat to external validity but is called "artificial research arrangements" in the text.

history A threat to internal validity that occurs when specific events, in addition to the treatment, intervene between measurements. This threat is a particular problem in studies in which a pretest is administered, followed by treatment and then a posttest. The specific events may be occurrences such as a playground fight, an accident, or similar *specific* intervening factors other than the treatment.

hypothesis A statement used in research to help clarify the research question. It is presented as a declarative statement of prediction. Two basic formats are used, the *null* hypothesis and the *directional* hypothesis. The null hypothesis predicts no difference, for example, "Subjects will not differ in mean correct responses as a function of teaching method." The directional hypothesis predicts a difference and the direction of that difference, such as "Subjects receiving teaching method A will make significantly more correct responses than those receiving teaching method B."

independent group design Group research designs in which different subjects are used for each group. A group of subjects receives only one treatment, and therefore the scores in one condition are presumed independent of scores in another condition. This is *in distinction* to studies in which subjects may receive two or more treatments (repeated measures), and the scores in one condition cannot be considered independent of scores in the other.

independent variable *See* experimental variable.

instrumentation A threat to internal validity that occurs when changes in the calibration of a measuring instrument result in alteration of the scores that are recorded. Instrumentation also refers to changes in calibration in human observers that may result as a function of systematic differences in the way they judge and record observations.

internal validity The technical soundness of a study. A study is internally valid or has high internal validity when all the potential factors that might influence the data are controlled except the one under study. This would mean that the concept of control had been successfully implemented. If, for example, two teaching methods were being compared, internal validity would require that all differences between groups (e.g., intelligence or age) were removed except the differences in teaching method, which is the experimental variable.

interval data A type of data that has all three properties of numbers—identity, order, and additivity. Interval data have known and equal distances between score units and also have an arbitrary zero point. With interval data, it is possible to determine greater than or less than and the magnitude of a difference in the property being measured. Examples of interval data include calendar time and temperature as measured on centigrade and Fahrenheit scales.

maturation A threat to internal validity that occurs when factors influence performance as a result of time passing. Such factors as growing older, hunger, and fatigue are considered maturational threats to internal validity when they are operating in a fashion that influence data *in addition* to the experimental variable.

mean A central tendency descriptive statistic obtained by adding the scores for all subjects together and dividing the total by the number of subjects in the group; the arithmetic average. This measure of central tendency may be used with data that have the property of additivity, which includes interval and ratio data.

median A central tendency descriptive statistic that is a point in the distribution with exactly the same number of scores above it as below it when all the scores are arranged in order. If there is an odd number of subjects (e.g., 9, 11, or 15), the median is the midmost score. If there is an even number of subjects (e.g., 10, 12, or 16), the median is the midpoint between the two scores that occupy the midpoint in the distribution. The median may be used with data that have the property of order (ordinal) as well as higher level data such as interval and ratio types.

mixed-group design A group research design in which two or more experimental variables are involved with independent comparisons (different groups) on one or more of the variables and repeated measures on the remaining variable or variables. The term "mixed" comes from the fact that in this type of design there is a mixing of components that are independent group comparisons with repeated-measures comparisons.

mode A central tendency descriptive statistic that is the score in the distribution occurring most frequently. The mode may be used with nominal data. It may also be used with higher level data such as ordinal, interval, or ratio, but it is the only central tendency measure that may be used in situations in which nominal data are collected.

multiple-baseline design A time-series research design in which data on more than one target behavior are recorded simultaneously. Phase changes from baseline to treatment are then staggered with each behavior serving as the sequential control for the previously treated behavior as in the diagram at the top of p. 316.

multiple-treatment interference A threat to external validity that occurs when more than a single treatment is administered to the same subjects. Because the effects of prior treatments are frequently not dissipated by the time later treatments are administered, the generalizability of results from later treatments is reduced.

N Generally, the total number of subjects in a sample. It is frequently used as a substitute for the term "number" (for example, "the total *N* for the study . . ." or "*N* equaled . . .").

n Generally, the number of subjects in a given treatment group or cell. For example, if a study has four groups, each with twenty subjects, then *n* would equal 20 (whereas *N* would equal 80).

nominal data A type of data that represents the most primitive type of measurement, designation of occurrences into categories; also known as categorical data. This type of data has only the property of identity; all that can be accomplished is the assignment of events to categories (e.g., yes or no, male or female, pass or fail). There is no assumed underlying continuum between categories.

nomothetic net The structure of a theory in which data or results from studies are logically linked together to form the theory.

nonparametric statistics A general type of inferential statistics that does not require rigorous attention to assumptions regarding the nature of the population from which scores (data) are drawn. Nonparametric statistics often may be used in sit-

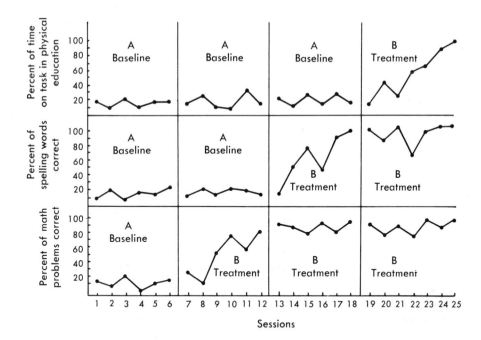

uations in which nominal and ordinal data are collected and in certain cases in which few subjects are used. These are useful tools in such situations, since other statistics (parametric) are often not applicable.

objects A term used by Nunnally (1967) referring to abstract phenomena that cannot be measured directly. For example, one cannot measure learning directly; learning is the abstract object. It is possible, however, to measure certain attributes of performance (such as number of correct responses on a test) and to infer that learning has occurred.

operational definition A process whereby the researcher specifies all the steps (operations) and details of a research problem. By operationally defining the problem, each term is taken in turn, and exactly what is meant by that term is specified.

ordinal data A type of data that is characterized by the ability to rank order events on the basis of an underlying continuum. The ranks then denote greater than or less than of the property being assessed. Ordinal data do not necessarily represent known magnitude of the property being assessed.

parametric statistics A general type of inferential statistics that requires attention to several as-

sumptions regarding the nature of the population from which scores (data) are drawn. Parametric statistics generally require at least interval data and usually necessitate a larger number of subjects than nonparametric analyses. When it is possible to apply parametric statistics, they are generally preferred because they are more powerful, efficient, and flexible in terms of application than nonparametrics.

performance range (of a task) The variation in responses possible within the limits imposed by uppermost and lowest possible performances on a task.

phase change A term used in time-series research designs to denote the point in time when experimental conditions are changed. There may be several phase changes, such as the point when the baseline condition is terminated and treatment is begun, when treatment is terminated and the baseline or untreated condition is reinstituted (in an A-B-A-B design), and so on.

population Any well-described set of people or events from which the researcher selects the sample of subjects.

population frame A complete list of all individuals in the population. It is from this list that sampling actually takes place.

proportional sampling A type of subject selection

procedure used to sample from subgroups in the same proportion that they exist in the larger population. For example, if individuals in the larger population were 80% brown-eyed and 20% blue-eyed, the sample would also be 80% brown-eyed and 20% blue-eyed.

quasi-experimental design A group study design in which the groups are formed from subject pools that are different before the experiment is begun, and this difference is the basis for the experimental variable. An example might be the comparing of groups from two levels of intelligence (group A with an IQ range of 75 to 90 and group B with an IQ range of 100 to 115). In this example, level of intelligence is the experimental variable under study, and the two groups are preexperimentally different. Such a design is in contrast to a true experimental design in which both groups are formed from the same subject pool and become different after they are administered the respective treatments.

random sampling Also known as simple random sampling or unrestricted random sampling. This term refers to a selection procedure whereby each individual in the population frame has an equal chance of being chosen as a subject. This procedure frequently is implemented using a random number table or other technique that ensures each individual an equal chance of being selected.

range A descriptive statistic that is a measure of dispersion and refers to the difference between the highest and lowest scores in a distribution. This is the simplest and most easily determined measure of dispersion but is of somewhat limited usefulness.

ratio data A type of data that has all three properties of numbers—identity, order, and additivity. Ratio data has known and equal distances between score units and has a zero point that is not arbitrary. A zero score on ratio data signifies total absence of the property being measured. Examples of ratio data include temperature measured on the Kelvin scale and time (to perform).

rationalism An approach to enquiry that primarily emphasizes an internal source of knowledge. Characteristic of enquiry in ancient Greek times, rationalism views the intellectual examination of ideas as the primary means by which knowledge progresses. Little if any emphasis is placed on the observable.

relationship question A type of research question that explores the degree to which two or more phenomena relate or vary together. For example,

such a study might focus on the relationship between height and weight. This type of study would essentially be asking "As height varies, what tends to happen to weight?" Relationship studies use correlation statistics for analysis of the data.

repeated-measures design A study design in which the researcher records data on the same subjects under two or more different conditions.

research A systematic way of asking questions that uses an orderly method of enquiry known as the scientific method.

reversal design See A-B-A-B design.

sample Those individuals or events that are selected from the population to serve as the subjects are known as the sample for a study. This term is also used as a verb (to sample), referring to the process of selecting individuals to serve as subjects.

semi-interquartile range A descriptive statistic that is a measure of dispersion and refers to half of the range in scores represented by the middle 50% of the scores. It is easily determined and may be used with ordinal as well as interval or ratio data.

sequential assignment A procedure for assigning subjects to experimental treatments when the investigator does not have the entire sample captive (the actual names are not all present before beginning the experiment).

skewed distribution A term used as a general descriptor for distributions of scores that are not symmetrical.

stable data A term that has primary relevance to time-series experiments. It is crucial that the data are stable (that is, the behavior rate is neither accelerating nor decelerating) before a phase change is implemented to accurately assess the effect of changing conditions.

standard deviation A descriptive statistic that is the most commonly used index of variability. Computation of the standard deviation requires at least interval data and may be conceptualized as a measure of the variability in scores around the mean.

statistical regression A threat to internal validity that occurs when subjects have been assigned to a particular group on the basis of atypical scores. If this occurs, a subject's placement in, say, group A may be in error, since the score is atypical and the subject's more normal performance may be like that of the subjects in group B. If the misclassified subject (or subjects) then regresses toward the average performance during the experiment, internal validity is threatened.

stratified random sampling A type of subject selection procedure used in situations in which representative samples must be drawn from two or more population frames for a single study. Population frames are formed for each type of subject (e.g., different age levels), and random samples are then drawn from each frame.

systematic sampling A type of subject sampling procedure in which every kth (e.g., every fifth) individual is selected from the list or population frame. Systematic sampling is convenient and useful if the list is arranged in a fashion whereby the sequence is unbiased.

test practice A threat to internal validity that occurs when the effects of taking a test substantially influence the scores of subjects on a second testing.

t **test** A parametric statistical analysis used for comparing two means. Certain t tests are appropriate for comparing means of independent groups, whereas other computational formulas are used for comparing related means (as in a pre-post design).

Feedbacks

CHAPTER FOUR
Simulation 4-1

The most obvious research ideas in the preceding discussion section are those preceded by the phrase "further research." This phrase is found in the last paragraph of the discussion, and if you noted this as the area for generating research ideas, you are right on target.

The first sentence of the last paragraph reads as follows: "Future research should be directed toward the problem of determining how parents may be encouraged to generalize the social learning principles, which they were trained to use for this study, to other child behaviors facilitative of intellectual development." This is rather straightforward. The present study trained parents in the area of child question-asking. The suggestion about future research simply indicates that the authors believe that the same skills taught the parents for this purpose may well be applicable in other areas of behavior, and the question or problem being suggested is, "How could parents be encouraged or taught to use the same principles with other behaviors?" How close were you with your answer?

The second sentence is the last paragraph actually suggests two research ideas. The first one involves a study to determine a way to "maintain the use of parenting skills" that were taught to the parents over a longer period. The second part of the same sentence suggests that it may be important to determine both "specific and general effects of home intervention over time." This idea implies that the authors would like to observe the effects over a longer period than was accomplished in the present study and that the time factor itself may generate some important effects.

Another idea that is suggested in this discussion section is somewhat less obvious, and you should not be overly distraught if you did not pick it up. It is the type of suggestion, however, that you should begin to look for in addition to the more obvious ones. This idea is found in the fourth paragraph of the discussion section. The first sentence of that paragraph indicates that the relationship between question-asking behavior under controlled conditions and curiosity-motivated question-asking "remains to be examined through controlled investigation." This, then, is open game for some researcher who is inclined to follow up. The authors also suggest that the curiosity-motivated questions may be the type that are of primary concern to educators.

Simulation 4-2

The most obvious research idea is mentioned specifically in the last paragraph of the section. Note the last sentence, which begins with the term "further research." This type of cue is a dead giveaway, and if you focused on it, that's great. The investigation that is suggested is essentially similar to the one that is reported, but the authors are suggesting two additional considerations: (1) the criteria for body build need to be refined and (2) more of the factors noted by Goldstein should be included. Particularly for the second area of expansion, the first part of the paragraph must be reviewed before you have much of an idea of what is involved. With no more information than is available here, it would seem that the factors would include some or all of the following: (1) some assessment of thyroid status, (2) some measure of emotional status, (3) assessment of intelligence, (4) a check for pituitary disturbance if you can devise such a thing, and (5) probably some observational assessment of restlessness. The authors give less guidance concerning how body build criteria might be refined, so you can do this if you are experienced in that area or have some notions other than what is provided here.

Simulation 4-3

Specific mention of research ideas in this discussion section begins in the third paragraph. The third sentence in this paragraph suggests the first idea ("It would be interesting to . . ."). In this sentence the authors are pondering the effect of the regular teacher implementing the management procedure each day during the week. The next sentence suggests another idea, which would combine control in the home setting by parents with the control in school setting. If you identified these two suggestions, you are on target.

The fourth paragraph suggests another research idea. Although it is fairly specific, the authors take the entire paragraph to articulate the suggestion. The implied investigation would involve using peer management as a procedure for controlling thumbsucking.

The fifth paragraph makes two specific suggestions, both of which deal with the area of reinforcement. In the first part of the first sentence, "the effects of the number of reinforcements given" are indicated as an area needing study. This is followed by a suggestion that "the method of presentation of such reinforcements" should be investigated. This thought is clarified in the next sentence as referring to reinforcement schedules.

Simulation 4-4

Although a variety of approaches may be taken with any given problem distillation, the most obvious in relation to the instructions would appear to be as follows:

1. The beginning point is the idea statement, "Assess the effects of variation in teaching experience on material evaluation."

2. The experimental variable is *teaching experience*. This will mean that differing amounts of teaching experience will be involved in the subject characteristics. Probably one would want two or three levels of teaching experience, such as beginning teachers in their first year of teaching, teachers in their third year of experience, and teachers in their fifth year of experience. Pressing this explanation just a bit further, one may wish to constitute three groups of teachers, one each with a different amount of experience. The diagram below might exemplify a pictorial illustration of this experimental variable.

3. From the diagram below it is evident that the three groups will be compared with regard to something. This leads to the principle of operational definition. Several parts of the idea require definition; one part is material evaluation, which is what will be measured. The subjects will be evaluating some material, and the researcher will be seeing if the different amounts of experience (the experimental variable) influence the way in which the material is evaluated. In other words, do teachers who are in their first year of teaching, as a group, evaluate material differently than those in their third year of teaching and likewise those in their fifth year of teaching? It will be necessary to define in operational terms what the material is to be and the evaluation. Exactly how will the researcher record or assess the teacher's evaluation of the material? You can see that this moves into the realm of what is to be measured. Are you going to have the teachers rate the material on some scale such as the following?

Excellent		**Average**		**Poor**
1	2	3	4	5

Begin thinking in operational terms as you distill the problem.

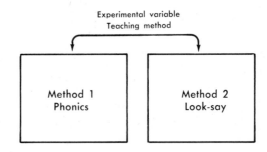

Simulation 4-5

As before, a number of different approaches may be taken in distilling a research idea. Some may result in different studies than others. The following approach is one that you may have developed.

1. Begin with the idea statement, "Compare the effectiveness of different methods of teaching reading."

2. The experimental variable is *teaching method*. Generally the researcher has a couple of specific methods in mind, but in keeping with the principle of generality the experimental variable should be stated in terms of the abstract variable rather than the specific methods being compared. In the process of distilling the problem it is necessary to specify what those methods are. Suppose for these purposes that method 1 is phonics and method 2 is look-say. A diagram for this study might appear as shown above.

To implement the study you may wish to form two groups of children, one that is taught using phonics and a second that is taught using the look-say method.

3. Now the term "effectiveness" needs to be operationally defined. The definition of this term will specify what is to be measured. One classic response to this is "reading comprehension." This is all right as a start, but is still too general. As you move through the text you will have to be much more specific to get to an observable criterion measure. In most cases reading comprehension is measured by counting the number of correct answers to questions on a test that covers a passage the children have read. It is frequently necessary to operationally define a number of factors in the research idea before it is distilled to the point that the study can be carried out.

Simulation 4-6

If you reacted to the statement with something like, "This one is really general," you were right. In its undistilled form this research idea is indeed vague. This makes your problem distillation task even more crucial. Additionally, because of the vague nature of the problem there are even more ways that this may be designed. Following is one possible distillation:

1. Begin with the idea statement, "Assess the effects of number of reinforcements given."

2. The experimental variable is this idea is *number of reinforcements given*. This is what the researcher will manipulate. Probably there will be two or three different experimental conditions, such as one reinforcement a minute, three reinforcements a minute, and six reinforcements a minute. Of course these are merely examples, and those actually selected would be determined by the specific situation and the type of subjects being used. Note that these examples specified the time frame during which the respective numbers of reinforcements were to be given. This would obviously be a necessary part of setting up the experimental conditions.

3. Operational definitions are particularly important in the distillation of this idea, since it is vague. The term "effects," once again, is a word that must receive attention. It will have to be distilled into sufficiently specific terms so that measurement is possible. In the present context, the definition of effects will also determine the setting that will be used, that is, it may determine whether the subjects will have to learn some material. If so, the amount they learn (assessed on some sort of test) is the way in which the effects of the experimental variable will be assessed.

4. Who will the subjects be? Description of the subjects may have to be accomplished rather soon to determine the reinforcement conditions as well as what is to be learned.

Simulation 4-7

Recall that a series of questions to yourself is frequently an effective means of preexperimental planning. A mental rehearsal of the entire procedure, as you visualize it, is often helpful. Such questions may include the following:

1. Where will you administer the task to subjects?
2. Where are the subjects, and how do you have access to them?
3. What furniture is necessary in the experimental room, and how should it be arranged?
4. Are the record sheets in order? What will you record?
5. Are the experimental materials in order?
6. What about instructions to the subject?
7. Is there a time limit for responses?
8. What will you say when the subject responds correctly? What will you say when the subject makes an error?
9. How will you dismiss your subject when the task is complete?
10. What about the unexpected?

Simulation 4-8

As before, a mental rehearsal is probably as an effective a device as exists for preexperimental planning for the data collection. You might be alerted to the fact that questionnaire studies frequently involve more problems than one might expect. Here are some factors that will probably need attention.

1. Initially, of course, you will need to have your instrument completely designed. This will require considerable thought concerning the content (both general and specific) on which you want data. Are your instructions clear? Careful considerations must be given to the wording of your stimulus items. Are there possible misinterpretations that might result in contaminated responses? A good safeguard against this is to have two or three friends (who are uninformed about your project) complete the questionnaire. This may suggest areas in which clarification is necessary.

2. How will you obtain your subjects? This is discussed in detail in Chapter 8, but be alerted that this must receive attention.

3. How will you administer the instrument? Are you going to mail it? Percentage of return is frequently poor on mail-out questionnaires. How about the campus mail service? Remember Murphy's Law! The Dean of Women was most upset that a certain type of content was being asked of her women the time I tried such an investigation. Plan ahead to circumvent such problems; if necessary get permission from the appropriate big wheels.

4. What will you do if you do not receive an equal number of returns from men and women? How equal must they be for your satisfaction?

5. Others?

CHAPTER FIVE
Simulation 5-1

In any group study, application of the concept of control is a clinical process. Recall that this concept essentially requires that groups be equivalent on all variables *except the one under study*. Certainly there will be some factors that one may not think about; however, it is important to attend to all that seem to require control and can be thought of at the time the study is planned. Some might be as follows with regard to the study in the feedback for Simulation 4-4.

1. The three groups should all evaluate the same material, with the same instructions and time limits and on the same instrument under the same or similar conditions.

2. There should be no reason to suspect systematic preference of one group for one type of material over another (such as might be the case if, say, the members of group 3 had all received intensive training in Distar on the writing of behavioral objectives and the other groups had not).

3. All groups should be from similar backgrounds, teaching in similar situations, with similar types of children.

4. Others?

Simulation 5-2

You will recall that the concept of control in group studies requires that the groups be equivalent on all factors except for the experimental variable. In the present example the groups are receiving two different teaching methods. Some factors that may need attention in terms of control are as follows:

1. The setting. The children from both groups should be taught in the same setting or in settings as similar as possible. This might include matters such as rooms, teacher-pupil ratios, and others.

2. The teacher. All precautions possible should be taken to prevent differences in teacher enthusiasm, experience, effectiveness, and so forth between the two conditions. This is a tough one to control. Perhaps the same teacher might be used for both. Still there is the possibility of preference differences. This problem plagues educational researchers endlessly.

3. The subjects. Both groups should consist of children with similar ability, from similar backgrounds, and of similar ages. This can frequently be accomplished by careful assignment procedures.

4. The instrument. The same test for reading comprehension should be used with both groups.

5. The time. There should not be any systematic difference in when the two groups are taught. If one group is always taught in the morning and the second in the afternoon, there is a problem. Also pay attention to the duration of the experiment; you do not want one group to receive more training than the other.

6. Others?

Simulation 5-3

Several problems are evident from the data display, mostly interrelated.

1. There is a preexperimentally determined period for both baseline and postintervention measurement periods. Although the importance of preexperimental planning has been emphasized, the length of time that observations continue should be determined by data stability in a time-series experiment, and a predetermined time period presents a problem.

2. Data stability has been emphasized as crucial in time-series designs. The data in phase A are certainly not stable at the time of intervention. Instead, an upward trend is evident in at least the last two performance observations. The performance level in phase B could well be caused by merely an extension of this trend rather than by the intervention. Likewise, data collection in phase B is terminated while the performance is still on an apparently increasing trend. Consequently you do not know how much change would ultimately result.

3. Because of the problems noted above, the concept of control is not apparently operative in these data. You would hope that change in performance level could be attributed to the intervention. Since the data were not stabilized at the

point of intervention, the postintervention performance level could well be caused by influences other than the treatment. This would seem to be a definite possibility in these data because of the upward trend in performance level, which began before the intervention and generally continued afterward.

Simulation 5-4

Since you were asked to draw the diagram in this simulation, considerable latitude is possible concerning exactly *how* your drawing might appear. Essentially it should resemble the data display diagram in Fig. 5-1.

The most crucial decision point in your hypothetical study is the phase change from baseline (A) to treatment (B). It is important that the data appear stable, which would require that your graph have essentially a horizontal line connecting the data points before change. The data stability should exist for several points before the phase change. Likewise the data should appear similarly stable at the end of phase B. How did you do?

Simulation 5-5

Recall that one of the crucial factors in any reversal design is the reversal itself. The present data do not evidence that essential reversal of performance under phase A_2. There was nothing that would have predicted this as the experiment proceeded. Baseline was stable; a dramatic performance change occurred under treatment phase 1 (B_1) and then stabilized nicely. Problems became evident as the reversal was attempted (A_2) and performance level did not return to the pretreatment level.

These data are difficult to interpret. Can the change in B_1 be attributed to the treatment? Not with any degree of certainty. Why? Review the discussion in your text and note the possible alternative explanations.

What problems may have generated these results? What would you do now? Would you replicate the experiment? Would you choose another behavior? Are there other alternatives?

Simulation 5-6

This particular data display presents a somewhat confusing situation. The crucial violation of design methodology occurred at the end of the B_1 phase when the data were not stabilized before reversal was implemented. Note the definite decelerating trend in the data during the last three observations. The apparent reversal in A_2 could therefore be caused by a continuation of this trend.

On an overall basis, the change in B_1 could be caused by influences other than the treatment. This is a possibility presented by the deceleration in B_1 and the ineffective B_2 reimplementation of treatment.

What should have been done differently? Once the data began to decelerate under B_1, this phase should have been continued until the data stabilized. This would have given more information concerning the effect of the treatment.

Simulation 5-7

Since you were asked to draw the diagram in this simulation, considerable latitude is possible concerning exactly *how* your drawing might appear. Essentially it should resemble the data display diagram in Fig. 5-2.

The phase changes are, of course, extremely important decision points. Hopefully your diagram portrays stable data for several observations before the change points.

In A_1 you should have the label of "baseline," and your hypothetical data should proceed essentially in a horizontal fashion before the phase change. There will often be variation from observation to observation in terms of the subject's performance, but the general trend should be neither accelerating nor decelerating. Phase B_1 should be labeled "treatment," and the treatment should be specified, such as "parental attention," "reinforcement applied," or some other indication that communicates what the treatment was. Depending on what the data are supposed to represent, this phase may show a rather dramatic change in performance level (if the treatment worked). It is also important in this phase that the data stabilize for several observations before the next phase change (to A_2).

Phase A_2 is the reversal phase or a return to baseline conditions. This should be so labeled in your diagram. Again, depending on how your hypothetical results turned out, this phase may show a dramatic change in performance level in which the data return to or near the baseline level in the first phase. This is assuming that you selected a reversible behavior. Did you do so? Check your label on the criterion measure side of the graph, which tells what performance or behavior is being assessed. It is something that will probably reverse to baseline when the treatment is withdrawn? If you have questions about this, review the text pages covering this problem. The data should again be stable in phase A_2 before the change to B_2. Phase B_2 should probably include a performance change that might resemble that which occurred in B_1 and then stabilize before observations are terminated. How did you do? Have your instructor inspect your diagram if you are unsure.

Simulation 5-8

Probably the most effective way to inspect a multiple baseline data display involves a sequential inspection from behavior 1 through behaviors 2, 3, and so on. One should also, however, attempt to view the total display to obtain an overall interpretation.

In this particular data display, the behavior 1 phase change sequence appears to be appropriate. Under Phase A, the baseline condition, the data appear to be stable in what could be called a stable low rate. There is probably no doubt that adequate data are available and that the phase change to B is appropriate. As the change occurs in behavior 1, it becomes dramatically evident that something has influenced the behavior rate in the subject. If one views only the data in behavior 1, there is little reason to believe that the treatment is not the effective agent generating the change.

In this data display behavior 2 is where problems become evident. The behavior is stable under the first baseline phase, which coincides with the baseline for behavior 1. However, during the second baseline phase (which coincides with the initiation of treatment in behavior 1), there is a dramatic change in the rate of behavior 2. In fact these data appear as though the treatment has been applied to behavior 2 as well as behavior 1. Consequently it is not certain that the implementation of treatment in behavior 1 generated the change, since a similar change appears in the data for behavior 2. It could be that something other than the treatment generated the change in behavior 1 and that it also was evident in behavior 2, since it was not specifically targeted on behavior 1.

Moving to behavior 3, there is evidence of stable behavior frequency under all three baseline phases with a general trend toward change under treatment, which would suggest that the treatment is effective. In an overall fashion the researcher should have some concern regarding the design of the study represented by this data display. He or she cannot be terribly confident that the treatment is generating the change in behavior although in two cases it appears to be so. That is, data for behaviors 1 and 3 would suggest that the treatment is probably the factor generating change. The problem that is evident in this display comes with behavior 2, where a rather substantial change in rate occurred when that particular behavior was still under baseline and behavior 1 was under treatment. Because the data did not fall nicely into the phase change pattern (since there was a change under baseline with behavior 2), the set of evidence is not terribly strong although the data are suggestive. Probably what occurred is that behaviors 1 and 2 were not sufficiently independent, and implementation of treatment in behavior 1 generalized to behavior 2. Of course there is no strong evidence for this—it is merely speculation—but one might suspect that this occurred with these data. This emphasizes the importance of selecting behaviors that are independent and that can be treated in sequential fashion, so that generalization does not change those behaviors not under treatment.

Simulation 5-9

The data display presented in this simulation provides what is probably a classic example of everything appearing to go right. For behavior 1 (math problems) there was a stable baseline evident at around the 10% correct level for seven sessions. This is certainly a sufficient amount of data to consider a phase change, which was initiated on behavior 1 at that time. Beginning with session 9 there is a rather dramatic increase in the percent of math problems correct, which moves all the way to 100% and, with three minor variations, remains at 100% for the remainder of the observation sessions.

Behavior 2 (spelling words) is somewhat less stable than behavior 1 but certainly is within a narrow enough range that an estimate of untreated performance level is evident. This is particularly the case since seventeen sessions are available under baseline before treatment is begun. Behavior 2 also responds rather darmatically to the treatment with the percent of spelling words correct approaching 100% and varying around that level until session 32, when it was determined that the behavior was probably as stable as it was going to be and observation was terminated.

Simulation 5-10

This is a difference question. The difference question essentially asks, "Is there a difference between . . ." and compares two or more groups or measures. The arrow is the symbol in this diagram that indicates that the performance of group 1 will be compared with the performance of group 2.

The experimental variable is material difficulty. Without knowing any more about the specifics of the study, the question can be stated as "Comparing subject performance as a function of material difficulty." Another way of looking at the same descriptive statement might be "The effects of material difficulty on subject performance." The principle of generality requires that the experimental variable be spoken of in terms of the abstract construct (material difficulty) rather than the particular levels or conditions within that variable (which would be like the material A versus material B approach, noted earlier as inappropriate).

This is an independent design, since different groups of subjects are compared (one group receives the low-difficulty material, and a second group receives the high-difficulty material). The repeated-measures design would require that the same subjects be tested under both conditions, which is not indicated by the diagram.

Simulation 5-11

Since you were asked to draw the diagram in this simulation, considerable latitude is possible concerning exactly *how* your drawing might appear. Essentially it should resemble the diagram shown below and should be labeled in the same fashion.

Simulation 5-12

This stimulation presented a series of questions related to the diagram that was included. Responses to those questions will be outlined in the same manner as they were presented. As you read the simulation feedback responses, refer back to the diagram and keep in mind your own responses to the questions.

1. This study is asking a difference question. As before, difference questions suggest comparisons between groups or groups of measures.

2. There are two experimental variables involved. Comparison A is designated as material difficulty, whereas comparison B is presentation speed. This would generally be called a two-factor design because there are two experimental variables involved. Each experimental variable has two levels or conditions within that variable. For comparison A, material difficulty, there is low-difficulty and high-difficulty material (also designated A_1 and A_2, respectively), and for comparison B, presentation speed, B_1 is a 2-second presentation, whereas the B_2 condition involves a 6-second condition.

3. This is an independent design, that is, for both experimental variables there are independent comparisons with a different group for each condition. This is evident from the indication that there are four different groups involved, groups 1, 2, 3, and 4. Each group functions under only one condition and is not measured under more than one condition, thus there is a totally independent design on both experimental variables. Group 1 receives condition A_1B_1, which is the intersection of low-difficulty material and 2-second presentation speed. Group 2, on the other hand, is operating under condition A_2B_1, in which high-difficulty material is presented at the 2-second speed. Group 3, condition A_1B_2, receives the low-difficulty material at a 6-second presentation speed, whereas group 4 receives high-difficulty material at the 6-second presentation speed. These types of notations are frequently helpful, as you proceed through an experiment, to prompt yourself and keep in mind exactly under what conditions each group is being tested (or which treatment is actually being administered).

Simulation 5-13

Although a variety of details may differ in the way your diagram is arranged, the following general format will hold.

If you have drawn this basic configuration, you are on target. Here is a brief review of certain information about this design. The stimulus question (part c) required that the design be totally independent, that is, that both experimental variables be set up as independent comparisons. What does that mean in terms of this experiment? Simply stated, it means a different group for each condition, which in this case resulted in six different groups of subjects (group 1 received condition A_1B_1, group 2 received A_2B_1, and so on). The two experimental variables are teaching method and amount of practice. Three methods of teaching are involved in the first experimental variable and two levels of practice are

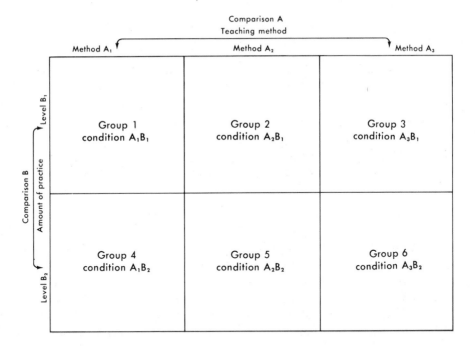

Comparison A
Teaching method

Method A₁   Method A₂   Method A₃

	Method A₁	Method A₂	Method A₃
Level B₁	Group 1 condition A₁B₁	Group 2 condition A₂B₁	Group 3 condition A₃B₁
Level B₂	Group 4 condition A₁B₂	Group 5 condition A₂B₂	Group 6 condition A₃B₂

Comparison B
Amount of practice

involved in the second. Because this is an experiment involving two experimental variables, it is generically called a two-factor design. Specifically you will see such a configuration called a three by two or 3×2, which refers to the different numbers of levels under each variable.

Proceed to the next simulation and become a bit more specific in terms of the details of your diagram.

Simulation 5-14

Because of the variety of possibilities in responses that you might have, this simulation should be checked with your instructor. This will be the quickest way of obtaining specific feedback.

In general you should have six different sets of conditions, one for each group. The conditions are dictated by the specifics that you attached to each level of the two experimental variables. If you called method A_1 the authoritarian method and level B_1 six practice trials, $A_1 B_1$ will receive the authoritarian teaching method and six practice trials. Your description should continue in this fashion for each group.

CHAPTER SIX
Simulation 6-1

First of all, assume that you have enough reserve (no pun intended) of tact that you do not lose your job. They really screwed up in a number of fashions, but you're not going to say that directly. The questionnaire was probably too long; they did not need that much information and it probably contributed to the low response rate. The other major problem was the lack of follow-up. As you recall, the text suggested that the use of appropriate follow-up procedures might increase response rate as much as 20% to 30%. This would only raise the response rate to a maximum of 40% however. Is that enough? Probably not. There is another, even more delicate issue that relates to sponsorship. How might the Monolithic Oil Corporation letterhead influence response rate? It might be better if the study were conducted by an independent research organization that did not suggest conflict of interest. This might be a very difficult point to make with the president. Good luck!

Simulation 6-2

The most obvious suggestion involves the population that is to be involved in the survey. If the interviews are to be conducted in an area that has a predominantly black population, the interviewers should most likely be black. This would hold for any particular ethnic or other subgroup. You may have to provide advice regarding the general factors influencing success or failure of interview studies such as grooming and dress for the interviewers, the appropriate presentation of credentials, and the manner in which sensitive questions should be presented. Although you might expect the researchers to know about these influences, you must remember that Northern Delta University is not exactly on the academic mainstream. How did you do? Would you have at least considered the general areas that should receive attention?

CHAPTER SEVEN
Simulation 7-1

The most obvious internal validity threat is to comparison A. Recall that there was no difference between the movement of subjects in brown versus beige rooms under A_2, in which subjects were aware that they were in an experiment. There was, however, a difference between the movement under brown and beige conditions when subjects had no knowledge of the experiment (A_1). So it appears that knowledge of the existence of an experiment had some influence. There is a problem with such an interpretation, however. If you inspect the report concerning the way in which subjects encountered the rooms, you will find a difference between A_1 and A_2 *in addition to the knowledge variable.* Subjects in the A_2 condition were administered the experimental task individually, whereas those in A_1 were in groups. This raises a red flag immediately. Even more of a threat is evident when one considers the criterion measure of movement speed and pattern. One would expect a difference on both of these measures depending on whether a person was in an art gallery alone or with someone. Thus the differential effects of A_1 and A_2 could have been a result of the knowledge variable, the way in which subjects were administered the task, or a combination of both.

To circumvent this threat one would merely hold the way in which the task was administered constant between A_1 and A_2 conditions. Either group or individual administration might be appropriate, but it should be the same for A_1 and A_2.

Simulation 7-2

The methodological issues involved in this study were discussed later in the review by Drew. Viewing the initial paragraph first, there is a subtle inference that may be inappropriate. The critique of this inference reads as follows:

"Rohles (1967) did not make specific inferences from his finding that high-anxiety individuals would not volunteer for his thermal stress experiment. The reader, however, may be inclined to draw unfounded conclusions relating anxiety level and thermal environment. Such an implication, although possibly forthcoming in future research, is not given sufficient support as yet to warrant such a conclusion. It is likely that highly anxious individuals would be reluctant to participate in any experiment they are aware of."

The most serious internal validity difficulties were then discussed in the following statement. If it is helpful, diagram the basic two-group comparison and then consider how the concept of control is violated and thus internal validity weakened.

"Further reservation is in order concerning Rohles' (1967) report of the behavioral tendencies of 'aggressive-prone' subjects as compared to graduate students in high temperature and crowded conditions. At least two systematic differences between these groups could be contaminating his between-group comparisons. One might suspect that a difference in intelligence existed between the two groups. Although this may have produced behavioral differences, the second problem would seem even more compelling to prompt further study. Graduate students are, by the fact of their status, substantially adapted to the environment of the university and its scholarly research orientation. In fact, it is possible that such students are experienced as subjects. It is doubtful that the same can be said for high-school dropouts, juvenile delinquents, parolees, and those awaiting the draft. In light of this possibility, it is not surprising that behavioral differences of the nature described were noted between these groups."

Simulation 7-3

Although a variety of potential problems are evident in this statement, the most serious involves the major comparison between retarded and nonretarded subjects. Without any additional information about the study, it is evident that there is at least a two-group comparison such as that illustrated on p. 336.

First of all, recall from your reading of the text that this would be known as

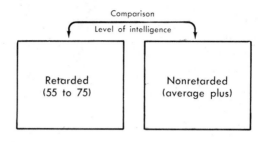

a quasi-experimental design, since the different levels of the experimental variable existed in the subjects before the experiment, rather than a true experimental design, in which the subjects would be equivalent initially and the treatment would be the sole difference. The major problem with this particular study is that the level of intelligence is far from being the only dimension on which the groups are different (which is necessary if the concept of control is to be operative, creating an internally valid investigation). Initially, consider the fact that the members of the nonretarded group of subjects were college students, whereas the retarded group was selected from an institutionalized population. Despite the fact that some would make the case that both sources of subjects are institutions, this is indeed problematic. Mentally retarded persons are institutionalized for many reasons beyond their intelligence level (as are college students). For example, social and behavioral problems are frequently compelling issues in the institutionalization of retarded persons. This would raise the possibility that there are substantial differences in the frequency of behavioral problems between the groups in addition to the intelligence variable. Also, what about cultural, ethnic, and socioeconomic status? It is not only possible but probable that a higher proportion of ethnic minorities, lower socioeconomic status (SES), and cultural subgroups are found among institutionalized retarded persons than the nonretarded college students. Of course if the researcher is studying level of intelligence, these other systematic differences between the groups represents threats to internal validity. How might you attempt to control these variables?

Beyond the more obvious noted above, other concerns should be addressed if the study is to be redesigned. The IQ level for the retarded group is defined and involves a 20-point range. However, since the members of the nonretarded group are in college, they are apparently assumed to be average or above average in intelligence. This is a rather sloppy manner to conduct a study, and it also offers the probability of much more than a 20-point range for the nonretarded group. The two groups should at least be defined in terms of a similar range spread so that one group does not automatically have a greater variability in terms of the descriptive characteristic(s).

Simulation 7-4

The researcher's observations about the reversal in A_2 are based on the basic assumption of the design (that if withdrawal of the treatment results in reversal, the treatment may be viewed as generating the effect). These arguments are not, however, entirely convincing. For the moment, suppose that the medication generated the behavior change in B. It is possible that physiological adaptation occurred after a period of time and the medication was no longer as effective as it was initially. If this adaptation began to occur at about the time that A_2 was instituted, the gradual change under the reversal condition may be a result of a lessening effectiveness of medication (rather than a withdrawal of the reinforcement contingencies). Thus the data under A_2 could support a medication influence as well as reinforcement contingencies.

Circumventing the problem would best be accomplished by a replication of the entire experiment and by studying the effects of the reinforcement without medication being involved. If the researcher had known of the problem before terminating the experiment, some strength could have been gained by adding a B_2 condition (making it an A-B-A-B design). This would have only been suggestive, however, and a clean replication without medication is the soundest alternative.

Simulation 7-5

It is unfortunate that so many precautions were taken to attain an internally valid investigation only to have it plagued by one threat that has been a constant problem for many drug studies. The same experimenter who administered treatment also recorded the data after treatment. Since it is not mentioned otherwise, it can be assumed that the experimenter was aware of which subjects were in the treatment group and which were in the placebo group. Particularly since the data were recorded by a checklist based on clinical judgment, there is the possibility that there was an unconscious biasing of the data, perhaps favoring the actual treatment over the placebo. This is a classic example of a situation in which a double-blind study should have been used, which would have "blinded" the data recorder from information as to which group any individual was in. How about other problems?

External validity is certainly questionable from the standpoint that the initial source of subjects for the sampling were volunteers with an admitted acne problem. Regardless of what influences may be operative to prompt the admission of such a problem (that might make them different from those individuals who did not or would not), it is doubtful that they are "like" the general population. Results are probably generalizable to other teen-age boys and girls who would admit such a problem, but it is doubtful that beyond those like the volunteers, the data are accurate with regard to external validity.

Simulation 7-6

A considerable amount of latitude was available to you in your work on this simulation. It would be impossible to anticipate all the possible details in responses that might occur. Consequently you should check with your instructor concerning aspects of your work that are not addressed below.

1. The research question being asked is a difference question, since you are comparing the effectiveness of two types of visual instruction.

2. The experimental variable is method of presentation. Depending on how you viewed the paragraph, you may have stated the variable as "degree of reality." This would certainly be appropriate, since this is the essential distinguishing characteristic between the two methods.

3. This material is probably best suited for a traditional experimental approach comparing two groups.

4. Your diagram should generally look like the one in Fig. 5-4 on p. 105. You would, of course, have different labels for the conditions and the experimental variable.

5. This is a particularly challenging study to attempt to control the necessary factors to achieve internal validity. This is an area in which you will want to exchange ideas with your colleagues and check with your instructor. You may want to be alert to such areas as content of the material, time or duration of the film, subject factors such as age, intelligence, and many others.

6. With regard to your response to this simulation, here is a clue. Remember Murphy's Law. Review the pages in the text that discuss these types of details.

CHAPTER EIGHT
Simulation 8-1

As indicated in your text, the population frame is constructed by designating all the potential subjects, by name, who have the characteristics indicated in the population definition. Recall that the population was defined as "all third-year male students enrolled in West Rebew State." From the partial list that you have, certain students should have an X by their name, thereby becoming part of your population frame. The students listed below should have an X by their name. These are male students with a code of 3 for year of enrollment.

Bach, Jay T.	3	Barker, James R.	3
Bacon, Robert F.	3	Barnes, Mike L.	3
Badger, Mike	3	Berg, William J.	3
Bailey, Bob Jo	3	Bigelow, Randy L.	3
Barber, George	3	Bigelow, Robert W.	3
Barclay, Larry	3	Bragg, Raymond J.	3

Other students in the original list did not combine the characteristics of both male and code 3. Occasionally you may encounter some difficulty determining characteristics from the information provided. For example, names have definite regional differences in terms of whether they are given to males or females (Bob Jo Bailey). If confusion exists, you must confirm sex by seeking additional information in some way. By the way, Bob Jo is from the South.

Simulation 8-2

The exact subjects who will become a part of your study will vary depending on which part of the random number table you use. Since you are instructed to begin in the upper left corner, here is a list of the subject codes that would appear from this approach.

10	63	54	14
22	9	32	36
24	7	29	69
42	51	15	40
37	2	46	61
77	1	39	12
85	52	6	
28	48	72	

The children whose names appear beside these code numbers are your subjects. Other digits were ignored (e.g., the number 99 in column 1, line 7) because they were not part of your population frame (which only went to 85) and were therefore not relevant.

Simulation 8-3

The exact assignment would, of course, differ depending on the random number table used (or the point of beginning in this table). Since you were instructed where to begin and how to proceed, here is a list of the names and numbers of the subjects once again with their group codes in parentheses. This would mean that since Robert has a (1) beside his name, he will be in group 1, and so on.

1. Robert (1)	14. David (1)	27. Carole (1)	40. Virginia (1)
2. Myrna (2)	15. Earl (2)	28. Phil (2)	41. Sonia (2)
3. Ralph (2)	16. Lorraine (2)	29. Don (1)	42. Anita (1)
4. John (2)	17. Maurice (1)	30. Walt (1)	43. Bruce (2)
5. Sally (1)	18. Terry (1)	31. Bonnie (1)	44. Suzanne (2)
6. Sherry (2)	19. Carl (1)	32. Doug (1)	45. Alice (2)
7. Lois (1)	20. Ken (2)	33. Steve (1)	46. Barbara (1)
8. Andy (1)	21. Wilmer (2)	34. George (2)	47. Clyde (2)
9. Joel (1)	22. Anne (1)	35. Mary Ann (1)	48. Karle (2)
10. Thomas (2)	23. Alan (1)	36. Sandra (2)	49. Kent (2)
11. Eugene (2)	24. Kevin (2)	37. Larry (1)	50. Travis (2)
12. Dennis (2)	25. James (1)	38. Rick (1)	
13. Anna (2)	26. Kay (1)	39. Joy (2)	

Note that Clyde, Karle, Kent, and Travis all received group 2 assignments. The reason for this (regardless of which numbers came up in the table) is that when Barbara was assigned to group 1, that made a total of 25 subjects in group 1. The remaining individuals were then placed in group 2 to make that group full.

Simulation 8-4

As before, the exact assignment would differ depending on which table you used and where you began in the table. If you did follow the procedure outlined before exactly, then you would obtain the following subject position assignments:

1. (1)	8. (1)	15. (2)	22. (1)
2. (2)	9. (1)	16. (2)	23. (1)
3. (2)	10. (2)	17. (1)	24. (2)
4. (2)	11. (2)	18. (1)	25. (1)
5. (1)	12. (2)	19. (1)	26. (1)
6. (2)	13. (2)	20. (2)	27. (1)
7. (1)	14. (1)	21. (2)	28. (2)

The complete listing of position assignments is not presented here, since it is exactly the same as that obtained in simulation 8-3 and presented in the feedback for simulation 8-3. Check back to see if you need further feedback. They are the same because you had the same number of subjects, and they were assigned to the same number of groups using the table in exactly the same way. If the situation were different in terms of any of these factors, the subject position sequence would also be different.

CHAPTER NINE
Simulation 9-1

As with any problem in which one is given a general task to perform, a variety of specific responses may be expected. The crucial issue here is whether you were sufficiently specific and operational that what you specified can be measured and is a logical criterion measure for the topic. Hopefully the following will serve to exemplify such specificity for at least one possible measure.

You have already had some practice that applies to this simulation. Remember Simulation 4-5? It dealt with a reading study. Pursue this same approach once again.

First of all, the criterion measure must be a way of determining effectiveness of the reading programs. One way of assessing effectiveness of reading instruction is to measure a student's reading comprehension. However, as noted previously, the term "reading comprehension" is not specific enought to tell you what you are going to count. Frequently reading comprehension is determined by counting the number of correct responses on a test dealing with a passage the students have read. Correct responses will serve adequately *if* reading comprehension is what you wish to assess. Do you have something else you want to measure? Is it specified in measurable form?

Simulation 9-2

As before, there may be a number of different responses that are appropriate for this simulation. You should check with your instructor to determine if what you listed is on target. A few guidelines are presented below for general feedback.

First of all, specificity and operational definitions are crucial. Not only are you faced with the issues of defining some behavior that is measurable and countable, you are also going to have to have that behavior sufficiently well described so an observer can reliably record frequency. This will require a precise description so that the observer will know the behavior (whatever it is) when it occurs. In this case you will want to select one or two countable behaviors involving the child's interaction with other children. Perhaps these could be verbal interaction or appropriate physical interaction such as cooperative play or sharing toys. Additionally it will be necessary to specify a time frame. This might involve a statement such as "frequency of verbal interactions per 2-minute observation." How did you do? Can you measure it?

Simulation 9-3

The problem with the data may be obvious to you immediately. The instruction to graph the data was included because I have found visual inspection of graphs to be helpful. Your graph might involve some specific characteristics that are different, but generally the data may be visually presented as below.

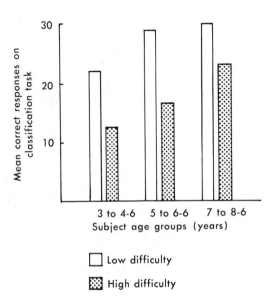

From the graphed data it becomes obvious that the previous study was plagued with a serious ceiling effect. This probably prevented at least the groups of subjects who were 7 to 8-6 and 5 to 6-6 years old from performing as well as they might have. If there are only thirty possible items, certainly means of 29.2 and 28.6 included scores of 30 from several subjects.

What does this mean for your study? You will obviously want to avoid the ceiling effect. Since the major focus of the research involves child development, your options would favor altering material in the task rather than the subjects' ages. One approach might entail changing the present high-difficulty material to the lower-difficulty task and developing another set of material for the high-difficulty condition. This would certainly be a possibility, since difficulty is only relative, and the means in the right-hand column of the table do not appear to be restricted by a ceiling.

Simulation 9-4

The graph for the data in this table would look something like that shown below.

What problem did you note with these data? If you said that a ceiling effect was operating, you were exactly right! If you said it was a floor effect, you fell into a trap. The trap was not set up to intentionally frustrate you; this is an area where even experienced researchers often have to take a second look. Here is what happened.

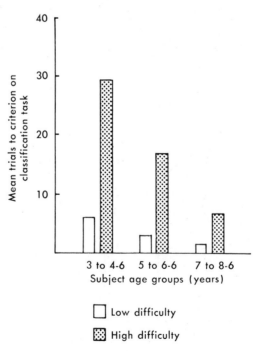

Essentially this set of data could be from the same study presented in Simulation 9-3, but the criterion measure that was recorded has been changed. Before, mean correct responses were used, which meant that the higher number indicated better performance. This time the measure is the number of trials that a subject takes to reach a proficiency criterion. Using this measure, the lower the number, the better the performance. If a subject takes only two trials to reach proficiency, he or she is performing better than a subject who takes five trials to reach proficiency. Consequently a ceiling effect is operating with the older group, who received low-difficulty material. Why? It is possible to reach proficiency in one trial (see the footnote to the table). If the older group has a mean of 1.5 trials, there are a good number of them who are reaching proficiency in one trial. Consequently their ability to perform is being restricted by the task.

What changes are in order for your study? Again the focus is child development, so the favored option probably involves a change in the material. The high-difficulty material looks all right, since the means are nicely distributed without an apparent restriction in performance range. Probably the same adjustment that was suggested in the feedback for Simulation 9-3 should not be made because if a still more difficult list were developed, a floor effect might result with the younger children (there is already a mean trials to criterion of 29.2 with them). Perhaps the best option would be to develop a new set of easy material that has a difficulty level somewhere in between the two that are presented in the table. This would hopefully avoid the ceiling and yet not present other problems. A pilot test will be in order before launching the experiment to see if the material appears appropriate.

Simulation 9-5

These questions present some obvious problems. First of all, question number one represents a classic example of two questions in one item. The tip-off here is the use of the term "and." The respondent may now regularly but not trim—so what response is appropriate? This problem could be solved by replacing "and" with "or." A second approach might involve writing two separate questions, one addressing lawn mowing and the second focusing on trimming. Question one also includes a vague term pertaining to how often the activity is undertaken. "Regularly" might mean one thing to one respondent and another to a second. It probably would be better to specify how often in the question itself (e.g., weekly, every two weeks, monthly).

The second question is one of those that uses a "four-bit" word that is unnecessary and likely unknown to most respondents. "Florous" is not a term that is in many individuals' vocabulary. The question could have simple said "Does your yard have flowers" and been much more appropriate.

How did you do on this simulation? Can you think of other similar examples?

CHAPTER TEN
Simulation 10-1

As noted in Chapter 10, the data generated by a rating scale such as this are ordinal in nature. This is the case because the different numbers on the scale denote greater than or less than in terms of the teacher's perception of the quality of the material. A rating of 1 indicates a more positive assessment than a rating of 3. This is, however, a relative statement, and you do not know what the difference between those two ratings means in terms of a quantity or amount.

The properties of ordinal data are identity and order. These are two of three possible properties that numbers may have, the third being additivity. Since ordinal data do not have the property of additivity, certain arithmetic operations cannot be performed (such as adding or subtracting). This is not necessarily "bad" because a rating does provide a relative indicator of the teacher's perception of the material. It does, however, have considerable importance for later decisions about what analysis should be applied.

Simulation 10-2

As noted in Chapter 10, the data generated by a categorical sorting are nominal in nature. What was accomplished was the assignment of events, in this case pupils, to a classification of either successful or unsuccessful.

Nominal data have the property of identity. Each category is unique from the other and any symbol (e.g., numbers or letters) could be used. The identification of such data as nominal is important for later decisions on analysis.

Simulation 10-3

The data generated by temperature as a criterion measure (at least assessed by thermometer) can be considered interval data. When you are working with such data, you have known and equal distances between score units and an arbitrary zero point. These are characteristics that are applicable to the criterion measure in this simulation.

Interval data have all three number properties—identity, order, and additivity. This provides considerable latitude in terms of what can be done with the data from an analysis standpoint.

Simulation 10-4

Despite the fact that the same dimension—age—is being assessed in all three examples, the types of data differ because of the way in which the measure is recorded. Example A is nominal data, since categories are used. Even though an underlying continuum exists, the subjects are only grossly classified into one of three categories. Example B involves ordinal data, since the subjects are ranked from youngest to oldest. Since only ranks are recorded, you have no information about the magnitude of age difference between ranks 6 and 7, or whether it is the same as the difference between ranks 3 and 4. Example C is at least interval data and perhaps ratio (depending on whether one can determine an actual zero age). If in doubt, it is frequently wise to be conservative in deciding the level of measurement (interval in this case). It makes little difference in this example, since most of what can be done with ratio data can be performed on interval data.

CHAPTER ELEVEN
Simulation 11-1

The data presented are ordinal data, since they are generated from a rating scale that does provide evidence of greater than and less than but does not provide information concerning the interval between any two scores. This is the type of example that was used in discussing ordinal data in Chapter 10 as well as in previous simulations.

The central tendency measure of choice for these data is the median. This choice is based on the fact that the median does not require arithmetic operations such as adding, subtracting, or dividing. These operations cannot be performed on ordinal data, since the property of additivity is not present. The median is preferable over the mode for ordinal data.

The score representing the median in this example is 4.

Simulation 11-2

First of all, assume that the instrument to be used in data collection is a thermometer, since this is the usual instrument. The data that will be collected can be considered to be interval data. In such cases one is working with known and equal distances between score units and an arbitrary zero point. These are the characteristics of interval data.

The central tendency measure of choice for these data is the mean. Since interval data include the property of additivity, the arthmetic operations necessary to obtain a mean can be appropriately performed. When this is possible, the mean is usually preferred because it makes use of as much information as possible (which the median and mode would not in this case).

Simulation 11-3

The dispersion measure of choice is most likely the semi-interquartile range because it is frequently viewed as a natural dispersion companion when the median is used. More important, however, is the fact that ordinal data will not permit the use of standard deviation, since additivity is not present. The semi-interquartile range will provide more information than the range, since more of the available data are used.

Simulation 11-4

Since you are so pressed on the phone, you are really likely to need a measure of dispersion that is quickly obtainable without much computation. For the purpose noted in the stimulus material, the range will probably serve adequately, and you can get the coach off the phone.

For your written report you may wish to use a measure that will use more of the information available. Your data are at least interval in nature and therefore have the property of additivity. With this in mind, the standard deviation would probably be the dispersion measure used on your report.

CHAPTER TWELVE
Simulation 12-1

The general category of nonparametric statistics would be appropriate for use in the study presented. The nonparametric choice is based on the type of data that are collected. The rating scale has been a recurring example of ordinal data throughout the text. Reference to Table 12-1, p. 270, indicates that nonparametric analyses are the only possibility with such data. The sample size was certainly adequate for parametric statistics, but the previously mentioned type of data consideration will not permit parametric statistics use, since the property of the additivity is not present.

Simulation 12-2

The general category of parametric statistics can be appropriately selected for the study presented. This selection is appropriate because both the type of data and the sample size will permit the use of parametric analyses. The data are at least interval (actually they are probably ratio), and the group size is more than ample.

Simulation 12-3

The general category of nonparametric statistics can be appropriately selected for this study. Nonparametrics are necessary because of the extremely small number of subjects. The data (frequency of upper lid flutters) are at least interval and probably ratio, since there really could be zero occurrences. Therefore, although the data are strong enough for parametric analyses, the small sample requires nonparametrics.

Simulation 12-4

As noted on p. 274, two statistical tests are appropriate for situations such as that presented in the stimulus material, the $\bar{z}$ *test* and the *t test for differences between independent means*. The $\bar{z}$ test may be used since the samples are over thirty, but the t test may also be used (in fact, the t test may be used for samples both above and below thirty). Either test may be used in the situation presented.

The *t* test is more popular and is probably one of the most widely used statistical tests because it can be more flexible in terms of sample size.

Simulation 12-5

First run through the questions in the stimulus material.

1. You have information in the stimulus material that indicates two groups of fifteen subjects each were formed. Consequently there is little reason to believe that the performances are not independent. It seems you have an independent comparison.

2. As you have noted throughout the text and previous simulations, a rating scale such as this is generally considered to be generating ordinal data. Reference to Table 12-1 on p. 270 indicates that nonparametric analyses should be used with ordinal data.

3. The sample size of fifteen per group is not terribly relevant, since you must use nonparametrics with ordinal data. It may, however, influence your choice of a specific test within the nonparametric category.

As noted on p. 275, two statistical tests are appropriate for ordinal data comparing two independent data points, the *median test* and the *Mann-Whitney U test*. Either test will be appropriate, although the Mann-Whitney U test is perhaps the more popular with samples under twenty.

Simulation 12-6

First run through the questions in the stimulus material.

1. The stimulus material indicates that one group of subjects will be evaluated before and after the pollution device is in operation. Essentially this is a pre-post study with data on the same subjects being gathered before and after the treatment is started. Thus there is a nonindependent comparison.

2. The data involve counting sinus symptoms before and after treatment. As you will recall from Chapter 10, this type of data presents a somewhat uncertain situation but is usually treated as interval data if it is not clearly ordinal. For your purposes, assume interval data are present, which means parametric analyses may be used if the sample size is adequate.

3. The sample size noted in the stimulus material is 100 subjects. This is more than adequate for using parametric statistics.

Reference to p. 276 indicates that the *t test for differences between nonindependent means* may be used in situations such as you have here. Reread this section to refresh your memory on this analysis; it is a popular test and appears frequently in the literature.

Simulation 12-7

Run through the questions in the stimulus material.

1. One experimental variable is involved in the study. As was noted in Chap-

ter 4, exactly what it is labeled may vary in terms of wording, but it probably would be called something like "type of drug compound." So you have one experimental variable and three specific conditions under it (compounds A, B, and C).

2. The comparison is independent, since three different groups of subjects were formed, one to receive each of the drug compounds.

3. The data can be considered to be interval data (in fact, temperature is one of the examples of interval measurement in the text). This suggests that parametric analyses may be considered if other requirements (e.g., sample size) are met.

4. The sample size noted in the stimulus material is twenty subjects in each group, which is generally considered adequate for parametric statistics.

Given the contingencies noted above, probably the most popular statistical test is the *one-way analysis of variance for comparing independent means*. Consequently the ANOVA will be used to determine whether there is a statistically significant difference in the mean temperature between the groups being treated with the different compounds.

Simulation 12-8

Run through the questions presented at the last of the stimulus material.

1. One experimental variable is involved. As before, the exact wording may vary, but it would probably be called something like "stage in weight loss program" (since you are dealing with assessment at three stages, pre-, mid-, and postprogram measures).

2. The comparison is a nonindependent design, since the same subjects are being assessed at three different times (pre-, mid-, and postprogram points).

3. The data may be considered as ratio (weight is one of the examples of ratio data in Chapter 10). This suggests that parametric analyses may be considered if other requirements are met (e.g., sample size).

4. The sample size of thirty is generally considered adequate for parametric statistics.

Given the contingencies noted above, probably the most popular statistical test is the *analysis of variance for repeated measures*. The ANOVA will be used to determine whether there is a statistically significant difference in group mean weight between the preprogram, midprogram, and postprogram assessment points.

Simulation 12-9

Run through the question in the stimulus material.

1. Two experimental variables are involved, type of drug (compound A compared with compound B) and dosage (5 ml. compared with 10 ml.).

2. The study is totally independent (both variables are independent comparisons), since four different groups of subjects were randomly constituted (one for compound A, 5 ml. dose; one for compound A, 10 ml. dose; one for compound B, 5 ml. dose; one for compound B, 10 ml. dose).

3. The data can at least be considered interval, perhaps ratio, in nature. This suggests that parametric analyses may be considered if other requirements are met such as sample size.

The sample size of thirty per group is generally considered adequate for parametric statistics.

Given the contingencies noted above, probably the most popular statistical test is the *two-way analysis of variance for comparing independent means*. The two-way ANOVA is suggested because two experimental variables are involved in the study, and the data and the sample are appropriate.

Simulation 12-10

Height and weight may both be considered to be at least interval data, and, in fact, they have been used as examples of ratio data. Reference to p. 292 indicates that when both measures to be correlated are either interval or ratio data, the *Pearson product-moment correlation* may be used. This is perhaps the most commonly known correlation technique and provides a stable estimate of relationship.

Simulation 12-11

Your first task is to somehow inform the superintendent in a tactful manner that he probably used the incorrect analysis last year. Reference to p. 292 suggests that *Kendall's tau* is perferred for correlating ranks when a small sample is available (N less than 10). Once this delicate task is completed, you can compliment him on his foresight in anticipating this year's study. With samples greater than ten, the *Spearman rank-order correlation* is preferred for correlating ranks. If your advice is presented tactfully, you may even receive a merit increase in salary. Good luck!

Author index

Subject index

DATE DUE

The Library Store   #47-0103